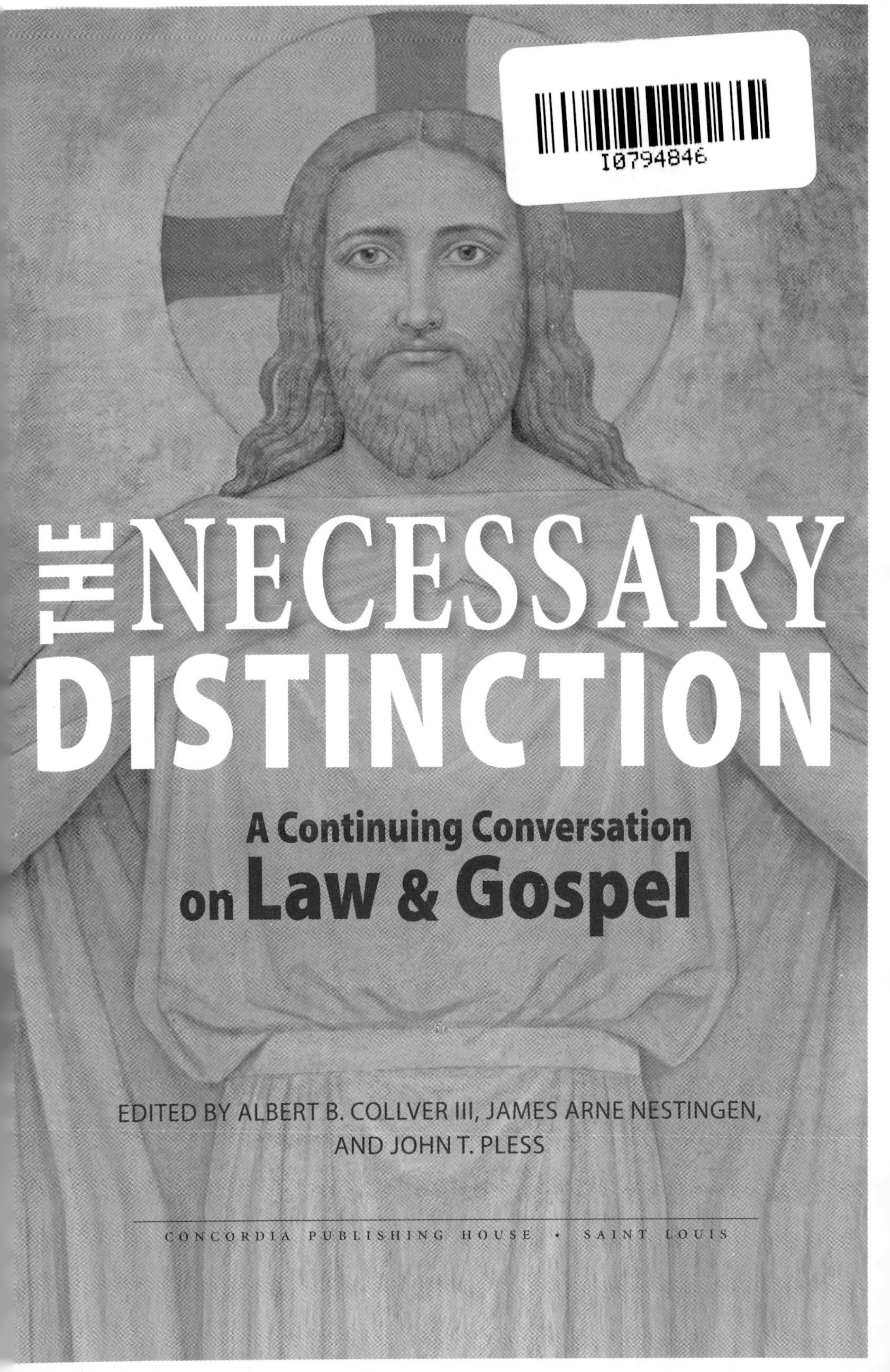

THE NECESSARY DISTINCTION

A Continuing Conversation on Law & Gospel

EDITED BY ALBERT B. COLLVER III, JAMES ARNE NESTINGEN, AND JOHN T. PLESS

CONCORDIA PUBLISHING HOUSE · SAINT LOUIS

3558 S. Jefferson Ave., St. Louis, MO 63118-3968
1-800-325-3040 • cph.org

Manufactured in the United States of America

2 3 4 5 6 7 8 9 10 11 26 25 24 23 22 21 20 19 18 17

A tremendous resource! All you want to know about the distinctive Lutheran witness to the proper relation of Law and Gospel is in this volume. It attends to the classic debates within Lutheranism about that relation, with special focus on the third use of the Law. The definitive essay by Stephen Hultgren alone is worth the price of the book.

—Dr. Robert Benne
Jordan-Trexler Emeritus Professor and Research Associate in the Religion and Philosophy Department of Roanoke College, Salem, Virginia

The Necessary Distinction has relevance not only for such American Lutherans as are broadly represented among its authors, but also ecumenical relevance. As non-Lutherans today increasingly become aware of the value of the Law/Gospel distinction, it is incumbent on those who were raised on it to speak out. And they do so here.

—Rev. Dr. des. Jacob Corzine
Assistant Professor for Systematic Theology, Concordia University Chicago
Secretary, International Loehe Society, English Language Section

If decisions on human sexuality in recent years illustrate how great segments of Lutheranism have lost their way, the essays included in *The Necessary Distinction* help guide you to anchors we all need. These authors take Christ, the Scriptures, and our confessions seriously. Pastors as well as informed lay theologians will profit from them. What a welcome contribution to the 500th Reformation anniversary year!

—Rev. Dr. Robert Bugbee, President, Lutheran Church—Canada
Vice-Chairman of the International Lutheran Council

For Martin Luther, it was a matter of highest priority to distinguish correctly between Law and Gospel. As Dietrich Bonhoeffer noted, this distinction has come into disrepute. Instead, we promulgate cheap grace. The Gospel is often wrapped into the Law to advance a moralistic message that neither condemns nor frees. Therefore, it is highly commendable that in this volume prominent theologians think through how the much-needed distinction between Law and Gospel can be used for preaching, pastoral care, liturgy, mission, and Christian living. This is a valuable resource for anybody who cares for the liberating voice of the Gospel.

—Hans Schwarz, Dr. theol. Dr. h. c. mult.
Prof. em. of Systematic Theology and Contemporary Theological Issues
University of Regensburg, Germany

A first-class resource. Anyone wishing to become more deeply acquainted with practicing a belief in Law and Gospel in the postmodern age does well to acquaint themselves with this primer on the ongoing dialogues between a variety of denominational bodies striving to be faithful American heirs to Luther's theology. Any scholar, pastor, or layman hoping to add his voice first owes it to himself to imbibe at the feet of these august students of Luther's greatest legacy: the proper distinction.

—Rev. Jonathan Fisk, on-air personality for KFUO radio, host and creative consultant for Worldview Everlasting, and author of Broken: 7 "Christian" Rules That Every Christian Ought to Break as Often as Possible

In our day, when many Lutherans seem to have lost their way biblically, this book is much needed. It is for those who preach the Word and those who hear the Word, for the theologically trained and those who aren't. It is a gift to our churches and to all who are committed to the "necessary distinction."

—The Rev. Dr. David M. Wendel, Assistant to the Bishop for Ministry and Ecumenism, The North American Lutheran Church

The Necessary Distinction is a sparkling collection of essays. The writing is done with clarity and conviction and, most of all, with a deep appreciation for the Lutheran tradition. This book is a cool drink for those thirsty for new perspectives on the proper relationship between Law and Gospel. It is a work that is indeed "necessary" for preachers and teachers seeking to proclaim God's radical grace in Jesus Christ.

—Dr. Mark D. Tranvik, Professor of Religion Augsburg College, Minneapolis, Minnesota

This collection of scholarship by an impressive array of theologians cuts to the heart of genuine Lutheran theology, the distinction between Law and Gospel, and demonstrates why this distinction has been, is, and must be the necessary distinction in biblical preaching and teaching if we are to maintain and proclaim the vibrant, Christian, saving message entrusted to the Church by Christ Himself. Both pastors and laypeople will benefit from the essays contained here, and, given that its relevance is rooted in the timeless treasure of the properly divided Word, it will hold its value on one's bookshelf for decades and beyond.

—Wade Johnston, PhD, Assistant Professor of Theology Wisconsin Lutheran College, Milwaukee, Wisconsin

The essays in this book call us back to the center of theological inquiry, pastoral care, and Christian living. When pastors and churches across denominational lines are tempted to cater to the culture or myopically react to it, the distinction between God's Law and Gospel is easily blurred, the Gospel is lost, and troubled consciences are left falsely secure in their own works or in terror of God's judgment. This collection of essays offers the Church at large a timely resource on the proper distinction of Law and Gospel that will challenge, edify, and, by God's grace, bring about repentance and the righteousness of faith in Jesus Christ.

—Dr. Jason D. Lane, Assistant Professor of Theology Concordia University Wisconsin, Mequon, Wisconsin

CONTENTS

Preface by Editors 9

1. Law and Gospel: An LCMS Perspective by John T. Pless 13
2. Rightly Dividing the Word of Truth: An Introduction to the Distinction between Law and Gospel by Mark A. Seifrid 25
3. Maintaining Law and Gospel in the Liturgy by William M. Cwirla 45
4. Law and Gospel in Pastoral Care: A View from the Parish by Peter J. Brock 65
5. Law and Gospel in the Christian Life by Larry M. Vogel 89
6. Properly Distinguishing Law and Gospel as the Pastor's Calling by Mark C. Mattes 109
7. Luther on Law and Gospel in His *Lectures on Galatians* 1531/1535 by Naomichi Masaki 135
8. Speaking of the End to the Law by James Arne Nestingen 169
9. The Problem of Freedom Today and the Third Use of the Law: Biblical and Theological Considerations by Stephen Hultgren 185
10. Preaching Law and Gospel: Repentance and Faith from the Penitential Psalms in Lent by John T. Pless 253
11. A Royal Ass by Steven D. Paulson 265
12. Law and Gospel in Mission Theology by Albert B. Collver III 285
13. What Happens When the Third Use of the Law Is Rejected? by Roland Ziegler 309

Appendix: "God's Word Forever Shall Abide: A Guiding Statement on the Character and Proper Use of the Sacred Scriptures" 332

AUTHOR BIOGRAPHIES

Peter J. Brock (MDiv, Concordia Theological Seminary, Fort Wayne), Pastor of St. John Lutheran Church, Bingen, Indiana, and adjunct instructor at Concordia Theological Seminary. He is the Secretary for the Indiana District of The Lutheran Church—Missouri Synod.

Albert B. Collver III (PhD, Concordia Seminary, St. Louis), Director of Church Relations and Assistant to the President of The Lutheran Church—Missouri Synod. He also serves as the Executive Secretary of the International Lutheran Council.

William M. Cwirla (MDiv, Concordia Seminary, St. Louis), Senior Pastor of Holy Trinity Lutheran Church in Hacienda Heights, California. Pastor Cwirla has also served as the president of Higher Things.

Stephen Hultgren (PhD, Duke University), Lecturer in New Testament at Australian Lutheran College—University of Divinity, Adelaide, Australia.

Naomichi Masaki (PhD, Concordia Seminary, St. Louis), Associate Professor of Systematic Theology at Concordia Theological Seminary. He is the author of *He Alone Is Worthy*.

Mark C. Mattes (PhD, University of Chicago), Professor of Theology and Philosophy and Department Chair at Grand View University, Des Moines, Iowa. Author of *The Role of Justification in Contemporary Theology* and *Martin Luther's Theology of Beauty*. He is also a coeditor of *A Dictionary of Luther and the Lutheran Traditions*.

James Arne Nestingen (ThD, St. Michael's College at University of Toronto), Emeritus Professor of Church History at Luther Seminary, St. Paul. Author of *Martin Luther: A Life* and along with Robert Kolb and Charles Arand, *The Lutheran Confessions: History and Theology of the Book of Concord*.

Steven D. Paulson (ThD, Lutheran School of Theology at Chicago), Professor of Systematic Theology at Luther Seminary, St. Paul. Author of *Luther for Armchair Theologians*, *Lutheran Theology*, and *A Brief Introduction to Martin Luther*.

John T. Pless (MDiv, Trinity Lutheran Seminary, Columbus, Ohio), Assistant Professor of Pastoral Ministry and Missions, Concordia Theological Seminary, and visiting professor at Lutheran Theological Seminary, Pretoria, South Africa. He is also the author of *Handling the Word of Truth: Law and Gospel in the Church Today*, *Praying Luther's Small Catechism*, and *Martin Luther: Preacher of the Cross*.

Mark A. Seifrid (PhD, Princeton Theological Seminary) is Professor of Exegetical Theology, Concordia Seminary, St. Louis. Among his publications are *The Second Letter to the Corinthians: The Pillar New Testament Commentary* and *Christ, Our Righteousness: Paul's Theology of Justification*.

Larry M. Vogel (MDiv, Concordia Seminary, St. Louis) is Assistant Executive Director of the Commission on Theology and Church Relations of The Lutheran Church—Missouri Synod. Prior to coming to his present position, he served as the pastor of congregations in New York City and New Jersey.

Roland F. Ziegler (Dr. theol., Eberhard-Karls-Universität Tübingen) is the Robert D. Preus Associate Professor of Systematic Theology and Confessional Lutheran Studies at Concordia Theological Seminary, Fort Wayne. Prior to joining the faculty in Fort Wayne, he served a congregation in Germany.

PREFACE

We must bring forth the voice of the law that men may be made to fear and come to a knowledge of their sins and so be converted to repentance and a better life. But we must not stop with that, for that would only amount to wounding and not binding up, smiting and not healing, killing and not making alive, leading down into hell and not bringing back again, humbling and not exalting. Therefore we must also preach the word of grace and the promise of forgiveness by which faith is taught and aroused. Without this word of grace the works of the law, contrition, penitence, and all the rest are done and taught in vain.

Martin Luther, *The Freedom of a Christian* (AE 31:364)

This collection of essays had its genesis in the ongoing discussions between representatives of the North American Lutheran Church (NALC), the Lutheran Church—Canada (LCC), and The Lutheran Church—Missouri Synod (LCMS). Early on in these conversations, we agreed that it would be of benefit to the pastors and laity of all three bodies to have an anthology of essays on the proper distinction of God's Law from His Gospel. Writers were recruited not only from the NALC and LCMS but from other Lutheran bodies as well who were known for their capacity to think through the implications of this distinction for preaching, pastoral care, liturgy, mission, and Christian living. We have also included "God's Word Forever Shall Abide: A Guiding Statement on the Character and Proper Use of the Sacred Scriptures" as an appendix to this volume. This statement, adopted by the dialogue committee made up of representatives from the NALC, LCC, and LCMS, asserts the necessity of rightly distinguishing the Law from the Gospel for a proper understanding of the Holy Scriptures.

In our conversations together, we have recognized that the significance of the Law/Gospel distinction is downplayed, questioned, and rejected by some within American Lutheranism. Others have misused the distinction to promote an allegedly more liberated sexual ethic. The place of the so-called "third use of the Law" remains a contentious issue in some circles. In the Smalcald Articles, Luther notes "that the law was given by God, in the first place, to curb sin by means of the threat and terror of punishment and also by means of the promise and offer of grace and favor" but "the foremost office or power of the law is that it reveals inherited sin and its fruits" (SA III 2).[1] These are commonly identified as the first two uses, or functions, of the Law. The Formula of Concord clarified a dispute that had arisen among Lutheran theologians over the place of the Law in the life of the Christian, asserting in Article VI a "third use" that is a guide to the good works that the Christian is obligated to do in his or her vocation. Several of the essays in this volume take up this topic.

The editors of this book are firmly committed to the Lutheran assertion that the distinction between the Law and the Gospel is a necessity if the Scriptures are, indeed, comprehended according to the mind of the Lord who inspired them. We are convinced that the words of the Apology of the Augsburg Confession are altogether accurate: "All Scripture should be divided into these two main topics: the law and the promises. In some places it communicates the law. In other places it communicates the promise concerning Christ, either when it promises that Christ will come and on account of him offers the forgiveness of sins, justification, and eternal life, or when in the gospel itself, Christ, after he appeared, promises the forgiveness of sins, justification, and eternal life" (Ap IV 5). Likewise, we wholeheartedly affirm the testimony of the Formula of Concord:

> The distinction between law and gospel is a particularly glorious light. It serves to divide God's Word properly [cf. 2 Tim. 2:15] and to explain correctly and make understandable the writings of the holy prophets and apostles. Therefore, we must diligently preserve this distinction, so as not to mix these two teachings together and make the

1 Book of Concord quotations in this preface are from Kolb-Wengert.

> gospel into a law. For this obscures the merit of Christ and robs troubled consciences of the comfort that they otherwise have in the holy gospel when it is preached clearly and purely. With the help of this distinction these consciences can sustain themselves in their greatest spiritual struggles against the terror of the law. (FC SD V 1)

We recognize that the right distinction of the Law from the Gospel is not a theoretical abstraction but a functional necessity for preaching and pastoral care lest sinners be left with their own attempts at righteousness, which can only lead to arrogance or despair. It is a difficult art taught by the Holy Spirit in the school of experience, to paraphrase Luther, this business of distinguishing the Law from the Gospel. But it is a necessary art if the Church is to live by faith alone. This art, Hermann Sasse reminds us, is not balancing or coordinating Law and Gospel but distinguishing them.

Each author is responsible for his own essay. They speak for themselves, and we offer this book to our respective church bodies for study, deliberation, and debate.[2] The essays by their very nature are exploratory. We particularly hope that they might be the basis for conversation and continued study by pastors in the NALC, LCC, and LCMS. If they draw their readers back into a deep look into the Holy Scriptures and the Lutheran Confessions so that Christ Jesus is preached with greater clarity and broken sinners given the full consolation of the forgiveness of sins, we will rejoice that this work has not been done in vain.

Albert B. Collver III

James Arne Nestingen

John T. Pless

The Fifth Week in Lent 2017

2 "This material is being released for study and discussion purposes, and the author(s) is (are) solely responsible for its contents. It has not been submitted to the process for doctrinal review stipulated in the Bylaws of The Lutheran Church—Missouri Synod and does not necessarily reflect the theology of the Lutheran Confessions or the doctrinal position of The Lutheran Church—Missouri Synod." (From the 2016 LCMS *Handbook*, Bylaw 1.9.1.1 [b], p. 35.)

LAW AND GOSPEL: AN LCMS PERSPECTIVE[1]

John T. Pless

The assertion that the Law must be rightly distinguished from the Gospel has certainly been a key theme in the history of the Missouri Synod, even as the implications of this distinction have not been without disputation and controversy. Distinctions matter. Where they are improperly made, the results can be deadly. The failure to distinguish between medications can be fatal. Pastor C. F. W. Walther (1811–87) knew that where God's Law is not rightly distinguished from His Gospel, the spiritual lives of people are endangered, driven either to futility and despair or to Christ-denying self-confidence and arrogance. The end result is the same: unbelief, which condemns. Where the Law and the Gospel are mixed together, faith is endangered and uncertainty rules the day.

Among the many gifts that we received from the Lord through Walther is the biblical truth that God speaks to human beings in two fundamentally different and even opposing ways. The Scriptures identify this twofold manner of speaking as Law and Gospel. The great twentieth-century theologian Werner Elert (1885–1954) observed that Walther was one of only two men, the other being Theodosius Harnack (1817–89), who genuinely grasped what was at stake with this teaching in the nineteenth century.[2] Walther, a careful student of Luther and the Lutheran Confessions followed the pattern of the Apology of the

1 This paper was originally presented at a meeting of the NALC, LCC, and LCMS Dialogue held in Dallas, Texas, on May 1, 2013.

2 Werner Elert, *Law and Gospel*, trans. Edward Schroeder (Philadelphia: Fortress Press, 1967), 2. Also see Robert C. Schultz, "The Distinction between Law and Gospel," *Concordia Theological Monthly* (October 1961): 591–97.

Augsburg Confession: "All Scripture should be divided into these two main topics: the law and the promises. In some places it communicates the law. In other places it communicates the promise concerning Christ, either when it promises that Christ will come and on account of him offers the forgiveness of sins, justification, and eternal life" (Ap IV 5).[3]

In a series of Friday evening lectures for seminary students delivered between September 12, 1884, and November 6, 1885, now published under the title *Law and Gospel: How to Read and Apply the Bible*, Walther echoes the teaching of the Lutheran Confessions when he writes, "The doctrinal contents of all Holy Scripture, both of the Old and the New Testament, consist of two doctrines that differ fundamentally from each other. These two doctrines are Law and Gospel."[4] Like Luther before him, Walther knew that the ability to rightly distinguish the Law and the Gospel was a hard and difficult art to learn; one that finally could only be taught by the Holy Spirit through God's Word as the believer lived under the cross of spiritual affliction. Far more than a technique or method acquired by academic study, the ability to know and apply both Law and Gospel comes only through the experience of hearing and trusting God's Word even as one lives in constant battle with sin and the devil.

Walther knew of this battle. He had experienced it in his youth as a university student in Germany exposed to the teachings of both Rationalism and Pietism. These two powerful movements blurred the distinction of the Law from the Gospel, leaving people in uncertainty over their standing before God. Rationalism would reduce God's Law to moral precepts capable of being fulfilled with the aid of natural, human wisdom, leaving no room for a Savior who would fulfill the Law for us in His obedient life and His sacrificial death. Subjecting Holy Scriptures to the judgment of human reason, the biblical Gospel was rejected as obsolete. If God's Word could not be trusted, then the sinner is left with his own strivings to lead a morally decent life. Ethics become more

3 Book of Concord quotations in this chapter are from Kolb-Wengert.

4 C. F. W. Walther, *Law and Gospel: How to Read and Apply the Gospel*, ed. Charles P. Schaum, trans. Christian C. Tiews (St. Louis: Concordia Publishing House, 2010), 11.

important than doctrine. Pietism would focus on the subjective experience of the believer, directing him to the testimony of his own emotions. Again this deprives struggling Christians of the certainty of salvation through Christ alone. As a young man, Walther had been tyrannized by the uncertainty created in his heart by the demands of Pietism. It was only as he heard the true Gospel of Jesus Christ preached as God's sure and certain promise to be the Lord of real sinners that Walther found peace for his tormented soul.

In his *Law and Gospel,* Walther demonstrates how God's Law is different from His Gospel in the way that they are revealed, in their content, in the way each either threatens or makes promises, in their effects, and in regard to the persons to whom they are to be preached. Walther wants Christians to know that the Law of God is not the way of salvation but that Word of God which reveals divine wrath over sin and threatens unrepentant sinners with condemnation. While the Law of God promises life to those who keep it and threatens punishment to all who break it, it is powerless to make a person righteous in the sight of God. It is only the Gospel that declares sinners to be righteous, not on account of their morality or good intentions but solely because of the work of Jesus Christ, who has fulfilled the Law, suffered under its condemnation in our place, and been raised from the dead as our Brother. Walther was insistent on rightly discerning the difference between the Law and the Gospel so that broken sinners might come to know and to trust God's ultimate word of good news, the promise that Jesus' blood and righteousness alone give us the forgiveness of sins. That is the Gospel, which makes and keeps us Christian, and it is to predominate in all preaching and teaching. Further, Walther sees that the life of good works is rooted in the promises of the Gospel and not the threats of the Law.

The continued use of Walther's *Law and Gospel,* now available in a fresh contemporary English, is evidence of its abiding significance in the life of The Lutheran Church—Missouri Synod. Walther's theses on the proper distinction of Law and Gospel are required reading for the first-year homiletics class at Concordia Theological Seminary. My book, *Handling the Word of Truth: Law and Gospel in the Church Today* (2004) was an attempt to bring Walther's theses in conversation with contemporary Christians. It was revised and expanded in 2015 to include the 2010 translation of Walther. Although written with a Lutheran audience in mind, *Handling the Word of Truth* has also been positively received in some circles of American Evangelicalism and Reformation-oriented American Anglicanism. The LCMS Sunday School teacher's magazine, *Teachers Interaction*,[5] featured a "Law Gospel Department," a column which applied Walther's material to teach the faith to children. CPH also published *Law and Gospel: The Lutheran Difference* by Korey Maas in 2005 as an adult education piece to assist laity in learning the Law/Gospel distinction.

Within the last decade or so, there have been significance publications and conferences on Law and Gospel, particularly with reference to the so-called "third use." Scott Murray's doctoral dissertation was printed by CPH in 2002 under the title *Law, Life, and the Living God: The Third Use of the Law in Modern American Lutheranism.* The Law/Gospel distinction would be part and parcel of the controversies in the LCMS leading up to Seminex in 1974. Even today, the aftermath of that conflict remains.

Law, Life, and the Living God focuses on this controversy. The book itself is well organized, beginning with an opening chapter that identifies the centrality of the Law/Gospel distinction in Lutheran theology, surveys the threat of antinomianism in the sixteenth century, and surveys the content of Article VI of the Formula of Concord. In the first chapter, Murray shows his hand as he identifies Elert as a culprit: "Elert set up a false alternative: Either the Law accuses or it is only didactic."[6] The bulk

5 *Teachers Interaction* ceased publication in 2014.

6 Scott Murray, *Law, Life, and the Living God: The Third Use of the Law in Modern American Lutheranism* (St. Louis: Concordia Publishing House, 2002), 29. Unfortunately, in the LCMS, Elert is often interpreted through the lens of those who translated and cited him for their own theological agenda in the 1960s and 1970s. This continues down to the present in some quarters of the LCMS. See Matthew Becker, "Werner Elert in Retrospect," *Lutheran Quarterly* (Autumn 2006): 249–302. Elert needs to be read and assessed independent of these interpreters. This point is made by a former student of Elert, Lowell C. Green. See Green, "The 'Third Use of the Law' and Werner Elert's Position," *Logia* (Eastertide 2013): 27–34. A yet unpublished paper by Roland Ziegler, "What Happens When the Third Use of

of the book is comprised of three chapters that look at the history of the debate according to three historical periods: (1) 1940–60, (2) 1961–76, and (3) 1977–98. A final chapter addresses the question "How Has the Third Use Fared?" Here Murray argues that the *lex semper accusat* need not rule out a third use of the Law in light of the fact that "the *simul justus et peccator* provides the anthropological shape to the application of Law and Gospel."[7]

Murray identifies T. A. Kantonen, Richard Caemmerer, and Jaroslav Pelikan as mid-century conduits of the Luther renaissance to American Lutheran soil; these men enabled theologians to identify and correct the Aristotelianism of Melanchthon and his seventeenth-century heirs. In particular, it was Richard Caemmerer (professor of homiletics at the St. Louis seminary from 1940 to 1974) who would serve as a catalyst in this time of theological ferment. Other factors identified by Murray are Missouri's participation in the Bad Boll conference of 1948 (especially the St. Louis systematician F. E. Mayer) and a number of Caemmerer's students who would go to Erlangen to study with Werner Elert. While Murray sees something of a parallel between this generation of Missourians (Edward Schroeder, Robert Bertam, Robert Schultz, et al.) and their counterparts in the Lutheran Church in America (George Forell and William Lazareth), he also notes distinct differences of approach. "While affected by existentialism and dialectical theology to this significant degree, Lazareth and Forell still accepted natural Law in the theological matrix. This represented a clear deviation from the trend set by Caemmerer and Pelikan, who identified the doctrine of an objective natural Law as a significant threat to Christ-centered Christian theology."[8]

Although Murray is critical of Schroeder and others primarily associated with Valparaiso University (hence the moniker "Valparaiso Theologians") for their rejection of the *usus tertius*, he is not unmindful of flaws within the Missouri Synod's traditional interpretation of the Law

---

the Law Is Rejected?" demonstrates that Elert's rejection of the "the third use" by no means indicates an embrace of antinomianism. {This is now chapter 13 of this book.}

7 Murray, *Law, Life, and the Living God*, 217.

8 Murray, *Law, Life, and the Living God*, 60.

that blunted the dynamic of the Law/Gospel distinction. For example, Murray offers this critique of an essay by R. Herrmann on the "The Decalog and the Close of the Commandments" in *The Abiding Word* (1946): "Herrmann reduced the Ten Commandments to information for humans about the will of God. This approach to the Law mutes the sinner's confrontation before the holy God (*coram Deo*). . . . The Law as information alone emasculates the real threat of the majesty and holiness of God against the whole person."[9] Again Murray writes:

> The theologians who provided articles for *The Abiding Word* were deeply affected by the orthodoxy they inherited from Walther and Pieper. They emphasized the Law as an objective standard that provides instruction for Christian holiness. Unfortunately, their viewpoint tended to accept a tamed Law. They also made a sharp division between the heart and the mind of the Christian. The Gospel affected the heart; the Law affected the mind of the Christian. These old Missourians emphasized the third use so strongly that they tended detrimentally to de-emphasize the second use. They also presumed that the Law was susceptible to human manipulation so the preacher controlled the uses of the Law. Later critics of these positions had ample room to chide the old Missourians.[10]

The decade of the 1960s witnessed a new generation of Missouri Synod theologians, many of whom had done doctoral work in Germany and now held teaching positions at Concordia Seminary (St. Louis), Concordia College (formerly River Forest, now Chicago), and Valparaiso University. Murray includes Edward Schroeder, Robert Bertram, Walter Bartling, Robert Hoyer, Paul G. Bretscher, Walter Bouman, and Robert Schultz in this group, although he devotes most of his attention to Edward Schroeder. Murray traces the development of Schroeder's theology from Werner Elert while arguing that Schroeder went beyond

---

9 Murray, *Law, Life, and the Living God*, 65.

10 Murray, *Law, Life, and the Living God*, 73.

Elert in making the Law/Gospel distinction "*the* biblical hermeneutic of the Lutheran church."[11] Murray concludes that "in varying degrees the defenders of Valparaiso theology were prone to attribute to the Gospel parenetic purposes so that the Law's work was subsumed under the Gospel. The denial of the third use of the Law leads to a redefinition of the Gospel to include legal concepts. The Gospel is no longer the gratuitous promises of God to the anxious sinner."[12] In other words, the Law simply returned in a legalized Gospel as the Gospel now becomes the guide to the ethical life.

One of the most insightful and perhaps provocative sections of *Law, Life, and the Living God* is Murray's investigation of the fate of the *usus tertius* among the theologians of the American Lutheran Church and the Lutheran Church in America and, more recently, the Evangelical Lutheran Church in America. In particular, Murray uses William Lazareth, Gerhard Forde, and William Horden as primary examples of theologians from these bodies who questioned the Law's third use. The 1963 *Dialog* article, "A Comparison of Melanchthon's and Luther's Doctrine of Justification" by the Finnish scholar Lauri Haikola is said to have "set the tone for the ALC and LCA approach to the third use of the Law."[13] However, Murray rightly notes the critical contribution of Forde's 1969 book, *The Law-Gospel Debate*, which takes up the nineteenth-century debate as a prelude for the controversy provoked by Barth. Here Murray could have paid more attention to the influence of Gustaf Wingren (especially *Creation and Law*), Hans Joachim Iwand, and Wilfred Joest (especially *Gesetz und Freiheit*) on Forde as these theologians lead Forde to understand the Law/Gospel distinction differently from Schroeder and his colleagues.

Henry Eggold, David Scaer, John Montgomery, Eugene Klug, Theodore Jungkuntz, and Kurt Marquart are selected as representatives of LCMS theologians who defended a third use of the Law in the 1960s

11 Murray, *Law, Life, and the Living God*, 103.

12 Murray, *Law, Life, and the Living God*, 114.

13 Murray, *Law, Life, and the Living God*, 115.

and 1970s. The defense of the *usus tertius* was part and parcel of a larger struggle in the LCMS over the authority of Scripture and the relationship of Gospel to doctrine. Several themes emerge in the apologetic for the third use mounted by the theologians faithful to the historic teaching of the Synod. The continuity between Luther and the Formula of Concord is stressed. The anthropological aspect of Christian existence as *simul justus et peccator* calls for the ongoing place of the Law in the life of the believer against what was seen as ethical permissiveness on the part of the advocates of "Gospel reductionism."[14]

Surveying the period of 1961–76, Murray opines:

> The more radical treatments of the Law by the theologians of the Valparaiso school might well have been a theological overreaction calculated to shock and irritate the stodgy orthodoxy of the Missourians. As the two groups faced off over momentous issues, the political situation required swift responses, often fraught with too much passion and too little deliberation. The Missourians rejected the hermeneutical implications of the Valparaiso position for methodological reasons, but they could also see the impact Gospel reductionism would have on any number of Christian doctrines, including the three uses of the Law. The ELCA theologians were not as deeply affected by the internecine fights wracking the LCMS and thus were more balanced in their consideration of the third use of the Law, though they clearly denied it a place in their theology. Forde's use of Haikola's thesis about the significance of the Law in Lutheran theology presents significant evidence of this balance.[15]

---

14 This phrase seems to have been coined by John Warwick Montgomery. See his book *Crisis in Lutheran Theology*, vol. 1 (Grand Rapids: Baker Book House, 1967), 81–123. Also see Edward Schroeder, "Law–Gospel Reductionism in the History of The Lutheran Church—Missouri Synod," *Concordia Theological Monthly* (April 1972): 1–17.

15 Murray, *Law, Life, and the Living God*, 145. In this light, it would have been interesting to hear the author's evaluation of Forde's "Law and Sexual Behavior" in *Lutheran Quarterly* (Spring 1995): 3–22, as Forde clearly demonstrates that he is no antinomian.

Chapter 4 takes up the period from 1977 to 1998 as Murray revisits Lazareth and Forde and then takes up the views of younger ELCA theologians usually identified as "evangelical catholics" (Scott Ickert, David Yeago) who are critical of the "practical antinomianism" (Yeago) spawned by Lutheran theologians of the twentieth century. Murray's narration of the debate between David Yeago and Walter Bouman prompts him to observe, "The younger ELCA theologians are now moving toward the Missourians on the third use of the Law. How this convergence will progress remains to be seen."[16] Murray does not take up the question as to what extent the evangelical catholic affirmation of the third use of the Law is motivated by an attraction to the "virtue ethics" made popular by Alasdair MacIntyre and John Milbank and reflected, at least to some degree, in the work of LCMS ethicist Gilbert Meilaender.[17]

Murray's book would be the centerpiece for engagement at the 2005 symposium on the Lutherans Confessions at Concordia Theological Seminary in Fort Wayne. Essayists Lawrence Rast, Larry Vogel, Louis Smith (died just weeks before the symposium, but his essay was read by Richard Niebanck), David Scaer, James Nestingen, Mark Mattes, and Carl Beckwith each provided critical and constructive responses to Murray's work demonstrating tensions and nuances in how the place of the third use is understood. These essays were published in the July/October 2005 issue of *Concordia Theological Quarterly.*

Other recent works which also provide ongoing engagement with the place of the Law in Lutheran theology and ethics have appeared within the last few years. Essays from the 2001 exegetical symposium at Fort Wayne in 2001 appear under the title *The Law in Holy Scripture* edited by Charles Gieschen. David P. Scaer's book *Law and Gospel and the Means of Grace* was published as volume VIII in the Confessional Lutheran Dogmatics series in 2008. Edward Engelbrecht's *Friends of the*

16 Murray, *Law, Life, and the Living God*, 218.

17 See, for example, Gilbert Meilaender, *The Freedom of the Christian: Grace, Vocation, and the Meaning of Our Humanity* (Grand Rapids: Brazos Press, 2006), 37–55. Also note a Lutheran critique of virtue ethics by Mark C. Mattes, "The Thomistic Turn in Evangelical Catholic Ethics," *Lutheran Quarterly* (Spring 2002): 65–100.

Law: Luther's Use of the Law for the Christian Life appeared in 2011. The chaotic decadence of our culture has evoked an interest in natural law in the wider Christian community and in the LCMS, spurring CPH to publish *Natural Law: A Lutheran Reappraisal* edited by Robert Baker (2011). Holger Sonntag's translation of Luther's complete "Antinomian Theses and Disputations" appeared in print from Lutheran Press in 2008 under the title *Solus Decalogus Est Aeterrnus.*

Much of the discussion in the Missouri Synod at the moment seems to center on the concern that the classical Law/Gospel distinction does not adequately address issues of Christian living. Two decades ago, this was reflected in a controversial book by Robert Nordlie and Philip Bickel, *The Goal of the Gospel: God's Purpose in Saving You.* Published by CPH in 1992 and then later withdrawn after a successful challenge of its doctrinal review status, the book defended the thesis that God's goal in saving sinners was that they might be obedient to His will for sanctified living. In the view of the authors, the Gospel goal is not simply the creation of saving faith but the empowerment of obedience for Christian life, especially mission. The influence of *The Goal of the Gospel: God's Purpose in Saving You* would be short-lived, but significant numbers of LCMS pastors and laity would be attracted to non-Lutheran popular works such as Rick Warren's *The Purpose Driven Life.* This would seem to indicate an inability to appreciate or apply the Law/Gospel distinction. One might also probe here with a view to detect if Karl Barth's insistence on the Gospel-Law sequence, with its accent on obedience evoked by the divine encounter as the goal of Christian existence, had any influence on homiletics and catechetical materials produced in the LCMS in the 1950s and 1960s. The unintended result was the blurring of Law and Gospel among that and the sequent generation of LCMS clergy and laity.

The recognition of the need to speak concretely of the Christian life in preaching and teaching has led to some probing into Luther's writings. Hence the provocative title of a continuing education course developed by Dr. Joel Biermann, "Two Kinds of Righteousness: A Better Paradigm than Law and Gospel?"[18] Luther's distinction between two kinds of righteousness is suggested as a more fulsome way of providing space for conversation about the Christian's life in the world. While "two kinds of righteousness" is surely an important aspect of Luther's overall theological approach, it seems to serve as a corollary drawn from the Law/Gospel distinction rather than an overarching and perhaps even competing alternative. There is also the concern that the preaching of so-called horizontal righteousness (active) can easily become disconnected from the vertical righteousness (passive) and become a platform for moralistic preaching. Luther's teaching of the two kinds of righteousness is to exalt the righteousness that alone saves—that is, the righteousness of Christ Jesus.[19]

CONCLUSION

The Lutheran Church—Missouri Synod has a theological legacy deeply imprinted with the necessity of the Law/Gospel distinction. As is the case with any heritage, it has suffered neglect, abuse, and distortion. There have been chapters which give evidence of legalism and others which indicate the presence of antinomianism, which only veils a rigid form of legalism. We in the LCMS are challenged today to reclaim and put to use the Law/Gospel distinction in preaching, teaching, liturgy, pastoral care, mission, and ethics. It is not irrelevant or incidental to any of these aspects of our life together. The distinction of the Law from the Gospel cannot be taken for granted for the sake of the doctrine of justification by faith alone. Here the warning of Hans Joachim Iwand first uttered well over a half-century ago is strikingly timely:

---

18 See Charles Arand and Joel Biermann, "Why the Two Kinds of Righteousness?" *Concordia Journal* (April 2007): 116–35. Also Robert Kolb and Charles Arand, *The Genius of Luther's Theology: A Wittenberg Way of Thinking for the Contemporary Church* (Grand Rapids: Baker Academic Press, 2008), 21–128. After this essay was first presented in 2013, Joel Biermann published a book, *A Case for Character: Towards a Lutheran Virtue Ethics* (Minneapolis: Fortress Press, 2014). In this book, Biermann clarifies his preference for virtue ethics.

19 See Hans Joachim Iwand, *The Righteousness of Faith according to Luther*, trans. Randi Lundell (Eugene, Oregon: Wipf & Stock, 2008) and Steven Paulson, "Categorical Preaching," in *Justification Is for Preaching*, ed. Virgil Thompson (Eugene: Wipf & Stock, 2012), 123–46. Used by permission of Wipf and Stock Publishers. www.wipfandstock.com.

An evangelical church that views the teaching of the righteousness of faith as self-evident—but about which no one should trouble himself and further because other issues are more important—has in principle robbed itself of the central solution by which all other questions are illuminated. Such a church will become increasingly splintered and worn down. If we take the article of justification out of the center very soon we will not know why we are evangelical Christians or should remain so. As a result we will strive for the unity of the church and will sacrifice the purity of the Gospel; we will have more confidence in church organization and church government and will promise more on the basis of the reform of Christian authority and church training than either can deliver. If we lose our center, we will court pietism and listen to other teachings and we will be in danger of being tolerant where we should be radical and radical where we should be tolerant.[20]

20 Iwand, *The Righteousness of Faith*, 18.

RIGHTLY DIVIDING THE WORD OF TRUTH[1]

An Introduction to the Distinction between Law and Gospel

Mark A. Seifrid

As *evangelical* Christians, we profess to be committed first and foremost to the proclamation and preservation of the Gospel. Yet it is worth asking ourselves afresh if the Gospel truly has grasped our hearts and lives. Indeed, that is the essence of being a Christian. Whether we find ourselves discouraged by failure or elated by success, we must again and again grasp the word of the Law and the word of the Gospel in their distinction from each other. This distinction is not a truth which may quietly rest in an outline of systematic theology, but bears fundamental hermeneutical implications. Through this distinction, the Bible offers its own interpretation,[2] and does not remain merely a book I read, but is "the book that reads me."[3]

1 The expression (sc. show yourself a worker) ὀρθοτομοῦντα τὸν λόγον τῆς ἀληθείας describes the proper *ministry* of the divine Word, not merely exegesis or interpretation, but picturing it as walking or cutting a straight path in the face of useless, yet popular distractions and heresies (cf. LXX Proverbs 3:6; 11:5). In context, this "word of truth," the "word of God" is clearly equivalent to the Gospel of the crucified and risen Christ, who is the seed of David (2 Timothy 2:8–13).

2 The distinction is implicit in the words of the risen Christ to the disciples on the Emmaus road (Luke 24:25–27) and on the evening of the day of the resurrection (Luke 24:44–49). The whole of Scripture is fulfilled in *His* suffering and resurrection, to which the Law of Moses indeed bears witness, but from which it is distinguished as a body of requirements (e.g., Luke 2:22; 16:19; Acts 13:38–39; 15:1–21).

3 The words come from a woman in an African village, who was asked by her neighbors why she reads only the Bible. See Hans-Ruedi Weber, *The Book That Reads Me* (Geneva: World Council of Churches, 1995).

In this light, it is worthwhile to listen to the complaint—in all its length—that at least one disappointed Christian has voiced concerning his own experience of an evangelical church:

> I experienced what happens when Law and Gospel are not understood and thus not distinguished. My Christian life, truly begun by grace, was now being "perfected" on the treadmill of the Law. My pastors did not end their sermons by demanding that I recite the rosary or visit Lourdes this week in order to unleash God's power; instead, I was told to yield more, pray more, care about unbelievers more, read the Bible more, get involved with the church more, love my wife and kids more. Not until . . . some 20 years later, did I understand that my Christian life had come to center around my life, my obedience, my yielding, my Bible verse memorization, my prayers, my zeal, my witnessing, and my sermon application. I had advanced beyond the need to hear the cross preached to me anymore. Of course, we all knew that Jesus had died for our sins, and none of us would ever argue that we were trying to "merit" salvation. But something had changed. God was a Father all right, but a painfully demanding one. I was supposed to show that I had cleaned up my life and was at least grateful for all the gifts that had been bestowed. . . . The Gospel was critical for me at the beginning, critical now to share with others, and still critical to get me into heaven, but it was of little other value. The "evangel" in Evangelicalism was missing.[4]

Would this person's experience have been any different at any other evangelical church? How many of our churches truly live up to the name "evangelical"? Should the Gospel be reserved only for the beginning of the Christian life, or an invitation at the close of the sermon? Is Charlotte Elliott's hymn "Just as I Am, without One Plea" to be reserved merely for

4 Craig A. Parton, *The Defense Never Rests: A Lawyer's Quest for the Gospel* (St. Louis: Concordia Publishing House, 2003), 18.

evangelistic crusades? Or is it for the daily life of every Christian? If this hymn and others like it become part of our daily thought and life, are we resigning ourselves to weakness and defeatism—an impotent faith that brings no growth?

Before we take up these questions, a brief confession is necessary. I omitted a brief, but central element of Craig Parton's story: it was, as he says, when he "came to the Lutheran Reformation" that he was able to see his way through the faults of the teaching to which he had been exposed. Although it is not entirely absent from the Reformed tradition, the insistence on a sharp distinction between Law and Gospel is much more characteristic of Lutheran thought. As an all-too-brief introduction to this topic, it is worth tracing some of the historical lines of thought centered upon the interpretation of Scripture as Law and Gospel. Naturally, we can only touch on the surface of matters that require discussion in considerable historical and theological depth. Yet perhaps it is possible to provide a basic orientation.

It was Luther who not only first formulated this distinction, but also associated it with his very conversion and reformational discovery:

> I learned to distinguish between the righteousness of the Law and the righteousness of the Gospel. I lacked nothing before this except that I made no distinction between the Law and the Gospel. I regarded both as the same thing and held that there was no difference between Christ and Moses except the times in which they lived and their degrees of perfection. But when I discovered the proper distinction, namely, that the Law is one thing and the Gospel is another I broke through.[5]

For Luther, "Law" expresses God's demand on us in all its clarity and as a result condemns us and delivers us over to death. He uses the term "Law" as an overarching description of God's demand on us, whether that demand is expressed in the Old Testament or the New, or written

5 The statement comes from the mature Luther (1542). I have drawn it in slightly altered form from AE 54:442.

in the heart of the human being by the Creator. Yet as Luther's own usage shows, this summary category contains plenty of room for both the variety of biblical terms which describe God's will for human conduct and for its own fulfillment outside itself in Jesus Christ.

A protest often already arises at this point, especially from Old Testament scholars: "the Law was an expression of God's grace given only after the Lord's deliverance of Israel in the exodus, as a *gift* to His people." Apart from a necessary qualification as to what is meant by "grace" in such a protest, Luther most likely would have gladly agreed with it—and nevertheless insisted that Law and Gospel must be kept as far apart from each other as "heaven and earth." Although it is not without its resonance in Reformed theology, as we shall see, this protest now often represents a reaction against a Kantian (or neo-Kantian) rejection of external moral constraints.[6] The protest is legitimate as such, but it entirely misses Luther's point. Scholars also are prone to speak of "negative" and "positive" statements about the Law in Paul's letters. But these categories, too, represent little other than a Kantian hangover. For Luther as for Paul before him, even in its strange, condemning work, the Law serves the proper and good purpose of God. For this reason, Luther speaks rightly of "the blessed death" worked by the Law.[7] We shall return to this matter further below.

It is important to observe first of all that Luther, along with other reformers, recognized that the Law appears in more than one "function" (or "office") within the Scriptures. It quickly becomes apparent in the

---

6 Scott R. Murray, *Law, Life, and the Living God: The Third Use of the Law in Modern American Lutheranism* (St. Louis: Concordia Publishing House, 2002), takes up the outworkings of these sorts of debates.

7 As, for example in Luther's mocking reply to Jerome Emser's interpretation of "the Spirit" and "the letter," which retains its validity for certain current readings of Paul (see AE 39:185.):

> Therefore, it is impossible for someone who does not first hear the Law and let himself be killed by the letter, to hear the Gospel and let the grace of the Spirit bring him to life. Grace is only given to those who long for it. Life is a help only to those who are dead, grace only to sin, the Spirit only to the letter. No one can have the one without the other. Therefore, what Emser calls the letter and death is, in reality, nothing but the veil, the harmful misunderstanding of the letter, and the damnable flight from this blessed death.

Decalogue, for example, that the Law reckons with the presence of evil in the human heart. Although it provides no means by which that evil may be removed, it does pronounce injunctions by which evil may be curbed. The commandments "You shall not murder" and "You shall not commit adultery" presuppose that hatred and lust reside in the human heart.[8] In a significant measure, these and other prohibitions (and threats) of the Law prevent human beings from acting upon those evil desires.[9] While the fallen world is not thereby tamed, the Law serves to preserve human society and to further its natural development as God's creation, even in its fallen condition.[10] This divinely ordained function of the Law came to be known as the "first" or "political" use of the Law (*usus civilis*). It is not to be confused with the "second" or "condemning" function of the Law, which serves God's larger saving purpose (*usus theologicus*). Simply because I refrain from murder under threat of punishment does not mean that I have been forgiven and redeemed from the evil of hating another human being in my heart! Out of his own particular theological perspective, Luther's fellow reformer Philip Melanchthon came to speak of a "third use of the Law," the use of the Law as instruction and pattern of life for the regenerate.[11] This category, although extraneous to Luther's understanding of Law and Gospel, nevertheless can be encompassed within it, so long as it is recognized that the "third use of the Law" in the end is nothing other than the first and second uses of the Law at work in the life of the believer.[12]

---

8 The Law, which also enjoins love of neighbor (Leviticus 19:18), thus bears an internal tension which points forward to Jesus' teaching (e.g., Matthew 5:21–26) and work.

9 The Law reflects the natural law, which however obscured is already written on the human heart (Romans 2:12–16). While this natural law is to be understood as universal (and not, for example, in terms of something like a nationalistic, German *Volksnomos*), the Law given to Israel retains its priority above all other cultural expressions of natural law (Deuteronomy 4:5–8), an observation relevant to Christian preaching and ethics.

10 See especially Oswald Bayer, *Martin Luthers Theologie: eine Vergegenwärtigung*, 2nd ed. (Tübingen: Mohr–Siebeck, 2003), 134–38.

11 Now it is not God who uses the Law, but the human being! See Timothy J. Wengert, *Law and Gospel: Philip Melanchthon's Debate with John Agricola of Eisleben over Poenitentia* (Grand Rapids: Baker, 1997).

12 The Epitome of the Formula of Concord, Article VI, nicely walks a very fine line, preserving Luther's position while allowing for a certain understanding of a *tertius usus legis* in the

In relation of the Law to the Gospel, we are first and foremost concerned with the condemning function of the Law, much as Paul was in his Letter to the Galatians. That condemning function, it must be pointed out, does not at all entail the idea that the Law is evil. Admittedly, for Luther the Law becomes the tool of sin and of the devil, who works sin and despair in us through it. Nevertheless, the Law remains in God's hand, just as sin and the devil also remain ultimately in God's hand. In the light of the Gospel, it becomes clear that the Law has a "strange," but necessary purpose. As Paul tells us, evil lies not in the Law, but within *me* (Romans 7:14–25). It is for this reason that the Law condemns me.

Yet another objection regularly arises: "Why would God give a Law that no one can fulfill?" We may respond with two observations on the usual function of civil law. In the first place, in making laws, the primary question is *not* whether human beings will be able to keep those laws, but whether the laws are just and beneficial for society. Unhappily, our sinfulness sometimes expresses itself in fraud, embezzlement, robbery, murder, and other crimes. Obviously, the criminalization of such behavior is intended to induce conformity to the norm through the threat of punishment. Nevertheless, some persons in some situations cannot keep themselves from acting in such ways. That does not normally hinder the development of law. It would hardly be appropriate, for example, to exempt alcoholics from drunk-driving laws because they may lack the ability to keep themselves from drinking and driving. The Law of God likewise was given because it is right and good: more on this point in a moment. Second, when a police officer has pulled over a driver who is obviously intoxicated, the officer nevertheless administers certain tests to that driver. Why should the officer ask the person to walk a straight line or attempt to touch their finger to their nose if they can see from the start that the person is not able to do so? They do so because it has to be *established* openly and publicly that the person is intoxicated.

The Law has the same function. The Lord's gift of the Law to Israel, which held the offer of life and blessing to Israel if Israel would only obey

---

wake of the debates which had broken out on the matter.

it, served to expose Israel's need for the Lord to make its heart new, so that Israel would love the Lord as the Law requires it to do. Yet from the very start, Israel's conduct in the wilderness anticipated its disobedience once it received the Commandments (Deuteronomy 8:2; 9:7; 29:2–4; 30:1–5). According to Deuteronomy, the Lord (and for that matter, Moses too) knows that Israel is a "stiff-necked" people who will rebel against the Lord and His good Law (Deuteronomy 9:6–7). But it was necessary to establish the matter openly, *so that Israel itself comes to know its condition*: that is one of the fundamental lessons of Israel's history of repeated rebellion, punishment, and restoration. Along with addressing Israel, the Law also addresses all human beings with the good and beneficial demands of God the Creator, even though we are unable to yield the obedience which they require from us. Our sinfulness is so radical, so fundamental to our person, that we are in a state of blindness, a sort of drunkenness on our own pride (and sometimes too, despair). We cannot see, feel, or know our sin without a voice from outside of us that exposes us for what we are. That is the function of the Law, not only at the beginning of the Christian life, but throughout our entire earthly journey. God's Law is like the knife in the hand of the surgeon with which He first must wound us in order to work our healing.

For Luther, the distinction between Law and Gospel was of such a fundamental nature that the ability to draw the distinction between them determined whether or not one was a "theologian" (i.e., whether or not one was a Christian):

> Therefore whoever knows well how to distinguish the Gospel from the Law should give thanks to God and know that he is a real theologian. I admit that in the time of temptation I myself do not know how to do this as I should.[13]

Elsewhere he in fact speaks of the ability to distinguish between Law and Gospel as an "art" which the Holy Spirit alone can work.[14] As Luther himself points out, at the theoretical level, the distinction between

13 AE 26:115.

14 AE 54:125.

demand and gift is not at all difficult to grasp. But Luther has in view the practical distinction between God's demand and God's gift that we must make in the temptations and trials of life. Although we unfortunately do not have space to pursue the matter here, the hermeneutical implications are large. Luther understands the distinction between Law and Gospel to be *fundamental* to Scripture, so that God speaks to human beings concerning salvation in the words of Scripture in these two distinct ways, and in no other way. God's address to us in these two ways in the Scriptures, moreover, is *direct*. The promise of Isaiah 54:13, that "all your sons will be taught of the Lord," is fulfilled in the words of Scripture themselves.[15] Interpretation and application cannot be separated from each other into two distinct acts, but remain together in the single act of faith, which grasps what God has done for us in Christ in its significance for the present moment of our life. Otherwise, the interpretation of Scripture and preaching almost inevitably become the presentation of ideal (or a warning drawn from a pattern of disobedience) that we then are encouraged to follow (or avoid), an image of truth which we are to bring to reality. Naturally, we generally are urged to do so "by the power of the Spirit" and not in our own strength. Nevertheless, as the disappointed evangelical sadly observed in the citation above, the crucified and risen Christ is now strikingly absent from such preaching.[16] As Christ is absent, so, too, is the work of the Law, which calls us to account and judges us, so that we might know freedom from our sins. Preaching which takes this form does nothing to further Christian living. In fact, insofar as it furthers the illusion that we are basically good and merely weak, it is detrimental.

Needless to say, this approach to Scripture calls for a radical revision of our usual pattern of thought, according to which we first complete our

---

15 See John 6:45; 1 Thessalonians 4:9. All Scripture quotations in this chapter are the author's translation.

16 Bonhoeffer found only this kind of preaching; in part, this experience led to his agreement with the thesis of Thomas Cunning Hall (in a manner that the author did not intend) that American Christianity represents "Protestantism without Reformation." See Dietrich Bonhoeffer, *Barcelona, Berlin, Amerika: 1928–1931*, ed. Reinhardt Staats, in Dietrich Bonhoeffer Werke, vol. 10 (Munich: Chr. Kaiser, 1991), 270–71, 276–77.

exegesis and then seek to apply it to life. Without in any way calling into question the need for careful, methodical study of the text, we may ask if the model to which we generally are accustomed properly acknowledges the way in which the Scriptures *interpret us* before we interpret them. To imagine that we can sit down with a text of Scripture, employing certain rules of study and using the linguistic tools at our disposal, determine the meaning of the text, and then go on to apply it prayerfully is to deceive ourselves. We imagine that we master the text, when in fact it discloses its meaning only as it masters us. If the reformational affirmation is true that *Scriptura sui ipsius interpres* ("Scripture interprets itself"), then we must follow the pattern which Luther commends to us. We begin with prayerful entrance into Scripture, continue in meditation on the words of Scripture, and experience the testing of the Gospel in us, in the trials and temptations of our life.[17] As those who believe and therefore already have been interpreted by the Word of God, and driven by our trials, we enter into Scripture praying that God will open us to the Scripture and the Scripture to us.[18] That prayer continues through the whole task of interpretation.

We have mentioned already that while the distinction between Law and Gospel is present within Reformed thought, it does not play the same role there as it does in a Lutheran framework. The difference on this matter goes back to Calvin himself. Calvin is able to speak of the condemning function of the Law with the same vigor as Luther himself (e.g., *Institutes* 2.7.1–7). Yet in his eagerness to resolve the question of the unity of Scripture, he speaks of the Law as functioning *within* a larger covenant of grace which comes to its fulfillment in Jesus Christ.[19] Apart from grace, the Law brings death (*nuda lex*), but seen within its larger setting, in its witness to Christ, the Law does not bring death but serves

---

17 See, e.g., the well-known preface to the Wittenberg edition of Luther's Works (AE 34:282–87).

18 As my own pastor, Chuck Fuller, often rightly prays before preaching.

19 Karl Barth, who was primarily concerned with *revelation* itself rather than Scripture, then brings all of God's dealings with the created order within the circumference of God's gracious dealings in Jesus Christ.

another purpose (*totus lex*). According to this perspective, Law and Gospel do not address the *believing* human being in radically different ways, but only in differing degrees according to the measures of "grace" present within them. Within the Reformed tradition, then, a kind of "salvation history" became the fundamental paradigm by which to explain the difference between Law and Gospel, a "difference" that could become either large or small. Either continuity or discontinuity between the Law and the Gospel could be stressed. There were times in which the Reformed tradition could approach the Lutheran paradigm, but rarely, if ever, do Law and Gospel appear there as "words" which are *irreconcilable* this side of glory.[20] The embedding of the Law within grace qualifies its demands: while the Law works the death of sinners, it has a different effect on the righteous. For them, the Law is no longer a "hard taskmaster" who exacts full payment. It rather urges believers on to the goal of their lives, exciting them to obedience. In describing how the regenerate experience the Law, Calvin appeals directly to the Scripture psalms, Psalm 19 and Psalm 119, to which we shall return below. In itself, of course, the Law is able to impart nothing. Charged with grace, however, the Law is "of utility to the regenerate" (*Institutes* 2.7.12–13). Consequently, *in his own way* Calvin takes up Melanchthon's "third use of the Law" and makes it the "principal use." In a manner distinctly different from the later Formula of Concord, the Law serves first and foremost to instruct the regenerate.

As a result, there is a certain instability within the Reformed tradition on the question of the relationship between Law and Gospel. A few brief examples will have to suffice for illustration. There are some who draw a sharp distinction between them, as does, for example, Isaac Watts

20 Although other factors were at work in it, Dispensationalism, particularly in its early form, may be regarded as an attempt to recapture the sharp distinction between Law and Gospel which one finds in Scripture *by means of temporal distinctions*. It may therefore be regarded as a radicalized form of the Reformed approach, despite its obvious distinctives. The strictly temporal "solution" had to be revised because of early errors (such as the idea that Old Testament saints were saved through the Law), yet even in its revised forms this reading tends to *separate* Law and Gospel rather than (properly) *distinguishing* between them. Again in this case, the attempt to explain the unity of Scripture fully here and now results in a hermeneutic that rests in a temporal scheme rather than solely in the incarnate, crucified, and risen Christ.

in the following hymn:

The Law commands and makes us know
What duties to our God we owe;
But 'tis the Gospel must reveal
Where lies our strength to do His will.

The Law discovers guilt and sin,
And shows how vile our hearts have been;
The Gospel only can express
Forgiving love and cleansing grace.

What curses doth the Law denounce
Against the man that fails but once!
But in the Gospel Christ appears
Pard'ning the guilt of num'rous years.

My soul, no more attempt to draw
Thy life and comfort from the Law.
Fly to the hope the Gospel gives;
The man that trusts the promise lives.[21]

Yet, especially in the wake of the development of covenant theology, there was also a tendency to take up the other side of Calvin's thought, and that in ways of which he would not have approved. The conjoining of grace and Law in a single "covenant of grace" led, for example, to the notion within the Church of Scotland in the late seventeenth and early eighteenth centuries that repentance and holiness were conditions of the covenant of grace.[22] The attempt by the "marrow men" to correct this error led to considerable controversy, including the charge against them of "antinomianism."[23] Although it has larger dimensions, the "new perspective on Paul" has been most fiercely debated within the Reformed

21 *The Lutheran Hymnal* 289. Public domain.

22 See James B. Torrance, "Covenant or Contract? A Study of the Theological Background of Worship in Seventeenth-Century Scotland," *SJT* 23 (1970): 51–76.

23 The Lutheran Reformation had already been forced to deal with this issue in Agricola's controversy with Melanchthon, and then again in a similar manner after Luther's death.

tradition: here, one might suggest, those who see an extreme continuity between the Law and grace have been opposed by those who recognize a clear distinction between them (at least with respect to the unregenerate).

Returning to Luther and Calvin, we may say that there are at least two fundamental differences between them on the relation of Law and Gospel. In the first place, they differ on the question as to where the unity of Scripture is to be found, a question which is profoundly related to God's identity. Calvin seeks to maintain the unity of Scripture through a covenantal structure by which the Law is encompassed within grace. Although there certainly is a mystery of God's grace for Calvin, for him the final unity of Scripture is perceptible and rationally available to us already on this side of glory. Luther, in contrast, while certainly affirming the unity of Scripture, especially as it is manifest to us in the crucified and risen Christ, leaves the final resolution of the relation between Law and Gospel *hidden in God*. The affirmation of the unity of Scripture is a matter of faith, not of sight. These differing approaches to Scripture entail, at least tendentially, differing conceptions of God. Does grace finally serve Law, so that in the last analysis God appears as the Law-giver who in the mystery of election grants grace in Christ? Or does the Law serve the Gospel, so that in the last analysis God appears as absolute Giver, who through the "strange" work of the Law opens the way to His "proper" work in the Gospel, by which He communicates His self-giving love to me, His fallen and condemned creature? Does the mercy of God point us beyond itself, so that we learn to contemplate God's majesty? Or does the mercy of God teach us to see, find, and know the majesty of God only as it is revealed to us in that mercy?

Luther and Calvin correspondingly differ in their conception of the human being, particularly the regenerate human being, who believes in Christ. As is apparent from his understanding of the "third use of the Law," Calvin regards the Law as addressing the believer *as a regenerate person*. This "regeneration" is not fully effective in us, but weak and impeded by the "sluggishness" of the flesh. Consequently, we require the exhortation and urging of the Law's commands, which no longer condemn us but show us God's goal and purpose for us (*Institutes* 2.7.12). Luther, on the other hand, finds within Scripture, especially within the letters of Paul, a radically different picture of the human being. In such passages as Galatians 5:17–26, "flesh" and "Spirit" do not appear there as capacities or qualities of a unified human person, but two different descriptions of the *whole* person. The old, fallen human being in Adam exists along with the new creation God has made us to be in Jesus Christ. We must hasten to add that the relationship between the two is unequal. Our sinful self, which is incapable of faith and obedience to God, has been crucified with Christ (see, e.g., Galatians 5:24–26; Romans 8:7–8). Although our fallen person, "the flesh," remains present until the end of our earthly life (Romans 7:24), that fallen existence is present now only as *a conquered reality*. Luther employs a number of images to communicate this rather difficult concept, none of which captures it fully: we now stand at the dawning of the day, so that from one perspective we stand in the light, yet from another the darkness is still with us; the new life is like Israel's conquest of the Promised Land—the battle already has been won, yet we must enter in to possess that which is already ours; the old Adam is like an outlaw, who once roamed freely wreaking havoc, but now has been placed in chains; we have a mortal illness, yet so long as we trust our Physician and remain under His care the illness shall be healed. Underlying all these images, and distinct from Calvin's perspective, is the understanding that God deals with sin in the human being, even the regenerate human being, not by removing sin from the human being, but by removing *the human being* from sin. The Christian life consists of our "putting to death" our former self by *our new self*, present in the Spirit who dwells in us (Romans 8:12–14; Galatians 5:16–17).

As is the case with Scripture and our understanding of God, so it is with us for Luther: the unity of our person lies outside of us in Jesus Christ. We grasp it now by faith, but it is only in the resurrection that it shall become visible.[24] Until then, we still live within the experience of the wretched person of Romans 7:24. At the same time, in faith, like Paul,

---

24 This is the emphasis above all else of the work of Rudolf Hermann. See his *Luthers These "Gerecht und Sünder Zugleich": Eine Systematische Untersuchung* (Gütersloh: C. Bertelsmann/ "Der Rufer" Evangelischer Verlag: Hermann Werner Nachfolger, 1930).

in the same breath we joyfully offer to God the shout of thanksgiving found in Romans 7:25: He has delivered us from our old self "through Jesus Christ our Lord." *Insofar as we are led by the Spirit*, we no longer need Law or instruction: the Spirit produces fruit in us, just as a healthy tree produces its fruit without any commandments or instruction. That is the sense of Paul's description of the "fruit of the Spirit" in Galatians 5:22–23: "against such things, there is no law." It is of critical importance, of course, that we do not imagine that we have rid ourselves of "the flesh" or that it is even possible to do so in this life. We cannot remove sin from our hearts; we must learn to daily overcome it by the Gospel. That means, of course, that we must also hear God's demands in all their force, so that they expose not merely our sin and guilt (as if they were extrinsic to us), but *us* in our sin and guilt. Only in this painful yet necessary look in the *mirror* of the Law do we see *ourselves* in such a way that we grasp the Gospel.[25] The Law remains absolutely essential to the Christian life, even though properly speaking it operates outside the new life which is given to us in Christ.

Especially with respect to the human being, the difference between Calvin and Luther on the distinction between Law and Gospel now becomes quite clear. Calvin regards regeneration to effect a new state within the human being, which is *partially* present and active. The "flesh" likewise is present as a power which exerts *partial* influence on us. His conception of the "third use of the Law" and the primacy which he assigns to it are bound up with this understanding of the human being. The most important function of the Law lies in its speaking to us as *regenerate persons*, urging us onward to the goal that lies before us. In speaking to the regenerate, the Law has lost its condemning function: it no longer works our death, but only furthers the new life which is partially present in us already. Luther, as we have seen, finds a radically different anthropology in Scripture. The old, fallen creature exists as a whole alongside the new creature, who is likewise a whole. The picture of the human being

25 Calvin very nicely describes the Law as a mirror in this sense. Yet he restricts its use in this way to the unregenerate in *Institutes* 2.7.7.

is radically darkness and light, without any shading of tones. There is no "intermediate state" in which we receive instruction but escape condemnation. Insofar as the Law deals with our salvation (and does not merely guide our outward conduct), it pronounces our condemnation. The Law speaks to us, even to us who are regenerate, *as fallen human beings*. Being a Christian means again and again, in all the trials and temptations of life, hearing and believing the Gospel, which overcomes the condemnation pronounced on us by the Law and by our own consciences in which that Law is written. Insofar as we are grasped by the Gospel and live by faith, we live beyond the Law.

There are at least three fundamental questions—or really, objections—that Luther's understanding of Law and Gospel regularly raises. Is this understanding of Law and Gospel, which appears most directly with the apostle Paul, confirmed or undermined by the rest of Scripture? Does it allow for progress and growth in the Christian life, or are we not left in a sort of ethical paralysis? Must not preaching which follows this paradigm become repetitive and mechanical, so that it becomes a bit like an exercise wheel on which a hamster runs? Obviously, the first question in particular requires a much lengthier answer than we can supply here. But perhaps we can trace a few lines of thought that may prove helpful.

Does the distinction between Law and Gospel run through Scripture? One might begin in Genesis 1–3, where both human existence and the entire creation (including the commandment concerning the tree of the knowledge of good and evil) appear as unmerited *gifts* of God the Creator, and the will of God later expressed in the Law is already present within the heart of human beings: the Gospel opens the door to paradise again so that we know, see, and give thanks to the Creator for His gifts.[26] We might then turn, as Paul does, to the saving work of the Creator in His unconditioned promise to Abraham, which not only came before the Sinai covenant, but in its unconditionality, stands apart

---

26 The work of Oswald Bayer, in which the creational dimension of justification plays a prominent role, is most fully accessible to English speakers at the moment in the summarizing work of Mark Mattes, *The Role of Justification in Contemporary Theology* (Grand Rapids: Eerdmans, 2004), 145–73.

from it as distinct. Or we might turn to the Sermon on the Mount, in which Jesus simultaneously sharpens the demands of the Law and announces its fulfillment in His own person. This latter text is of particular relevance, since here it becomes clear, as Luther recognized, that the new covenant does not abrogate the Law, but brings it to fulfillment *outside of us in Jesus Christ.* Yet for our purposes at the moment, it is useful to glance briefly at the Scripture psalms, which seem to many interpreters to be at odds with Paul's own experience of the Law as he describes it in Romans 7, at least if we understand him to speak of an aspect of his life as a believer. But is that the case? Psalm 119 strikingly ends on the same note as Romans 7:24: "I have gone astray like a lost sheep. Seek Your servant! For I do not forget Your word" (Psalm 119:176). The whole psalm is summarized in this closing statement. The one who delights in the Law of God—who recounts it, meditates on it day and night, and clings to it—nevertheless does not yet *know* it in heart and experience, and repeatedly appeals to the Lord to *teach* him. As he implicitly confesses in the opening of the psalm, his ways are not yet "established" in keeping the Lord's statutes. He still is ashamed when he considers them (Psalm 119:5–8). In view of these petitions and the closing of the psalm, there is good reason, contrary to usual practice, to render the whole of Psalm 119:9 as a question: "How shall a young man purify his way? How shall he keep it according to Your word?" This petition recurs in varying forms, as the psalmist looks *beyond the Law* to the Lord, whom he asks to teach, instruct, and revive him (e.g., Psalm 119:12, 18, 25–26, 29). The condition of the psalmist is not essentially different from that of the believing Paul, who likewise delights in the Law of God, but finds a different Law at work in him that makes him a prisoner of sin. What the psalmist sought from the Lord (and undoubtedly in faith received) is found, Paul with joy announces, in the crucified and risen Christ (Romans 7:25).

In Psalm 19, too, the psalmist, even after his exalted praise of the Law which "refreshes the soul" (i.e., brings refreshment and delight to the heart; Psalm 19:7), confesses that *a saving work of God beyond the Law is necessary in his heart*: "Who can discern (their) errors? Make me innocent of hidden sins. . . . Then I shall be blameless and innocent of great transgression" (Psalm 19:11–13). Admittedly, Psalm 1 lacks this element of confession. But the shadow of the cross lies across this psalm: who among us can claim to be that person here and now? As the psalm itself suggests in its promise that "his leaf does not wither," the path of one righteous one whom it describes leads through testing and trial on its way to the "season" of fruit. These brief reflections by no means answer the larger question as to how the distinction between Law and Gospel fits the whole of Scripture. But perhaps they provide some hints.

Does the distinction between Law and Gospel represent a sort of defeatism that leads to laxity in Christian living? Undoubtedly, when it is loosed from its biblical moorings, it can lead to this result, as Luther himself was aware. Yet the alternative, which supposes that the regenerate merely need instruction in their sluggishness and not the radical remedy of the Gospel, is the more dangerous thought. Here it is appropriate to point yet again to Romans 7. We fail miserably to understand Paul if we imagine him to be telling us that we should simply surrender to our sins and wallow in the misery of them. That is not how the deceptiveness of sin works. We generally are insensate to the sins operating in our hearts and lives: "The heart is desperately perverse and incurably ill, who can understand it?" (Jeremiah 17:9). The sins of which we are aware, dangerous though they may be, are not the most dangerous ones. These hidden faults are more deeply rooted in our person and being than we can imagine, and finally consist in the desire to do away with God and to possess that which properly belongs to our neighbor. This sin, in all its various forms, repeatedly requires the mirror of the Law to expose it. It is this encounter with the commandment of God which brings Paul to see the awful truth about himself, which he describes in Romans 7. In the hand of God, the Law exposes our sin not in order that we might despair, but in order that we see and believe what He has done for us in Christ, as again Paul himself does in Romans 7:25. Without in the least detracting from our conversion, we must not imagine that the turn from unbelief to faith is behind us and complete. It lies before us at every moment.

But where does progress lie in this encounter with the Law? Admittedly, this perspective robs "progress" of its ultimacy. The goal and end of the Christian life is given to us already at its beginning in Jesus

Christ. But this displacing of "progress" from its place of primacy prevents us from taking upon ourselves burdens that we were never meant to bear. We "progress" in that we progress into that which already is given and done for us by God in Christ. That is the sense, for example, of Paul's image of being clothed with Christ. Christ has become ours (and we His) at the start of the Christian life in faith and Baptism (Galatians 3:27–29). Yet Paul also exhorts mature believers to "put on the Lord Jesus Christ" (Romans 13:14). He is not playing some strange mental game. We have Christ, and yet we must *more fully enter into the experience of having Him*: the Word of God has to be tested in our heart and lives. We must taste it. As Paul tells the Philippians, progress in the Christian life is progress *in faith*, in which we more fully grasp that which is already given to us (Philippians 1:25; 3:8–11). That progress in faith is in all our trials and temptations a turning again and again away from unbelief and to God in faith as He gives Himself to us in the Gospel. Our progress is *not* progress away from the cross and resurrection of Christ, as common thinking about sanctification would lead us to think (as if we were working ourselves away from needing Christ). Our progress is progress *into* the cross and resurrection of Christ. We enter more deeply into the beginning of our Christian life rather than becoming ever more distant from it. Is it any wonder that Christians—especially older, more mature Christians—never tire of singing about the cross?

That brings us finally to the question of preaching Law and Gospel. If Luther is right, as I think he is, we will never master this art here on earth. We desperately need the Holy Spirit to teach us how to "rightly divide the word of truth." One matter is certain: this preaching cannot rest with mere abstractions or doctrinal formulas. Those who gather as a church for worship often (but not always!) already know and confess that they are sinners in need of grace. What they need, and what those need who do not feel themselves to be sinners, is the careful, gentle, yet direct exposure of *their* sins, corporately and individually: not merely the faults of our society or problems in our culture or merely sinful activities (although now more than ever pastors have to confront churches with what the Scriptures teach about our created sexuality). What those gathered to worship need to hear is the root sins of self-seeking, pride, lust, envy, and greed by which we deny God and mistreat one another. The "practical atheism" which infects our daily lives without our seeing it must be exposed and judged so that we see afresh precisely what it is that Christ has done *for us.* While form and order of presentation may vary, the preaching of the Law would be incomplete and perverted without the clear announcement of the Gospel, God's unconditioned gift of Himself to us in Jesus Christ. As Luther underscored, the preaching of the Gospel is not merely the preaching of Christ in a general way, but the preaching of Christ *for you and for me.* If we are to avoid useless abstraction and generalities, this "for you and for me" must also be quite specific: it must, so to speak, name us as those persons whom the Scriptures confront with their sins here and now, in our concrete circumstances. As Nathan once confronted David, Scripture must say to us, "You are the one!" (2 Samuel 12:7). *Then,* as those whom the Law concretely and definitely condemns, we may hear the Gospel afresh that gives us life and makes us new creatures. *Then,* faith in the Gospel means quite concrete acts in our hearts and lives, that only the Holy Spirit, not the preacher, can communicate to us. *Then,* we must ask, as Paul himself did, "Who is sufficient for these things?" And *then,* finally, we may echo Paul's confident answer.

MAINTAINING LAW AND GOSPEL IN THE LITURGY

William M. Cwirla

As Lutherans, we are accustomed to speaking of the proper distinction of the Law and the Gospel as it applies to the tasks of preaching and teaching. C. F. W. Walther literally wrote the book on this topic for the Missouri Synod, and the distinction of the Law and the Gospel is considered a hallmark of Lutheran preaching. Less obvious, however, is the proper distinction of the Law and the Gospel in the liturgical life of the congregation. The focus of this essay will be to reflect upon the role and responsibility of the pastor to maintain the proper distinction of the Law and the Gospel in the worship life of the congregation entrusted to his care.

THE WORD OF GOD AS LAW AND GOSPEL

To speak of the "proper distinction of the Law and the Gospel" is to say something that is at once distinctively Lutheran yet not exclusively Lutheran. Lutherans hold no monopoly on this distinction, but the proper distinction of the Law and Gospel is at the heart of Lutheran theology centered in the justification of the sinner by grace through faith in Jesus Christ. "Since the beginning of the world these two proclamations have continually been set forth side by side in the church of God with the proper distinction" (FC SD V 23).[1] Indeed, Law and Gospel are the very rhythm of the Word of God that "kills and brings to life . . . brings down to Sheol and raises up" (1 Samuel 2:6).[2]

1 All quotations from the Book of Concord in this chapter are from the Tappert edition.

2 All Scripture quotations in this chapter are from the RSV.

The proper distinction of the Law and the Gospel is the necessary distinction of God's commands from His promises, our works from God's work, our sacrifices from Christ's sacrifice without which the Scriptures remain a closed book and the once for all sacrifice of Jesus Christ is obscured by the works of man. Law and Gospel are not merely categorical distinctions, as though one can place each verse of Scripture into one bucket or the other as "Law" and "Gospel," but it is the inherent bipolarity of the Word of God that places God's wrath against sin in paradoxically polar tension with His mercy toward the sinner. They are two doctrines held in dynamic tension through which the double-edged Word of God is properly heard and applied.

Law and Gospel are not static, abstract concepts but the living and active Word of God. These are live wires of opposite polarity that kill and make alive. The Law always accuses, condemns, instructs, and kills both sin and the sinner. The Gospel always forgives, justifies, raises up, and renews the sinless saint. Only as these are kept opposite and in dynamic polar tension will they be heard rightly and have their killing- and making-alive way with the hearer.

The distinction of the Law and the Gospel must be carefully and diligently maintained in preaching, teaching, and worship as the Formula of Concord says: We must therefore observe this distinction with particular diligence lest we confuse the two doctrines and change the Gospel into law. This would darken the merit of Christ and rob disturbed consciences of the comfort which they would otherwise have in the holy Gospel when it is preached purely and without admixture, for by it Christians can support themselves in their greatest temptations against the terrors of the law (FC SD V 1). This deep pastoral concern is what drove Luther and the reformers in their reformation of the canon of the Western Mass and their critique of abuses of the Western Catholic tradition. Unlike reform movements before and after it, the Lutheran Reformation was decidedly conservative in its approach to reform, seeking to introduce nothing new or contrary to the Scriptures or the universal tradition of the Church catholic. At the Reformation's center was the justification of the sinner before God by grace through faith for Christ's sake. This alone brought comfort to terrified consciences, as Luther himself experienced personally. The centrality of justification is also necessarily the centrality of Jesus Christ crucified, for His blood and His righteousness alone avail before God. Therefore, keeping the proper distinction of the Law and the Gospel is to keep Christ at the center, and failure to do this in the liturgy will inevitably result in man becoming the center and object of his own worship.

THE PASTOR AS STEWARD AND *SEELSORGER*

The pastor stands uniquely as both steward of the mysteries of God and as *Seelsorger*, the physician of the souls entrusted to his care. As steward, he is entrusted with the care and distribution of the possessions of Christ, whose office he holds in the congregation. The gifts he administers do not belong to him but to Christ. The forgiveness he speaks is not his forgiveness but Christ's forgiveness. The Baptism he administers is not his Baptism but Christ's. The Supper he distributes is not his Supper but Christ's. The task of the steward is to see that the household servants each receive their proper portion at the proper time. A steward is mindful both of the mandate and institution of the Lord and also of the condition of those to whom the gifts are being administered so that he gives them the proper food at the proper time. This is the *Seelsorge* aspect of pastoral care, which not only involves personal one-on-one care such as personal confession, counseling, and visitation, but also corporate care of the congregation as a whole through the liturgy of God's Word and Sacrament. Like the physician who makes a diagnosis and prescribes a course of treatment, the pastor as *Seelsorger* must be attentive to the spiritual condition of the individual members and of the congregation as a whole. A body composed of many members has both an individual and a collective spiritual condition.

This is nicely demonstrated in St. Paul's First Letter to the Corinthian congregation, a congregation beset with multiple issues ranging from division to immorality to disordered worship. By centering the entire letter on Jesus Christ and Him crucified, the apostle is able to address the manifold difficulties of the congregation while avoiding harsh legalisms and apostolic authoritarianism. In addressing abuses at the Lord's Supper involving the agape meal, the apostle simply squares the Corinthians up to the Words of Institution and their implications. When confronting the charismatic issue and the ecstatic speaking in tongues, he simply notes the evangelical need for five coherent words concerning Christ and the fact that God is a God of order, whose prophets are in control of themselves.

St. Paul's pastoral approach to the troubles of Corinth run remarkably parallel to Luther's perceptive approach to liturgical reform in his Invocavit sermons of 1522 preached in Wittenberg. The driving force of the Reformation must always be the Gospel of Jesus Christ crucified or everything will come to naught. Radicals such as Andreas Karlstadt and others who pushed for accelerated reformation in the interest of purifying the church and opposing the papacy met with stern opposition from Luther himself, who recognized that the proper distinction of the Law and the Gospel required much more careful discernment. His willingness to tolerate even the practice of Communion under "one kind" until people could be properly instructed and receive it in a Gospel manner bears witness to Luther's confidence that the Gospel must always be the driving force in the church's worship or, having purged the spirit of the papacy, seven spirits worse than the first would take up residence.

> Although I hold that it is necessary that the sacrament should be received in both kinds, according to the institution of the Lord, nevertheless it must not be made compulsory nor a general law. We must rather promote and practice and preach the Word, and then afterwards leave the result and execution of it entirely to the Word, giving everyone his freedom in this matter. Where this is not done, the sacrament becomes for me an outward work and hypocrisy, which is just what the devil wants. But when the Word is given free course and is not bound to any external observance, it takes hold of one today and sinks into his

heart, tomorrow it touches another, and so on. Thus quietly and soberly it does its work, and no one will know how it all came about.[3]

The pastor as steward and *Seelsorger* is confronted with a myriad of issues in the congregation, many of which come to bear in the congregation's worship. His guidance and oversight of the liturgy is itself an exercise in the proper application of the Law and the Gospel. Hymn selection, preaching lectionary, the seasonal and festival celebrations, the choice of music, and the employment of the arts all come to bear. Is the congregation focused on Jesus Christ and Him crucified? Is the justification of the sinner front and center in the congregation's hymnody as well as the pastor's preaching? Is the Law proclaimed to the death of the sinner? Is the Gospel proclaimed to the resurrection of the saint? Moreover, the pastor must be aware of the liturgical attitude as well as aptitude of the congregation. Are they a congregation that "does the liturgy" or are they a "liturgical congregation" who is at ease with the church's liturgical traditions and forms? Are they justifying themselves by their liturgical precision and performance? Are they itching to try something new and innovative to amuse their bored old Adam? Are they acting out of indulgence of self or love of neighbor? The *Seelsorger* must ever be the keen diagnostician in his liturgical principles. Rigid rubricism is as poor a Law/Gospel prescription as "anything goes" liturgical license.

This calls for a compassionate understanding of one's people, something that can be acquired only through long familiarity, in season and out of season, not only through the seasons of the liturgical year but also the seasons of life with its births, Baptisms, marriages, deaths, and funerals. Pastoral visitation along with individual conversation in the home and workplace are essential to the *Seelsorger's* diagnoses. Along this line, much can be said in favor of long-term pastorates. A pastor's familiarity with the flock increases dramatically with time, as does his ability

3 AE 51:90.

to sense the nuances and subtleties of congregational life. Many a new pastor has mistakenly enacted a hasty change in his first year to address an issue which by his tenth year might appear quite trivial.

As important as conversations with individual members are the observations of congregational meetings. The pastor as *Seelsorger* must retain a certain outside perspective as one who "watches over" (*episkopos*) the flock with a horizon-to-horizon view. Very often, the congregation's peculiar Law/Gospel dynamic can be discerned more clearly in a congregational meeting than it can in its Sunday-to-Sunday liturgical life. *How* a congregation decides and does things is as revealing, and perhaps more symptomatically diagnostic of its condition, than *what* it does. Do they seek to maintain the unity of the Spirit in the bond of peace? Do the stronger concede to the weaker? Does the majority bully the minority through an exercise of power and control? What are the congregation's own idolatries, its "high places" and "sacred groves" that threaten to crowd out the Gospel? While seemingly not connected to worship and the liturgy, such observations are essential to the proper pastoral care of the congregation as a whole and to its individual members. The same body of baptized believers that argues and votes as an assembly must also come together as the Church, the Body of Christ, and be able to set aside their individual differences and preferences and to forgive one another as God in Christ has forgiven them.

THE WORSHIPER AS *SIMUL*

A physician is always thinking diagnostically of his patients. This is also true for the *Seelsorger* as a spiritual physician. One of the most important insights of the Lutheran Reformation is the diagnosis from the books of Romans and Galatians that the baptized believer is at one and the same time a saint and a sinner—*simul justus et peccator*—at once righteous, clothed in the righteousness of Christ, and sinful, corrupted through and through with Adam's original sin. He is, as it were, a holy saint trapped in a sinner, life trapped in a body of death, the spirit of Christ wearing the flesh of Adam, a new "inner man" hidden in, with, and under an old "outer man" (cf. 2 Corinthians 4:16).

What does this mean for the worshiper and the presider of worship? It means that according to his new nature in Christ, he is glad when they said, "Let us go to the house of the Lord." But according to his old nature in Adam, he'd rather pull the cover over his head, catch another hour of sleep, and go out for Sunday brunch with his friends. In short, to be *simul* is to be horribly conflicted. "For the desires of the flesh are against the Spirit, and the desires of the Spirit are against the flesh; for these are opposed to each other, to prevent you from doing what you would" (Galatians 5:17). He wants to be there and doesn't want to be there. He delights in the Law of the Lord, and he doesn't. He hears the Gospel of justification by grace through faith for Christ's sake as freedom to serve the neighbor on the one new hand and license to sin on the old hand.

The pastor as preacher and presider must be thoroughly acquainted with the baptismal paradox of being *simul*, or he will never understand his hearers or himself. They, and he, are flesh born of flesh and spirit born of Spirit. As children of God, they are without sin (1 John 3:1), and yet, if they say they have no sin, they deceive themselves and the truth is not in them (1 John 1:8). While the old man in Adam has been declared dead, he remains for the moment very much alive. And while the new man in Christ has been declared alive, he remains a mystery hidden under the old. It is precisely for this reason that the Law must continue to be preached and heard by the baptized believer in Christ.

> For the Old Adam, like an unmanageable and recalcitrant donkey, is still a part of them [Christians] and must be coerced into the obedience of Christ, not only with the instruction, admonition, urging, and threatening of the law, but frequently also with the club of punishments and miseries, until the flesh of sin is put off entirely and man is completely renewed in the resurrection. There he will no longer require either the preaching of the law or its threats and punishments, just as he will no longer require the Gospel. They belong to this imperfect life. (FC SD VI 24)

External disciplines such as liturgy and lectionary are for the sake of our old nature in Adam, the old, recalcitrant ass, who must be coerced by threats and punishments to go along with the program. In the preface to his 1526 *Deutsche Messe*, Luther observed that liturgical orders and the like "are needed for those who are still becoming Christians or need to be strengthened, since a Christian does not need Baptism, the Word, and the sacrament *as a Christian*—for all things are his—*but as a sinner*."[4] The maintenance of the dynamically polar tension of Law and Gospel in liturgy and preaching is entirely on account of the existential reality of the Christian being *simul justus et peccator*. To suggest that one may worship "in the Spirit" without liturgical forms or preach "as the Spirit moves" is to engage in a kind of liturgical antinomianism, which denies the reality of the old man who wants to order worship his way and does not want to get out of the way and die.

God's way of dealing with things is death and resurrection, not renovation and rehabilitation. The old Adam cannot be rehabilitated. He must die. This is the work of the Law, which outwardly curbs and restrains the old Adam through the various authority structures of the temporal kingdom, reveals and diagnoses the depth of sin as a condition, and disciplines the old man by punishments and rewards to cooperate with the Spirit of Christ so long as he lives, until the Christian is "completely renewed in the resurrection."

The pastor must ever be on guard against moralism, legalism, and pietism that would attempt to renovate or fix his hearers by use of the Law. The Law always accuses (*lex semper accusat*), and it accuses in all of its functions and uses. The purpose of the Law is not to provide a template for moral improvement, but to silence every self-justifying argument before God and amplify sin. Adam must die; Christ must rise. Dying and rising is the daily, baptismal life of the *simul* Christian. Conversely, the pastor must also be on guard against what is generally termed "antinomianism"—that is, the notion that the Christian no longer needs the Law because he is now born of God, covered with Christ, and free from the Law's condemnation. This is to deny the reality of the *simul*, that the Christian remains in this life a sinner.

4 AE 53:62, emphasis added.

The proper distinction and application of the Law and the Gospel is not simply a matter of compromise between legalism and license, nor is it a "balance" with the scales tipped in favor of the Gospel. It is more the way a sailor guides a sailboat into the face of the wind, tacking skillfully from one side to the other, sometimes leaning toward the Law, sometimes toward the Gospel, always cognizant of the condition of the congregation, always recognizing that the Law kills and the Gospel brings life. The pastor may diagnose a spirit of libertinism that needs to be reined in, or a spirit of legalism that needs to be freed.

He also will be aware that each *simul* hearer will have a *simul* hearing of the Word as Law and Gospel. The sinner in Adam will hate the Law and respond with religious bargaining, denial, and anger in view of his own death. He will justify himself or make excuses for his sin. He will blame those around him. On the other hand, the saint in Christ will delight in the Law as a description of who he already is in Christ and how he appears before God clothed in Christ's righteousness. He will strive to become who he already is in Christ, albeit approximately and imperfectly, and use the Law to mortify the sinful nature together with its lusts and desires (see Ephesians 5). The old Adam will hear the good news of free forgiveness as a license to sin. "Let us sin that grace may abound! Let us sin for we are not under Law but under grace" (see Romans 6). But the new man in Christ responds, "May it never be!" Forgiveness in Christ is never license to sin but liberty to serve God and neighbor free from fear of judgment. "There is therefore now no condemnation for those who are in Christ Jesus" (Romans 8:1).

THE LITURGY AS WORD OF GOD IN ACTION

The liturgy is God's Word in action—killing and making alive, bringing down to Sheol and raising up. By His Word, God created and ordered all things in the beginning. By His Word Incarnate, He redeemed us in the death and resurrection of the Son. And by His Word and Spirit, He sanctifies us by means of the birthing and cleansing water of Baptism, the bread and wine that are the sacrificial body and blood of Christ, and the authoritative word of Absolution that looses the sinner from captivity to sin and death by Christ's own authority. So tied to the Word is the pastoral office that our Confessions are willing to give both holy order (*ordo*) and holy ordination (the laying on of hands) the categorical label of "sacrament":

> If ordination (*ordo*) is interpreted in relation to the ministry of the Word, we have no objection to calling ordination a sacrament. The ministry of the Word has God's command and glorious promises: "The Gospel is the power of God for salvation to every one who has faith" (Rom. 1:16), again, "My word that goes forth from my mouth shall not return to me empty, but it shall accomplish that which I purpose, and prosper in the thing for which I sent it (Isa. 55:11). If ordination is interpreted this way, we shall not object either to calling the laying on of hands (i.e., ordination) a sacrament. The church has the command to appoint ministers; to this we must subscribe wholeheartedly, for we know that God approves this ministry and is present in it. (Ap XIII 11–12)

The pastor as the congregation's preacher and presider is much more than a communicator or a master of ceremonies. He is a conduit and instrument connecting the Word of God with God's people. He represents not himself or his own person, but the person of Christ as His authorized representative (*shaliach*, *apostolos*). "He who hears you hears me" (Luke 10:16). This lays a particular burden on the pastor by virtue of the office to which he is called and ordained. Christ requires him "to teach in such a way that he might be heard, because he says, 'hears me'" (Ap XVIII 19). Maintaining the Law and the Gospel in the liturgy means being watchful that it is the dynamic and powerful Word of God that is being preached and not the traditions and opinions of men. The Office of the Word is responsible that the Word be preached and heard in the Church so that the sheep may hear the voice of their Shepherd (see SA XII).

Nowhere else in the liturgy is this more apparent than in the sermon. The pastor's sermon is an event of the living and active Word of Law and Gospel, breaking down and building up, humbling the high and lifting up the low. The plow of the Law crushes and breaks down the hard-packed soil so that the seed of the Gospel might be fruitful. Even when the pastor is exhorting the baptized to holiness and new life, the focus is ever on Christ and not the believer. Our holiness, innocence, and righteousness are not our own nor do they come about because of our works. They are Christ's by His active obedience, and they are ours by imputation through faith. The holiness, innocence, and righteousness we do is our being who we already are in Christ. Every sermon is a struggle between Adam and Christ, between the old man and the new. It is a continual call to repentance, a "re-cognition" (*metanoia*) of our being baptismally dead to sin but alive to God in Christ (Romans 6:11).

The tyranny of the "urgent" and "late-breaking news" that invade our consciousness by way of television, talk radio, and social media conspire to drown out this living and active Word of God for other, more "important" and "relevant" words. As one of the three orders of the temporal kingdom, the Church (*ordo ecclesiasticus*) does not live in monastic seclusion from what goes on in the home (*ordo domesticus*) and civil society (*ordo politicus*) (Small Catechism, Table of Duties). Just as John the Baptizer confronted King Herod over his illicit marriage to Herodias, his brother Philip's wife, so the Church is constantly tempted to comment on the ills and immoralities of the Herods of our own day with the same righteous indignation. And we should not be surprised if she loses her head in the process!

Righteous causes may be both good and right, but they are not salutary. The Word of God must have free course and be preached and not be corralled and co-opted by the urgency of things temporal. This is not to advocate for "quietism" on the part of the Church with respect to the temporal kingdom, but for the Church to assume her proper role and function among the temporal orders, which is to proclaim the reign of Jesus Christ crucified, risen, and ascended, who lords His death and resurrection over the entire created order as the One who has all authority in heaven and on earth. The Church in this world is a foreign embassy of the eternal King of kings and Lord of lords at whose name every knee will bow on the Last Day. While the protection of the unborn, the plight of the poor, the proper stewardship of the environment, the cause of the widowed and orphaned, justice for the worker, and the upholding of marriage as the celebration and protection of the one-flesh union of man and woman are all laudable and even godly causes, they dare not deflect from the Church knowing and hearing nothing but Jesus Christ and Him crucified. While the activists may charge that the Church is fiddling as Rome burns, they need to be reminded that while ancient Rome was falling apart at the seams, the Church was vigorously debating the doctrine of the Trinity and the two natures of Christ. The pastor must ever be on guard, lest the Church lose sight of things eternal for the sake of things temporal.

To this end, liturgy and lectionary come to the rescue and assist the pastor in his work as guardian and steward of the Word. The origins of the liturgy are mysterious. While one can trace various liturgical forms through the ages and the various families of liturgies, there is no single ur-liturgy from whence all Christian worship flows. Parts came from the synagogue service, parts from the Sabbath and Passover tables. The closest we have toward any insight into the worship of the earliest Church is a simple sentence in the Book of Acts: "And they devoted themselves to the apostles' teaching and fellowship, to the breaking of bread and the prayers" (Acts 2:42). Of this much we can be certain: Christian worship always has at its core the apostolic Word, the fellowship (communion, *koinonia*) in the breaking of the bread, and prayer. These impart to Christian worship a transtemporal and transcultural character. The worship of the Church, like the Lord whom she worships, is the same "yesterday, today, and forever."

The introduction to *Lutheran Worship* (1982) captures the essence of liturgy as a living tradition, something handed down and handed on to the next generation of believers.

> We are heirs of an astonishingly rich tradition. Each generation receives from those who went before and, in making that tradition of the Divine Service its own, adds what best

may serve in its own day—the living heritage and something new.[5]

The liturgy, as living tradition, helps to maintain the Law and the Gospel by holding fast to the prophetic and apostolic Word as its content. It has often been observed that nearly all the words spoken, chanted, and sung in the liturgy are Scripture words. *Lutheran Service Book* (2006) does us the valuable service of providing some of the Scripture references. We are reminded that these are not men's words but God's Word spoken through the prophets, apostles, and evangelists and faithfully handed down to us.

The stability of the liturgy provides something more as well. It connects the present with the past and those who have fought the good fight of faith before us. We are not the first to believe and, should the Lord tarry in His appearing, we won't be the last. The churches who confessed at Augsburg could boast before the emperor and the pope, "we have introduced nothing, either in doctrine or in ceremonies, that is contrary to Holy Scripture or the universal Christian church" (AC Conclusion). This was the confidence of the Lutheran churches that they were not a sect or some cult of personality but could lay claim to the "catholic tradition," citing not only Scripture, but also the ancient creeds and liturgies.[6]

Liturgical stability in form and content also promote a pedagogical purpose. From the youngest to the eldest members, all learn the same words, the same rhythms and rhymes. Like the catechism, the liturgy shapes the "primary theology" of the worshiper as it unites the Body of Christ in one common language and confession. The rhythm of the liturgy itself maintains the killing- and making-alive distinction of the Word as a double-edged, Law-Gospel sword, moving from confession to benediction, from diagnosis of the condition to administration of the medicine, from darkness to light, from death to life. With repetitious urgency, the liturgy demands that the worshiper be forgiven in Christ, not

5 See *LW*, p. 6.

6 See Kurt Marquart, "Corporate Worship of the Church," in *Lutheran Worship—History and Practice* (St. Louis: Concordia Publishing House, 1994), 63–64.

just once but several times during the course of the Divine Service. The life of the Christian is one of constant repentance, continual return and renewal in Baptism, and constant dependence upon Christ as Redeemer and Mediator. The liturgy teaches the baptismally born child of God to mortify the old Adam with his sinful lusts and desires and to put on the new man in Christ.

The liturgy emphasizes the externality of the Word of God, which was of paramount concern for the reformers against the enthusiastic radical reformation, over and against the internality of the heart curved inward (*incurvatus est*) and corrupted by sin. "Accordingly, we should and must constantly maintain that God will not deal with us except through his external Word and sacrament. Whatever is attributed to the Spirit apart from such Word and sacrament is of the devil" (SA VIII 10). There is something radically external about the liturgy. It imposes the Word of God on the worshiper. It does not ask that the worshiper "feel" a particular way, nor does it drive the worshiper to look inward for enlightenment. The readings are assigned for the Sunday, as is the chief prayer of the day. The hymns are not selected by majority vote or as a preservice hymn sing, but are selected to fit the assigned readings of the day. Even the prayers do not arise spontaneously but have been prepared for the moment when the liturgy summons, "Let us pray." We hear, eat, and drink; we confess, pray, praise, and give thanks, whether we feel like it or not. It is all gloriously *extra nos,* outside of ourselves, precisely where things must be if the Law and the Gospel are to have their way.

The same can be said of the lectionary, the system of assigned readings for the Church Year. The origins of the lectionary, like the liturgy, are obscure, yet it's clear that a system of readings was used even in the synagogue that came before. The discipline of assigned readings from the Old Testament, an epistle, and one of the Gospels frees the preacher from the tyranny of the urgent "here and now." Never mind what they're talking about in the newspapers and on television, "thus says the Lord." The assigned readings also protect the preacher against charges of using the Scripture to serve his own purposes or what he perceives the congregation "needs to hear." Preacher and hearer are both under the same discipline in the lectionary. Should the preacher strike a sensitive nerve, he can say with all honesty, "I was just preaching on the text assigned for the day. I just work here." Many a seasoned preacher can attest that the Spirit works even with an assigned text!

The lectionary links the preacher to those who have come before him and also to what is being preached in other pulpits at the same time. The proper distinction of the Law and the Gospel is a high and subtle art, taught by the Holy Spirit in the school of experience, C. F. W. Walther noted.[7] It is good for both preacher and hearer to draw upon the experience of the Church Fathers, of Luther and Lutherans of the past, and of the whole Church who has proclaimed this text. Believers do not believe in isolation, nor do preachers preach in solitary confinement, deaf to what others have said. To do so is to risk sectarianism and even heresy while creating a cult of personality rather than shepherding a congregation of Christ. While a system of assigned readings does not guarantee the proper distinction of the Law and the Gospel or its proper application to a specific group of hearers, it does help to ensure that the preaching of the Church does not occur in obscure isolation.

The lectionary system of readings also provides a helpful seasonal emphasis for the Word. Every Sunday may be a little Easter, but every season of the Church isn't Lent. There is a time for mourning and a time for rejoicing. The seasonal accents of Advent, Christmas, Epiphany, Lent, Easter, and Pentecost punctuated with festival and feast days serve to draw attention away from our selves and to the Lord and His gifts. The coming of Christ, His incarnation and epiphanies, His work of redemption and the exchange of our sin for His righteousness, His dying, rising, and ascending to glory, His breathing out His Spirit and the fruitful life of the Spirit—all of these have their place and time in the cycle of readings. The Church Year is a veritable romp through the articles of the Creed, touching on every aspect of the faith in an annual cycle. How vastly superior this is to the "topical series" or even the expository style

7 C. F. W. Walther, Thesis IV in *Law and Gospel* (St. Louis: Concordia Publishing House, 2010).

of preaching where one can be bogged down in one thing for weeks if not months or years. How many sermons on financial responsibility or sexual fulfillment can one possibly endure? Faith comes by hearing the proclamation of Christ (Romans 10:17), not common sense and advice, no matter how "biblical" it might be.

Liturgy and lectionary unleash the Word of God from its captivity to our notions of what is "relevant" and "urgent," that it may be preached and heard to the joy and edification of Christ's holy people. To maintain the Law and the Gospel in the liturgy is for the pastor to be a steward of these textual traditions, handling them skillfully as a workman with his tools. While possession of good tools does not guarantee good work, the absence of good tools most certainly ensures shoddy workmanship.

DIVINE SERVICE AS SACRAMENT AND SACRIFICE

Worship is a two-way conversation, a dialogue between God and man in which God speaks first and the worshiper responds to what he has heard. "Our Lord speaks and we listen. His Word bestows what it says. Faith that is born from what is heard acknowledges the gifts received with eager thankfulness and praise."[8] To maintain the proper distinction between the Law and the Gospel in the liturgy is to maintain the proper distinction between sacrament (God's saving action toward us) and sacrifice (faith's response toward God and neighbor). Our Lutheran Confessions identify proper worship in the Gospel as God's gifts received through faith: "Faith is that worship which receives God's offered blessings; the righteousness of the law is that worship which offers God our own merits. It is by faith that God wants to be worshiped, namely, that we receive from him what he promises and offers" (Ap IV 49). Divine service begins with God's service to us.

Creation is God's first act of divine service. He creates cosmos and congregation. He orders a concentrically oriented garden with death and life in the center and installs man, His image, as priest of creation. The

---

8 *Lutheran Worship*, p. 6.

first worship was to receive the fruit of all the trees of the garden as food, including the tree of life, but to refrain from eating the fruit of "knowing good and evil," the tree of death. Man's taking what was not given him to take resulted in his fall and banishment to the wilderness. The faithless priest was defrocked, having reached into the center, the garden's "holy of holies." No longer was he the image of his Creator; now he was "like God," knowing good and evil. Now he must die in the wilderness, cut off from the garden and its tree of life.

Christ comes as the Second Adam, the new High Priest of creation, the "image of the invisible God" (Colossians 1:15). Where the First Adam brought death, Christ brings life. Where the First Adam brought condemnation, Christ brings justification. He alone offers the once-for-all atoning sacrifice on the cross, His own flesh for the life of the world (John 6:51; Hebrews 9:26). His death and life, His body and blood are at the center of worship. His cross is the tree of life from which a sinner may eat and live. The baptized believer, as a priest in Christ's royal priesthood, offers his body as a living sacrifice (Romans 12:1–2), acceptable to God through the all-atoning sacrifice of Jesus.

The Lutheran understanding of worship makes two key distinctions: sacrament and sacrifice, and propitiatory and thanksgiving sacrifice. To maintain the proper distinction of the Law and the Gospel in the liturgy, these distinctions must be rigorously maintained.

> The theologians make a proper distinction between sacrament and sacrifice. The genus common to both could be "ceremony" or "sacred act." A sacrament is a ceremony or act in which God offers us the content of the promise joined to the ceremony; thus Baptism is not an act which we offer to God but one in which God baptizes us through a minister functioning in his place. Here God offers and presents the forgiveness of sins according to the promise (Mark 16:16), "He who believes and is baptized will be saved." By way of contrast, a sacrifice is a ceremony or act which we render to God to honor him. (Ap XXIV 17–18)

There is much more going on than meets the eye in God's sacramental activity. Our eyes see a man baptizing, speaking, forgiving, and distributing the bread and the wine. Therefore, we are tempted by what we see to turn God's sacrament into our sacrifice, in effect turning Gospel into Law, and gift into ordinance. However, the Word joined to the outward ceremony reveals something more hidden in, with, and under man's speaking and actions: God is at work delivering all that Christ won for us by His death and resurrection. "To be baptized in God's name is to be baptized not by men but by God himself. Although it is performed by men's hands, it is nevertheless truly God's own act" (LC IV 10).

The distinction of sacrament and sacrifice, like the distinction of the Law and the Gospel, is not a categorical distinction by which certain actions in the liturgy can be labeled "sacrament" while others are labeled "sacrifice." "One action can have several purposes" (Ap XXIV 74). While God is speaking sacramentally through the reading and preaching of the Word, the act of reading and preaching is also a vocational sacrifice of praise on the part of the preacher. While God is giving sacramentally in the Supper, the act of conducting the ceremony and distributing the Sacrament are also a sacrifice of praise on the part of the presider. This means that the preacher and presider's words and actions must always draw attention to Christ and His gifts and not the servant who is distributing them. The table server does not try to upstage the chef or the food, especially in the Lord's Supper, where the Lord is both chef and food.

The pastor, who is as responsible for the congregation's song as he is for its preaching, must be ever-vigilant to the content and form of the hymns employed for worship. The Church is not a concert hall or performance stage. Here the text is master and music its servant. Music serves to deliver the text to the ear. A successful hymn is one that leaves you singing the text not just humming the melody. Solid, sturdy hymnody both proclaims and praises: it is sacramental and sacrificial, focusing attention on Christ and His gifts and away from the worshiping self. The old Adam can be deceptively religious, turning our attention to our praise, our prayer, and our thanksgiving, putting the "I" and "we" ahead of God. Even the venerable *Te Deum laudamus* becomes "We praise You, O God."

Musical form, while technically an adiaphoron, is not completely a matter of indifference and has Law/Gospel implications. The old Adam is a rugged individualist who wants to worship on his own terms and in his own way. The new man in Christ is a member of a Body, a priest in a priesthood, a child of God's household. He is a corporate person, united with Christ and with his fellow baptized believers. Musical forms can bring together a group as one or isolate the individual. There is a vast difference between "singing along with" and "singing all together" as one voice. We "sing along with" the lead singer on stage as a crowd of individuals. We "sing all together" as one voice in a congregation. Sadly, our culture has few examples outside of church of true corporate singing. One may hear it occasionally with the singing of the national anthem or "God Bless America" at sporting events or the singing of ballads in Irish pubs. Beyond that, corporate singing in American culture seems to have disappeared after the Vietnam War–protest era, replaced by the crooning contestant on *American Idol*. This makes congregational singing a largely countercultural activity for most Americans. The liturgy and hymnody of the Church require musical forms that enable the congregation to sing all together as one voice, whether in unison or harmony, so that the individual becomes a part of a greater whole.

As liturgical servants, musicians and their music may not overshadow the text they are given to deliver. While popular music tends to be tune-driven, the Church's music is radically text-driven. Musicians who draw attention to theirselves, their talents, and even their piety are pandering to the religious ego of the old Adam. This applies as much to high classical as it does to hip-hop. There is a difference between performance and liturgy, and the pastor and musicians must know and heed that difference lest the servant eclipse the Master.

God acts sacramentally; faith responds sacrificially. Our Confessions speak of two types of sacrifices—*propitiatory*, by which sins are atoned for and the sinner reconciled by the sacrifice of another, and *eucharistic*, by which those who have been reconciled give thanks or show their gratitude for the forgiveness of sins and other blessings received (Ap XXIV 19). Christ alone offers the one propitiatory sacrifice, once for all. The Christian as priest offers eucharistic sacrifices, thank offerings in the form of prayer, praise, thanksgiving, confession, and faithfulness in vocation. Since these sacrifices are offered with the coerced cooperation of the old Adamic flesh, they can never be pleasing to God on their own merits but only by mercies and merits of Christ through faith. "Without faith it is impossible to please [God]" (Hebrews 11:6).

SUMMA

Maintaining the proper distinction of the Law and the Gospel in the liturgy is a profoundly pastoral act of *Seelsorge*. The proper care of souls calls for careful diagnosis and discernment. It requires that the dynamic tension of Law and Gospel be preserved in every aspect of worship—liturgical form, reading, sermon, ceremony—in order to hold the worshiper as sinner/saint in the dynamic tension between death and life, sin and grace, sacrament and sacrifice. It is to keep Christ crucified for the justification of the sinner central in all things, and to hold the baptized believers on the faith-receiving side of the gifts of salvation, teaching them to hold fast and cling to all that Christ has entrusted to His Church and her ministry.

It is not easy work; in the end, it is not our work at all. We are but servants of the Lord and stewards of His mysteries. "Through these [the Word and the sacraments], as through means, he gives the Holy Spirit, who works faith, when and where he pleases, in those who hear the Gospel" (AC V 1).

LAW AND GOSPEL IN PASTORAL CARE

A View from the Parish

Peter J. Brock

I. INTRODUCTION

> Charity is the power of defending that which we know to be indefensible. Hope is the power of being cheerful in circumstances which we know to be desperate. It is true that there is a state of hope which belongs to bright prospects and the morning; but that is not the virtue of hope. The virtue of hope exists only in earthquake and eclipse. It is true that there is a thing crudely called charity, which means charity to the deserving poor; but charity to the deserving is not charity at all, but justice. It is the undeserving who require it, and the ideal either does not exist at all, or exists wholly for them. For practical purposes it is at the hopeless moment that we require the hopeful man, and the virtue either does not exist at all, or begins to exist at that moment. Exactly at the instant when hope ceases to be reasonable it begins to be useful.[1]

> And take they our life, Goods, fame, child, and wife,
> Though these all be gone, Our victory has been won;
> The Kingdom ours remaineth. (*LSB* 656)

1 G. K. Chesterton, *Heretics* (London: Butler & Tanner, 1928), 157–58. I am indebted to the lectures and writings of Gilbert Meilaender, the Phyllis and Richard Duesenberg Professor of Christian Ethics at Valparaiso University, for introducing me to the work of G. K. Chesterton in general and this reference in particular.

The data distresses, and the budget beleaguers. The school is stressed, and families are fighting. No matter the rat residing in the church basement, I smell death in the state of the sanctuary. Thanks be to God; it smells like Baptism just as it always has. In the church today, reasons to panic abound, and panic is the pastime of despair. However, while the specific sights, sounds, and smells may seem slightly different through the ages, the church's life remains unchanged. In this and every age, the Bride requires her Bridegroom.

"It is at the hopeless moment," G. K. Chesterton writes, "that we require the hopeful man. . . . Exactly at the instant when hope ceases to be reasonable it begins to be useful." Jesus Christ, the word of the cross, proclaims unreasonable peace in circumstances precisely like ours, to locked rooms filled with cowardly Christians, to dying men justly facing the consequences of their crimes, to men and women hiding their sin and shame from the God who died to forgive it. Christ's Body, the Church, remains wholly dependent on her Head, and her servants would sever themselves from the Savior by forgetfully rejecting this reality.

In his inaugural lecture at Cambridge in 1954, C. S. Lewis remarked that "it is not the remembered but the forgotten past that enslaves us," and such forgetfulness leads to arrogance, to the presumption that the current age needs something more or different than those that came before.[2] The resulting arrogant effort to fabricate freedom leads only to slavery, for while the proclamation of that forgotten past is forsaken, quixotic efforts to treat the day's symptoms with a disease replaces it. Forgetfulness breeds panic. Nevertheless, now no less than the first century after Jesus' ascension, when the "Epistle of Ignatius to the Ephesians" was written, the antidote that destroys the disease itself is Christ Himself, the "medicine of immortality," whose body and blood is given and received for His remembrance to those who would forget without it.[3]

---

2 C. S. Lewis, *They Asked for a Paper* (London: Geoffrey Bles, 1962), 23. (THEY ASKED FOR A PAPER by C. S. Lewis © CS Lewis Pte Ltd 1962.)

3 "The Epistle of Ignatius to the Ephesians," in *Ante Nicene Fathers*, vol. 1, ed. Alexander Roberts and James Donaldson (Peabody, MA: Hendrickson, 2004), 57.

Ten years ago, John Pless, assistant professor of pastoral ministry and missions at Concordia Theological Seminary, observed how "we live in a decaying culture where good is called evil and evil good."[4] The Church in such an age, Pless explains, faces the twofold temptation of antinomianism and legalism, both of which forsake Christ and despise His cross. Martin Luther made the same assessment five hundred years earlier in the twenty-first thesis of the Heidelburg Disputation: "A theologian of glory calls evil good and good evil. A theologian of the cross calls a thing what it actually is."[5] Both Pless and Luther identify a distinction first made in the Garden of Eden, the distinction between Satan's "Did God really say?" and the Lord God's "Where are you?" The former bespeaks a theology of glory; the latter the theology of the cross. The devil's question cajoles the hearer to doubt and despair. The Lord's question kills the hearer in order to raise him to a new life of faithful hope. The theologian of glory twists the Gospel into Law and loses everything. The theologian of the cross properly divides Law and Gospel and gains everything.[6] In other words, the theologian of glory speaks neither Law nor Gospel, for the theologian of glory speaks not for God but for Satan.[7] The theologian of the cross speaks the word he himself suffers, and the word spoken to Adam and Eve in the garden therefore remains the very word the Lord speaks today, "an eternal Gospel to proclaim to those who dwell on earth" (Revelation 14:6).[8]

Rightly divided, that Word of God kills and makes alive. Mishandled, it convinces a corpse that all is well and destroys forever. Indeed, the sanctuary may look, sound, and smell like death, much like a delivery room resembles a battlefield. But rather than "alas," faith confesses an

4 John T. Pless, *Handling the Word of Truth: Law and Gospel in the Church Today* (St. Louis: Concordia Publishing House, 2004), 8.

5 *AE* 31:40. For further reflection on the "theology of the cross" in Luther's writing, see Gerhard O. Forde, *On Being a Theologian of the Cross* (Cambridge: Eerdmans, 1997).

6 I do not here attempt to offer an exhaustive treatment about the proper distinction between Law and Gospel. For that, see C. F. W. Walther's *The Proper Distinction between Law and Gospel* (St. Louis: Concordia Publishing House, 1986) and Pless's excellent commentary, cited above, *Handling the Word of Truth*.

7 See Matthew 16:13–23.

8 All Scripture references are from the ESV.

"amen," for faith perceives more than the eye can see. Faith recognizes the reality of these sights and smells, the birth and life of Baptism given and preserved by the promised proclamation of God's rightly divided Word.

This proper distinction between Law and Gospel therefore belongs to pastoral theology, to the study of the preaching and practice of Christ's office by which He serves His Body, the Church.[9] Moreover, while this distinction can and should be studied both by the pastor and the people the pastor serves, its use, or application, cannot be achieved or comprehended through study. The Christian, including the pastor, suffers the distinction between the Law and the Gospel, for both Law and Gospel are God's Word, His doing, address, and revelation to fallen mankind, that humbles the hearer by killing and making alive.

Christology therefore predicates the proclamation of Law and Gospel, for the historical person and work of Jesus are the content and substance of the Word proclaimed, the faith suffered, and the righteousness received.[10] Thus, any opposition, contradiction, or tension experienced between the proclamation of the Law and the proclamation of the Gospel lie not in God or His Word but in sinful man who is addressed by God and the paradox of man's existence as simultaneously justified and sinful. Christ alone resolves the contradiction, and any preaching or pastoral care that tries to ease or eradicate the tension apart from Christ and His cross necessarily fails to distinguish between Law and Gospel. In so doing, the confusion of Law and Gospel loses both by suggesting a naively optimistic anthropology and a desperately pessimistic Christology.

The confusion of Law and Gospel in pastoral care, the idolatrous refusal to suffer the death of the old and the birth of the new, leads only to despair and its twin of hypocrisy, both of which attack the Christological ecclesiology that humbly clings to the means by which the Lord creates, sustains, and preserves His Church. The proper distinction between Law

---

9 See David P. Scaer, *Law and Gospel and the Means of Grace*, vol. 8 of Confessional Lutheran Dogmatics, ed. John Stephenson (St. Louis: The Luther Academy, 2008), 57.

10 See Scaer, *Law and Gospel*, 61.

and Gospel, by contrast, proclaims patience in place of panic and faithfulness instead of fanaticism, for, properly divided, God's Word delivers His Church on earth from the condemnation of measurable success and creates His people to live in love by the faith that is free from metaphysical pressure. From the pulpit to the parish hall and from the bedside to the boardroom, the Lord's proclamation of Law and Gospel directs, informs, and gives the Church's life, as the parish and her pastor humbly suffer God's Word and receive faith's content in Christ.

II. THE PROPER DISTINCTION AND PASTORAL THEOLOGY

> There's no man living on earth who knows how to distinguish between the law and the gospel. We may think we understand it when we are listening to a sermon, but we're far from it. Only the Holy Spirit knows this. . . . Because I've been writing so much and so long about it, you'd think I'd know the distinction, but when a crisis comes I recognize very well that I am far, far from understanding. So God alone should and must be our holy master.[11]

> The cross is the doing of God to us.[12]

In what is perhaps one of the most oft-quoted theses of his lectures, C. F. W. Walther asserts that "rightly distinguishing the Law and the Gospel is the most difficult and the highest art of Christians in general and of theologians in particular. It is taught only by the Holy Spirit in the school of experience."[13] The *doctrine* of Law and Gospel is accessible even to young children, Walther explains, who can learn to recite the words of the catechism and describe the difference between the Word of God that makes demands *of* us and the Word of God that makes promises *to* us. Law and Gospel are confused, however, when the Christian mistakes a *description* of God's Word with its *proclamation*. "At the present time,"

11 AE 54:127.

12 Forde, *On Being a Theologian of the Cross*, 4.

13 Walther, *The Proper Distinction*, 42.

Walther continues in his lectures, "we are studying the *application* and the *use* of this doctrine. The practical application of this doctrine presents difficulties which no man can surmount by reasonable reflections."[14] Thus, though the doctrine may be (and ought to be) learned through study, man suffers the distinction daily as God addresses him through the Word of Law and Gospel.

German Lutheran theologian Oswald Bayer explains:

> Admittedly, the authors of the Lutheran confessions tried to formulate precise doctrinal statements giving "rules" for the proper distinction between Law and Gospel, as we see from the *Formula of Concord*. But the proper application of these rules to the Christian conscience in a time of spiritual crisis depends on the particular situation. Because this situation varies from person to person and cannot be known in advance, it is very difficult to make the proper application of Law and Gospel the topic of a disputation which, by its very nature, demands precision of formulation and has no room for the element of the unknown. God Himself is the Lord of both the distinction and the unity of Law and Gospel, not we. However, in order not to forget this, we must dare to teach Law and Gospel theologically. By this I mean that we must teach it in such a way that the distinction between them is considered in the light of its context (*Sitz im Leben*).[15]

Because "the difficulties of mastering this art confront the minister, in the first place, in so far as he is a Christian; in the second place, in so far as he is a minister," the proper distinction between Law and Gospel finds its place in pastoral theology.[16] In daring to wield "the sword of the Spirit, which is the word of God," the pastor must himself continually be

---

14 Walther, *The Proper Distinction*, 43. Emphasis original.

15 Oswald Bayer, *Theology the Lutheran Way*, ed. and trans. Jeffrey G. Silcock and Mark C. Mattes (Cambridge: Eerdmans, 2007), 74.

16 Walther, *The Proper Distinction*, 43.

slain by it (Ephesians 6:17). The old Adam is too strong to suffer, so he must die. He is too smart to listen, so he must be silenced. This hurts, and in hurting it humbles. Thus the aim of pastoral theology, Gerhard Forde notes, "is to *become* a theologian of the cross, not merely to talk or write *about* it. . . . Theologians of the cross therefore come to understand that the only move left is to the proclamation that issues from the story. The final task is to *do* the story to the hearers in such a way that they are incorporated into the story itself, killed and made alive by the hearing of it. The hearers are to be claimed by the story."[17] Since God Himself does the story to the hearer in Jesus Christ, the pastor himself suffers the distinction between Law and Gospel as he is daily killed with Christ and daily raised with Him.

In this passivity of pastoral theology comes the promise to the pastor. "Behold, I have given you authority to tread on serpents and scorpions, and over all the power of the enemy," Jesus says to the seventy(-two), "and nothing shall hurt you. Nevertheless, do not rejoice in this, that the spirits are subject to you, but rejoice that your names are written in heaven" (Luke 10:19–20). Preaching at my ordination, Pastor Douglas Bauman of St. Paul Lutheran Church in Columbus, Indiana, proclaimed to me this promise of Christ, reminding me that the greatest work of the Lord on that day, the most wonderful word that I heard and would continue to hear years later, was not "I ordain you," but "I forgive you all your sins in the name of the Father and of the Son and of the Holy Spirit." That baptismal proclamation, the very word and work of Christ Himself, makes the pastor a participant in the story of the cross and humbles him to suffer the Word that God speaks through him.

The theologian of glory calls this work of God through the office of Christ arrogant, for the theologian of glory calls good evil. Pride is a pernicious temptation for the pastor, so insidious that boasting of self often masquerades as the pursuit of humility. The theologian of glory not only mistakes opinions for the words of the Lord, the words of the Lord are even replaced with opinions, confusing personal sentimentalities with

---

17 Forde, *Theologian of the Cross*, 4, 13–14. Emphasis original.

the certain promises of Christ. For example, the question "Who is he to forgive sins?" gives the pastor too much credit. The theologian of the cross, recognizing that of himself he has nothing lasting to offer, humbly speaks the words he is given to speak even in the face of satanic accusations and lies that would distract the hearer from the cross of Jesus and the means by which God's grace is given. This suffered humility trusts that while the pastor's person is not worthy to bind and loose sin, Jesus is. The office and its authority belong to Christ, not to the man commanded to fill it. All of this means the pastor himself must die.

No less than the Christian in general, the pastor in particular meets his end and his new beginning in the proclamation of God's Law and Gospel, in dying with Christ and being raised with Him. "The justification of God promised in Jesus is not an 'offer' made to us as old beings," Forde notes, "it is our end, our death. We are, quite literally, through as old beings. . . . All of the questions and protests that we raise are really just the death rattle of the old Adam and Eve who sense that their kingdom is under radical and final attack. No doubt that is why the defense is so desperate, and why it even quite innocently takes such pious and well-meaning forms."[18] The old self is put to death with Christ and thereby freed from sin and its ignorant arrogance that presumes to make claims about and to God rather than suffer God's claims about and to us. That distinction, the distinction between Law and Gospel, the Lord makes most plain in His twofold work of Baptism that destroys attempts to avoid the cross and frees the pastor to preach it in all severity and sweetness. Baptism teaches an honest anthropology, "because it means that for the first time we shall have to be reborn not as gods but as human beings, shorn of all our defenses, projects, and claims."[19]

---

18 Forde, *The Preached God*, ed. Mark C. Mattes and Steven D. Paulson (Cambridge: Eerdmans, 2007), 232.

19 Forde, *The Preached God*, 227; citing Ernest Becker, *The Denial of Death* (New York: Free Press, 1973), 58.

III. THE PROPER DISTINCTION AS CHRISTOLOGICAL ANTHROPOLOGY[20]

> The remedy for curing desire does not lie in satisfying it, but in extinguishing it.[21]

> Superficial optimism breeds ultimate despair. . . . The addict/sinner is not coddled by false optimism but is put to death so that a new life can begin. . . . The theologian of the cross preaches to convict of sin. The addict is not deceived by theological marshmallows but is told the truth so that he might at last learn to confess, to say, "I am an addict," "I am an alcoholic," and never to stop saying it. Theologically and more universally all must learn to say, "I am a sinner," and likewise never to stop saying it until Christ's return makes it no longer true.[22]

As noted above, forgetfulness of the past breeds panic in the present. The setting in which the contemporary Church finds herself remains the same as in Luther's day. In essays such as "Rupture of Times: Luther's Relevance for Today"[23] and "With Luther in the Present,"[24] Bayer explains the continued necessity and relevancy of Luther's theology, specifically his confession of justification by grace and its proclamation in the distinction between Law and Gospel. "The singular historical experiences moving Luther," Bayer notes, "impelling him from the inside, extend to a meaning reaching beyond their original situation."[25]

The Church and her pastors continue to live in the midst of conflict, for "this history of the world is marked by the war of all against all. All

---

20 Portions of this section summarize and apply suggestions made in my essay "Space to Be Secular: The Thought of Oswald Bayer as Resource for the Church's Theology of Mercy," in *Toward a Theology of Mercy* (St. Louis: LCMS World Relief and Human Care, 2008), 1–20.

21 AE 31:54.

22 Forde, *Theologian of the Cross*, 16–17.

23 Bayer, "Rupture of Times: Luther's Relevance for Today," *Lutheran Quarterly* 13 (1999): 35–50.

24 Bayer, "With Luther in the Present," *Lutheran Quarterly* 21 (2007): 1–16.

25 Bayer, "Rupture of Times," 39.

fight to live or die in the struggles for mutual recognition."[26] The reality of this conflict must not be forgotten or ignored as it is in the attempt to ease or eradicate the tension between Law and Gospel in the life of the believer. With devastating results, Law and Gospel are confused when works of civil righteousness are mistaken for sanctification and the threats of the Law are quieted. "Now, living morally is indeed an important, wise, and good thing," Forde comments;

> There is no need to knock it. But it should not be equated with sanctification, being made holy. . . . Sanctification is the result of the dying of the old and the rising of the new. . . . On the level of human understanding, the problem is that we attempt to combine the unconditional grace of God with our notions of continuously existing and acting under the Law. In other words, the old being does not come up against its death, but goes on pursuing its projects, perhaps a little more morally or piously, but still on its own. There is no death of the old and thus no hope for a resurrection of the new. The unconditional grace of God is combined with the wrong theological anthropology. That is always disaster. . . . Justification by faith alone demands that we think in terms of the death of the old subject and the resurrection of a new one, not the continuous existence of the old.[27]

Ignoring the existence of the old world and old Adam as they stubbornly persist, thereby forgetting the place and proclamation of Law and Gospel in this world, results in either a pessimistic antinomianism or an optimistic legalism, both of which lead to hopeless despair and idolatry. Bayer contends that

> This realistic perspective distinguishes Luther sharply from the harmlessness of modern theologians of love. The theologians of love transform the original Christian confession,

26 Bayer, "Rupture of Times," 39.

27 Forde, *The Preached God*, 227–28.

> God is love, into a principle of both knowledge and systematic construction in order to build an internally coherent dogmatic system. The price paid for this transformation is to render harmless the enemies referred to in the prayers of the Psalms, to let them fade into paper tigers. They are allowed to disappear through the effort of subsuming evil under a theory of love. Luther's life and work, contrary to what modern theologians of love think, is determined throughout by the trials and temptations (*Anfechtungen*) suffered at the hands of these enemies and by the fight against them.[28]

As Bayer helpfully observes, Luther's address "redirects our eyes to Christ crucified on the cross, who 'was assailed by the images of death, sin, and hell just as we are.' Focusing on the crucified one, Luther encourages us to 'look at death while you are alive and see sin in light of grace and hell in the light of heaven.'"[29] In this regard, the pastor is given to understand that the distinction between Law and Gospel is, both objectively and subjectively, the proclamation of Jesus. It is Jesus' preaching of Jesus. Thus the distinction between Law and Gospel will necessarily be lost whenever and however Law or Gospel is considered or proclaimed apart from Christ's historical incarnation, death, and resurrection. David Scaer, chairman of systematic theology at Concordia Theological Seminary, observes how positions advocated by theologians such as Karl Barth and Rudolf Bultmann confound Law and Gospel by rejecting the history of Jesus into which the preached Word brings the hearer. "Gospel is more than a proclamation of forgiveness," Scaer insists,

> But finds its presupposition in the historical reality of Israel and Jesus. . . . Without the reality of the incarnation, atonement, and resurrection, the Gospel becomes a meaningless theological abstraction, even when the Law and Gospel are carefully distinguished and forgiveness preached. . . . Gospel is proclamation, but it presupposes the absolute

28 Bayer, "Rupture of Times," 38.

29 Bayer, "Rupture of Times," 40.

> necessity of the history of Jesus of Nazareth in whose death the atonement is encased. . . . Law and Gospel as a principle has no autonomous life of its own.[30]

Moreover, both Law and Gospel are the Word of God, and Jesus is God's address to the world.[31] As Scaer correctly notes, "the chief function of the Law for man in the state of sin should not be confused with God's original intentions for the Law or what the Law is in itself. Man and not God is responsible for seeing the Law as a horrible affliction on the sinner. Law is not oppressive because of its character as Law but because of man's depravity."[32] The Law always accuses because man remains a sinner in this life even when, by faith in Christ, the Law is fulfilled in Christ and the righteousness of Christ is reckoned to him by grace. Because the Christian remains simultaneously sinful and justified for Christ's sake, the Lord's Word of Law and Gospel is experienced as a contradiction or tension even as God remains "the Lord of both the distinction and the unity of Law and Gospel."[33] The same God whose wrath against sin cannot be escaped is the very God "who accepts him in Christ and sanctifies him by his Spirit."[34] This tension, along with the *simul*, ends in Christ now by faith when unbelief still remains in need of daily drowning, and it will end in Christ soon by sight when the Christian is raised forever to that life where the Law is indicative and the Gospel innate.[35]

In the meantime, a sober anthropology reflects a proper Christology and therefore a proper distinction between Law and Gospel. Seeing what Christ became for sinners, what He suffered for sinners, shows sinners the depth of their depravity. "Because in Adam we mounted up towards equality with God," Luther writes, "he descended to be like us, to bring us back to knowledge of himself. That is the sacrament of the

---

30 Scaer, *Law and Gospel*, 14, 61.

31 See Martin Luther, "The Distinction between Law and Gospel: A Sermon by Martin Luther," trans. Willard L. Burce, *Concordia Journal* 18 (April 1992): 153–63.

32 Scaer, *Law and Gospel*, 91. See also SD V.

33 Bayer, *Theology the Lutheran Way*, 74.

34 Scaer, *Law and Gospel*, 46–47.

35 See Scaer, *Law and Gospel*, 45.

incarnation. That is the kingdom of faith in which the cross of Christ holds sway, which sets at naught the divinity for which we perversely strive and restores the despised weakness of the flesh which we have perversely abandoned" (WA 5.128.31–5.129.4).[36] In this Christological proclamation of Law and Gospel, one finds Luther's relevance for today. The "rupture of the times," which for the Church begins to explain the conflict in which it must engage, is for Luther not a rupture between two historical ages. Rather, Bayer explains, "the rupture of the times between the new and the old eon has occurred once and for all on the cross of Jesus Christ" where the old world meets its end and the new world, the renewed creation, breaks in:

> The crucial point of Luther's understanding of time consists of the folding into one another of pivotal events in time, it consists in an interweaving of times (*Verschrankung der Zeiten*). The last judgment, the consummation of the world, and the creation of the world are perceived simultaneously. The future of the world comes from God's present and presence. God's new creation establishes the old world as old and restores the original world. Salvation communicated in the present is seen in view of Christ on the cross. The salvation effected on the cross guarantees the coming consummation of the world. In between the times, the suffering and groaning of the creatures of the old world are experienced in painful contradiction to the creation originally created by the promise.[37]

Baptism places the Christian in this rupture, and, as Forde says, makes of sanctification "the art of getting used to the unconditional justification wrought by the grace of God for Jesus' sake. . . . It is the justified life. It is what happens when the old being comes up against the end of its self-justifying and self-gratifying ways, however pious. It is life lived

36 Cited in Forde, *Theologian of the Cross*, 14.

37 Bayer, "Rupture of Times," 45.

in anticipation of the resurrection."[38] Baptism destroys my desire to be like God that I should hear how God became like me. Faith finds hope in God's baptizing, for faith finds its future in Jesus whose death, resurrection, and ascension is the promise of our own. Again in the words of Bayer, baptismal life is lived in "freedom in response" to God's promise—"for human action does not start with itself; it draws its life from freedom that has already been given."[39]

In the third chapter of *Living by Faith,* "The Passive Righteousness of Faith," Bayer notes that because the baptismal life of faith is entirely the work of God, "we experience it in that we suffer it. . . . The passive righteousness of faith takes place when justifying thinking (metaphysics) and justifying doing (morality), together with the unity of both that some seek, are all radically destroyed."[40] Again, God's action of killing in order to raise remains consistent with His historical dealings with His people. Throughout Israel's history, God was persistent in His task of killing and raising. Indeed, it was no different for His Son, the one Israel, upon whom God looked and declared, "I chastise and crush You."[41] This word of God is not the final one, however, for in fact Christ has been *raised* from the dead, the firstfruits of those who have fallen asleep. And in Christ, God's pronouncement to His people is the same: "I hereby kill you and raise you." Through this Word of Law and Gospel, through this Christ, "we receive the death and resurrection that marks [this] 'Israel.'"[42] "For in Adam all die, so also in Christ shall all be made alive. . . . Christ the firstfruits, then at His coming those who belong to Christ" (1 Corinthians 15:22–23).

In this death, the Lord destroys our need "to gain recognition by what we can afford and accomplish."[43] So, too, does He destroy the

38 Forde, *The Preached God*, 226.

39 Oswald Bayer, *Freedom in Response: Lutheran Ethics, Sources, and Controversies*, trans. Jeff Cayzer, Oxford Studies in Theological Ethics (Oxford: Oxford University Press, 2007), 1.

40 Bayer, *Living by Faith: Justification and Sanctification*, trans. Geoffrey W. Bromiley (Cambridge: Eerdmans, 2003), 20–21.

41 See Isaiah 53:10.

42 Timothy E. Saleska, "Pastors Who Play God," *Concordia Journal* 31, no. 1 (2005): 24.

43 Bayer, *Living by Faith*, 21.

"justifying thinking that tries to settle the conflict of justifications and to fashion a concept of the 'unity' of reality. . . . The death of the old nature lies last but not least in the fact that the illusion of a totality of meaning, even if only hypothetical and anticipatory, has been overthrown."[44] Bayer does not exclude works from the new life which is given and lived in response to this death. On the contrary, the freedom from justifying thinking and action that comes with the death of the old Adam grants space to live and to act—a space free from metaphysical pressure.

To speak of Christ as "space" into which one is baptized recognizes the sacramental character of the Christian life as the new creation relates to the old world. Citing Jörg Bauer, Bayer explains the "alien righteousness" that comes as gift from another and "by virtue of whose life I live (Gal 2:19–20):"[45]

> That the sinful human being can be brought into a right relation with the righteous God by being torn free from sin and transposed in God's righteousness—God's Kingdom—has as its presupposition and abiding implication that God and the human being are bound together in one 'person,' that is, that they come together in a communicative event that reaches the sinful human being in a human manner, . . . rearranges, transposes, and radically transports them (Col. 1:13), and in this way determines and defines the human being anew. Only because Jesus Christ is simultaneously God, only because God is this human being, can one speak of Jesus Christ as a "space," into which I am baptized, into which I enter in faith, in which I gain a share. In Christ, then, "God and human being do not stand as closed entities over against one another. They communicate with one another without restriction." This transposition of human existence into Jesus Christ takes place, "through the God who always speaks and promises concretely, who draws the

44 Ibid., 22–23.

45 Bayer, "With Luther in the Present," 12.

> trust unto himself which formerly was based on the self, and thus awakens faith as the consummation of absolute eccentricity."[46]

Bayer writes elsewhere that "the course of this world and that of their own lives are so concealed even from those who are justified by faith that they cannot conceive or experience the divine and the human concern for the world as a harmonious relationship. This ambiguity extends even to the works of the justified done in the new obedience."[47] Rather than condemning the Christian to a life of inactivity or quietism, however, this truth frees the Church and her members to live and love spontaneously, as the need arises and is discerned. Concern over the "success" and permanency of active faith—love—does not plague Christians' action, for their justification has already been accomplished and deeds are pure and joyous response. The Christian is not condemned to measurable success, as Bayer notes, and neither is the community of saints on earth.

IV. THE PROPER DISTINCTION AS PASTORAL CARE

We wonder about baptizing infants, puzzling over how they can possibly have faith. And we strain for answers when others object to such a practice. Infants, we say, are part of "all nations," and Jesus says to baptize all nations. True enough. But it is as if we have forgotten that the whole of the baptized life from start to finish is a life of faith—a life of trust in what we can neither see nor fully comprehend. As if the very best image we could find of such trust in ordinary life were not that of a baby in the arms of its mother—uncomprehending, but secure. We talk as if the marvel and mystery of baptism were that a baby should be able to believe like an adult. Whereas the real marvel and mystery—the mystery of

---

46 Ibid., 12–13; citing Jörg Bauer, *Das reformatorische Christentum in der Krise* (Tübingen, Mohr, 1997), 17–18.

47 Bayer, *Living by Faith*, 38.

grace—is that in baptism we should receive permission to trust, to be as "newborn babes," and to believe what we do not see.[48]

Therefore, since we have been justified by faith, we have peace with God through our Lord Jesus Christ. Through Him we have also obtained access by faith into this grace in which we stand, and we rejoice in hope of the glory of God. Not only that, but we rejoice in our sufferings, knowing that suffering produces endurance, and endurance produces character, and character produces hope, and hope does not put us to shame, because God's love has been poured into our hearts through the Holy Spirit who has been given to us. For while we were still weak, at the right time Christ died for the ungodly. (Romans 5:1–6)

The Lord commands the pastor to preach the Word the pastor suffers, and only in suffering that Word of Law and Gospel does the pastor divide it rightly. The pastor speaks; the Lord applies. The pastor speaks; the Lord comforts. The pastor speaks; the Lord uses the Word of Law and Gospel to kill and make alive when and where God wills. Since the old Adam does not want to die, the pastor is given continually to be in God's Word, in study and meditation, continually in prayer for himself and the people he serves, and continually with the people under his care.

The Divine Service provides the primary place of this activity. There the Lord confronts His people, showing them that their failings and shortcomings have not merely strained relationships with others and undermined some vague sense of self, their words and deeds have crucified Christ.[49] The word of Law cuts through the fence that is built by feeling ashamed and reveals the real problem. The sinner is guilty before God.[50] The Lord's divine service to His people brings those people up against

48 Gilbert Meilaender, *Love Taking Shape: Sermons on the Christian Life* (Cambridge: Eerdmans, 2002), 13–14.

49 See Acts 2:14–41.

50 See David F. Wells, *Losing Our Virtue: Why the Church Must Recover Its Moral Vision* (Cambridge: Eerdmans, 1998), 180–96.

the absolute God, and, as Forde has well explained, "the only solution to the problem of the absolute is absolution. . . . That is to say that the only solution to this systematic problem is the *pastoral* one, the move from the abstract to the concrete, from the hidden to the revealed God, from, we might say, the lectern to the pulpit, font, and altar. Only if the absolute actually absolves here and now can our bondage be broken and we be *saved*."[51]

The theologian of the cross properly divides Law and Gospel by humbly confessing the central place of worship in pastoral care and there receives the "greater work" of God in the forgiveness of sins (Matthew 9:1–8; John 14:12). The theologian of glory fixates on penultimate attainments and loses both Law and Gospel in the desperate effort to be relevant to those whose idol is self. Christ's death, resurrection, and ascension inaugurate the end of all things, and "according to the testimony of the word of God," Walther preaches, "the closer we come to the end of all things, the greater the world's security and lust will become. . . . We have obviously entered that midnight hour when even the wise virgins sleep."[52] "The contemporary church," David F. Wells contends,

> is whoring after this god as assiduously as the Israelites in their darker days. . . . The Church needs to recover some old habits now much discarded, like learning to think of sin as moral failure before God and the self as needing to be restrained, displaced, and forgotten, and seeing God not for his value to us as consumers but for the value he has in himself. . . . Humility is that freedom from our self which enables us to be in positions in which we have neither recognition nor importance, neither power nor visibility, and even experience deprivation, and yet have joy and delight. That is the pattern of humility modeled in the incarnation (Phil. 2:5–11). It is the freedom of knowing that we are not

51 Forde, *The Preached God*, 155. Emphasis original.

52 C. F. W. Walther, *God Grant It*, trans. Gerhard P. Grabenhofer, comp. August Crull (St. Louis: Concordia Publishing House, 2006), 445–46.

> the center of the universe, not even in the center of our own private universe. Those who have best learned this kind of godliness know that what may seem like the most awful loss is actually true freedom.[53]

Recalling again the words of C. S. Lewis, "it is not the remembered but the forgotten past that enslaves us," the proper distinction between Law and Gospel locates pastoral care where the Lord has always located Himself to kill and make alive, while forgetful arrogance confuses God's Word by turning the church into a sanctuary for the old Adam where he is coddled instead of killed. In *Worship as Pastoral Care*, William Willimon recalls these "old habits" that Wells begs the Church's servants to recover:

> In an earlier time, a pastor caring for his flock, engaging in the activities related to the cure of souls meant, in great part, leading them in worship. . . . A major difference in the pastoral care of previous ages of the church and that of our modern era is the switch from care that utilized mostly corporate, priestly, liturgical actions to care that increasingly limited itself to individualistic, psychologically-oriented techniques heavily influenced by prevailing secular therapies for healing, personal fulfillment, and self-help addressed to the needs of that twentieth-century creation, Philip Rieff's "psychological man."[54]

Referencing Willimon's insight about this peculiar change in pastoral care, or perhaps the *exchange* of pastoral care for utilitarian tactics intended to accomplish penultimate goals, Pless reminds the Church and her pastors of the primary place of Word and Sacrament, including Confession and Absolution, in pastoral care: "The pastoral care of the individual is done in the context of the congregation gathered around word and sacrament. . . . Only in the context of Law/Gospel preaching will the value of private confession be appreciated and the gift of holy absolution

53 Wells, *Losing Our Virtue*, 204.

54 William H. Willimon, *Worship as Pastoral Care* (Nashville: Abingdon, 1979), 35–36.

be treasured. The practice of private confession is actually an extension of such preaching. . . . In catechizing his people the pastor will need to make it clear that confession/absolution is the ordinary means of pastoral care in the church. It need not be reserved only for extraordinary circumstances or situations."[55] Properly distinguishing between Law and Gospel means remembering the task the Lord gives to His pastors. "If you have a broken leg," Forde explains, "you would likely be served better by a medical doctor than a preacher. If your anxieties arise from conditional causes, you are better served by a therapist than a theologian."[56] But if you are dead in your trespasses and sins, you require the service of the Savior, by whom sin is forgiven and death defeated.

The proper distinction between Law and Gospel thus declares the end of religious fascination with the so-called "postmodern population" or whatever the current label happens to be. Searching for a secret word that resonates relevancy to unbelievers offers a false Gospel. We should preach in English to English speakers and in Spanish to Spanish speakers, in plain prose to toddlers, straightforward speech to teenagers, and profounder polemics to those whose vocation is teaching. We should not, however, make relevance our goal. "Seeking to be relevant to the age," Forde states of churches transformed into secular organizations, "they just succumbed to it. Claiming to be wise, as St. Paul put it, they became fools. The most serious mistake of theological attempts to understand the age is the assumption that the Gospel could somehow be made to appear relevant to old beings."[57] Efforts to convince the old Adam that dying is a good idea do not kill him. Drowning is no fun.

Pless helpfully reminds the Church of this, stating that properly distinguishing Law and Gospel in pastoral care includes catechizing people about expectations:

---

55 John T. Pless, "Your Pastor Is Not Your Therapist—Private Confession: The Ministry of Repentance and Faith" (paper presented at the Seventh Annual Symposium on Catechesis, Sussex, WI, June 15, 2000). Available here: http://www.ctsfw.net/media/pdfs/PlessPastornotTherapist.pdf.

56 Forde, *The Preached God*, 166.

57 Forde, *The Preached God*, 166.

> Absolution delivers an eschatological reality. It is not a quick fix for psychological disorders or difficulties. It does not follow that one will "feel better" after confession and absolution. The opposite may be true. The penitent may still need psychological counseling from those whose calling it is to provide this service in the kingdom of the left hand. The pastor will want to shepherd the penitent in such a way as to guard against false expectations regarding the effects of absolution so that he or she learns to hold fast to this Word even under the crosses and afflictions which still must be borne in this life.[58]

All other expressions of pastoral care flow from this divine service of God to His people *and direct them back to it.* This rhythm of the Christian life, as Luther called it, cannot be escaped on this side of the resurrection. Efforts to overcome or move past the need for forgiveness, to have a measurable answer to every question and secular solution for every problem, seek ultimate meaning in penultimate actions, making the pastor a mechanic and Christ his toolbox.

Jesus is the end for which we long, not the means to meet the challenges we face. The proper distinction between Law and Gospel is not an explanation but an address, not a trouble-shooting manual but the "hammer of God" that destroys our projects and replaces them with Jesus (Jeremiah 23:29). Teaching Christian stewardship, for example, must not have as its goal meeting the budget. May God be glorified when the budget is met, but the trumpet is blown in heaven for the widow's faith, not the Pharisees' offerings (Mark 12:41–44). Outreach and missions, too, have Jesus and His Means of Grace as their reason, content, and goal, not self-assurance in the work as falsely dichotomized against other daily vocations or the idolatrous attempt strategically to manage the Word outside of Christ's "strategy" to baptize and teach. As Pastor Paul Doellinger of St. Paul Lutheran Church in Cassopolis, Michigan, once reminded me, many Samaritans in the town of Sychar believed in Jesus

58 Pless, "Your Pastor Is Not Your Therapist."

because of a sinful woman's testimony that Christ "told [her] all that [she] ever did" (John 4:39). Her evangelism, her confession of the Christ, was the confession of sins to which the Word made flesh had brought her.

Though numbers may be necessary, numbers are not the Gospel. Neither do numbers necessarily reflect the Word's efficacy in this or any age.[59] Programs may be appropriate at certain times and in certain circumstances, particularly those that organize and support the Church's works of mercy that imperfectly incarnate the care of God for daily needs, but programs are not the "holy, precious blood and the innocent suffering and death" that purchased us "from all sins, from death, and from the power of the devil" (SC 355:4).[60] By God's grace, only on account of Jesus Christ crucified for the sin of the world, the Lord's Word of Law and Gospel accomplishes the purpose for which the Lord sends it "even when steeples are falling" (*LSB* 645).

This promise of God attached to His Word and Sacraments creates patience for both people and pastor as the Law kills our efforts to be like God and the Gospel gives life freed from the fanaticism that grasps at the garbage of works instead of clinging to the cross of Christ. Again Walther:

> What does Peter say in cautioning Christians about such a time? He says, "The end of all things is at hand; therefore be self-controlled and sober-minded for the sake of your prayers." This does not mean that when the end of all things is near, Christians should no longer make use of the world, that they should deprive the body in self-chosen spirituality and humility and not provide for the necessities of the flesh. Nor does it mean they are not allowed to rejoice in the bodily refreshment God gives them in this last time. No, says the apostle, we should be serious and watchful only in our prayers. Even in the nearness of the Last Day, we can eat and drink, but we should not weigh down our hearts

59 See John 6:60–69.

60 Book of Concord quotations in this chapter are from Kolb-Wengert.

> in these pursuits. We can like something in this world, but we must be prepared to sacrifice it readily to God. We have and continue to accumulate gold and silver, but we should not attach our heart to them, not rely upon them, and not mourn when we lose them. We can build dwellings for ourselves, but they must be considered as lodgings for the night from which we will set out the following morning (in other words, we must always prefer to go to the house of our heavenly Father than cling to our earthly abodes). We can continue to plant and sow in the face of the Last Day, but we must be prepared not to reap the harvest, if that is what the Lord desires. We can also care about the future, but only in such a way that our heart does not become burdened with worry. . . . We must seek first the kingdom of God and His righteousness. And we must pass through this world like strangers and pilgrims, pausing here and there to rest and refresh ourselves, but soon thereafter hastening on toward our heavenly goal. Our entire life must be, as Luther expressed, an eternal Lord's Prayer in which our principal desire is for God to deliver us from evil. And may we add, "Come, Lord Jesus, take us out of this evil world, and take us to Yourself."[61]

The sober mind for which the apostle calls comes with the proper distinction between Law and Gospel—a sober-minded anthropology reflecting a thorough-going Christology, the condemnation of sin and its forgiveness, the only expression of pastoral care worthy of the name. Regardless of the reasons to panic, and there remain countless reasons, the unreasonable man, Jesus Christ, preaches peace to His people on earth, peace that surpasses worldly understanding and thereby guards our hearts and minds for a future secured by the forgiveness of sins.

---

61 Walther, *God Grant It*, 446–47.

LAW AND GOSPEL IN THE CHRISTIAN LIFE[1]

Larry M. Vogel

There is no Christian, much less "Christian life," without the Law and the Gospel. In seeking "to show that the theology taught in Wittenberg remained true to the catholic tradition,"[2] Philip Melanchthon pointed to the Law's conclusive truth of human inability—"we cannot obtain forgiveness of sin and righteousness before God through our merit, work, or satisfactions"—and of the corollary Gospel truth "that we receive forgiveness of sin and become righteous before God out of grace for Christ's sake through faith" (AC IV). Hence we are justified only by grace through faith in the Gospel's promises for Christ's sake. Through the proclamation of the Gospel, the Holy Spirit produces faith (AC V) and the Church is established (AC VII). There is no Christianity, no Church, and no Christian without Law and Gospel.

It is important to emphasize what is plain from the title—that this chapter is a consideration of Law and Gospel in the life of *Christians*. By that I mean to emphasize the ongoing work of Law and Gospel in the lives of those who, by the proclamation of Law and Gospel in preaching and in the sacraments, are believers. That is to say, this is an essay primarily about God's *sanctifying* work in Law and Gospel, rather than His *justifying* work. Or put differently, it is less about Law and Gospel in conversion than it is in the context of holy living.

---

1 This chapter makes some use of a previous article, "Doing Ministry between Law and Gospel," *Lutheran Forum*, 40, no. 4 (Christmas/Winter 2006): 10–25.

2 "Editors' Introduction to the Augsburg Confession." All Book of Concord quotations in this chapter are from Kolb-Wengert.

I. LAW AND GOSPEL—PROPER DISTINCTION

In terms of justification, the Law of God can only identify sin and thereby crush and condemn proud sinners; and the Gospel can only declare crushed and repentant sinners forgiven and righteous for Christ's sake. But in the matter of holy living, sanctification, or the daily lives of God's newly redeemed sons and daughters, the Law and Gospel have a wider role to play. That wider role is what we are exploring here.

Please note, what this addresses is a different context, not a different Law or Gospel. Luther says with characteristic aplomb: "The confession is clear: 'Christians are sinners.'"[3] It is ever and always the Law that makes that clear—whether the first time we have heard or the last time. It is ever and always the Gospel that assures forgiveness, never "progress in sanctification," never good works that prove our salvation, or anything else. Robert Benne: "It is important to note here that Lutherans see the whole process of salvation and ensuing sanctification as the work of the Holy Spirit in their lives."[4] Yet, although sin is sin, God does not deal with it in a singular fashion. In detail, Luther tries to teach Latomus (and the Louvain faculty):

> Now we finally come to the point. A righteous and faithful man doubtless has both grace and the gift [faith in Christ]. Grace makes him wholly pleasing so that his person is wholly accepted, and there is no place for wrath in him any more, but the gift heals from sin and from all his corruption of body and soul. It is therefore most godless to say that one who is baptized is still in sin, or that all his sins are not fully forgiven. For what sin is there where God is favorable and wills not to know any sin, and where he wholly accepts and sanctifies the whole man? However, as you see, this must not be attributed to our purity, but solely to the grace of a favorable God. *Everything is forgiven through grace, but as*

3 AE 12:330.

4 Robert Benne, "Law and Gospel: A Lutheran Perspective on Personal and Political Existence," *Reformation and Revival Journal* 14, no. 2 (January 1, 2005): 142.

yet not everything is healed through the gift. The gift has been infused, the leaven has been added to the mixture. It works so as to purge away the sin for which a person has already been forgiven, and to drive out the evil guest for whose expulsion permission has been given. In the meantime, while this is happening, it is called sin, and is truly such in its nature; but now it is sin without wrath, without the law, dead sin, harmless sin, as long as one perseveres in grace and his gift. *As far as its nature is concerned, sin in no way differs from itself before grace and after grace; but it is indeed different in the way it is treated.* It is now dealt with otherwise than before. *How was it treated previously? In such a way that it was existent, known, and overwhelmed us; but now it is treated as non-existent and as expelled.* Despite this, it is truly and by nature sin. Indeed, it is ingratitude and injury to the grace and gift of God to deny that it truly is sin. To be sure, for grace there is no sin, because the whole person pleases; yet for the gift there is sin which it purges away and overcomes. A person neither pleases, nor has grace, except on account of the gift which labors in this way to cleanse from sin. *God saves real, not imaginary, sinners, and he teaches us to mortify real rather than imaginary sin.*[5]

Several things deserve comment here. Luther refers to "grace and the gift," denoting faith as "the gift." Then Luther distinguishes the work of the Law and Gospel for the Christian in a couple of ways. First, he distinguishes forgiveness from healing: "Everything is forgiven through grace, but as yet not everything is healed through the gift." Second, he distinguishes how God treats sin (and the sinner) before and after grace: "How was it treated previously? In such a way that it was existent, known, and overwhelmed us; but now it is treated as non-existent and as expelled." Real sinners are saved by grace through faith. Redeemed, real sinners struggle, not with something less than sin, but with real sin.

5 AE 32:229. Emphasis added.

It is sin that "has already been forgiven" yet remains as an "evil guest for whose expulsion permission has been given."

Luther can also be far less subtle in making this same point. In comments on 1 John, he says: "The remission of sins has not been instituted in order that we may have permission to sin or that we may sin; it has been instituted in order that we may recognize sin and know that we are in sin, that we may fight against sin."[6] The Lutheran Confessions therefore recognize the necessity of distinguishing justification and sanctification or renewal, but not to isolate them from each other (see FC SD III 41). Rather, to quote one of the confessors, Martin Chemnitz, the distinction is necessary because

> [J]ustifying faith is not always or in all people a brightly burning light; often it is a scarcely smoking flax. It is not always a loud noise, but often an obscure desire and a hidden groaning. Here this distinction is pertinent: There is a great faith, such as in the centurion and the woman of Canaan; there is a weak faith as in Matt. 14:31. Faith is strong and robust; it is weak and infirm, Rom. 14:1. This weakness may be in the area of knowledge, as when the apostles did not sufficiently understand several articles of faith; or it may be in the area of trust, Matt. 6:30; 14:31. Yet Scripture says that the smoking flax is not put out [Matt. 12:20], the groanings are unutterable, Rom. 8:26, that is, weak faith is still true faith, and it justifies.[7]

The distinction is not merely theoretical nor is it a mere intellectual conundrum. Rather, it is vital for this topic.

II. LAW AND GOSPEL—PERSONAL AND INDIVIDUAL

Law and Gospel work in the lives of *individuals,* changing them by the power of the Word. The "foolishness of preaching" reveals its

6 AE 30:245.

7 Martin Chemnitz, *Loci Theologici I* (St. Louis: Concordia Publishing House, 1985), 105–6.

surprising power as people listen to words, but not as passive hearers or "mere" listeners. Long after I had forgotten the sermon, a doctor who worked in the rough and often vulgar world of Camden medical care said something like this: "I couldn't stop thinking about what you said about how God cares about words—when we talk to and about Him and the same with people. I'm trying to clean up my mouth." Pastors experience that kind of surprise with some regularity—someone reveals that what has begun to feel almost humdrum for us touches someone deeply. Other times the surprise is less gratifying, but not less powerful, when someone indicates how a word we spoke hurt or offended them unnecessarily. We have nothing but words and nothing, seemingly, is more easily ignored than "mere words," yet the Word in words has great power despite that and despite its faltering speakers. And we know the effect of the words of God. His words do two things. They indict and they promise. They lead, again and again, against all odds, to confession and faith.

This effect occurs in "personal" life—that is, individually. Although there may be times, like Pentecost, when large numbers of people are burdened with guilt only to seek the sure hope of forgiveness (Acts 2:37), the work of Law and Gospel is, nonetheless, an individual work. The miracle of repentant faith happens as individuals take personally the words spoken in sermon, absolution, sacrament, and in the mutual consolation and conversation of brothers and sisters. Miraculously, here and there, to our surprise, individuals hear a human word as "what it really is, the word of God" (1 Thessalonians 2:13). It tears hearts and then heals them.

> "Come, let us return to the Lord; for *He* has torn us, that *He* may heal us;
>
> *He* has struck us down, and *He* will bind us up" (Hosea 6:1, emphasis added).[8]

The Law and Gospel are God's words, words to the entire world, yet words that are always thoroughly personal. We can never adequately consider the theme of Law and Gospel in the Christian life unless we

8 All biblical quotations in this chapter are from the ESV.

begin individually. So the biblical paradigm, rightly, is so often an individual. Consider Hosea's bride—the stained woman who is type for Lady Israel. Consider the woman of Romans 7:1–6 who is set free only after her first husband dies, so that she can be married to Christ. Consider Ephesians 5 and the Bride cleansed only by the washing of water with the Word to become radiant without stain or spot or blemish.

The spotless Lady Church, Christ's Bride, is made real as individuals die from a Word of Law and rise by a Gospel Word. This finally includes all who believe, even you and me. Only personal words cut and heal hearts. Only personal words bring us to confess with Paul:

> For we know that the law is spiritual, but I am of the flesh, sold under sin. For I do not understand my own actions. For I do not do what I want, but I do the very thing I hate. . . . Wretched man that I am! Who will deliver me from this body of death? Thanks be to God through Jesus Christ our Lord! (Romans 7:14–15, 24–25)

III. PERSONAL, BUT NOT SUBJECTIVE

That Law and Gospel have their primary effect on the individual—that the work of God's Word is profoundly *personal*—may lead to a false understanding. The individual who is rightly the intended hearer of God's Word in Law and Gospel, thinks, wrongly, that he or she is also the primary speaker of this Word and the one to decide whether to "preach" Law or Gospel to the self. In effect, the individual may be tempted to assume the role of pastoral care for himself or herself.

> *Therefore whoever knows well how to distinguish the Gospel from the Law should give thanks to God and know that he is a real theologian. I admit that in the time of temptation I myself do not know how to do this as I should.* The way to distinguish the one from the other is to locate the Gospel in heaven and the Law on earth, to call the righteousness of the Gospel heavenly and divine and the righteousness of the Law earthly and human, and to distinguish as sharp-

> ly between the righteousness of the Gospel and that of the Law as God distinguishes between heaven and earth or between light and darkness or between day and night. Let the one be like the light and the day, and the other like the darkness and the night. If we could only put an even greater distance between them![9]

The right distinction of Law and Gospel in an individual life is a tall order and Luther admits as much: "I admit that in the time of temptation I myself do not know how to do this as I should." In Christian living—in seeking to put off the old self and put on the renewed self (Ephesians 4:22–24)—the individual Christian certainly applies the Word of God to himself or herself and therefore tries to distinguish Law and Gospel. One rejoices in the Gospel's forgiveness as he repents. Another aches over how God's Law identifies her sins and failures.

Each of us *personally* seeks to apply Law and Gospel whether consciously or unconsciously. Yet a danger lies close to hand. It may work something like this. A man's conscience accuses him of sin and he feels guilty. However, because he knows that Christ died for the sins of the world, he tells himself not to worry and he "forgives himself." It is all quite neat and easy. Guilt's resolution comes by means of self-assurance under a Law-Gospel veneer.

Or, perhaps it takes a different direction. A woman's conscience accuses her of sin and she feels guilty. She knows that Christ died for the sins of the world, but she also knows that she needs to repent and because the sin persists, she wonders if she is fully repentant. Her conscience provides no clear assurance. A personal*istic* approach to Law-Gospel fails her in her need.

The danger on the one hand is that one becomes a David without a Nathan—comfortable and secure in oneself (2 Samuel 12). Like David, no sinner is equipped to recognize the depth of his sin without the aid of a Word that comes from *outside* us. Each of us is instead the hapless man

---

9 AE 26:115. Emphasis added.

who approves his hair with a check in the restroom mirror, only to march forth unaware of the toilet paper stuck to his backside. The Law is indeed a mirror, but sinners need a Nathan to reflect the Law's illumination in the places we are unable (or unwilling) to see. After all, a central weapon in sin's arsenal is self-deception: "Not the least of the errors which have entered the world because of sin is the fact that we sin and want to sin and yet do not want to acknowledge or bear the guilt of our sin."[10]

The danger on the other hand is that one becomes a Cephas without Jesus to restore us to confidence in His grace and mercy (John 21). Faith is not a psychological gimmick or an act of self-therapy for convincing myself that "I'm still okay." Faith comes by hearing a voice other than my own—the voice of Christ—declaring forgiveness and grace.

> Ezekiel (34:3–4) is right when he says that the prophets who frighten the heart of a righteous person with lies commit sin, for these are the smoking flax that should be tended and not altogether extinguished. And they sin in the other direction too, because they strengthen the hands of the wicked and do not rather accuse and condemn them.[11]

Thus our gracious God does not leave us "real, not imaginary sinners" to our own devices—to shepherd our own souls or prophesy to ourselves. Rather, He sends prophets, preachers, shepherds, and everyday saints to call us to repentance and to proclaim our Savior. So, although every believer personally wrestles with the Word, he need not and ought not do it in isolation from the household of faith and the office of preaching and teaching that Christ has established for the shepherding of His flock.

---

10 Martin Chemnitz, *Loci Theologici I* (St. Louis, Concordia Publishing House, 2008), 323.

11 AE 3:223.

IV. LAW AND GOSPEL IN DAILY LIFE

"Therefore, as you received Christ Jesus the Lord, so walk in Him, rooted and built up in Him and established in the faith, just as you were taught, abounding in thanksgiving." In these words from Colossians 2:6–7, the apostle reveals that the root or foundation for Christian living is no different from that on which salvation itself is established—just as justification is by faith in Christ, so also is sanctification. Thus he urges in 3:16, "Let the word of Christ dwell in you richly, teaching and admonishing one another in all wisdom, singing psalms and hymns and spiritual songs, with thankfulness in your hearts to God." These verses are a helpful reminder that Christian living is anchored in specific practices: solid catechesis ("just as you were taught"), regularly hearing the Word ("Let the word of Christ dwell in you richly"), and the rhythm of prayer and thanksgiving ("abounding in thanksgiving," "singing . . . with thankfulness").

A young man from a former congregation, Stephen Lee, recently acknowledged to me and others that he has homosexual desires. He also provided an article in which he explains publicly and quite thoroughly why he does not intend to act on those desires. Though he cannot deny the desire, he also cannot affirm it as appropriate to Christian life. He says, relative to Romans 1:

> My own experience illustrates this logic of God's creation of male and female. Desiring to love other men, I turn to the romantic and sexual love extolled by contemporary culture. However, the men to whom I am attracted, whether straight or gay, cannot genuinely give or receive love in this form. Homosexual desires treat men as women or women as men, of which they can only be a counterfeit. Even a gay man is never a woman. For these men to give and receive romantic and sexual love from me would only be a counterfeit of the actual gifts they can give as male friends.[12]

---

12 Stephen N. Lee, "Homosexuality: Why Does It Matter?" unpublished manuscript attached to email message from the author, May 14, 2014, page 3. Accessed July 24, 2014.

Yet, it is not only an understanding of creation or natural law that prevents Stephen from an affirmation of homosexuality. He refuses to evade texts of Scripture—words of Law—and instead acknowledges them. Above all, he parallels his desire to Paul's own frustration in Romans 7. Referring specifically to 7:15 and 7:19, he comments:

> These statements about actions resonate particularly with my frustration over my homosexual desires; I desire the very thing I hate. Even homosexuals who hate their homosexual tendencies will continue to have homosexual desires and even, in moments of weakness, to commit homosexual acts.[13]

But, emphatically, Stephen also rejoices in the Gospel of God's redeeming gracious love, not as a love that affirms his homosexual desire, but instead a love that is found in Christ and His redeeming work. It is the grace of God alone that answers the wrath of God.

> In Romans 1, Paul precedes his discussion of God's wrath with "I am not ashamed of the Gospel; it is the power of God for salvation to everyone who has faith" (Romans 1:16). In 1 Corinthians, Paul follows his statement "wrongdoers will not inherit the kingdom of God" (1 Corinthians 6:9) with "And this is what some of you used to be. But you were washed, you were sanctified, you were justified in the name of the Lord Jesus Christ and in the Spirit of our God" (1 Corinthians 6:11).[14]

This is the love that he, as a Christian living under God's Word of Law and Gospel, pleads for himself and for all with homosexual desire.

In significant ways, the struggle of this young man illustrates Law and Gospel in the Christian life. It is, first, a reminder of the necessity of foundational catechesis.[15] The young man spoke of his gratitude for the

13 Lee, "Homosexuality," 4.

14 Lee, "Homosexuality," 5.

15 Note Arthur Just's Christological definition of catechesis: "catechesis involves instruction in how Jesus thinks . . . and how Jesus lived, particularly the mercy and compassion He showed

teaching he had received—specifically, teaching about Law and Gospel, which is for him, with the confessors, a "particularly glorious light."[16] The catechisms of Luther have rightfully earned a place as a primary tool for Christian living in Lutheran churches. The Small Catechism simply and concisely lays out Law and Gospel and the life of faith—without any theological jargon or even, for that matter, the phrase "Law and Gospel." Instead, we encounter God's commands explained simply, in a way that shows what is proscribed and prescribed in His enduring Law.[17] Then we learn the Creed—the revelation of a gracious tri-personal God revealed as Father, Son, and Spirit; who alone gives life to the world, alone redeems human life in Christ Jesus, and alone creates and sustains faith and new life by His Spirit. Let Luther explain the distinction:

> From this you see that the Creed is a very different teaching than the Ten Commandments. For the latter teach us what we ought to do, but the Creed tells us what God does for us and gives to us. The Ten Commandments, moreover, are written in the hearts of all people, but no human wisdom is able to comprehend the Creed; it must be taught by the Holy Spirit alone. Therefore the Ten Commandments do not succeed in making us Christians, for God's wrath and displeasure still remain upon us because we cannot fulfill what God demands of us. But the Creed brings pure grace and makes us righteous and acceptable to God. Through this knowledge we come to love and delight in all the commandments of God because we see here in the Creed how

---

toward our dying world, which needs to be freed from its bondage." See *Heaven on Earth: The Gifts of Christ in the Divine Service* (St. Louis: Concordia Publishing House, 2008), 176.

16 "The distinction between law and gospel is a particularly glorious light. It serves to divide God's Word properly [cf. 2 Tim. 2:15] and to explain correctly and make understandable the writings of the holy prophets and apostles" (FC SD V 1).

17 In his *Commentary on Galatians*, Luther identifies the basis for the Law's enduring quality in natural knowledge rather than scriptural revelation: "Therefore there is one law which runs through all ages, is known to all men, is written in the hearts of all people, and leaves no one from beginning to end with an excuse, although for the Jews ceremonies were added and the other nations had their own laws, which were not binding upon the whole world, but only this one, which the Holy Spirit dictates unceasingly in the hearts of all" (AE 27:355).

> God gives himself completely to us, with all his gifts and power, to help us keep the Ten Commandments: the Father gives us all creation, Christ all his works, the Holy Spirit all his gifts. (LC II 67–69)

The Commandments and Creed fit so seamlessly with our theme of Law and Gospel that we might leave the catechism at this point. But Luther, from the start of his catechetical endeavors, understood that commandments and creed always stand together with prayer:

> Three things a person must know in order to be saved. First, he must know what to do and what to leave undone. Second, when he realizes that he cannot measure up to what he should do or leave undone, he needs to know where to go to find the strength he requires. Third, he must know how to seek and obtain that strength.[18]

Thus, in his explanation of Exodus 20:5, Luther identifies both the Creed *and* the Lord's Prayer as the aids we require in our failure to keep the Law's commands (LC I 316).[19] As he moves on from the Creed to the Lord's Prayer, he says:

> We have now heard what we are to do and believe. The best and most blessed life consists of these things. Now follows the third part, how we are to pray. We are in such a situation

---

18 AE 43:13. Note the footnote on page 13: "In the Middle Ages the four items everyone was to know by heart were the Hail Mary, the Ten Commandments, the Creed, and the Lord's Prayer. The most common traditional order in the period from 1450 to 1500 was: the Lord's Prayer, the Creed, and the Ten Commandments on the ground that the Lord's Prayer in the rosary was valueless without the faith of the Creed, and the faith of the Creed was of no effect without the keeping of the commandments. Luther consciously reversed the order with the purpose of showing that the gospel is the source of vitality and power for morality. Luther did not seek here to show a new way to salvation which omits the keeping of the law. Rather, the law is to show man that he is powerless to fulfill God's will by himself. See Johannes Meyer, *Historischer Kommentar zu Luthers kleinem Katechimus* (Gütersloh: C. Bertelsmann, 1929), pp. 82–83." Although Luther greatly simplifies this, it is noteworthy that Luther is still directly addressing the mortal sins, "strange sins," "crying and silent sins," etc. (ibid., 21).

19 This does not, however, suggest that prayer is a "means of grace." See Commission on Theology and Church Relations, *Theology and Practice of Prayer: A Lutheran View* (St. Louis: The Lutheran Church—Missouri Synod, 2011), 18.

> that no one can keep the Ten Commandments perfectly, even though he or she has begun to believe. Besides, the devil, along with the world and our flesh, resists them with all his power. Consequently, nothing is so necessary as to call upon God incessantly and to drum into his ears our prayer that he may give, preserve, and increase in us faith and the fulfillment of the Ten Commandments and remove all that stands in our way and hinders us in this regard. That we may know what and how to pray, however, our LORD Christ himself has taught us both the way and the words, as we shall see. (LC III 1–3)

The catechism directly connects "what we are to do and believe" (i.e., Law and Gospel) with prayer. Luther grounds prayer in both Law and Gospel, beginning with the command to pray which we are to obey,[20] going on to the Gospel promise that God will hear, answer, and give to those who ask in faith (LC III 19–20), and then to the pure initiative of God who "puts into our mouths the very words and approach we are to use" in prayer (LC III 22). Then, as he explains "the very words and approach" in the Small Catechism, Luther emphasizes how we are led in the first three petitions to pray for the pure teaching of the Word and for holy lives, for the Holy Spirit's grace that we might believe the Word and be empowered for holy living, and for steadfastness in His Word and in faith until the end of our lives (SC III 5, 8, 11).

After addressing the three historic parts of Christian catechesis, Luther goes on to speak of the sacramental Word whereby faith and new life are sustained: Baptism, Absolution, the Supper. Baptism is God's promise of salvation made personal and individual—a call to "faith, which trusts this Word of God in the water" (SC IV 9). It signals (signifies) to

---

20 The contemporary "Lutheran" antinomianism that rejects all commands in Christian life will gain no ally in Luther, who is never chary of demanding obedience from Christians. "This is the first and most important point, that all our prayers must be based on obedience to God, regardless of our person, whether we are sinners or righteous people, worthy or unworthy. We must understand that God is not joking, but that he will be angry and punish us if we do not pray, just as he punishes all other kinds of disobedience" (LC III 17–18).

us that Christian living is within Law and Gospel—"daily contrition and repentance" (SC IV 12). And so we are also invited to the confessional where the *individual* confesses sin and is *personally* absolved and also "comfort[ed] and encourage[d] to faith" (SC IV 29). In the fifth part, Luther sounds once more this same personal note, emphasizing that the body and blood of Christ we eat and drink are "given for you" (SC V 7–8).[21]

Such is the foundational teaching—the catechesis—of Christian faith and life as our churches understand it. To be grounded in such truth is not optional—so the Church has always rightly emphasized the necessity of imparting foundational doctrines.[22] But the catechesis that a new or maturing Christian requires hardly satisfies the whole of her need for God's Word of Law and Gospel. Faith comes by hearing (Romans 8)—and not just once. Again, I point to my young correspondent. None of the concerns he expressed would matter in the least for one who had not—by the power of the Word—come to know both his sin and his Savior in a way that was habitual and internalized. Such internalization happens not by a course of catechesis alone. The faith that first comes by hearing, remains, is sustained, and grows by continued hearing.

So it is that Paul urges that the Word dwell in us *richly.* The phrase "word and sacrament" is more than a mantra. It is a way of living, the way of Christian living. It is life in the Church, not as mere institution but as the specific setting in which "believers and saints" assemble (AC VIII 1) to hear the Gospel "preached harmoniously according to a pure understanding" and to receive the sacraments as they "are administered in conformity with the divine Word" (AC VII 2). That Gospel and those sacraments are the only reason there are believers and saints, and it is the only setting in which sinners are sustained as believers and saints. This

21 Although I will not discuss herein the prayers for morning and evening or the Table of Duties, it should be obvious that these also fit directly within the schema of Law and Gospel.

22 See "Catechesis, II (Medieval)" and "Catechesis, III (Reformation)" in *New Catholic Encyclopedia*, vol. 1 (Farmington Hills, Michigan: 2002), 228–36. Also see Michael Reu, Dr. Martin *Luther's Small Catechism: A History of Its Origin, Its Distribution and Its Use* (Chicago: Wartburg, 1929), 1–4. Luther's catechisms are arguably as ecumenical as they are confessional.

is also the setting in which believers and saints are formed, established, and sustained in "the Christian life."[23] Thus the Lord's Day is hallowed, devoted "to holy words, holy works, and holy living" as we "make use of God's Word and exercise ourselves in it" (LC I 87–88).

The Word of Law and Gospel is not confined, however, only to the Church's assemblies. We ought "to occupy ourselves daily with God's Word and carry it in our hearts and on our lips" (LC I 89). In the rhythm of daily reading and prayer, we hear the same Word of Law and Gospel and pray for the Holy Spirit, by whom alone God works in us "conversion, faith in Christ, rebirth, renewal, and everything that belongs to the actual beginning and completion of these things" (FC SD II 25).

This means, simply, a reaffirmation of the importance of personal piety. The excesses of *Pietism,* have, I fear, turned some in contemporary Lutheranism against *piety.* Orthodox pastors, professors, and church officials undermine their offices and the truths they proclaim when they fail to practice or encourage life that humbly hears the Word, grieves over sin, prays devoutly, and remembers Luther's admonition to hallow the name with holy teaching *and holy lives.*[24]

Right piety starts with the disciplined hearing of the Word and prayer. The Church's daily office—whether followed strictly or loosely—can hardly be excelled for it instills a rich habit of expansive readings from the Word of Law and Gospel together with prayers from the Holy Spirit Himself in the Psalter and from the Spirit-given catholic inheritance bequeathed to us. Coupled with personal prayers, concerns, and pleas, such daily practice sustains Christian life day by day.

Though such devotional life is, in the very best sense, habitual, it will foster neither a somnambulant life of spiritual ease and *faux* calm, nor any sort of supercilious sanctity. Rather, the Word's character as Law and

---

23 For an insightful argument regarding the importance of Christian worship in ethical formation, see Gifford A. Grobien's "Righteousness, Mystical Union, and Moral Formation in Christian Worship," *Concordia Theological Quarterly* 77, nos. 1–2 (2013): 141–63.

24 "Likewise, this petition is for ourselves who have the Word of God but are ungrateful for it and fail to live according to it as we ought. If you ask for such things from your heart, you can be sure that God is pleased" (LC III 47–48).

Gospel and the rhythm of daily encounter with God's hammer and His healing—this daily foray into Scripture's theology of the cross—will keep us unsettled and humbled. It will have us ever acknowledging that we are sinner saints. Benne remarks that "the theology of the cross prevents undue optimism about our own sanctification. Even though the Spirit imputes to us and indwells in us the righteousness of Christ, the old Adam in us never dies. We are sinners and saints all the days of our life on earth. In fact, we regress as well as progress. The struggle goes on."[25] Just as preaching does, so also will the daily office make plain that struggle.

V. LAW AND GOSPEL IN CHRISTIAN VOCATION

"So, Lutheran theology affirms that faith not only fastens to Christ for salvation but also discerns a deeper meaning in the ordinary structures of life. They are, in spite of all, blessings of God to be accepted with gratitude and joy. Further, they are the places in which we discern our special missions in life—our callings. They provide roles for Christians to play in the drama that God is unfolding. They provide the context, the locale, in which Christians are to play out their temporal destinies."[26] Robert Benne's discussion of Law and Gospel in Christian vocation is a thorough consideration of this vital concern. It is in vocation that Benne chiefly identifies the "personal" dimension of Law and Gospel in Christian life. I have emphasized a different aspect of the Law/Gospel effect above, but that should not be viewed as disagreement with Benne's vocational focus.

In the vocational dimension, one sees the role the Law plays in Christian life in particular ways. It is in their vocations that Christians most helpfully apply the commandments of God together with Scripture's other rich admonitions and directions toward holy living. Note the heading of Luther's "Table of Duties" or "Household Chart": "The Household Chart of Some Bible Passages for all kinds of holy orders and walks of life, through which they may be admonished, as through lessons

25 Benne, 145.

26 Benne, 143.

particularly pertinent to their office and duty."[27] These pertinent lessons of Scripture address us in the everyday world of the home, the office, the political arena, and the church's polity (its institutional shape). They are words of Law and so admonition. They are sobering words of duty, yet they also are gladly received for all who live under the freedom of the Gospel, for as they structure life and direct our days they free us from the aimlessness of "making it up as we go along."

These words define the priesthood of 1 Peter 2. Note that, in context, Peter's priestly appellation for believers emphasizes not only the *spiritual* character of the priesthood, but also its *practicality.*

> As you come to Him, a living stone rejected by men but in the sight of God chosen and precious, [5]you yourselves like
> living stones are being built up as a spiritual house, to be a holy priesthood, to offer spiritual sacrifices acceptable to
> God through Jesus Christ. [6]For it stands in Scripture: "Be-
> hold, I am laying in Zion a stone, a cornerstone chosen and precious, and whoever believes in Him will not be put to
> shame." [7]So the honor is for you who believe, but for those who do not believe, "The stone that the builders rejected
> has become the cornerstone," [8]and "A stone of stumbling, and a rock of offense." They stumble because they disobey the word, as they were destined to do.
>
> [9]But you are a chosen race, a royal priesthood, a holy nation, a people for His own possession, that you may proclaim the excellencies of Him who called you out of darkness into His
> marvelous light. [10]Once you were not a people, but now you are God's people; once you had not received mercy, but now you have received mercy.
>
> [11]Beloved, I urge you as sojourners and exiles to abstain from the passions of the flesh, which wage war against your

27 See Kolb-Wengert, p. 365.

soul. [12]Keep your conduct among the Gentiles honorable, so that when they speak against you as evildoers, they may see your good deeds and glorify God on the day of visitation.

[13]Be subject for the Lord's sake to every human institution, whether it be to the emperor as supreme, [14]or to governors as sent by him to punish those who do evil and to praise those who do good. [15]For this is the will of God, that by doing good you should put to silence the ignorance of foolish people. [16]Live as people who are free, not using your freedom as a cover-up for evil, but living as servants of God. [17]Honor everyone. Love the brotherhood. Fear God. Honor the emperor.

It is in the context of "every human institution" that the royal priesthood serves. Luther's defense of the royal priesthood in his *Letter to the Christian Nobility of the German Nation* emphasizes the spiritual dignity of the universal priesthood, but also emphasizes that distinctiveness within the priesthood is dependent on office or specific calling.[28] That is precisely the connection one sees in 1 Peter 2. All priests are to "proclaim the excellencies" of the One who called us. We do that in the places *where* He has called us. So Peter speaks of the life we sojourner priests are to live "among the Gentiles" in terms of subjection to authority, doing good, and honor for all.

So the priestly wife and husband serve each other in subjection and honor and love. The priestly son or daughter serves in honor and obedience. The priestly citizen serves in responsibility toward government even as the priestly employee or employer serves in the workplace. In every setting, we are called to live as those who have received mercy (2:10), conducting our lives honorably (2:12), and proclaiming the excellencies of our Lord (2:9).

---

28 See AE 44.

Such is the way of Law and Gospel in Christian vocational life. "As far as that goes, we are all consecrated priests through baptism, as St. Peter says in I Peter 2[:9], 'You are a royal priesthood and a priestly realm.' The Apocalypse says, 'Thou hast made us to be priests and kings by thy blood' [Rev. 5:9–10]."[29]

CONCLUSION

The same Luther who challenged the legalism of Rome came to abhor the antinomianism that some adopted under the name of reformation. Both enemies were evident because of the twofold Word of Law and Gospel. The enemies of Christ never change their tunes, and they have but two. The one is spiritual smugness—the self-congratulatory "spirituality" of human accomplishment according to one's own standard of obedience and goodness. The other is spiritual licentiousness—the nonsense of false freedom under a Gospel of permission rather than a promise of forgiveness for Christ's sake. The weapons of Christ also never change—they are ever His Word of Law and Gospel.

29 AE 44:127.

PROPERLY DISTINGUISHING LAW AND GOSPEL AS THE PASTOR'S CALLING

Mark C. Mattes

It is the charge and privilege of Lutheran pastors properly to distinguish Law and Gospel. It is no exaggeration to say that the proper distinction between Law and Gospel is the native air in which Lutheran pastors live, move, and have their being. As shepherds of peoples' consciences, pastors must consistently and courageously discern how the Law binds people in their sin and how such bound people can be set free through the Gospel. The proper distinction between Law and Gospel is thereby the interpretive lens through which Christians understand both Scripture and the world. But even more, it is the way in which God works with sinners. Through the Law God accuses sinners, renders His verdict of death upon them ("the wages of sin" [Romans 6:23]), and through the Gospel God forgives repentant sinners and imparts to them new life in Christ risen and victorious over death. Indeed, our Lord Jesus was "delivered up for our trespasses and raised for our justification" (Romans 4:25).[1]

NALC pastors are directed properly to discern Law from Gospel since this doctrine is brought to the fore in the Common Confession (2005): "We believe and confess that the Bible is God's revealed Word to us, spoken in Law and Gospel."[2] On the basis of this confession, all members of the NALC should be familiar with and exercise this classic teaching of Evangelical faith. In congregations where laypeople are not

1 All Scripture quotations in this chapter are from the ESV.

2 Find the full text at http://thenalc.org/nalc-constitution/.

familiar with this doctrine, pastors should teach it to them. The proper distinction between Law and Gospel is the framework through which Lutheran pastors read the Holy Scriptures, peoples' consciences, and the world. The Lutheran tradition has acknowledged three uses of the Law: (1) the civil or political use, whereby God orders society; (2) the theological use, whereby God kills sinners all for the purpose of remaking them to be people of faith; and (3) a parenetic guide for Christian living, whereby God indicates the path upon which His children walk. The focus of this paper deals with the second use of the Law.

THE TWOFOLD NATURE OF GOD'S ACTION

All Christian doctrine should be interpreted through the lens of Law and Gospel. Expounding Luther's theology, Bernhard Lohse writes that "dealing with any doctrine in a formally correct manner is never enough unless we also express the proper distinction between Law and Gospel in the *double nature* of God's activity as well as our *twofold relationship* to God as people who are both judged and who have experienced mercy."[3] For example, Christians affirm that God is omnipotent. In terms of Law, God's omnipotence is a threat to humanity's presumption of autonomy. But freedom after all is a divine attribute alone, proper to God, and not something people can claim for themselves before God. God is almighty. We are not. Any power or agency that humans have is purely a gift from God's "fatherly and divine" goodness and mercy. Even so, sinners are bound to claim their own independence from God, and thus succumb to God's judgment. In contrast, from the perspective of the Gospel, God's omnipotence is precisely His power to rescue sinners from sin, death, the devil, and even His own Law as accusatory. So, as Lohse notes, God's activity is that of a double nature, accusing and comforting. And our relationship to God is twofold, that of our old rebellious nature as being accused and our new liberated nature as being released from such accusation.

---

3 Bernhard Lohse, *Martin Luther: An Introduction to His Life and Work*, trans. Robert C. Schultz (Philadelphia: Fortress, 1986), 158. Italics mine.

The proper distinction between Law and Gospel is central to Luther's own "reformation discovery." Both early and late in his career, Luther was concerned with how people properly honor God, acknowledge His deity.[4] Intuitively, one would think that God is most properly honored when we observe His Law in thought, word, and deed. But with this perspective, Luther could never find a God he could love, but instead only a God he could hate. If God is only a judge or evaluator of human behavior and never a loving Father who wants to care for and provide for His children, then this God can never be the object of love, but only fear. Through intense study of the Psalms, Romans, Hebrews, and Galatians, the early Luther came to realize that God provides two kinds of righteousness, one of the Law and the other of faith. The first kind of righteousness exists to establish and secure healthy community. The second is the way God works to right-wise sinners before God and thus permit them to honor God. In a late Table Talk, Luther said,

> For a long time I went astray [in the monastery] and didn't know what I was about. To be sure, I knew something, but I didn't know what it was until I came to the text in Romans 1 [:17], "He who through faith is righteous shall live." That text helped me. There I saw what righteousness Paul was talking about. Earlier in the text I read "righteousness." I related the abstract ["righteousness"] with the concrete ["the righteous One"] and became sure of my cause. I learned to distinguish between the righteousness of the law and the righteousness of the gospel. I lacked nothing before this except that I made no distinction between the law and the gospel. I regarded both as the same thing and held that there was no difference between Christ and Moses except the times in which they lived and their degrees of perfection. But when I discovered the proper

4 Compare David Yeago, "The Catholic Luther," in *The Catholicity of the Reformation*, ed. Carl Braaten and Robert Jenson (Grand Rapids: Eerdmans, 1996), 17–18.

distinction—namely, that the law is one thing and the gospel is another—I made myself free.[5]

Pastors are at the forefront of discerning the word that frees from the word that binds (Matthew 16:19; 18:18); this is their great charge and privilege. No other vocation is specifically set aside to exercise this power. It is not that others cannot make this distinction. Indeed, some laypeople make this distinction better than many pastors do. But the pastoral office is charged with this privilege of properly distinguishing Law and Gospel in preaching and pastoral care. Along with administering the sacraments, this is the core identity of the pastoral vocation. It is the foundation for all evangelistic endeavors. For Luther, the proper distinction between Law and Gospel in preaching and pastoral care is an art, and so it is a practice in which all pastors can grow. Since other Christian traditions ignore, distort, or downplay this distinction, the proper distinction between Law and Gospel is the most important ecumenical challenge and gift which Lutherans offer other Christians. For that reason, it should never be ignored, distorted, or downplayed when dealing with Christians of other confessional traditions. Indeed, it is a nonnegotiable item at the forefront in any ecumenical discussion.

The Common Confession (2005) simply restates the thrust of the Apology of the Augsburg Confession. This binding confessional document indicates that Law and Gospel are at the heart of the Evangelical-Lutheran witness. In the Apology, Philip Melanchthon noted that "these are the two chief works of God in human beings, to terrify and to justify the terrified or make them alive. The entire Scripture is divided into these two works. One part is the law. . . . The second part is the gospel."[6] The upshot of the proper distinction between Law and Gospel is to make the truth of the doctrine of justification by grace alone through faith alone clear: "Accordingly, justification takes place through the Word, just as Paul notes [Rom. 1:16]: the gospel 'is the power of God for salvation to everyone who has faith.' . . . If justification takes place

5 AE 54:442. Dated to the winter of 1542–43.

6 Ap XII 53. All Book of Concord quotations in this chapter are from Kolb-Wengert.

only through the Word and the Word is grasped only by faith, it follows that faith justifies."[7]

For greater clarity in how Law and Gospel are different, we can look to Martin Chemnitz, one of the chief authors of the Formula of Concord. Chemnitz articulated three important ways that the Law is different from the Gospel. First, the Law, at least to some degree, can be known by nature since its commands are imprinted on human behavior. For instance, people recognize that some things, such as murder, theft, and lying, are destructive, while other things, such as thrift, hard work, and collegiality, promote life. In contrast, the Gospel is a "mystery hidden to reason" and which God "has revealed only through His Word" in the preaching of Jesus Christ as our justification. Second, the Law points out, censures, and rebukes sinners, while the Gospel "offers and bestows life eternal to all that apprehend it by faith." Finally, the attempt to secure salvation through the Law can be had only through achieving perfection. But given human corruption, such perfection is impossible. In contrast, the Gospel offers "true righteousness as imputed and given to us freely, without our merit, solely for the sake of Christ and through faith."[8]

THE SCRIPTURAL BASIS

It is not confessional authority alone which sustains the Lutheran conviction of the centrality of Law and Gospel. Instead, the Confessions, along with Luther, are simply pointing to the core truth of the Scriptures' presentation of how God works with sinners throughout. Law and Gospel are the means by which God has always worked and continues to work with people. Mary, the mother of our Lord, encapsulated the difference between Law and Gospel: "[God] has brought down the powerful from their thrones and exalted those of humble estate" (Luke 1:52). Mary testifies that God does a *twofold* work: bringing down the powerful and

7 Ap IV 67.

8 Martin Chemnitz, *Ministry, Word, and Sacraments: An Enchiridion*, trans. Luther Poellot (St. Louis: Concordia Publishing House, 1981), 72.

lifting up the lowly.[9] This is no different than the job description which God provided for the youthful prophet Jeremiah, "Behold, I have put My words in your mouth. See, I have set you this day over nations and over kingdoms, to pluck up and to break down, to destroy and to overthrow, to build and to plant" (Jeremiah 1:9–10). In Jeremiah's preaching, God worked to destroy prideful claimants but also to comfort the oppressed and fearful.

The entire history of Israel can be read through the lens of Law and Gospel. When Israel was self-secure, she became idolatrous; she looked to her own resources and not to God. Thereby, she violated the basis of the covenant in which God promised to be God for her and allow her to live as His people. She incurred God's judgment. The execution of her punishment reduced her to nothing. She suffered through famines or foreign invasions. The most definitive experience of such judgment in Israel's history was the exile or Babylonian captivity from 586 to 516 BC. During times of judgment, any resources which Israel could claim for herself were insufficient. Israel was reduced to a state which Luther later described in the Heidelberg Disputation (1518): "It is certain that man must *utterly despair* of his own ability before he is prepared to receive the grace of Christ."[10] Reduced to nothing, utterly despairing of herself, Israel then could look to God alone. And God was there to claim her. Specifically during the exile, the word of absolution in Isaiah (Isaiah 40:1–2), as well as the prophecy of a coming Suffering Servant, encouraged and empowered those who were exiled (Isaiah 52:13–53:12).

But an important caveat must be noted. Wise pastors will recognize that judgment is not to be confused with God's hiddenness. Even when God was not overtly judging Israel for infidelity, injustice, and waywardness, God's kindness was not always apparent. This is a feature of God's way with the world that we cannot rationalize or figure out. But it is a common experience in a faith walk with God. An example in the Scriptures is when the people of Israel were enslaved in Egypt.

9 See Luther's magisterial and devotional "The Magnificat" in AE 21:297–358.

10 AE 31:51. Italics mine.

Their enslavement was not a punishment per se. They had done nothing specifically wrong to deserve enslavement. Under the leadership of the patriarch Jacob, they had gone to Egypt for food during a time of famine. The fact that over a period of time they had been enslaved by a pharaoh "who knew not Joseph" ran counter to God's promise given to Abraham that his descendants would enjoy the land promised to them. Undoubtedly many Hebrews wondered where God was in their enslavement. In response, God called Moses to lead the Hebrews out of slavery and back to their homeland. God's liberation of the slaves was surely Gospel. The Hebrew celebration of Passover, which commemorated the family meal eaten before their journey back to the Promised Land, foreshadows the Lord's Supper. But here the Gospel was not a response to Law or punishment per se but instead to God's hiddenness. God's promise to provide for His people was incommensurate with the people's enslavement; God's mercy was hidden under the duration of slavery. People encounter God's hiddenness precisely at the juncture of such incommensurability between the promise and present experience.

Administering the Gospel entails that pastors must discern whether their parishioners are experiencing God's accusing Law or instead God's hiddenness. In the Scriptures, it is clear that God will be faithful to His promise—even if this fidelity does not happen within the time frame desired by His people. The proper distinction between Law and Gospel is appropriate for sinners caught in the trap of their own guilt. But it should not be employed with those wrestling with God as hidden. In those cases, people are not especially guilty of overt sin but instead are wrestling with the question of where God is in their suffering. If they wrestle with doubt, it is an honest wrestling. For such men and women, lamentation or even complaint is appropriate. Most important, God's promise should be upheld. God will rescue them and has indeed already healed them in the resurrection of Jesus Christ. Pastors and others should not treat those suffering God's hiddenness as Job's "comforters" treated Job by blaming Job for his trials. The wise pastor not only distinguishes Law from Gospel but also distinguishes Law from God's hiddenness and responds accordingly in pastoral care.

LAW AND GOSPEL AT WORK IN JESUS' MINISTRY

Law and Gospel not only determine the breadth of Scripture but also its center: the Passion of our Lord. Jesus, the Suffering Servant foretold by Isaiah, was crucified at the hands of sinners. We sinners are all responsible for His death. But His death is also the execution of a divine verdict—again, the execution of the wages of sin. Even though Jesus committed no sin, He so identified with sinners, became one with them, fellowshiped with them, cast His lot in with theirs, gave His whole being for them, that He bore their sins. As John the Baptist proclaimed, He was the Lamb of God who takes away the sin of the world (John 1:29). As Luther put it, in bearing sin, Jesus was the "greatest sinner."[11] The fact that Jesus was not only a man but also the Son of God would not let Him off the hook. In John 7:53–8:11, when Jesus defended the woman caught in adultery, He opposed not only her accusers and assailants but also God's very Law. "Teacher, this woman was caught in the very act of committing adultery. Now in the Law Moses commanded us to stone such women. Now what do You say?" When Jesus defends this woman ("Let anyone among you who is without sin be the first to throw a stone at her"), He goes against not only her accusers (who after all were really after Him, not the woman) but the Law of Moses itself. The Law, of course, is not just Moses'. It is God's.

Here there are multiple levels of conflict, but one stands out in a striking way. First, there is conflict between those claiming righteousness

---

11 Luther writes, "For Christ is innocent so far as His own Person is concerned; therefore He should not have been hanged from the tree. But because, according to the Law, every thief should have been hanged, therefore, according to the Law of Moses, Christ Himself should have been hanged; for He bore the person of a sinner and a thief—and not of one but of all sinners and thieves. For we are sinners and thieves, and therefore we are worthy of death and eternal damnation. But Christ took all our sins upon Himself, and for them He died on the cross. Therefore it was appropriate for Him to become a thief and, as Isaiah says (53:12), to be 'numbered among the thieves.'" See AE 26:277. "Now He is not the Son of God, born of the Virgin. But He is a sinner, who has and bears the sin of Paul, the former blasphemer, persecutor, and assaulter; of Peter, who denied Christ; of David, who was an adulterer and a murderer, and who caused the Gentiles to blaspheme the name of the Lord (Rom. 2:24). In short, He has and bears all the sins of all men in His body—not in the sense that He has committed them but in the sense that He took these sins, committed by us, upon His own body, in order to make satisfaction for them with His own blood" (AE 31:51).

for themselves in opposition to the adulteress. Second, there is conflict between Jesus as an advocate and the woman's self-righteous accusers. But most important, there is conflict between God's Law which calls for the woman's death and God's mercy as expressed in Jesus' advocacy. The woman has forfeited her life not only with respect to her peers but also with respect to God's Law. Jesus does not let her off the hook and claim that she is innocent. But neither will He give her opponents heed. Her life is in Jesus' hands. Jesus, the woman's advocate, will forfeit His own life, if need be, to defend this woman. It is mercy which the woman's accusers refuse to give. But in contrast, ultimately, it is God's mercy and not His judgment which expresses God's very nature as love, especially to this particular adulteress. Jesus bears this woman's sin, identifies with her, exposes the sinful, self-righteous mercilessness of her accusers, and thereby brings the Law to its limits. This woman is a sinner—but, running counter to the Law, Jesus is for her.

In being-for-sinners, in identifying with them, in becoming Himself the "greatest sinner"—far more a sinner than what you or I or anyone ever could be—Jesus succumbs to the Law's accusation: crucify Him! But it is this advocate that God in mercy receives, raises from the dead, and so establishes an end to the Law's accusations (Romans 10:4). The Law has its say, has its place, does its job, and does so rightly. But it is not God's final, ultimate, even true word. That true word—God's faithfulness even to those who do not deserve it—is this: for Jesus' sake repentant sinners are forgiven. And that divine judgment cannot be overthrown. "For the law was given through Moses; grace and truth came through Jesus Christ" (John 1:17).

Law and Gospel thus indicate conflict within the divine life itself, conflict between God's wrath and God's mercy, and overcome only as Jesus takes this wrath away as He bodily bears our sin. In God's own inner-trinitarian counsel, the eternal Son in full agreement with the Father and the Spirit elected Himself to ransom sinners but in so doing He bears the full effect of the punishment of God's own Law.[12] God's

---

12 "God said to His beloved Son: / 'It's time to have compassion. / Then go, bright jewel of My

Law rightfully condemns sinners for their self-assertion in opposition to God. But ultimately God will have His sinners nonetheless. For it is to such sinners as the adulteress whose self-assertion is entirely broken, who have no backup plan, who have "utterly despaired" of themselves, and so are utterly dependent, that God's mercy can come. As such, they can sing with Mary that God exalts those of humble estate.

What also is exposed is that those self-righteous ones seeking the adulteress's stoning violate God's mercy. They who think that they are not sinners, that the "designated sinner" or reject is right in front of them on her knees, are proven wrong. Their legalism—justification by works of the Law—is just as vile before God as the woman's libertinism. Neither libertinism with its antinomianism or legalism with its nomism counts before God; instead, only a pure, clean heart, rid of self-defense and self-righteousness does. And it is that kind of heart which the Holy Spirit is out to create with any sinner with whom He has to do (Psalm 51). Just as Jesus tells the woman "go and sin no more" is this new, clean, and pure heart created. God will have nothing of a sacrifice of human purity any more than He will tolerate human lawlessness and rebellion. It is faith alone that properly honors God. To use Luther's terms, the Law as accusing is disclosed as God's *alien* work. It exists for the Gospel, God's *proper* work. The Law brings sinners of all sorts—whether libertines or legalists—to repentance, to the end that they might believe the good news, trust in God for Jesus' sake, and so rightly fear, love, and trust in God above all things. What is also disclosed is that the person of a human is to be distinguished from his or her works. Works avail nothing before God. God does not need them. The neighbor instead needs them. God justifies the person—claims a sinner as His own. Works helping our neighbor are an outgrowth of the renewal of the claimed sinner, whose righteousness before God is established on the basis of God's favor of the sinner for Jesus' sake.

crown, / And bring to all salvation; / From sin and sorrow set them free; / Slay bitter death for them that they / May live with You forever.'" See "Dear Christians, One and All, Rejoice" (*LSB* 556).

That one would attempt to justify oneself by means of the Law, that living a good, clean life could feed self-righteousness, and thus be tantamount to sin, is counterintuitive. But it is a hallmark of Lutheran discerning between self- and divine-righteousness. Sin comes not only in the variety of the accused adulteress but also her accusers. What the Law does is to shatter all presumption before God. And it is more a trait of a Pharisee than a prodigal—as bad as that is—to offer such presumption. In his classic treatment of the proper distinction between Law and Gospel in *Lectures on Galatians* (1535), Luther expressed this truth in this way:

> Therefore the proper and absolute use of the Law is to terrify with lightning (as on Mt. Sinai), thunder, and the blare of the trumpet, with a thunderbolt to burn and crush that brute which is called the presumption of righteousness. Hence God says through Jeremiah (23:29): "My Word is a hammer which breaks the rock in pieces." For as long as the presumption of righteousness remains in a man, there remain immense pride, self-trust, smugness, hate of God, contempt of grace and mercy, ignorance of the promises and of Christ. The preaching of free grace and the forgiveness of sins does not enter his heart and understanding, because that huge rock and solid wall, namely, the presumption of righteousness by which the heart itself is surrounded, prevents this from happening.
>
> Therefore this presumption of righteousness is a huge and a horrible monster. To break and crush it, God needs a large and powerful hammer, that is, the Law, which is the hammer of death, the thunder of hell, and the lightning of divine wrath. To what purpose? To attack the presumption of righteousness, which is a rebellious, stubborn, and stiff-necked beast.[13]

13 AE 26:310.

Luther is fully aware that the tendency with the Law is either to reject it altogether or to use it to justify ourselves. God takes that risk of such responses to the Law because neither way will work and in fact both ways lead to culs-de-sac from which only the Gospel can deliver us.

THE HERMENEUTICS OF JUSTIFICATION

The core of Luther's articulation of the proper distinction between Law and Gospel is grounded in his overall "reformation discovery." Luther discovered a new outlook on language. Oswald Bayer notes that since the Stoics it had been assumed that words are signs referring to reality outside of language. In other words, language either describes things or feelings or it directs behavior though imperatives or commands. In his study of penance, Luther along with thinkers before him had understood the priestly word of absolution, "I absolve you of your sins," as an act of declaration acknowledging a state of affairs. When the priest sees a penitent's remorse and takes it as a sign of divine justification—"the divine absolution occurring already in the one being absolved but unknown to him—and lets this appear as such. He states it for the assurance of the one being absolved. By this means the word of absolution is understood as a judgment in the classical sense of a statement."[14] Luther came to an entirely different view.

> That the linguistic sign is itself the reality, that it represents not an absent but a present reality, was Luther's great hermeneutical discovery, his "Reformation Discovery" in the strict sense. He made it first (1518) in reflection on the sacrament of penance. That the sign itself is the reality means, with reference to the absolution, that the sentence "I absolve you of your sins!" is no judgment which only ascertains what already exists, therefore assuming an inner, divine, proper absolution. Rather, the word of absolution

14 See Oswald Bayer, "Luther as an Interpreter of Holy Scripture," trans. Mark Mattes in *The Cambridge Companion to Luther*, ed. Don McKim (Cambridge: Cambridge University Press, 2003), 76–77. In this section, I follow Bayer's language closely.

> is a speech-act that first establishes a state of affairs, first creates a relationship—between the one in whose name it is spoken, and the one to whom it is spoken and who believes the promise.[15]

In other words, God's words are powerful and active. The Law is a word which actually does something. It kills sinners. And the word of absolution is a word which does something. It reclaims sinners. In Luther's new hermeneutic, we deal with words that do what they say and say what they do. These words do not merely describe a situation or express a command. Instead, a word such as the promise is a gift-word, a word which delivers the reality of forgiveness. Here the sign is the reality—and the reality delivered is Christ Himself.

AN INNOVATION?

While grounded thoroughly in the Scriptures, Luther's distinction between Law and Gospel comes across to many as something of an innovation. In a sense, it is. The concern to distinguish Law from Gospel, so important to Lutheran preachers, is not as explicit in other Christian traditions. For instance, Calvin has no locus treating this subject in his *Institutes*. As the late J. A. O. Preus observed, "the doctrine of the proper distinction between Law and Gospel is a doctrine which developed almost entirely and only on Lutheran soil."[16] The NALC is concerned for the orthodoxy of faith—that is, that her teaching conforms to the benchmark of the Ancient Church Fathers in the first several centuries of the Christian faith. Is the proper distinction between Law and Gospel a departure from orthodoxy?

Of course, it is the Scriptures that must assess the tradition of the Church and not vice versa. To the point, Luther's "discovery" of the proper distinction between Law and Gospel was not a therapeutic response to his own anxious conscience but instead due to his thorough saturation in Scripture. In a sense, the proper distinction between Law and Gospel

15 Ibid., 76.

16 J. A. O. Preus, "Chemnitz on Law and Gospel," *Concordia Journal* 15.4 (October 1989): 409.

serves to make the doctrine of justification by faith alone through grace alone operative and concrete in daily ministry. The doctrine is not merely a standard or benchmark of true faith but primarily an articulation of how God deals with sinners. In summary, for Luther, justification by faith is (1) for the sake of Christ and His righteousness; (2) by virtue of the imputation of this righteousness through the forgiveness of sin for our benefit; (3) through the faith that receives this forgiveness, not as a new quality in us but as a laying hold of the gracious promise; (4) happening as an instantaneous act and not gradually; (5) offering a renewal of life based on this forgiveness; and (6) bound to the proper distinction between Law, which brings an end to the old being, and the Gospel, which creates the new.[17]

With respect to the catholicity of Luther's teaching, we can affirm that Luther's perspective on justification *sola fide* was not unknown to the Church Fathers. While there are different stands of theology in the Fathers, and their theology of justification was seldom expressed as clearly as found in Paul or Luther, the language of justification *sola fide* can be found in the Ancient Church. Commenting on Ephesians 2:8–9, fourth-century Greek theologian Theodoret of Cyrrhus noted that "it is not of our own accord that we have believed, but we have come to belief after having been called; and even when we had come to believe, He did not require of us purity of life, but approving mere faith, God bestowed on us forgiveness of sins." And commenting on Romans 3:28, Origen of Alexandria said,

> I think it must suffice to mention the thief on the cross, who asked Christ to save him and was told: 'Truly, this day you will be with me in paradise' (Luke 23:43). . . . A man is justified by faith. The works of the Law can make no contribution to this. Where there is no faith which might justify the believer, even if there are works of the Law these are not based on the foundation of faith. Even if they are good

17 Mark Mattes, *The Role of Justification in Contemporary Theology* (Grand Rapids: Eerdmans, 2004), 9.

> in themselves they cannot justify the one who does them, because faith is lacking, and faith is the mark of those who are justified by God.[18]

And further quotes could be added from ancient Western theologians such as Clement of Rome, Augustine, Prosper, and Fulgentius indicating their agreement.[19] Clearly their thinking was not duplicated in those theologians most influential in Luther's early study, such as Gabriel Biel or John Duns Scotus, who argued that God can elevate the love we have for finite things to the eternal and so enable our cooperation to earn grace by doing our very best. It was this latter thinking which Luther found dishonorable to God.

Luther's teaching, so indebted to Paul, was shared to one degree or another by the most able of the ancient theologians. But even so, those thinkers did not articulate the proper distinction of Law and Gospel as Luther expressed it. And there were other voices in the tradition that put Law and Gospel on a kind of continuum, with the Gospel as a kind of "new Law." Luther's call was to challenge such impurities within the Christian tradition and call the tradition to be accountable to Scripture. Properly distinguishing Law and Gospel guarantees that we are justified through Christ alone without any contribution on our part. If the tradition prior to Luther had been able to articulate Law and Gospel in terms similar to his, then Christ would have been proclaimed in the Church consistently as gift (*sacramentum*) and not only as example (*exemplum*). But because it was not so proclaimed, Luther was forced to bring this scriptural truth to the fore. Speaking in terms of Law and Gospel becomes then an innovative way to present ancient truth, grounded in the Scriptures and testified to by many of the patristic and early medieval

---

18 See Thomas C. Oden, *The Justification Reader* (Grand Rapids: Eerdmans, 2002), 44–45. See also the commentary on Ephesians 2:8–9 in *Galatians, Ephesians, Philippians,* ed. Mark J. Edwards in *Ancient Christian Commentary on Scripture*, New Testament VIII (Downers Grove: InterVarsity Press, 1999), 133–34.

19 Oden, *The Justification Reader*, 45–49.

theologians. Again, in any ecumenical discussion, Law and Gospel is a nonnegotiable truth which must be brought to the table first with any other Christian groups.

MARGINALIZATION AND RENEWAL

If it is so important, then why has not the proper distinction of Law and Gospel guided all versions of American Lutheranism? Why is this teaching not at the fore among all American Lutherans? There are specific historical reasons for the absence or downplaying of the doctrine due to movements in Europe such as Pietism and Rationalism or as a response to Lutheranism's transplantation in North America such as Evangelicalism and mainline Protestantism. For instance, in the late seventeenth century a highly influential movement arose in Germany called Pietism, led by Philipp Jakob Spener. All branches of Lutherans throughout the world have been influenced by Pietism in one way or another. It was from Pietism that Lutherans became interested in world missions, small-group Bible study, institutions of mercy for the orphans and the aged, and many educational institutions. Pietists were distraught over the lack of holy living among many in Germany and Scandinavia and pushed for reform in the church. These reforms encouraged people in greater spiritual renewal.

Many goals of the Pietists were praiseworthy, and in fact live on in our current focus on "discipleship," but they undermined the proper distinction between Law and Gospel by presenting the Christian life as a program for continuous spiritual growth, urging spiritual perfection insofar as it is possible, instead of a daily return in repentance and faith to God.[20] Since the proper distinction of Law and Gospel situates the Christian life in terms of a daily dying of the old Adam or Eve and a raising of the new person in faith in Christ, it acknowledges a discontinuity of the self. The self exists not on its own but instead exists solely moment to moment by God's gracious mercy. There is no continuous self

---

20 See Mark Mattes, "Discipleship in Lutheran Perspective" in *Lutheran Quarterly* 26 (2012), 142–63.

which can grow in higher degrees of perfection. Nor are there benchmarks by which to nail down spiritual progress.[21] Our life is hidden with Christ in God (Colossians 3:3). As hidden in Christ, we have no access to determine our growth and progress. Luther agrees that we make some progress in this life.[22] But our progress is of no concern to us. Faith directs us to live outside ourselves in God and in the neighbor, serving the neighbor as "little Christs." Finally, the tendency of Pietism is not to rely on God's external Word but instead on one's feelings with respect to God. In Lutheranism, we are directed not to trust in our own conscience or feelings but instead God's evaluation of us in God's Word. While many of the measures established by the Pietists are helpful for fostering daily discipleship, the overall portrait of the Christian life as a program of spiritual perfection is to be rejected, if the proper distinction of Law and Gospel is to be honored.

Another movement, arising concurrently with Pietism, is Rationalism. Rationalists agreed with early modern philosophers such as Descartes, who looked not to the Scriptures for truth but instead to reason alone. Increasingly, modern philosophers felt that truth could not be found in particular narratives such as we find in the Scriptures, but instead should be found in general or universal truths like mathematics or logical reasoning which render ideas "clear and distinct." This movement also advocated for individual autonomy and self-expression in reaction to the entrenched status of the nobility and the Church. As such, it was one of several forces which helped give birth to democratic forms of government. With respect to faith, however, along with Pietism, it centered

---

21 Carter Lindberg writes, "the holiness of *novus homo* is, like justification, an alien holiness. This does not preclude growth and progress but views it as the gift of God rather than the achievement of the person. It is, in short, always progress under the sign of the *simul*. Just as justified sinners are real, not fictitious, sinners, so the *novus homo* is a real, not fictitious, *nova creatura*. The progress of the *novus homo*, however, is not measurably growth in holiness but as life in repentance. It is a life lived between the times, between the now and the not yet. The new life is in progress because it is life under the time of the coming Christ, but like justification it is passive because the person is "being acted upon." See "Justice and Injustice in Luther's Judgment of 'Holiness Movements'" in *Luther's Ecumenical Significance: An Interconfessional Consultation*, ed. Peter Manns and Harding Meyer (Philadelphia: Fortress, 1984), 165, note 5.

22 AE 31:358.

faith in feelings, not the Scriptures. It saw faith as either a private matter or honored a view of God which was generic, not explicitly Trinitarian, similar to the God we find printed on our money. Like Pietism, Rationalism undermined the proper distinction between Law and Gospel because it argued for continuous self-guidance by reason uninformed by particular traditions. Its Achilles' heel is that it failed to see that reason must operate within a wider context than what it can generate from its own resources and that this context is itself a given. Likewise, reason has its limits when it deals with ultimate matters. Similarly, the freedom it sought, while properly eschewing inherited traditions from the nobility, failed to acknowledge that humans are to be not only lords but also servants. In its quest to undermine authority for the sake of independent thinking, it failed to recognize that freedom and authority are partners. All human life depends upon authoritative persons, offices, or institutions for life to function, and apart from freedom (*coram mundo*) we are not able to exercise our humanity. The question of course is to establish a humane authority which can complement a responsible freedom.

With respect to the North American context, the proper distinction of Law and Gospel has not fared well. Among Protestants, that context has been dominated by two movements, Evangelicalism and mainline Protestantism. In a sense, Evangelicalism is the American version of Pietism. Its roots are in revivalism, such as the two Great Awakenings of the 1740s and the 1820s. Of late, it has fled from the "turn or burn" mentality of these bygone days and has replaced that message with a saccharine Gospel preaching a Christ who enables greater self-acceptance or grants a "purpose-driven" life. Like Pietism, it posits a continuous self and focuses not on how God works to condemn us as sinners and justify us for Jesus' sake but instead on faith as a program for greater spiritual self-improvement. It has made inroads into all branches of Lutheranism. True to its roots in Puritanism, it seeks to establish a "Christian America," in which all branches of education and government would be grounded in a kind of theocratic kingdom. Lutherans have tended to eschew this latter venture since they are apt to see God as working differently in the state, whose task should be to uphold social order and health, than in the church, whose task is to state God's expectations and administer God's mercy. For Lutherans, there is no secular turf that must be Christianized. Instead, we presume that God works through the government by establishing order and providing for families and commerce whether or not people acknowledge it.

More problematic for the NALC has been "mainline Protestantism." The roots of mainline Protestantism are in Evangelicalism.[23] In a sense, they are secularized Evangelicals, rejecting the need for conversion advocated by their ancestors but adopting the goal of Christianizing the secular realm, usually under the rubric of peace and justice. They undermine traditional doctrines as too irrational and miraculous to the enlightened mind and tend to reinterpret those doctrines in terms of their existential effects upon the individual. More than anything, they seek a world guided by a kind of millenarianism where injustice is vanquished and harmonious, egalitarian relations exist among all. In essence, the bulk of Lutherans in North America, those groups which amalgamated into the ELCA, followed this trend. The history of the persons and forces which led to this transformation of the faith has yet to be written. Especially for Lutheran groups in the Upper Midwest and many Eastern Lutherans, whose roots were in the General Council, there was nothing inherent in their confessional witness to have made this a natural move.[24] It is likely that the leadership of these groups in the 1950s sincerely believed that a mainline approach to faith would be the wave of the future and so they positioned young leadership in teaching and administrative offices who would work toward fulfilling such mainline goals. That the assessment of these leaders of nearly six decades ago was wrong is proved by the fact of staggering membership loss in the ELCA over the last twenty-five years.

By its very nature, mainline Protestantism undermines the evangelistic thrust of the church since the goal is not to win people for Christ

23 For a survey of the rise of mainline Protestantism, see Gary Dorrien, "The Christian Century" in *First Things* 273 (November 2013), 27–34.

24 With of course the exception of the General Synod. Compare Milton Valentine, "The General Synod" in *The Distinctive Doctrines and Usages of the General Bodies of the Evangelical Lutheran Church in the United States* (Philadelphia: Lutheran Publication Society, 1893), 34–61.

but instead to use the church at the national level to pressure governmental agencies to conform to its version of peace and justice. Such an approach undermines the proper distinction of Law and Gospel in numerous ways. But at its worst, it dismisses Law and Gospel as dealing solely with a private matter of the conscience (which could be dealt with in good therapy) and moves on to really important matters such as social injustices or the environment. No doubt the concerns brought to the fore by mainliners are important and presumably all citizens want justice and peace. The problem is that in the public realm not all will agree on how to achieve justice and peace. Nor is the church designed to do the work of advocacy given the fact that in a democracy all do not see eye to eye. Such work is best done by agencies devoted to that task. Individual Christians are always invited to be involved in such ventures. Their advocacy needs to be informed by Scripture and at its best such advocacy will always seek the protection of the unborn and the aged, the sanctity of marriage, humane working conditions for all employed, along with a fair wage, and the very best in education for all.

The renewal of thinking in Law and Gospel terms was occasioned by emigration from Germany in the 1840s by those opposed to the union of the Lutheran and Reformed churches in the state of Prussia. This government-staged union sparked confessional renewal in Germany and Scandinavia and led to a more conservative approach to Lutheranism. All these emigrants had been influenced by Pietism to one degree or another. However, they sought a Lutheranism that did not accommodate to the influence of Rationalism and one in which Pietism would be accountable to the Law and Gospel distinction and not vice versa. Most influential among these emigrants was the founder of the Missouri Synod, C. F. W. Walther. His book *The Proper Distinction between Law and Gospel*,[25] lectures which he informally offered students while serving as professor at Concordia Seminary, was to impact not only the Missouri Synod, but many other Lutherans as well. Other than Luther, this book, more than any other, taught North American Lutherans to think in terms of

25 Online edition: http://lutherantheology.com/uploads/works/walther/LG/.

distinguishing Law from Gospel and reinforced Luther's teachings. By the 1930s–1950s, this work was augmented by newer studies among Luther researchers in Europe that eventually impacted North American preachers and Luther scholars.[26]

THE QUESTION OF GOD'S WRATH

To properly distinguish Law from Gospel implies that the question of God's wrath cannot be avoided. More than likely, this is the most troublesome issue involved in distinguishing Law and Gospel. That God is a God who judges and who exercises wrath is not a popular topic. While many Americans believe in God, they have a hard time believing that He could be wrathful. For many, the fact that the Bible teaches that God is wrathful is not enough to make them believe it. All too many Americans approach faith as a kind of buffet line where they can pick and choose those aspects of spirituality they find most fulfilling.[27] Even twelve-step programs encourage people to envision a God of their "own understanding." Undoubtedly, many who respond to the call to become pastors are at heart deeply caring people and their nature is to resist any talk of God's wrath which could come across as judgmental or negative to the people for which they are called to care.

Such sentiment needs to be challenged. In the Bible, God is not pictured as throwing arbitrary temper tantrums. God's wrath is nothing other than people experiencing the consequences of their sin. God judged those building the tower of Babel not because He is impetuous and maliciously vindictive but because it is not fitting for the human to seek divine attributes or traits. Humans are called to be human, and that is exactly what the proper distinction between Law and Gospel does: humanizes men and women. It chops down their self-centered attempts to be gods for themselves, as that first theologian, the devil, advocated in Eden, and opens a path of trusting that God can and will be God for

---

26 See Gerhard Forde, *The Law-Gospel Debate* (Minneapolis: Augsburg, 1969).

27 See Ingolf Dalferth, "'I Determine What God Is!': Theology in the Age of 'Cafeteria Religion'" in *Theology Today* 57.1 (April 2000), 5–23.

them. The effective preacher of God's wrath is not like the street preacher condemning people at the local farmer's market. Such a man is easily caricatured and dismissed. No doubt the populace only perceives such a man as himself self-righteous. Instead, the classical example of effectively preaching God's wrath is that of Nathan rebuking David after his taking Bathsheba and setting up Uriah to be killed (2 Samuel 12:1–7). Nathan's strategy is remarkably effective in its subtlety. Remember his parable?

> "There were two men in a certain city, the one rich and the other poor. The rich man had very many flocks and herds, but the poor man had nothing but one little ewe lamb, which he had bought. And he brought it up, and it grew up with him and with his children. It used to eat of his morsel and drink from his cup and lie in his arms, and it was like a daughter to him. Now there came a traveler to the rich man, and he was unwilling to take one of his own flock or herd to prepare for the guest who had come to him, but he took the poor man's lamb and prepared it for the man who had come to him." Then David's anger was greatly kindled against the man, and he said to Nathan, "As the Lord lives, the man who has done this deserves to die, and he shall restore the lamb fourfold, because he did this thing, and because he had no pity."
>
> Nathan said to David, "You are the man!"

Now, that is remarkably effective preaching of the Law, God's wrath; it is David who bespeaks the judgment upon himself. The key to preaching God's wrath is not to step up on a soapbox and hurl anathemas at people. Instead, it is simply to tell the truth—and in ways which people actually hear it as truth.

For Luther, the key factor indicating God's wrath is bodily death "in so far as the natural man in it experiences the wrath of God; whereas believers, delivered from wrath, find in death only a gentle sleep . . . pass blissfully away before realizing the presence of death. Thereafter, in hell, is really experienced the 'eternal' death of those accursed of God. . . . In this condition are all the children of Adam, without exception, until they are delivered by grace in Christ."[28] Death then is no natural phenomenon; instead it is, as Karl Rahner put it, "guilt made visible."[29]

What Carl Braaten wrote over three decades ago continues to be as true for today as it was then:

> People are not looking for a gracious God but a good deal, and preachers are helping them. According to the confessions, other alienating concepts must be introduced to make the Gospel qua Gospel stand out. Not only the Law but such positively negative symbols as sin and Satan, wrath and hell, in whatever modern idiom, must be preached to put starch into the Gospel. The twin process of demythologizing and psychologizing has ferreted these negative terms out of usage in most preaching today. We do not know how to speak of the realities to which they point. But this we can say: if the Gospel is not placed in bold relief against the background of the demonic, sin, wrath and hell, it degenerates into a saccharine-sweet message of civilizing aphorisms. When Jesus Christ is pictured in the confessional writings, he is the fulfiller of the Law, the appeaser of wrath, the victor over Satan, the conqueror of death, the atoner of sin—all concepts which have suffered an erosion of meaning in our monistic universe of discourse.[30]

Talk of wrath and judgment cannot be avoided or the Gospel is trivialized and rendered devoid of its content. At the core of such talk is the willingness to admit moral accountability. Helping people admit their accountability—as painful as that may be—is the truth which can begin the process of setting people free. When people do not come clean with their accountability, when they try to hide from their shortcomings, misdeeds, injustices, and self-righteousness, they remain trapped

28 Julius Köstlin, *The Theology of Luther in Its Historical Development and Inner Harmony*, trans. Charles Hay (Philadelphia: Lutheran Publication Society, 1897), II 358.

29 See Peter C. Phan, *Eternity in Time: A Study of Karl Rahner's Eschatology* (Selinsgrove, Pennsylvania: Susquehanna University Press, 1988), 106.

30 Carl E. Braaten, *Principles of Lutheran Theology* (Philadelphia: Fortress, 1983), 112.

in these very things. By coming clean with one's own violence and admitting one's responsibility and culpability, one breaks free from a life of blame. Claimed by the Gospel, forgiven in Christ, one can live free of such blame.

FREEDOM AND THE THIRD USE OF THE LAW

Paul indicates that in Christ we are free of the Law (Romans 10:4). What could that mean? Again, it is valuable to look to Martin Chemnitz. We are free in that we (1) are not obliged to do good works for our salvation but instead receive it by apprehending Christ alone, (2) are no longer are under God's condemnation, and (3) may do good works readily apart from the constraint that the Law previously obliged us.[31]

Naturally, this raises the question of a third use of the Law which has long been in dispute among Lutherans. We should stand with the Book of Concord on this matter.[32] Otherwise there is no way coherently to read apostolic parenesis throughout the New Testament. Likewise, there is no coherent way to understand the delight in the Torah which is advocated by the psalmist and many of the prophets. Indeed, the best presentation of the third use of the Law is to be found in both of Luther's catechisms. Especially the Small Catechism is addressed to Christian youth and families. The presentation of Law there is given not as its civil or political use but as a path in which Christians are to walk.[33] Youth especially have need for such catechesis. We cannot assume that the political use of the Law alone is sufficient for the education of Christian young people.

---

31 Martin Chemnitz, *Ministry, Word, and Sacraments*, 100.

32 Solid Declaration V.

33 By presenting the Ten Commandments before the Creed in the catechisms, Luther situates Law before Gospel in a formal way. However, the content of his interpretation of the Law in both catechisms is clearly that of the third use. Another way of looking at how God works in the world is that He has established "three estates": the home, the government, and the church. These estates are intertwined with the Commandments. "God lays hold of us from the outside . . . by casting us into His creative institutions, and He protects the latter by means of the Commandments. Thus the estates and the Commandments are the grip by which God sustains His creatures against the cunning attacks of the forces of destruction and preserves them into the eschaton." See Albrecht Peters, *Commentary on Luther's Catechisms: Ten Commandments*, trans. Holger K. Sonntag (St. Louis: Concordia Publishing House,2009), 82–83.

Undoubtedly, some find a third use of the Law inconsistent with the second use because in their mind any talk of Law indicates the supposition of a continuity of the self. But that is not the case. Such continuity need not be assumed when we admit that the new person comes forth in faith each day. This new person in Christ truly delights in God and in His ways, how God has ordered the cosmos and the limits He has established for our behavior which fosters our own well-being as well as the well-being of others. Too many practitioners of the Law and Gospel distinction have a robust view of God's killing function in the Law but too limited a view of the power of the Gospel to raise believers into the new life in Christ. We are reborn so that we might do good works—to the glory of God and the good of our neighbor. The third use indicates that very path and presupposes a new motive (the "new obedience" as the Augsburg Confession calls it[34]) for walking that path.

CONCLUSION

As pastors increasingly wonder how they fit into the wider culture, whether or not they are to imitate therapists, social workers, or CEOs, the Lutheran confessional heritage sets a clear path for their calling—to properly distinguish Law and Gospel with all to whom they minister. This vocation is crucial and is not to be compromised—it delivers in specific and concrete ways God's actually dealing with sinners. It brings a word which does not merely describe matters or provides directives but instead does what it says and says what it does. While the office of ministry is not to be exalted over other vocations, it is set apart for this specific task—a task which brings about the in-breaking of God's mercy and grace. Pastors never need doubt what their vocation is all about: it is discerning those who need the word that afflicts those who are smug and self-secure—seeking independence from God's grace—from those who desperately need God's comfort because they are wrestling either with God's accusatory Law or with God as hidden. May God strengthen pastors in this most important of tasks.

---

34 Article VII.

LUTHER ON LAW AND GOSPEL IN HIS *LECTURES ON GALATIANS* 1531/1535

Naomichi Masaki

INTRODUCTION

Luther's death in February 1546 presented the occasion for his closest associates to speak of him. Justus Jonas, Michael Coelius, and John Bugenhagen preached at his funerals, and Philip Melanchthon spoke a eulogy.[1] When they touched on Luther's most important contribution

1 Jonas preached the first funeral sermon at St. Andrew's Church in Eisleben in the afternoon of February 19. *Zwo Tröstliche Predigt / Uber der Leich / D. Doct: Martini Luther / zu Eisleben den XIX. und XX. Februarii gethan / Durch / D. Doct Justum Jonam, M. Michaelem Celium, Anno 1546* (Wittenberg: Georg Rhau, 1546), Aiijv–Cr, Diijr–Eijr. Hereafter referred to as *Zwo Tröstliche Predigt*. An English translation is available in E. Greenwald, trans., *Two Funeral Sermons on the Death of Dr. Martin Luther, Delivered at Eisleben, February 19th and 20th, 1546* (Lancaster, PA: The Junior Missionary Society of the Church of the Holy Trinity, 1883), 5–30. Hereafter referred to as *Two Funeral Sermons*. On the next day, Coelius delivered the second funeral sermon before Luther's body was moved to Wittenberg. *Zwo Tröstliche Predigt*, Eiijr–Iiiijr. An English translation is available in *Two Funeral Sermons*, 31–59. When the funeral procession reached Wittenberg on February 22, Bugenhagen delivered a funeral sermon in the Castle Church. *Eine Christliche Predigt / uber der Leich und begrebnis / des Ehrwirdigen D. Martini Luthers / durch Hern Johan Bugenhagen Pomern / Doctor / und Pfarherr der Kirchen zu Wittemberg / gethan* (Wittenberg: Georg Rhau, 1546). Hereafter referred to as *Eine Christliche Predigt*. An English translation is available in Kurt K. Hendel, trans., *A Christian Sermon over the Body and at the Funeral of the Venerable Dr. Martin Luther, Preached by Mr. Johann Bugenhagen Pomeranus, Doctor and Pastor of the Churches in Wittenberg* (Atlanta: Pitts Theological Library, 1996), 6–55. Hereafter referred to as *A Christian Sermon*. This was followed by a eulogy by Melanchthon in the name of the university. Philip Melanchthon, *In funere Lutheri: Oratio in funere D. Martini Lutheri* (no. 89). CR 11: 726–34. A German translation of Johannes Fünck is found in *Eyn Sermon uber der Leich / des Erwirdigen Herrn Doctor Martin Luthers zu Wittenberg gethon von Phillippo Melanthon* (March 13, 1546). Hereafter this work is referred to as *Fünck*. English translations are found in James William Richard, *Philip Melanchthon The Protestant Preceptor of*

to the life of the Church, they did not show any hesitation to say that it was his articulation of the doctrine of the proper distinction between Law and Gospel. The Lord had a good use of him, they would say, because through this doctrine the entire Scripture was opened.[2]

Amusingly and even astonishingly, however, even though Luther dealt with this weightiest doctrine in such vital works as the Heidelberg Disputation (1518), How Christians Should Regard Moses (1525), Theses Concerning Faith and Law (1535), The Disputation Concerning Justification (1536), and The Antinomian Theses and Disputations (1537–40), not to mention his catechisms (1529)[3] and the Smalcald Articles (1537) in the Book of Concord, he never crafted a major work on it.[4] Rather, as

---

Germany, 1497–1560 (New York: G. P. Putnam's Sons, 1898), 381–92, which is reprinted as "Melanchthon: Funeral Oration over Luther," in Lewis W. Spitz ed., *The Protestant Reformation* (Englewood Cliffs, NJ: Prentice-Hall, 1966), 68–76; and in J. Unwin, trans., "Elegy on the Death of the Rev. Martin Luther, D. D., From the Latin of Philip Melanchthon" in *The Life and Acts of Martin Luther*, 32–46. Cf. James Michael Weiss, "Erasmus at Luther's Funeral: Melanchthon's Commemorations of Luther in 1546," *Sixteenth Century Journal* 16 (1985): 91–114.

2 Jonas pointed out that only when Luther's expositions of Galatians, Psalms, Genesis, and John's Gospel have been read, "would [people] rightly comprehend what kind of man and treasure they have lost in Dr. Martin Luther." *Zwo Tröstliche Predigt*, Aiij–Aiiij; *Two Funeral Sermons*, 6–7. Coelius summarized Luther's contribution as "opening the Holy Scripture by the true distinction between Law and Gospel" by which he also restored "both doctrine and true Divine Service." *Zwo Tröstliche Predigt*, Fiij, Gj; *Two Funeral Sermons*, 34, 41. Bugenhagen recognized that Law and Gospel are "two parts of Dr. Martin Luther's doctrine . . . through which the whole Scripture was opened and Christ, our righteousness and eternal life, was recognized." *Eine Christliche Predigt*, Aiiij, *A Christian Sermon*, 18–19. And Melanchthon praised Luther's greatness in his hearing Jesus and bringing to light the true doctrine of repentance, justification, and the proper distinction between Law and Gospel. *CR* 11: 728–32; Fünck, a3–b2; *The Protestant Reformation*, 71–74; *The Life and Acts of Martin Luther*, 36–42.

3 Cf. Charles P. Arand, *That I May Be His Own: An Overview of Luther's Catechisms* (St. Louis: Concordia Publishing House, 2000); Janz Denis, *Three Reformation Catechisms: Catholic, Anabaptist, Lutheran*, Texts and Studies in Religion, vol. 13 (New York and Toronto: The Edwin Mellen Press, 1982); Gottfried G. Krodel, "Luther's Work on the Catechism in the Context of Late Medieval Catechetical Literature," *Concordia Journal* 25 (October 1999): 366–404; Timothy J. Wengert, "Wittenberg's Earliest Catechism" *Lutheran Quarterly* 7 (Autumn 1993): 247–60; Wengert, "Forming the Faith through Catechisms: Moving to Luther and Today," in *Formation in the Faith: Catechesis for Tomorrow*, Symposium Papers Number 7 (St. Louis: Concordia Seminary, 1997), 25–48.

4 While Luther never composed a major treatise on Law and Gospel, he preached on it twice to the saints in Wittenberg. Robert Kolb gives a good analysis of those two sermons which found their way into publication under titles "How Law and Gospel Are to Be Fundamental-

the Formula of Concord observes, the doctrine of the proper distinction between Law and Gospel *permeates* all his writings.[5] Yet, the importance of his *Lectures on Galatians* (1531/1535) is indisputable.[6] Together with the above mentioned Antinomian Theses and Disputations,[7] one cannot simply talk about Law and Gospel without referencing it.

Luther himself located the rediscovery of the doctrine of the proper distinction between Law and Gospel at the moment of the breakthrough in his theological development.[8] As his conviction of this doctrine was deepened over the course of his career as the preacher and the doctor of the church, the Gospel became increasingly clearer to him.

LAW AND GOSPEL DEBATE WITH GALATIANS

The popularity of Luther's *Lectures on Galatians* meant that they were the recipients of not only positive but also negative reviews. Luther himself needed to deal with such opponents as not only the papacy, enthusiasts, sacramentarians,[9] and Anabaptists,[10] but also sectarians and

ly Distinguished" (1532) and "A Fine Sermon on Law and Gospel" (1537) in "'The Noblest Skill in the Christian Church': Luther's Sermons on the Proper Distinction of Law and Gospel," *Concordia Theological Quarterly* 71 (2007): 301–18.

5 FC SD V 22.

6 Cf. FC SD III 67. Luther's *Lectures on Galatians* that was published in 1535 contains forty-one lectures he delivered between July 3 and December 12 in 1531.

7 WA 39 I:342–584, WA 39 II:124–44. English translation is available in Holger Sonntag, ed. and trans., *Only the Decalogue Is Eternal: Martin Luther's Complete Antinomian Theses and Disputations* (Minneapolis: Lutheran Press, 2008). Timothy Wengert gives a detailed account and evaluation of the earlier controversy between Johann Agricola and Melanchthon over the role of the Law in the Christian life as found in his *Law and Gospel: Philip Melanchthon's Debate with John Agricola of Eisleben over Poenitentia* (Grand Rapids: Baker Books, 1997).

8 WA TR 5:210.12–16, no. 5518, AE 54:442.

9 Ronald F. Thiemann pointed out that the source of much of Muentzer's dissatisfaction with Wittenberg theology stemmed from his different perspective on the relationship between Law and Gospel. Muentzer emphasized the continuity and congruence of Law and Gospel so that the whole of God's work is summarized under the rubric of the Law. He understood justification of sinners takes place as a process. "Law and Gospel in the Thought of Thomas Muentzer," *The Lutheran Quarterly* 27 (November 1975): 347–63.

10 According to Menno Simons, the Law does not only convict man of his sin and drive him to despair, but it also brings about repentance itself. Such extension of the function of the Law was possible for him because of his insistence on free will by which man can turn from sin to Christ. Richard C. Detweiler, "The Concept of Law and Gospel in the Writings of Menno

antinomians. John Wesley sharply criticized Luther's *Lectures on Galatians*, even though he had a wonderful experience with Luther's *Lectures on Romans*.[11] To Wesley, Luther's teaching in the area of "sanctification" did not appear to have met his expectations. Two centuries later, Paul Tillich devised a method of correlation.[12] Man's questions are taken seriously; man's questions are answered. It is through the structures of human life that God condescends to come to man and make Himself real to him. But "man cannot receive answers to questions he never asked."[13] Wayne G. Johnson observed that Luther's Law reappeared as Tillich's questions, and Luther's Gospel was restated in Tillich's Christian answers.[14]

In recent time, since the last third of the twentieth century, there have not been any other movements that challenged Luther's understanding of the doctrine of the proper distinction between Law and Gospel more than the ecumenical dialogue which resulted in the Joint Declaration on Doctrine of Justification (JDDJ) between the Roman Catholic Church's Pontifical Council for Promoting Christian Unity (PCPCU) and the Lutheran World Federation (LWF), the New Perspective on Paul (NPP), and the New Finnish Interpretation of Luther developed by Tuomo Mannermaa (NFIL).

Simons, Viewed against the Background of Martin Luther's Thought," *The Mennonite Quarterly Review* 43 (July 1969): 191–212.

11 It comes as something of a surprise to read Wesley's negative reaction to Luther's *Lectures on Galatians* only three years after his positive and formative experience with the reformer, because it was while listening to a reading of Luther's preface to Romans in May 1738 when Wesley felt his heart "strangely warmed" and was given assurance of salvation. Wesley maintained that Luther was deeply affected by mysticism and that he was ignorant of sanctification. Luther blasphemed good works and the Law. Jerry L. Walls examined Wesley's *Journal* from June 15–16, 1741, against the background of Luther's Galatians lectures themselves and demonstrated that Wesley's critique of Luther was far off the mark and it was based on his misunderstanding of Luther. Jerry L. Walls, "John Wesley's Critique of Martin Luther," *Methodist History* 20 (October 1981): 29–41.

12 Tillich defined the method of correlation as one which "explains the contents of the Christian faith through existential questions and theological answers in mutual interdependence." Paul Tillich, *Systematic Theology*, vol. 1 (Chicago: The University of Chicago Press, 1951), 60.

13 Ibid., 65.

14 Wayne G. Johnson, "Martin Luther's Law-Gospel Distinction and Paul Tillich's Method of Correlation: A Study in Parallels," *The Lutheran Quarterly* 23 (August 1971): 287.

The traditional Roman Catholics' charge against the Reformation was that to them Luther's understanding of the doctrine of justification was a "legal fiction." In addition, Luther was said to have not understood the role of works in justification (James 2:24; Matthew 5:20; 1 Corinthians 13; Galatians 5:6). In contrast, ecumenically minded Roman Catholics make the opposite claim, that there really is no essential difference between their position and the Reformation. Of course, since the supporting documents of the JDDJ from the Roman Catholics' side made it clear that they did not change their doctrine at all, it was the LWF which was more ready to abandon the doctrine of forensic justification as confessed in the Book of Concord. The JDDJ was a result of more than thirty years of dialogue. It was further spread into the World Methodist Council (WMC) which adopted it in 2006. The same year, a new exegetical-ecumenical study project on the doctrine of justification was started by the LWF, the PCPCU, together with the WMC and the World Communion of Reformed Churches (WCRC).[15] The WCRC is reportedly moving toward the adoption of the JDDJ in 2017.[16] In the meantime, the LWF and the PCPCU jointly published a booklet, *From Conflict to Communion*, in 2013 to prepare the way for full communion and the joint commemoration of the Reformation in 2017.[17]

---

15 A Task Force of Biblical Scholars and Systematic Theologians from the Lutheran World Federation, the Pontifical Council for Promoting Christian Unity, the World Communion of Reformed Churches, and the World Methodist Council, *The Biblical Foundations of the Doctrine of Justification: An Ecumenical Follow-Up to the Joint Declaration on the Doctrine of Justification* (Mahwah, NJ: Paulist Press, 2012).

16 Cf. Thomas Söding, "Justification and Participation: Ecumenical Dimensions of Galatians," in *Galatians and Christian Theology: Justification, the Gospel, and Ethics in Paul's Letter*, ed. Mark W. Elliott, Scott J. Hafemann, N. T. Wright, and John Frederick (Grand Rapids, MI: Baker Academic, 2014), 62–81; William G. Witt, "Anglican Reflections on Justification by Faith," *Anglican Theological Review* 95 (Winter 2013): 57–80.

17 The Lutheran World Federation and the Pontifical Council for Promoting Christian Unity, *From Conflict to Communion: Lutheran-Catholic Common Commemoration of the Reformation in 2017, Report of the Lutheran-Roman Catholic Commission on Unity* (Leipzig: Evangelische Verlagsanstalt and Bonifatius, 2013).

The NPP's challenge has focused extensively on Luther's understanding of Paul in the Epistle to the Galatians, and thereby it redefined justification completely. Beginning with Krister Stendahl's publication of "The Apostle Paul and the Introspective Conscience of the West" in 1963,[18] the new interpretation of Paul has advanced through such major contributors as E. P. Sanders,[19] James Dunn,[20] and N. T. Wright.[21] Basic to the NPP is a claim that Luther had misinterpreted both Paul and Judaism by reading his own psychological struggles with the Law into Paul and his own context of a legalistic sixteenth-century Roman Catholicism into the Judaism of first-century Palestine (Stendahl). Since God's gracious election of Israel had already established the covenant, the Law had nothing to do with meriting salvation but a means of maintaining the elect (Sanders). Paul was concerned with the social function of circumcision, dietary laws, and Sabbath observance. The Law functioned as the "boundary markers" that served to distinguish Jews from Gentiles (Dunn). Jesus as the faithful One, the true Israel, fulfilled the task that the nation was unable to perform. He also took upon Himself the curse (the exile) of their failure to perform it. The Christians are those who belong to this Messiah by incorporation. Justification in Galatians cannot mean for the sinners to be declared righteous before God but for the Gentiles to be given the same status as true members of God's family so that they can share Table fellowship in the church (Wright). Richard Hays supports the subjective genitive reading of Galatians 2:16 by

---

18 Krister Stendahl, "The Apostle Paul and the Introspective Conscience of the West," *Harvard Theological Review* 56 (July 1963): 199–215. This work originates in his essay he delivered at the annual meeting of the American Psychological Association in September 1961. Stendahl's works on Paul from the early 1960s including this essay are found in *Paul among Jew and Gentiles* (Philadelphia: Fortress, 1976).

19 E. P. Sanders, *Paul and Palestinian Judaism: A Comparison of Patterns of Religion* (Minneapolis: Fortress, 1977), remains central to the NPP undertaking.

20 James D. G. Dunn, *The Theology of Paul the Apostle* (Grand Rapids: Eerdmans, 1998); Dunn, "The New Perspective: Whence, What and Whither?" *The New Perspective on Paul: Collected Essays* (Tübingen: Mohr Siebeck, 2005), 1–88.

21 N. T. Wright, *What St. Paul Really Said* (Grand Rapids: Eerdmans, 1997); Wright, *Justification: God's Plan and Paul's Vision* (Downers Grove, IL: IVP Academic, 2009); Wright, *Paul for Everyone: Galatians and Thessalonians* (Louisville: Westminster John Knox, 2004), 3–83; Wright, "Messiahship in Galatians?" in *Galatians and Christian Theology*, 3–23.

claiming that the "faithfulness of Christ" is more a Christological reading because it expresses Christ's obedience to the cross to carry out His calling than the objective genitive reading which focuses on the anthropological act of believing.[22] The NPP is not *new* anymore.[23] Yet it remains as one of the chief contenders against Luther's *Lectures on Galatians*.[24]

---

22 Richard B. Hays, *The Faith of Jesus Christ: The Narrative Substructure of Galatians 3:1–4:11*, 2nd ed. (Grand Rapids: Eerdmans, 2002); Hays, "Apocalyptic Poièsis in Galatians: Paternity, Passion, and Participation," in *Galatians and Christian Theology*, 200–219.

23 The apocalyptic readings of various kinds followed the NPP, according to Bruce McCormack, which have been promoted by J. Louis Martyn, Martinus de Boer, Beverly Gaventa, and Joel Marcus. Bruce McCormack, "Can We Still Speak of 'Justification by Faith'?: An In-House Debate with Apocalyptic Readings of Paul," in *Galatians and Christian Theology*, 159–84. In Martyn, the root problem of man lies not in his sins but in the powers of the present evil age. The solution is deliverance from the powers that hold the human race in bondage. Martyn translates Galatians 2:16 with a subjective genitive like other NPP proponents. He also uses "rectification" language ("setting things right") in the place of traditional "justification." "Even we ourselves know, however, that a person is not rectified by observance of the Law, but rather by the faith of Jesus Christ. Thus, even we have placed our trust in Christ Jesus, in order that the source of our rectification might be the faith of Christ and not observance of the Law; for not a single person will be rectified by observance of the Law." Martyn describes redemption in terms of God's invasion of enemy-held territory with a war of liberation. The decisive event in the war of liberation was the crucifixion. There Jesus' death was not oriented toward personal guilt and forgiveness but toward corporate enslavement and liberation. The fundamental contrast in Galatians is not between the works of the Law and the faith of an individual but between works of the Law and the faith of Christ. Paul's message in Galatians is not about forgiveness of the sinners but about God's liberating invasion of the cosmos. J. Louis Martyn, "The Apocalyptic Gospel in Galatians," *Interpretation* 54 (July 2000): 246–66; Martyn, *Galatians: A New Translation with Introduction and Commentary*, Anchor Bible 33 (New York: Doubleday, 1997), 97–105.

24 A variation of recent engagement and critique of the NPP are found in the following works: Mark A. Seifrid, "Paul, Luther, and Justification in Galatians 2:15–21," *Westminster Theological Journal* 65 (2003): 215–30; Robert G. Artinian, "Luther after the Stendahl/Sanders Revolution: A Responsive Evaluation of Luther's View of First-Century Judaism in His 1535 Commentary on Galatians," *Trinity Journal* 27 (Spring 2006): 77–99; Stephen Chester, "When the Old Was New: Reformation Perspectives on Galatians 2:16," *Expository Times* 119 (2008): 320–29; Chester, "It Is No Longer I Who Live: Justification by Faith and Participation in Christ in Martin Luther's Exegesis of Galatians," *New Testament Studies* 55 (2009): 315–37; Erik M. Heen, "A Lutheran Response to the New Perspective on Paul," *Lutheran Quarterly* 24 (Autumn 2010): 264–91; Kristian Holm, "Beyond Juxtaposing Luther and the 'New Perspective on Paul': A Common Quest for the 'Other' Way of Giving?" *Lutherjahrbuch* 80 (2013): 142–58; Stephen Westerholm, *Justification Reconsidered: Rethinking a Pauline Theme* (Grand Rapids: Eerdmans, 2013); and A. Andrew Das, *Galatians*, Concordia Commentary (St. Louis: Concordia Publishing House, 2014), 238–52, 273–75, 310–16.

Tuomo Mannermaa published a monograph in 1979, *In ipsa fide Christus adest*,[25] which broke the ground for the development of what we now know as the NFIL. Mannermaa was concerned about the task of the ecumenical dialogue with the Eastern Orthodox Church, and he thought he found a common ground in the idea of *theosis*/deification. At the center of Mannermaa's thinking was Christ's *real presence* in the faith of believers. Salvation comes by participating in Christ's person. Christ is both the *favor* and the *donum* without separation and confusion. Mannermaa interpreted Luther, especially his *Lectures on Galatians* 1531/1535, in this way, with a result that he condemned the Formula of Concord because it teaches forensic justification.[26] It is to be noted that in *In ipsa fide Christus adest*, a discussion on Law and Gospel is absent. For Mannermaa, the focal point of the atonement is not Jesus on the cross. It is in His incarnational victory of His divine attributes over the human attributes.[27]

---

25 The full title of this work is *In ipsa fide Christus adest: Luterilaisen ja ortodoksisen kristinuskokäsityken leikkauspiste [In ipsa fide Christus adest:* "The Point of Contact between the Lutheran and Orthodox Understanding of the Christian Faith"] (Helsinki: Missiologian ja Ekumeniikan Seura, 1979). An English translation of *Christ Present in Faith: Luther's View of Justification* (Minneapolis: Fortress, 2005) by Kirsi Stjerna is based on the German edition, *Der im Glauben gegenwärtige Christus: Rechtfertigung und Vergottung zum ökumenischen Dialog* (Hannover: Lutherisches Verlagshaus, 1989), 11–93.

26 To reject the Formula of Concord means to disregard the Augsburg Confession and the whole Book of Concord. FC SD III 67 recommends the readers to review "the wonderful, magnificent exposition by Dr. Luther of St. Paul's Epistle to the Galatians." The source of this statement comes from the Torgau Book of 1576. Irene Dingel ed., *Die Bekenntnisschriften der Evangelisch-Lutherischen Kirche Quellen und Materialien* (Göttingen: Vandenhoeck & Ruprecht, 2014), II: 407.29–33. The mention of Luther's *Lectures on Galatians* in SD III reflects Nikolaus Selnecker's recommendation to adopt it in addition to the three ecumenical creeds, the unaltered Augsburg Confession, the Apology, the Smalcald Articles, the Small and the Large Catechisms as the new corpus doctrinae at the Lichtenberg Conference a couple of months earlier to replace the Wittenberg Catechism, the Consensus Dresdenis, and Corpus Philippicum. Friederich Bente, *Historical Introductions to the Lutheran Confessions*, 2nd ed. (St. Louis: Concordia Publishing House, 2005), 575.

27 Cf. Timo Laato, "Justification: The Stumbling Block of the Finnish Luther School," *Concordia Theological Quarterly* 72 (October 2008): 327–46; Javier A. Garcia, "A Critique of Mannermaa on Luther and Galatians," *Lutheran Quarterly* 27 (Spring 2013): 33–55; Garcia, "'Not an Idle Quality or an Empty Husk in the Heart': A Critique of Mannermaa on Luther and Galatians," in *Galatians and Christian Theology*, 132–42.

These three major contentions against Luther's confession of Law and Gospel did not appear without warning. They carried with them many of the major theological approaches that had developed over the course of several centuries, at least.

For example, although he did not aim at analyzing these three particular movements, Gerhard O. Forde pointed out that the Law-Gospel debate of the twentieth century found its root in the theology of Johannes C. K. von Hofmann and his attack on the doctrine of vicarious atonement in the name of a *heilsgeschichtliche* theology.[28] For Hofmann, the doctrine of forensic justification was too legalistic and objective because justification then must be considered as what God alone has done in the past, which excludes any involvement of man. In addition, it calls for credibility of the historical sources and scriptural infallibility, which he did not appreciate. Hofmann wanted to have Christianity that was not a matter of subscribing to doctrine but an experience. But unlike in Pietism and Synergism, and even in Luther, Hofmann's "experience" follows the Schleiermacherian sense of consciousness of being incorporated into a new existence, the Body of Christ.[29] The object of faith is not Christ and His salvific work on Calvary but a historical realization of the divine will of grace itself, which Hofmann believed to have been unfolded through a chain of successive stages of family—Abraham and his descendants, the Israelite nation, Christ, and the Church.[30] In Hofmann's system, the Law has a place only in passing, limited within the stage in the *Heilsgeschichte* where Israel existed as a nation. As a result, the Law was identified only by that which gave the nation its distinctive structure and character.

28 Gerhard O. Forde, *The Law-Gospel Debate: An Interpretation of Its Historical Development* (Minneapolis: Fortress, 1969, 2007). Hofmann developed this theology in his major work *Der Schriftbeweis*, 2 vols. (Nördlingen: C. H. Beck, 1852–55; 2nd rev. ed., 1857–60). One of the major critiques against these works from the confessional Lutheran position is found in Theodor Kliefoth, *Der Schriftbeweis des D. J. Chr. K. v. Hofmann* (Schwerin: Stiller'sche Hofbuchhandlung, 1860; first appeared in *Kirchliche Zeitschrift*, 1858–59). Lowell C. Green gives an account of the reception of Hofmann's theory of the *Heilsgeschichte* and the atonement among the Erlangen colleagues in his *The Erlangen School of Theology: Its History, Teaching, and Practice* (Fort Wayne: Lutheran Legacy, 2010), 105–33.

29 Hofmann, *Der Schriftbeweis*, 2nd rev. ed., I:8.

30 Ibid., I:40–45.

Hofmann also interpreted sacrifices of both the Old Testament and of Christ differently than Luther. Since grace was already ensured by the covenant, sacrifice did not have to earn it. Rather, the sacrifice was meant to function merely as a sign of the fact of man's sins and God's awareness of them. God did not punish the animal as man's substitute. The sacrifice merely covered man's sins.[31] Hofmann did not need Christ to die substitutionally to achieve man's forgiveness. Rather, the cross was the place where Christ demonstrated His steadfast faithfulness to His calling because He was *the* realization of the divine will to love mankind.[32] By His resurrection, Jesus established a new humanity. Christians are those who have become conscious of being incorporated into it.[33]

Albrecht Ritschl followed Hofmann's thinking in many ways, as he also rejected the doctrine of the proper distinction between Law and Gospel.[34] In place of the dialectic of Law and Gospel, he put forward the Kantian emphasis on practical reason and moral judgment. Ritschl was a theological positivist even more than Hofmann. He merged Christians' freedom in Luther's theology into a Kantian notion of categorical imperatives so that within the new community which Jesus established man freely engages in ethical activities out of love and independently from coercion and reward. Ritschl was concerned to foster actual ethical renewal in the present, and that is where he located the atonement. Jesus did not die for the sins of the world. Rather, the cross was the place where He drew near to God as the priestly representative in faithfulness to His calling. By His death, He founded a new community, in which He continues to carry out the actual work of the atonement by way of His personal and religious influence.[35] In this view, repentance comes from the love

---

31 Hofmann, *Der Schriftbeweis*, 1st ed., IIa:145, 154.

32 Hofmann, *Der Schriftbeweis*, 2nd rev. ed., IIa:123.

33 Cf. Forde, *The Law-Gospel Debate*, 3–48.

34 Albrecht Ritschl, *Die Christliche Lehre von der Rechtfertigung und der Versöhnung*, 3 vols. (1870–74). See the English translation of vol. 1: *A Critical History of the Christian Doctrine of Justification and Reconciliation*, trans. John S. Black (Edinburgh: Edmonston and Douglas, 1872) and vol. 3: *The Christian Doctrine of Justification and Reconciliation: The Positive Development of the Doctrine*, trans. H. R. Mackintosh and A. B. Macaulay (Clifton, NJ: Reference Book Publishers, 1966).

35 Ritschl, *Der Rechtfertigung und der Versöhnung*, 3rd ed., I: 620.

of Jesus and not from the fear of the Law.[36] Ritschl exerted a far-reaching influence on later Luther scholars in this connection by making a decisive difference between the young Luther and the old Luther. Ritschl maintained that in the young Luther true repentance had come from the love of righteousness. But as he grew older, he abandoned this earlier view by adopting a Melanchthonian legalistic position on penance.[37]

In Hofmann's view, we see a Hegelian color in his presupposition of a historical process of God's self-realization. In Ritschl's outlook, we sense a Kantian influence of moral law. And in both Hofmann and Ritschl, Schleiermacher's impact is decisive.[38] It lies in the background of their denial of original sin and forensic justification, their belief in salvation by union with Christ rather than forgiveness, and their understanding of

---

36 Ritschl's anthropocentric doctrine of justification was not left unchallenged. Theodosius Harnack (1816/17–89) in his *Luthers Theologie* criticized Ritschl for having overlooked some of the key teachings of Luther, such as the doctrine of the wrath of God, the proper distinction between Law and Gospel, and the question of the hiddenness of God. Harnack, *Luthers Theologie mit besonderer Beziehung auf seine Versöhnungs- und Erlösungslehre*, 2 vols. (Erlangen: Theodor Blaesing, 1862, 1886). Forde, *The Law-Gospel Debate*, 81–95. According to Harnack's assessment, Ritschl simply did not understand either Luther or the doctrine of justification. Werner Elert observes that Ritschl "wanted to banish this concept (the wrath of God) entirely from Christian dogmatics." Elert, *Morphologie des Luthertums*, vol. 1: *Theologie und Weltanschauung des Luthertums hauptsächlich im 16. und 17. Zahrhundert* (Munich: C. H. Beck, 1931), 37; cf. *The Structure of Lutheranism: The Theology and Philosophy of Life of Lutheranism, especially in the Sixteenth and Seventeenth Centuries* (St. Louis: Concordia Publishing House,1962), 42. Paul Althaus comments that Harnack's *Luthers Theologie* "remains the best presentation of Luther's doctrine of the wrath of God." Paul Althaus, *The Theology of Martin Luther* (Philadelphia: Fortress, 1966), 169. Ironically, a generation later, Theodosius's own son, Adolf (1851–1930), took side with Ritschl instead of his father and radicalized Ritschl's project. Karl Holl (1866–1926), too, in his attempt to harmonize Ritschl and Theodosius Harnack on the doctrine of justification, favored Ritschl's position. Holl interpreted Luther's doctrine of justification to be both declaration and transformation. It was Melanchthon who narrowed justification to be only forensic. Holl maintained that the righteousness that we possess is the reason for God to declare us justified. There were many Lutheran theologians who did not accept Holl's reading of Luther. They republished Theodosius Harnack's *Luthers Theologie* in 1927 to confess the forensic justification over against Ritschlian and Holl's view. At the Fourth Assembly of the Lutheran World Federation in Helsinki in 1963, Holl's view and Theodosius Harnack's view on justification were pitted against each other. Carl E. Braaten, *Justification: The Article by Which the Church Stands or Falls* (Minneapolis: Fortress, 1990), 10–15.

37 Cf. Forde, *The Law-Gospel Debate*, 96–119.

38 Concerning Schleiermacher's understanding of the doctrine of justification, see Naomichi Masaki, "The Doctrine of Justification in the 19th Century: A Look at Schleiermacher's *Der christliche Glaube*," *Concordia Theological Quarterly* 76 (July/October 2012): 213–30.

the centrality of religious community where Jesus provides generic influence so that man may gradually move away from his consciousness of sin, which is produced not by the preaching of the Law but by the love of Jesus, to his consciousness of being adopted as a child of God. The atonement was relocated from Calvary to the new community of the Church. The meaning of Jesus' death on the cross was not vicarious atonement but His faithfulness to His calling.[39]

A number of similarities between the theologies of Schleiermacher, Hofmann, and Ritschl and those of the JDDJ, [40] the NPP, and the NFIL are apparent. But one cannot ignore the impact of Karl Barth in his *Evangelium und Gesetz* (1935)[41] when we consider the vitality of Luther's confession of Law and Gospel. Especially in North America, Barth's work stimulated a renewed dispute over the third use of the Law.

As the title of his work shows, Barth reversed the traditional order of Law and Gospel to Gospel and Law. He explains that he did it because Paul in Galatians 3:17 does so.[42]

The starting point of Barth's understanding of the Law is the fact that Jesus has already satisfied and kept the Law.[43] This means that whenever the Law's demand is manifested, it comes with its fulfillment in Jesus. For example, Barth explains that the Ten Commandments with their exposition in the Sermon on the Mount are the proclamation of the Law.

---

39 Friedrich Schleiermacher, *Der christliche Glaube nach den Grundsäzen der evangelischen Kirche,* 2nd edition of 1830 (Berlin: Georg Reimer, 1861); *The Christian Faith*, trans. from 2nd edition, H. R. Mackintosh and J. S. Stewart (Edinburgh: T & T Clark, 1989). See the following propositions in particular: 68.3, 70.2, 71.2, 72, 81.2, 87, 88, 92, 100, 101.3, 104.2–4, 107.1, 109.2.

40 William G. Witt observes that in Hans Küng's book *Justification: The Doctrine of Karl Barth and a Catholic Reflection* (Louisville: Westminster John Knox Press, 2004) Küng argues that Karl Barth's position was not incompatible with that put forward at Trent. See Witt, "Anglican Reflections on Justification by Faith," 58.

41 Karl Barth, *Evangelium und Gesetz, Theologische Existenz Heute,* vol. 32 (Munich: Chr. Kaiser Verlag, 1935); ET is found as "Gospel and Law," in Karl Barth, *Community, State, and Church: Three Essays* (Gloucester, MA: Peter Smith, 1968), 71–100. For most Barth scholars, the year 1935 belongs to "later Barth."

42 Barth, "Gospel and Law," 71. See Hermann Sasse's critique of Barth on this point in his "Lutheran Doctrine and the Modern Reformed Theology of Karl Barth," in *Here We Stand* (Adelaide: Lutheran Publishing House, 1966), 161–78.

43 Ibid., 76–77.

But they are a proclamation of grace at the same time because they come with the fact of Jesus' fulfillment of it.[44] The Law and the Gospel are inseparable for Barth. The Law is the form of the Gospel and the Gospel is the content of the Law.[45] It follows that for Barth the fact of the Word of God addressed to man is already grace regardless of what it says.[46]

Contrary to Luther's understanding, Barth maintains that man acknowledges his sin when he is illumined by the grace of God.[47] Man is a sinner not only because he is unable to hear the Gospel in the Law but also because he is never willing to believe in the grace itself.[48] Precisely because of this, Jesus became human in order to become man's representative. Vicariously, Jesus confessed man's lostness and sinfulness, and received the due judgment of God.[49] Jesus bore our punishment in this faith, and for our justification He was raised from the dead. He now intercedes for humanity by believing in its place, so that man may become alive *in Christ*. Man's faith, in turn, is obedience to God's Law because believing in Christ means acknowledging His representative faith.[50] Justification is not by faith, but by Jesus' faith.[51] Man finds his salvation when he is incorporated into the faith of Jesus. This is why Barth paraphrased Galatians 2:20 when he wrote: "I live, not somehow in my belief in the Son of God, but in the fact that the Son of God believed."[52] As in Hofmann and Ritschl, Barth takes Romans 3:22 and Galatians 2:16 as a subjective genitive, emphasizing the faithfulness of Jesus.[53] Barth's conviction is conclusive: the faith of Jesus is "the heart and star of the Gospel."[54]

---

44 Ibid., 78.
45 Ibid., 80.
46 Ibid., 72.
47 Ibid., 76, 81, 84.
48 Ibid., 76, 84–85.
49 Ibid., 74–76.
50 Ibid., 83.
51 Ibid., 78.
52 Ibid., 76.
53 Ibid., 74.
54 Ibid., 81.

In Barth's system, however, there is no place where a sinner is properly dealt with as a sinner. When a sinner is approached with grace instead of Law, man can still hide himself under the place of false security. Barth's assertion of salvation comes without repentance and forgiveness, and without Baptism. There seems to be an organic relation between his view and the Calvinistic doctrine of election.

LUTHER'S THEOLOGICAL BREAKTHROUGH AND HIS *LECTURES ON GALATIANS*

When one approaches Luther's *Lectures on Galatians* today in light of modern and contemporary discussion on Law and Gospel, two important differences immediately become evident. The first is the most obvious. Luther confesses the proper distinction between Law and Gospel,[55] while all others have not and still do not. Luther recalled later in his life about his theological development: "But when I discovered the distinction—namely, that the Law is one thing and the Gospel is another—then I had the break-through."[56] The Law is one thing, and the Gospel is another. The distinction between Law and Gospel was at the heart of Luther's confession of Christ. As we have seen, his closest colleagues recognized this. Luther enthusiastically taught it throughout his lectures.

The second is perhaps less obvious than the first, but equally important. It is about Luther's standpoint—that is, literally where he stands in

55 Luther emphasized with a strong language that the doctrine of the proper distinction between Law and Gospel is "our theology." It contains, he maintained, "the summary of whole Christian doctrine," and "keeps all genuine theology in its true use." Therefore, "whoever knows well how to distinguish the Law and the Gospel is a theologian." WA 40 I:45.24–27, AE 26:7; WA 40 I:209.11–12, AE 26:117; WA 40 I:511.31–32, AE 26:331; WA 40 I:207.17–18, AE 26:115. Cf. WA 40 I:204.11–15, AE 26:113; WA 40 I:207.19–28, AE 26:115; WA 40 I:208.16–25, AE 26:116; WA 40 I:209.16–23, AE 26:117; WA 40 I:336.32–337.22, AE 26:208–9; WA 40 I:486.17–487.14, AE 26:313; WA 40 I: 519.34–520.24, AE 26:337; WA 40 I:617.24–30, AE 26:406–7.

56 WA TR 5:210.12–16, no. 5518 (1542–43), AE 54: 442 (slightly adapted from) ". . . *aber do ich das discrimen fande, quod aliud esset lex, aliud euangelium*, da riß ich her durch." Since the text in Weimar edition gives the sentence in both German and Latin mixed together, I put Latin in italics for clarification. In his *Lectures on Galatians*, Luther said that the Law and the Gospel are "two entirely contrary doctrine." "Ideo lex et Evangelium duae prorsus contrariae doctrinae sunt." WA 40 I: 336.35–337.14, AE 26:208. Cf. WA 40 I: 520.25–27, AE 26:337.

expounding on the Epistle to the Galatians and in addressing his students in Wittenberg. He does not engage in theological tasks by removing himself from the world to which God came in His Son. For him, theology does not deal with some abstract notion, concept, or ideal. Just as he clearly professed in his *Lectures on Psalm 51* a year later, the subject of theology was never God in Himself or our projection of who God should be,[57] but the fact of man as sinning and of Jesus as justifying the sinner.[58] Luther himself knew from experience under the preaching of the Law and the preaching of the Gospel that he was a baptized saint yet a bottomlessly[59] sinful man at the same time. The place where Luther spoke in his *Lectures on Galatians* was life under *tentatio*.[60] That was the place from which Luther viewed his Savior. That was the place from which Luther heard the voice of Jesus. Luther consistently stayed under the Word. For him, to stand above the Word or beside the Word would be a show of man's pretension and the devil's illusion.

Luther's focus was on concrete ways in which Jesus deals with sinners, especially those who are baptized.[61] Luther's repeated use of the word *conscientia* (conscience) indicates where his attention lay. Unlike the modern and common usage of the term as a sense of right and wrong, for Luther, conscience meant more than moral principles; it was the sense of man's standing in relation to God.[62] Because the battleground of

---

57 Luther warns against imposing our ideas on the Word of God in reading and hearing the Scripture. WA 40 II:36.24–37.25; AE 27:28–30.

58 WA 40 II:328.17–18, AE 12:311. "Nam Theologiae proprium subiectum est homo peccati reus ac perditus et Deus iustificans ac salvator hominis peccatoris." These lectures on Psalm 51 came from June to August of 1532. Cf. WA 40 I:406.24–25, AE 26:259: ". . . Cum tamen iustificare peccatorem sit solius Christi proprium officium."

59 Here, the expression "bottomless (*grundlos*)" was employed out of Luther's Smalcald Articles III II 4.

60 WA 40 I:318.12, AE 26:193; WA 40 I:321.27–33, AE 26:196.

61 The Formula of Concord gives a brilliant summary of how Jesus as both God and man wants to deal with the saints in a manner of bestowing them His own flesh and blood. "He instituted his Holy Supper as a certain assurance and confirmation of this, that also according to the nature according to which he has flesh and blood he wants to be with us, to dwell in us, to work in us, and to be efficacious to us" (FC SD VIII 79).

62 For example, Luther speaks of the location of Christian freedom in the conscience. "This is the freedom out of which Christ has set us free, not from some human slavery or tyrants but from the eternal wrath of God. Where? In the conscience. This is where our freedom

the conflict between God and the devil was precisely in the conscience, Luther doesn't speak of a cosmic arena as a place of such struggle.[63] The proper distinction is to be made at the most difficult place. It is not in the words but in the conscience where one's grounding relationship with the living God is located.[64] Luther in his lectures frequently mentioned that the papacy, enthusiasts, sectarians, and the antinomians failed to understand either the Law or the Gospel. Such an observation emerged out of his diagnosis that although they desired to pay attention to the "real life" they ended up being incapable of helping people in such "real life" because they stood only outside and never touched on the doctrine of Law and Gospel.[65] If Luther were alive today, he would speak the same negative words toward all who have no regard for the doctrine of the proper distinction between Law and Gospel. "As soon as reason and the Law are joined, faith immediately loses its virginity."[66] Luther's insightful words such as these only reveal Luther's profound awareness of the context in which man is given to exist.

---

comes to a halt; it goes no further. For Christ has set us free, not politically or physically but theologically and spiritually, that is, to make our conscience free and joyful, unafraid of the wrath to come. This is the most genuine freedom; it is priceless" (WA 40 II:3.20–25, AE 27:4). Cf. WA 40 I:47.26–48.20, AE 26:8–9, etc.

63 Cf. WA 40 I:95.19–96.11, AE 26:40–41; WA 40 I:539.34–541.35, AE 26:352–53; WA 40 II.178.16–179.24, AE 27:139–41.

64 Luther says: "Ideo quisque diligenter discat discernere legem ab Evangelio, non tantum verbis, sed etiam ipso affectu et experientia, hoc est in corde et conscientia ista duo bene distinguat. Alioqui quantum ad verba attinet, facilis est illorum distinctio. Sed quando ad experientiam venit, tum invenis Evangelium rarum et e contra legem assiduum esse hospitem in conscientia." "Let everyone learn diligently to distinguish the Law from the Gospel, not only in words but in feeling and in experience. That is, in his heart and in his conscience let him distinguish well between these two. As far as the words are concerned the distinction is easy. But when it comes to experience, you will find the Gospel a rare guest but the Law a constant guest in your conscience" (WA 40 I:209.17–22, AE 26:117). Luther also says: "Sic pulchre distinguit Paulus tempus legis et gratiae. Discamus et nos recte distinguere utriusque tempus, non verbis sed affectu, id quod est omnium difficillimum." "Thus so beautifully does Paul distinguish between the time of Law and (the time) of grace. Let us learn to distinguish the times of both, not in words but in feeling, which is the most difficult" (WA 40 I:527.21–23, AE 26:343). Cf. WA 40 I:47.26–29, AE 26:8–9.

65 WA 40 I:480.32–483.13, AE 26:309–10; WA 40 I:485.9–22, AE 26:312.

66 WA 40 I:204.17–18, AE 26:113. "Quam primum autem Lex et ratio coniunguntur, statim virginitas fidei violate est."

SIN AND THE PROPER OFFICE OF THE LAW

Luther's confession of Law and Gospel is grounded in the reason Jesus went to Calvary—to bear our sin and to be our Savior. Luther does not construct his theology by using the Law as its basic structure. He is not interested in taking the love of God as the organizing principle. Luther does not attempt to systematize his theology. Rather than the Law or the Gospel, his point of departure was man's condition before God as a sinner.[67]

Over the course of his *Lectures on Galatians*, Luther repeated a simple statement that the Law was not given to justify but to terrify, accuse, and kill.[68] This was not a mere critique of works-righteousness for Luther, but was his observation of an overarching problem in all of his theological opponents, the papacy, the enthusiasts, the sacramentarians, and the antinomians alike.[69] Luther was also fighting against the most powerful and attractive opinion that is inherent in man at the same time: the Law as the original way of salvation. This is what human hearts say.[70] This was also the entire theological tradition both before and after Luther.

Luther's harsh criticism of the merit of congruity and the merit of condignity as speculations and the tricks of Satan[71] should be construed

---

67 In the Smalcald Articles too, before confessing the Law and the Gospel, Luther deals with sin. SA III I–IV. In the *Lectures on Galatians*, Luther observes that man is indifferent to sin, regarding sin as something trivial, a mere nothing. Man does not know the weight and force of sin, with a result that he supposes that some little work or merit of man will remove it. That the word *sin* includes the eternal wrath of God and the entire kingdom of Satan is foreign to him. WA 40 I:84.12–24, AE 26:33.

68 WA 40 I:44.12–16, AE 26:6; WA 40 I:48.16–17, AE 26:9; WA 40 I:73.21–22, AE 26:26; WA 40 I:403.21–23, AE 26:256; WA 40 I:479.12–13, AE 26:308; WA 40 I:480.32–481.25, AE 26:309–10; WA 40 I:482.12–483.15, AE 26:310; WA 40 I:486.13–16, AE 26:313; WA 40 I:511.24–30, AE 26:331; WA 40 I:529.11–14, AE 26:345; WA 40 I:554.27–555.19, AE 26:363; WA 40 II:8.18–20, AE 27:7–8; WA 40 II:16.20–23, AE 27:14, etc.

69 Luther did a similar thing when he dismissed all the heretical doctrine of the Lord's Supper by saying that for them the sacrament was "something that we do" (*ein ding, das wir thun*) LC V 7. Whether playing some effective role before God through works/ethics (Rome), mysticism/emotions (Karlstadt), or reason/speculation (the Swiss), Luther discerned that his opponents had the common point of departure, *something in us*.

70 WA 40 I:474.21–24, AE 26:305.

71 WA 40 I:220.4–237.24, AE 26:124–35; WA 40 I:290.33–296.22, AE 26:172–76; WA 40 I:302.32–305.13, AE 26:181–83; WA 40 I:453.22–456.16, AE 26:291–93; WA 40 I:468.17–22,

within such a theological diagnosis of Luther. The scholastic theology culminated in the tradition of Gabriel Biel carried with it the ongoing attempts to structure theology under the shadow of Platonic, Aristotelian, and Nominalistic philosophies. In Plato, the always-changing (becoming) physical and empirical world was contrasted with the ever unchanging (being) world of the eternal ideas. The former is the shadow or copy of the latter. In turn, the latter exists as a goal and purpose of the former. Since the world of eternal ideas is sufficient in itself, if these two worlds should relate with each other it was the sensible world that has to move toward the nonsensible by way of imitation. This upward movement of drawing near to the world of ideas takes place because the sensible world yearns for the return to the nonsensible world where it used to belong (*anamnesis*). Plato thought that man is living in both worlds. Man's happiness is achieved when his soul is freed from the physical world of imprisonment as his reason disciplines his fleshly desires. Yet man's happiness is not fully accomplished individualistically. The nation to which he belongs should also follow the same pattern of movement and maintaining a common good order.

Aristotle rejected his master's idea of the world of ideas. He reduced the two independent worlds into one, seeing the ideas only within the *ousia* in the empirical world. For Aristotle, each substance consists in matter and form. And every substance is changing (becoming) in a movement of a matter (*dynamis*) to a form (*energeia*). Because every substance has a movement, there has to be the beginning point and the ending point. Aristotle called the most elemental and imaginative matter that subsists without a form as the prime matter, and the highest substance which exists without a matter as the unmoved mover. When Aristotle devised the unmoved mover as god, his notion moved closer to Plato. In both, god is immaterial substance. In both, god never moves toward the empirical world. The movement of things in the world is only upward, toward the goal of this unmoved mover or the world of ideas.

AE 26:301; WA 40 I:511.12–24, AE 26:330–31; WA 40 I:571.15–573.20, AE 26:374–75; WA 40 II:34.10–20, AE 27:28. Cf. Ap IV 19, 146, 167, 356.

God is self-sufficient. His activity consists in eternal self-contemplation. In terms of the living thing, Aristotle thought it to be a union of body (matter) and soul (form). Again, there is a hierarchy within the living thing. The plant (the lower soul) is lower than the animal (the higher soul) because the lower soul engages in actions related to nutrition and reproduction alone, while the higher soul possesses emotions and desires also. Man is placed as the highest in the hierarchy, because only man possesses reason, which is related to the self-contemplation of the unmoved mover. For Aristotle, the highest goodness is found in a life guided by this reason. Reason controls emotions and desires, and in this way man spends a morally upright life for the common good of a nation.

When philosophies of Plato and Aristotle were used to organize Christian theology, the church naturally rejected their notion that there is no Creator. Nevertheless, the basic structure of a movement from lower to higher or from a cause to an effect was retained. God was thought to preserve the perfect eternal order in the world. When scholasticism moved up to its late period, Nominalism destroyed the firm relation between faith and reason of the earlier periods by freeing God from acting by necessity. But the basic structure remained the same. The Law existed to preserve everything in its place and protect the entire structure in the world from chaos. But disorder was inevitable. Christ came to the world to fix the muddle by providing a new Law. In all of these, the Law was viewed as inherently good. It was given to conserve God's eternal order and to protect man from descending to a lower order in his sin. Everything was legal. The Law was the ultimate. The goodness of man's life was considered in a realm of moral achievement.[72]

When Luther confessed that the Law was not given to justify but to terrify, accuse, and kill, he put himself in enmity against the rest of the theological world. For Luther, the Law was not a description of what man

72 Cf. Takeo Iwasaki, *Seiyo Tetsugaku Shi*, rev. ed. (Tokyo: Yuhikaku, 1975), 10–120; Diogenes Allen, *Philosophy for Understanding Theology* (Atlanta: John Knox, 1985), 15–169; James A. Nestingen, "Changing Definitions: The Law in Formula VI," *Concordia Theological Quarterly* 69 (2005): 259–70; Robert Kolb, *Martin Luther: Confessor of the Faith* (Oxford: Oxford University Press, 2009), 11–71.

is supposed to do within the structure of the eternal order. Instead, he viewed the Law as what it actually does. It kills.[73] Luther observed how man in his weakness and sinfulness is capable of reducing the Law to a mere command, a rule, a system, a structure; a neat little package that is not threatening. He lamented that not only the sophists and monks but also the majority of those who hear the Word do not struggle with sin, death, and the devil.[74] The Law, indeed, does give requirements. But beyond the commandment, the Law exercises power and force.[75] Man can no longer make use of the Law to organize his life and take control of his way of living. The Law kills and condemns, and it does so in a number of ways.

When Luther presented two righteousnesses at the beginning of his *Lectures on Galatians*, he demonstrated how many forms the Law can take. Christian righteousness is only one. It is the doctrine of faith, grace, and forgiveness. It is *passive*. Man works nothing, renders nothing to God. Man only receives and suffers someone else to work in him. This passive righteousness comes to man as rain, a free gift of God in Christ. But outside this Christian righteousness, there is a multitude of other righteousnesses, such as political righteousness, ceremonial righteousness, human traditions of parents, teachers, moral discipline, and the Decalogue. These righteousnesses are all *active*.[76] Luther expressed the

73 WA 40 I:336.32–337.22, AE 26:208–9; WA 40 I:257.28–32, AE 26:148–49.

74 WA 40 I:84.12–24, AE 26:33; WA 40 I:618.11–17, AE 26:407; WA 40 II:90.12–21, AE 27:71. Cf. WA 40 I:236.17–22, AE 26:134; WA 40 I:484.32–485.22, AE 26:312.

75 Luther summarizes his thinking of the Law in *The Theses concerning Faith and Law* (1535) when he expounds on Romans 3:28. "34. It is firmly established, therefore, that Paul is speaking *not only of moral Law, but also of its total power* (potenta) *and force* (vi). 35. Man, the rational animal, does not even understand its *force*, much less is he able to judge and teach it. 36. Its *force*, however, and *power* is to slay (occidere), or *to show that sin must be punished with eternal death*. 37. When a man really begins to feel this force, with the Spirit reproving him, he soon despairs of God's mercy. 38. But despair of God's mercy is the greatest sin and is unforgivable unless grace cancels it in suitable time. 39. Such then truly are these greatest works which man does according to God's moral Law. 40. This is what Paul says, that through the Law sin is made sinful beyond measure; through the Law sin slays me; and the Law brings wrath [Rom. 5:20–21; 4:15]. 41. A man never sins more terribly than in that moment when he begins to feel or understand the Law." Emphases added. AE 34:116, WA 39 I:50.20–35. Cf. FC SD V 10–27.

76 WA 40 I:41.15–51.34; AE 26:4–12.

same thought when he stated later in his lectures: "*Whatever* is not grace is Law, whether it be judicial, ceremonial, or the Decalogue."[77]

According to Luther, the proper office of the Law is to make guilty those who are smug and at peace.[78] By using the term *proper*, he contrasted another use of the Law in the political and civic realm.[79] The Law in its proper office and use reveals to man his sin, blindness, misery, wickedness, ignorance, hate and contempt of God, death, hell, judgment, and well-deserved wrath of God.[80] The Law accuses and terrifies the conscience. The office of the Law is only to kill.[81]

In the lectures, we encounter Luther's employment of many illustrations on this chief office of the Law. His favorite one is that of the hammer of God drawn from Jeremiah 23:29. Man has a huge rock and a solid wall to protect (imprison) himself in the presumption of his own righteousness, immense pride, self-trust, smugness, hate of God, contempt of grace and mercy, ignorance of the promises and of Christ. This huge and horrible monster must be crushed and completely broken. If not, man suffers from two crucial consequences. First, he will never come to know himself as a sinner, not merely civically and morally but also theologically, not only outwardly but also in his conscience, and not only before men but also before God. And second, he will never experience that the proclamation of the forgiveness of sins enters his heart and understanding.[82] Luther takes this latter point rather seriously. He went on to diagnose that a lack of understanding of the proper office and

---

77 WA 40 I:218.7–8, AE 26:122. An emphasis added. In the second set of theses in his second disputation against the antinomians (1538), Luther stated in thesis 18: "*Whatever* shows sin, wrath, and death exercises the office of the Law, be it in the Old or in the New Testament." WA 39 I:348.25–26, Sonntag ed., Only the Decalogue Is Eternal, 80. An emphasis added. FC SD V 12 also states: "Everything that proclaims something about our sin and God's wrath is the proclamation of the Law, however and whenever it may take place." Emphases added.

78 WA 40 I:257.19–22; AE 26:148.

79 Luther presents two uses of the Law: (1) political/civic, and (2) theological/spiritual. Both confine men in a prison. But the latter is the "true and proper use of the Law." WA 40 I:519.34–520.24, AE 26:337.

80 WA 40 I:480.32–481.25, AE 26:309–10.

81 WA 40 I:517.26, AE 26:335.

82 WA 40 I:482.12–483.13, AE 26:310. Luther repeated the illustration of the Law as the hammer in SA III III 2.

use of the Law was the reason for the papacy, the sacramentarians, and the Anabaptists alike to blaspheme the body and blood of Christ. They turned the Lord's Supper from the Gospel into the Law.[83]

Luther predicted that after his time this true and proper use of the Law would be obscured again and would be completely wiped out.[84] Unfortunately, this frightening prediction seems likely to be fulfilled in our time.

THE PROPER OFFICE OF CHRIST

When the proper office of the Law approaches man, it strips the self-righteous, self-excusing sinner of every credential and covering. It strikes him dumb. It makes him guilty. It humbles him. It leads him to hell.[85] However, this is not the end of the story. The Lord does this work to a sinner so that He may be able to make him alive.[86] He strikes in order to heal. He kills in order to make alive. When the user of the Law is the Lord God Himself, the proper office of the Law is not separated from the proper office of the Gospel.

According to the Smalcald Articles, such a proper office of the Gospel is the preaching of the forgiveness of sins.[87] In the *Lectures on Galatians*, however, instead of the office *of the Gospel*, Luther speaks of the office *of Christ*. This office is twofold.

First, Luther confesses that the proper office of Christ is "to wrestle with the Law, sin, and death of the whole world, and to wrestle in such a way that He endures them, but, by enduring them, conquers them and abolishes them in Himself, and in this way frees us from the Law

83 WA 40 I:485.9–22, AE 26:312.

84 WA 40 I:484.32–485.9, AE 26:312.

85 WA 40 I:519.11–12, AE 26:345.

86 WA 40 I: 517.26–30, AE 26: 335; WA 40 I: 529.11–14, AE 26: 345; WA 40 I: 534.17, AE 26: 348.

87 SA III IV. "Erstlich durchs mündlich wort, darinn gepredigt wird vergebung der sunde inn alle wet, welchs ist das eigentliche Ampt des Evangelii." "... primum per verbum vocale, quo iubet praedicari remissionem peccatorum in universe mundo. Et hoc est proprium officium Evangelii."

and from every evil."[88] Here we observe Luther's understanding of the relationship of Christ with the Law. Although Jesus is the Lord of the Law, He is confessed as the receiver of the Law and not the giver. Christ relates to the Law *passively*. He was born under the Law. He voluntarily (*sponte*) subjected Himself to it in His ministry. This He did so that the Law may rage against Him as much as it does against an accursed and condemned sinner, and even more fiercely. The Law accused Jesus of blasphemy and sedition. It found Him guilty before God of all the sins of the whole world. It frightened Him to the point of the bloody sweat in Gethsemane. Finally, it sentenced Him to death, even to the death on the cross.[89] Luther confesses that in such a passive way Jesus achieved the forgiveness of sins for all people. It was not through force and might but through weakness and powerlessness. Against his sin, Luther found another sin, that which is in the flesh of Christ.[90] Christ *is* "my Law, my sin, and my death," Luther exclaimed.[91] In His own body, Jesus destroyed the wrath of the Law.[92]

The true office of Christ is to *bear* our sin, not only some of our sins but all of our sins and sinfulness; not only small sins, but also sins of any size and magnitude. For Luther, Jesus is not the Savior because He overlooks our sins or ignores them as if they did not exist. Jesus did not merely perform what we were unable to do either. Man's sins and his sinfulness are as real as Jesus, who suffered and shed His blood on the cross. Jesus wrestled with the Law, sin, and death, and by doing so He answered for them all vicariously and as our substitute.

> And all the prophets saw this, that Christ was to become the greatest thief, murderer, adulterer, robber, desecrator,

---

88 WA 40 I:569.18–21, AE 26:373. "Quare Christi verum et proprium officium est, luctari cum lege, peccato et morte totius mundi, et sic luctari, ut ista sustineat et sustinendo in Semetipso vincat et aboleat et hoc modo nos a lege et omnibus malis liberet." By asserting this, Luther explains that teaching the Law and performing miracles are His accidental offices; they are not the chief reasons for His coming. WA 40 I:568. 25–569.14, 569.21–24, AE 26:372–73.

89 WA 40 I:564.26–565.17, AE 26:369–70.

90 WA 40 I:273.17–32, AE 26:159–60.

91 WA 40 I:278.20–29, AE 26:163.

92 WA 40 I:503.19–504.21, AE 26:325.

> blasphemer, etc., there has ever been anywhere in the world. . . . He is a sinner, who has and bears the sin of Paul, the former blasphemer, persecutor, and assaulter; of Peter, who denied Christ; of David, who was an adulterer and a murderer, and who caused the Gentiles to blaspheme the name of the Lord (Romans 2:24). In short, He has and bears all the sins of all men in His body—not in the sense that He has committed them but in the sense that He took these sins, committed by us, upon His own body, in order to make satisfaction for them with His own blood.[93]

When Luther expounds the office of Jesus in the lectures, he gets so excited that he forgets teaching, which he was supposed to do in the university classroom, and begins to preach. The proper office of Christ is not a description of a thing. It is the preaching of Christ crucified. It does not belong to a classroom, but to a liturgical assembly where the Lord's liturgy goes on!

Second, Luther speaks of Christ's office not only as bearing our sin but as justifying. "It is the proper office of Christ alone to justify the sinner,"[94] he says. Here is summarized all that Luther wished to say about Christian righteousness. Jesus achieved the forgiveness on the cross by passively receiving all the accusations and attacks of the Law and its associates, sin, the devil, death, and the world. But He was not done for when He died on the cross. He was raised from the dead and now is seated at the right hand of God. Luther frequently spoke of Jesus as "going to the Father." This was a designation of not merely the victory of Jesus as such but also His victory which made it possible for His ongoing ministry of bringing the forgiveness of sins from the cross to the whole world.[95] Jesus alone is the One who is justifying the sinners now. From our human point of view, Christian righteousness is to receive His justification. It is, once again, completely passive.

---

93 WA 40 I:433.26–434.12, AE 26:277–78.

94 WA 40 I:406.24–25, AE 26:259. ". . . iusitificare peccatorem sit solius Christi proprium officium."

95 E.g., WA 40 I:361.12–362.14, AE 26:227–28.

How does Jesus justify the sinner now? Or as Luther poses the question differently, "Why should we listen to the Gospel? What need is there of the sacrament and of absolution?"[96] By inquiring in such a way, Luther has already answered the question. Jesus justifies the sinner through preaching.[97] He also preserves the saints by preaching justification.[98] The Gospel comes to sinners in more than one way. It is delightful to read how Luther cheerfully teaches on Baptism, the Lord's Supper, and Holy Absolution in this context.[99] For example, when Luther presents Baptism as a new birth and a new creation, he dismisses a *signum* theory (*non signum*) and calls Baptism the garment of Christ[100] and Christ Himself (*ipsum Christum*).[101] In baptizing the sinner, Jesus is the Justifier (*Iustificator*), Lifegiver (*Vivificator*), and Redeemer (*Redemptor*). To put on Christ in Baptism does not mean to imitate Him by the works of the Law but to receive "an inestimable gift of the forgiveness, righteousness, peace, comfort, joy in the Holy Spirit, salvation, life, and Christ Himself."[102]

The way of the Gospel is not by coercion. The Gospel does not demand; it bestows His gifts freely. The Gospel *bids* us (*iubet nos*) hold out our hands and receive what is being offered.[103] Jesus gives. We only receive. We don't even *permit* Him to work in us and toward us. Faith passively *suffers* (*patimur*) His gracious work in us and for us.[104] In this

96 WA 40 I:538.13–14, AE 26:350. "Quid igitur audiamus Evangelium, quid opus est Sacramento et absolution?"

97 WA 40 I:336.32–337.22, 343.33–345.30, AE 26:208–9, 214–15.

98 WA 40 I:534.30–538.35, AE 26:349–51.

99 E.g., WA 40 I:51.14–17, AE 26:11.

100 WA 40 I:539.34–541.35, AE 26:352–53.

101 WA 40 I:541.32–33, AE 26:353.

102 WA 40 I:540.33–541.20, AE 26:352–53.

103 WA 40 I; AE 26:208. "Contra Evangelium non exigit, sed donat gratis et iubet nos porrectis minibus oblate accipere." In the Gospel-delivery context such as this, we prefer the language of bidding rather than command as a translation of *inbeo* in order to avoid an impression of demand and coercion. The Lord bids us to hear His comforting voice of the Gospel. He bids us to come to the Lord's Table to receive His body to eat and His blood to drink.

104 WA 40 I:41.17–21, AE 26:4–5.

way, the baptized get to live in the fellowship of the Church,[105] where Jesus' ongoing ministry of delivering His gifts takes place.[106]

Luther's understanding of Christ's office as justifying is never complete without his confession of the Office of the Holy Ministry. He acknowledges that when he was a young theologian and doctor he did not understand that the *rite vocatus* was such a weighty matter.[107] Luther exhibits that as his understanding of the doctrine of the proper distinction between Law and Gospel became clearer, his confession of the Office of the Holy Ministry also matured.[108] Following Paul in the first two chapters of Galatians, Luther confesses that the certainty of the call and ordination gives comfort to both pastors and hearers. People are comforted to know that even though they see only the pastor and hear only his human voice, it is actually Jesus who preaches and administers the Sacrament. The pastor is also comforted when he realizes that the reason he preaches and administers the Sacraments is that his Lord Jesus called him, sent him to this particular field of service, and assured him of the promise that He is there in the office with him and carries out the ministry Himself. As in the Book of Concord on the *Predigtamt*, Luther confesses the doctrine of the Office of the Holy Ministry by bringing in such New Testament passages as Matthew 28:19–20; Ephesians 4:11–12; and Titus 1:5.

Christ's proper office as justifying the sinner is a description of the Christian righteousness for Luther. It is totally passive on the side of the sinners. Even faith that receives Jesus' proper office and work is the gift from the Lord. Luther articulates that faith is not an idle quality or an empty shell. It is a sure trust in the heart that takes hold of Christ[109] in such a way that if Christ is removed from faith nothing would remain

---

105 WA 40 I:576.21–25, AE 26:378.

106 WA 40 I:387.21–388.17, AE 26:245–46.

107 WA 40 I:63.19–22; AE 26:20.

108 WA 40 I:54.15–64.12, 66.14–71.28, AE 26:15–21, 22–26; WA 40 I:183.25–187.15, AE 26:101–3; WA 40 I:357.14–30, AE 26:224–25; WA 40 II:148.31–153.29, AE 27:116–20; WA 40 II:161.30–36, AE 27:126.

109 Cf. AC XX 23–26.

in the heart.[110] Faith in Christ plays such a vital role in Christian life. And yet, for Luther, there exists something more important than faith in the heart—the imputation.[111] The vitality of faith is never diminished in Luther's lectures. However, that saving faith is still imperfect. It is very weak. In fact, Luther describes it as barely a little spark. It is through this weak and imperfect faith and on account of it that Jesus reckons the sinner as righteous. God does not see the sin that is remaining in man, as a result. He covers the remnant of sin in the justified saint. He forgives it. The emphasis of imputation goes with another favorite term Luther uses in confessing Christ. The Christian righteousness is the *happy exchange.*[112] Jesus took upon Himself our sin and sinfulness. In turn, He grants us His innocence and victory—the vicarious atonement and the imputation. Luther refused to move beyond Jesus the crucified.[113]

THE CHRISTIAN LIFE AS *SIMUL IUSTUS ET PECCATOR*

What we observe from Luther's confession of the doctrine of the proper distinction between the Law and the Gospel is that unlike the medieval scholastic theology that had gone before him and the default position of the human heart that goes on as long as man exists in the world, the Law is not the ultimate any longer; the Law is not the way of salvation. The Law is now replaced by Christ. He alone is the way of salvation. As Paul says it in his Epistle to the Romans that Christ is the end of the Law (Romans 10:4), so in his *Lectures on Galatians* Luther confesses with Paul that the time of the Law ends with Christ's intervention.[114] Christ is the *telos*. He is not only the fulfillment of the Law, but also its end.

---

110 WA 40 I:228.27–229.32, AE 26:129–30.

111 WA 40 I:363.28–368.25, AE 26:229–32.

112 WA 40 I:442.31–443.34, AE 26:283–84. "Sic *feliciter commutans* nobiscum suscepit nostrum peccatriccem et donavit nobis suam innocentem et victricem personam." An emphasis added.

113 WA 40 I:564.11–14, AE 26:369. ". . . immergo conscientiam meam in vulnera, sanguinem, mortem, resurrectionem et victoriam Christi, praeter hunc nihil plane videre et audire volo."

114 WA 40 I:556.23–27, AE 26:364. ". . . non tamen desperes, sed credas in *Christum qui est finis legis* ad iustitiam omni credenti." An emphasis added.

According to Luther, the Christian is divided into two times: the time of the Law when he is under the accusation of the proper office of the Law, and the time of grace when the Law's accusing voice is stopped by the forgiveness of sins.[115] The Christian is to learn to distinguish the times of both, not in words but in the feelings,[116] because the accusation of the Law and the freedom of the Gospel are both experienced in the conscience.[117] When the Christian fails to distinguish these two times, Luther considers that he has abused the Law.[118]

Luther does not regard the time of the Law and the time of grace as a chronological order as if there were two dispensations, one of the Law and another of the Gospel. Luther borrows Aristotelian language of *forma* and *formalis* to point out that the Christian righteousness is not in the saint in a formal sense, but outside of him in His imputation.[119] Such a description resembles Luther's statement in his Antinomian Disputation's fifth set of theses, numbers 46 through 48 (1538). There Luther asserts that the antinomians are convinced that sin is formally (*formaliter*) and philosophically eliminated in Christ because they are completely ignorant of the fact that it is only eliminated in the reckoning and forgiveness of the merciful God. Thesis 48 says: "For *relatively*, not *formally* or substantially is sin eliminated, Law abolished, death destroyed."[120] Luther does not deny that salvation is fully accomplished by Christ on Calvary.

115 WA 40 I:523.31–529.14, AE 26:340–45. Cf. WA 40 I:454.30–33, AE 26:292; WA 40 II:19.25–26, AE 27:17.

116 WA 40 I:527.21–23, AE 26:343.

117 WA 40 II:3.20–4.12, AE 27:4.

118 WA 40 I:528.23–34, AE 26:344–45. Here Luther describes three ways in which the Law is abused. The first is when the self-righteous imagine that he is justified by the Law. The second is the sectarians (antinomians) who want to excuse Christians from the Law altogether. And the third is when the Christians feel the terror of the Law and do not understand these are to last only until Christ.

119 WA 40 I:370.28–32, AE 26:234. "iustitiam *non esse formaliter* in nobis, ut Aristoteles disputant, sed extra nos in sola gratia et reputatione divina, Et nihil *formae* seu iustitiae in nobis esse praeter illam imbecillem fidem seu primitas fidei, quod coepimus apprehendere Christum, interim tamen vere peccatum in nobis manere." Emphases added.

120 WA 39 I:356.27–32, Sonntag ed., *Only the Decalogue Is Eternal*, 135. Thesis 48 reads: "*Relative* enim, non *formaliter* aut substantialiter est peccatum sublatum, lex abolita, mors destructa." Emphases added.

Yet when it comes to His justifying office in the Means of Grace, Christ is the end of the Law in a relative sense (that is, dependent on His daily coming in the conscience). The structure of the Law remains. But the accusing voice of the Law ends in the conscience relationally when the living voice of the Gospel arrives to the sinner and frees his conscience with Christ's forgiveness.

All this is another way of putting Luther's weighty recognition that "the Christian man is righteous and a sinner *at the same time*, holy, profane, an enemy of God and a son of God."[121] As long as a Christian lives, both remain as fact. He is completely righteous. He is thoroughly a sinner. Luther says: "Thus if I look at Christ, I am completely holy and pure, and I know nothing at all about the Law. . . . But if I look at my flesh, I feel greed, sexual desire, anger, pride, the terror of death, sadness, fear, hate, grumbling, and impatience against God."[122] The Christian, not the unbaptized, is in need of hearing the Gospel and receiving the Lord's Supper precisely because there is sinfulness remaining in him and so there is a time of the Law to accuse and terrify the conscience. The Christian is *simul iustus et peccator*. Luther speaks of the Church in the same way.[123]

For Luther, therefore, it is inconceivable that the Christian would ever come to the point when he does not need Christ. The Christian is not progressively sanctified.[124] Rather, as he matures as a Christian he will increasingly discover the fact that he is indeed more deeply sinful than he has ever realized before. The battle between flesh and spirit, between old and new Adams continues. Luther says: "In fact, the godlier

121 WA 40 I:368.26–27, AE 26:232. "Sic homo Christianus *simul* iustus et peccator, Sanctus, prophanus, inimicus et filius Dei est." An emphasis added.

122 WA 40 I:537.24–28, AE 26:350.

123 WA 40 I:445.16–18, AE 26:285; WA 40 II:106.34–107.21, AE 27:85.

124 Today, even though many people view Jesus as the taskmaster, as at the time of the Reformation, so that they are to keep the Law, to obey Him, and to be good as He is good, yet unlike Luther's days such popular teaching doesn't seem to lead them to a terrified conscience. Instead of terrifying, the Law seemed to have been turned into a comfort. But this is nothing new. Luther was critical in his lectures of those who attribute to the Law what properly belongs to Christ. In short, for them the Law becomes Christ (*Lex fit Christus*). And in turn, Christ is the Law (*Christus est Lex*) to them. WA 40 I:248.22–30, AE 26:142.

one is, the more he feels this battle."[125] The true saints are not people who never experience the desires of the flesh.[126] They are not those who perform works that give the appearance of brilliance or grandeur. But they are the ones who are called by the Gospel, baptized, and forgiven.[127] "A Christian is not someone who has no sin or feels no sin; he is someone against whom, because of his faith in Christ, sin is not reckoned by God."[128] Moreover, a Christian under *tentatio* is under Christ's marvelous pastoral care. By appealing to the common experience of people that the head is more sensitive and responsive in its feeling than the other parts of the body, Luther comforts the hearers: "Christ, our Head, makes our afflictions His own, so that when we, who are His body, suffer, He is affected as though the evils were His own."[129]

Luther confesses the centrality of Christ in Christian life through the *simul*. There is no time when Christians would grow beyond Him so that they may spend an independent life away from Him. Christ may be seen as an example to imitate. But that happens only at the time of rejoicing when the Christian is out of the reach of *tentatio*.[130] But when the Christian is under the Law, which is the majority of his life,[131] Christ remains as a gift.[132]

In expounding on good works of the Christian, Luther never divorces them from the fact of the *simul*. Everything that has to do with good works belongs to faith, Luther observes, because works must not be looked at in a moral sense; they must be looked at in a theological

---

125 WA 40 II:94.14–15, AE 27:74. "Imo quo quisque magis pius est, hoc plus sentit illam pugnam."

126 WA 40 II:96.17–97.16, AE 27:76.

127 WA 40 II:18–28, AE 27:82.

128 WA 40 I:235.15–17, AE 26:133. "Definimus ergo hunc esse Christianum, non qui non habet aut non sentit peccatum, sed cui illud a Deo propter fidem in Christum non imputatur."

129 WA 40 II:171.32–172.14, AE 27:134.

130 WA 40 II:42.24–26, AE 27:34.

131 WA 40 I:209.20–22, AE 26:117. "Sed quando ad experientiam venit, tum invenis Evangelium *rarum* et e contra legem assiduum esse hospitem in conscientia." Emphasis added.

132 WA 40 II:42.29–32, AE 27:34.

sense.[133] "To do" includes faith at the same time (another *simul*!).[134] Faith takes the doer himself and makes him into a tree, and his deeds become fruit. First, there must be a tree, then the fruit. When the accusing office of the Law is ended by Christ,[135] the Law is deprived of this right and begins to work as a companion. But here, the Law does not work by coercion but it entices and charms the saints to do the works of vocations.[136] Just like Luther described Christian righteousness as rain from heaven so that while Christ is active we remain completely passive in receiving His gifts, so the reformer uses the same illustration of rain to speak of a Christian's service to his neighbor in love.[137] There, a Christian is completely active. His attention goes to the neighbor's need and never to his own need and interest, so long as he does those works as a Christian. Obviously, there is a big difference between Christ as rain and Christians as rain. Christians are in the *simul*. In doing good works, his struggles in his conscience are relentless.

When the whole Christian life is depicted as faith toward God and love and works toward the neighbor, that love and those works are never detached from faith.[138] It is amusing to note that Luther does not use the Calvinistic sense of the third use of the Law to describe the Christian life. In the place of the third use, Luther speaks of the *simul*.

CONCLUSION

For Luther, the proper distinction between Law and Gospel was never a static idea, a mere principle in theology. When it is lost, the whole Christian doctrine and life are undermined. When it is not faithfully

---

133 WA 40 I:417.13–15, AE 26:266.

134 WA 40 I:402.13–14, AE 26:255. "Ut facere includat simul fidem."

135 WA 40 II:97.29–34, AE 27:77. "Itaque pii non sunt sub lege, scilicet Spiritu, *lex enim non potest accusare* et ferre sententiam mortis contra eos, etiamsi ipsi peccatum sentient et fateantur se peccatores esse, *quia ius ademptum est legi per Christum*, 'qui factus est sub legem, ut eos, qui sub lege errant, redimeret.' Ideo hoc, quod vere peccatum est contra legem, *lex pro peccato non audet accusare in piis*." Emphases added.

136 WA 40 I:51.21–31, AE 6:11–12; WA 40 II:76.13–78.23, AE 27:60–62.

137 WA 40 I:43.18–28, 51.21–31, AE 26:6, 11–12.

138 WA 40 II:37.26–30, AE 27:30.

preserved, Jesus is diminished and the comfort for sinners is taken away. The doctrine of the proper distinction between Law and Gospel is essentially all about our sins having been answered for by Jesus, who continues with His Spirit to deliver the forgiveness of our sins through preaching, Baptism, Absolution, and the Lord's Supper.

In recent times, there emerged strong voices against the doctrine of the proper distinction between Law and Gospel as we have seen. These views may give an impression that this doctrine is unique only to Luther and therefore it is to be dismissed. Luther's historical view is to the contrary. He observes that this doctrine finds its root at the beginning of creation. Satan attacked this solid rock in Paradise when he persuaded our first parents to hear and follow another voice than that of the giving God. Then, a series of persecutions of the doctrine took place through Cain and his sons, in the world after Noah, in the people of Israel, in the Church of the Gentiles (Rome), and new sects including the antinomians.[139] Luther recognizes that Augustine taught the proper distinction between Law and Gospel "to some extent" (*aliqua ex parte*). Jerome and others like him knew nothing at all about it. And for many centuries there had been a remarkable silence.[140]

Since the devil constantly proposes new doctrines and new christs in each generation and even each day,[141] the *concordia* of doctrine is something the Church prays ceaselessly.[142] Luther himself mentions that he confesses this doctrine with greater certainty (*maiore certitudine*) at the time of the lectures than ever before. His conviction was deepened through "study, practice, and experience, as well as through great and frequent temptations." It was his prayer that Christ would keep him and

139 WA 40 I:33.12–36.27, AE 27:145–49; AE 40 I:36.28–27.20.

140 WA 40 I:486.21–25, AE 26:313. J. A. O. Preus observed that Chemnitz, who was "probably the greatest student of patristics Lutheranism has ever produced," made no use of the Church Fathers to support the doctrine of Law and Gospel. J. A. O. Preus, "Chemnitz on Law and Gospel," *Concordia Journal* 15.4 (October 1989): 409.

141 WA 40 I:321.31–33, AE 26:196; WA 40 I:563.22–26, AE 26:369.

142 WA 40 I:627.13–18, AE 26:413; WA 40 II:46.16–49.19, AE 27:37–39, 41–42; WA 40 II:136.20–137.10, AE 27:107–8.

strengthen him in that faith and confession to the end.[143] We certainly witnessed that through the record of his last days as well as the funeral sermons and an oration given by his closest colleagues. Melanchthon concluded his oration by urging those who were in the Office of the Holy Ministry to follow Luther's footsteps: to be diligent and faithful in the study, confession, preaching, and teaching of Law and Gospel.[144]

Even five hundred years after the Reformation, our prayers follow Luther's and Melanchthon's. We pray that the Lord Jesus may ever keep the Church in the concord of doctrine so that Jesus may never be diminished and the comfort for the sinner may never be taken away. May the distinction of the Law from the Gospel be preserved among us not only in words but also in feeling and in experience.[145]

---

143 WA 40 II:135.24–136.8, AE 27:106–7.

144 CR 11:734; Johannes Fünck, *Eyn Sermon uber der Leich / des Erwirdigen Herrn Doctor Martin Luthers zu Wittenberg gethon von Phillippo Melanthon* (March 13, 1546), b3; Lewis W. Spitz, ed. *The Protestant Reformation* (Englewood Cliffs, NJ: Prentice-Hall, 1966), 76; J. Unwin trans. *The Life and Acts of Martin Luther by Philip Melanchthon* (Malone, TX: Repristination Press, 1990), 45–46.

145 WA 40 I:209.17–19, AE 26:117; WA 40 I:511.31–32, AE 26:331.

SPEAKING OF THE END TO THE LAW

James Arne Nestingen

In public culture, both European and North American, two different declarations of the end of the Law stand at odds. One goes back to the Reformation in the sixteenth century. Though heavily criticized by theologians of other traditions and generally not well understood within its own heritage, the first has the authority of Luther and still surfaces on occasion. The other has its origins in the Enlightenment. Though it can claim no denominational or confessional loyalty and is fundamentally questionable, since the Second World War it has been culturally established and true to form, reflexively undercutting appeals to biblical or moral law and marginalizing those who make them.

Given the controversy and misunderstandings commonly attached to Luther's declarations of the end of the Law, the first purpose of this paper is to define his statement in the context of the Reformation. That done, second, the currently established assertion of the end of the Law as rooted in the Enlightenment should be examined, particularly in terms of its impact. Then third, it is to be hoped that these historical considerations will provide a basis for some implications for the contemporary biblical and confessional witness of the Church.

LUTHER ON THE END OF THE LAW

The origin of Luther's repeated assertions of the end of the Law, which show up with particular force in the 1535 Galatians commentary, is in Romans 10:4, where Paul states that "Christ is the end of the law that all who believe may be justified."[1] Paul uses a Greek term, *telos*, which wraps together a double connotation, very much like the English word *end*. The telos or end of the Law involves both its termination and its fulfillment. Thus, in Paul's original argument, the Law had lost its force or value and so terminates in Christ because He has fulfilled it. As Luther said, the fulfillment of the Law brings its termination.[2]

As simple and straightforward as this sounds, the sense of termination proved particularly problematic for the Augustinian tradition. Augustine, with the Early Church, took the Greco-Roman tradition of natural law. An order built into the shape of life by creation, in the Christian interpretation of it, arranges everything that has being in a hierarchical order from top to bottom. The law, the *lex aeterna*, preserves this order so that all things will move toward the end assigned to them by their status in the hierarchy of being. Natural law is thus inherent in life and necessary to the shaping of existence.

This has important consequences theologically. To begin with, it makes the Law the original way of salvation. The Law must be fulfilled if human beings, who hold a status just below the angels, are to come into the unity with God that is their ultimate purpose. The Law lays down the categories within which grace functions. As St. Augustine said, "Grace gives what the law demands." Further, the Law's work in the ordering of things has particular importance morally. Charged with the distribution of God's grace, the Church at the same time must preserve the moral order demanded by the Law.

Given such assumptions, the problem with the sense of termination in Paul's term *telos* appears quickly. A law that inheres in creation and keeps all things in order, showing the way to grace while morally ordering the community, cannot possibly stop or end without undermining the whole structure. So theologians and moralists in the Augustinian tradition, such as Erasmus, Zwingli, Bucer, and Calvin, seek to set aside

---

1 Scripture quotations in this chapter are the author's own translation.

2 Citations to Luther's Antinomian Disputations are identified by the disputation number, 1–6, followed by the thesis number and then the page number in the Weimar Edition, so 2:47, WA 39.1, 348.

the sense of termination, insisting on terms like fulfillment or goal. In traditional Catholicism, Christ brought the old law of Judaism to its termination to bring in the new law. Calvin, likewise, holds out for Christ's rehabilitation of the Law. As Wilhelm Niesel once observed, the disputed third use in Lutheranism becomes in Calvinism the Law's essential function.[3]

Thus Luther's insistence on the full, double connotation of *telos* sets him apart from the ecumenical tradition defined by Augustine. He found himself alone among his theological colleagues as well. Moving another direction theologically in the 1530s, Philip Melanchthon became increasingly convinced of the necessity of the Law for salvation and with that, developed the language of third use that became definitive for Lutheran orthodoxy.

Three different sources account for Luther's differences with the Augustinian tradition and his own heritage on the Law. First, as Heiko Oberman commented, Luther was shaped by the biblical apocalyptic which had gained particular significance in his time.[4] This shifted the traditional emphasis of the church from human participation and appropriation to God as the final actor in history. Second, Luther was a thoroughgoing nominalist. His teacher at the University of Erfurt was one of the great logicians of the time and instructed Luther in the assumptions and practices of what was then the prevalent philosophical school of thought. This made Luther skeptical about arguments such as Augustine's hierarchy of being and its emplacement of universal law. Instead of moving top down, from an eternal order to individual instances, Luther was trained to think more from the bottom, in terms of what was right in front of him. Claims to an eternal, all-encompassing law can be falsified by a single contrary instance—Jodocus Trutfetter at Erfurt taught Luther to think more pragmatically, in terms of how things actually work, close to the ground.

---

3 Wilhelm Niesel, *The Theology of Calvin* (London: Luttwerworth, 1951).

4 Heiko Oberman, *Forerunners of the Reformation* (Cambridge: Harvard University Press).

But second, instead of approaching the Law on traditional philosophical grounds, moving from Law to Gospel, Luther turned things around theologically. The Law comes before the Gospel in human experience—the Gospel is an alien word, sounding from without. But epistemologically, in terms of knowing and speaking theologically, the Gospel takes priority over the Law. For example, when Jesus says, "I am the way, and the truth, and the life," He is effectively also saying "the Law is not." Paul puts it even more baldly in Ephesians 2:15, "He has abolished the Law, with its commandments and ordinances." The Gospel, as the ultimate word, reduces the Law to a penultimate word. So Luther wrote in the Antinomian Disputations, set out against John Agricola between 1536 and 1540, "the Law was not given that it might justify or vivify or prescribe anything for the righteous."[5] The Law was not given to save—that is Christ's work, and His alone.

Reduced to terms, defined in the light of the Gospel, known by what it actually does in human experience, the Law's characteristic, idiosyncratic marks are its capacity to restrain and accuse. These are the uses. The Law sets limits and to some extent, encourages conformity to its requirements. But its genius, its hallmark, happens in accusation. "*Lex semper accusat*," the Law always accuses. So as Luther defines the Law in the Antinomian Disputations, "Anything that accuses has and holds the office of Law."[6] The anything, as it says, includes all. So for example, the accusation may take the form of a formal statement. But accusation can also arise out of an unresolved memory or, in a famous example, the sound of a rustling leaf.

Once the Law starts to accuse, it commonly knows no limit. Like a wheel spinning in snow or mud, it keeps throwing up indictments, sometimes explicitly in what might be termed "actual guilt," but more often implicitly in an unresolvable sense of having done wrong or worse yet, being wrong. In a telling phrase, Luther calls this "the Law ascending into the conscience and seeking to rule there." He uses the word

---

5 4:38, WA 39.1, 354. See also page 347.

6 WA 15, 228: BC 560.

conscience in a wider sense, not so much to speak of a moral agency at work in the self but to describe a person's sense or self-awareness in relation to the neighbor, to God, to life itself. When the Law ascends into the conscience, it quickly moves from act to person, from deed or misdeed to self-worth in relationship and from there it jumps to both past and future: "I have always been this way"; "it will never be different." Significantly, describing how the Law literally runs away with the self, Luther often cites the biblical suicides, Saul and Judas. Then, too, he will sometimes address the Law directly, as though it were a sentient power: "Here, Law, see that you do not jump your fences. You were not meant to be a murderer but a teacher."[7]

Defined this way, the Law is a power related to the other powers loose in fallen creation: it allies with sin, death, and the devil.[8] Luther takes this over from Paul's argument in Romans, "I should not have known sin if it had not been for the Law" (Romans 7:7). Sin, death, the Law, and the devil leapfrog over one another to curve the self in upon itself, binding the will, turning the creation against itself and its Creator.

Most important, as much as Luther speaks of the Law's uses, he does not clearly identify the Law's user, as Gerhard Ebeling pointed out in a classic essay.[9] While it is commonly assumed that the Law is available to the pastor in its uses, in fact, Luther is not so confident of this. As a power loose in the creation, the Law cannot so readily be domesticated. It may very well get away, as many pastors have experienced, turning on its deluded user to exact its independence. The devil may be the Law's user, as above, using it to lead the believer to unbelief, despair, and other great and shameful sins. Or the Holy Spirit may take over the Law, bringing it to harness through the Gospel so that it leads to its proper end in repentance and faith. For this to happen, however, the Gospel must take over from the Law to stop the indictment and bring the heart to rest in faith.

---

7 From the public discussion of the disputation, WA 39.1, 445.

8 5:7, WA 39.1, 354.

9 Gerhard Ebeling, "The Doctrine of the *Triplex Usus Legis* in the Theology of the Reformation," in James W. Leitch, trans., *Word and Faith* (Philadelphia: Fortress Press, 1963), 75.

Defined in this way, the Law can only end when it is fulfilled. There is only one who has fulfilled and does, who can by this fulfillment bring the Law to heel, putting it under control: that is Christ Jesus. He is the only one who ever kept the First Commandment, who fears, loves, and trusts God above all things, right to His own death. So doing, He has "bought and freed us, lost and condemned persons, not with silver and gold but with his suffering and death."[10] When God raised Him from the dead, the Law lost the ultimate standing it claimed for itself. So *tetelestai*, "it is finished," as Jesus said in a last victorious cry (John 19:30). The Law has lost its claim.

Now, Luther says, Christ finishes the Law in two ways.[11] He enters the conscience through the absolution, through the proclaimed Word and the administered Sacrament to effect the forgiveness of sins. This is the true substitutionary atonement, happening here and now. Christ Jesus takes upon Himself the sinner's sins, the sinner himself or herself, and in a marvelous exchange, as Luther calls it, becomes the victim for us so that while He bears our sins and our death, we arise in His righteousness.

With this, the risen Christ sends His Holy Spirit to begin keeping the Law in the faith He creates in the believer. This obedience is "incipient," as Luther calls it, a beginning that is not complete within this life. Axiomatically, without a doubt, there can be no point in the Christian life where the believer's obedience carries that person beyond Christ's service in the absolution. That would make Christ superfluous. Still, there is progress, even improvement, as the Spirit carries the self beyond itself, ever deeper into grace. Here, as Luther says, the Christian does without the Law what the Law requires.[12] This is the blessed ignorance of the Law that Luther describes in the Galatians commentary—faith is so fixed on Christ and His gifts that Moses has lost his voice.

But now there is another dimension here that is often overlooked.

10 See SC II 2.

11 2:24, 3:35, WA 39.1, 349, 354.

12 3:37, WA 39.1, 354.

"The Law says, Do this, and it is never done," as Luther writes in the Heidelberg Disputations. "The Gospel says, Believe in this, and it is done already." The Law works by signification, naming the deeds or conditions that it requires by pointing to them. This is the Law's limit—it can signify, illustrate, name, but it cannot produce what it requires. Thus its significance always remains. The Gospel, on the other hand, gives what it declares—when Jesus speaks the word, the sinner's chains drop, the deaf hear, the lame walk, the dead arise. The Law ends.

Terminated by the Gospel, the Law can no longer accuse in the conscience. For faith, it is dead and finished. But its significance continues, in fact, Luther will say for all eternity.[13] As my longtime friend and colleague Gerhard Forde pointed out, this is the key to understanding Luther's statements on the eternal quality of the Law. The Law is not eternal in the sense of Augustine's *lex aeterna* doctrine—then it would displace the Gospel. But it is eternal in the eschatological sense. Its significance points ahead of itself to the shape of life God intends for the creation and the new creation. The significance of the Law is that it points ahead to the shape of life when God completes what He has begun in Christ Jesus.

One way to think of this is to examine the grammar of the Decalogue. The Commandments are translated in the imperative: "you shall" or "shall not." But in the Hebrew, the tense of the verb is future. That is the true significance of the Commandments. You should have no other gods, the imperative, so you should fear, love, and trust God above anything else. Now the First Commandment, which Luther called the whole sum of the Gospel, remains at the same time the whole sum of the Law. When Christ has completed His work in the believer and the new creation, the indictment will be gone, never to return. So as Christ takes hold of you and through His Spirit continues in you now, as the Law falls silent you can catch glimpses of what Christ is shaping in the new self individually. There is coming a time, in the new creation, when you really will fear, love, and trust God above anything else, when these words will be so written in your heart that you have no alternative but to fear, love,

13 3:40–41, WA 39.1, 354. See also 2:47, 348.

and trust God above anything else. Then, as Luther says, the Law will remain "as fulfilled in the blessed." Then, as in the words of the Apocalypse of St. John, there will be no more weeping nor tears anymore. The Law and with it sin, death, and the devil, will be no more. The creation will be what God created it to be. The garden will once more bloom.

Here lies the difference between Luther and the antinomians of his time and any other. John Agricola, Luther once said, was putting on a play in an empty theater. He used language to create an illusionary or conceptual end to the Law among people, both outside the theater and within it, who were under relentless accusation. That is no end. Instead, the best it can do is to drive the Law underground, below conscious awareness, where it becomes even more desperately lethal. "A Law that does not kill is a mythological construction."

ANOTHER END OF THE LAW?

Though the conflicts of the Reformation were officially settled with the Peace of Augsburg in 1555, it didn't last indefinitely. Where there had been one legally recognized church in Europe, there were now two with a third pushing for similar standing. Roman Catholicism held in the Mediterranean; the Lutherans had their strength in Germany, Scandinavia, and Finland. The Calvinists, originating in French-speaking Switzerland, moved quickly into France, parts of Western and eventually Northern Germany, and the Netherlands. Roman Catholics and Lutherans refused them standing in the Peace of Augsburg, a factor in the eruption of further conflict.

When war broke out, it quickly escalated across Germany. Roman Catholic forces pushed all the way to the Baltic, only to be driven back by the Snow King, Gustavus Adolphus, who was finally killed in battle. The war became a minor holocaust, seesawing back and forth in an agony of death. It was finally settled in 1648 with the Peace of Westphalia. This time Calvinism gained official standing.

All three churches were determined to preserve what they had achieved theologically during the Reformation. Catholicism had defined itself in the Council of Trent, which ended in 1560, its holdings being officially ratified by the papacy. A new order, the Jesuits, swearing loyalty to the papacy, took over the task of enforcement, entrenching itself politically and academically. After extended controversy among themselves, among other things about the place of the Law in the Christian life, Lutherans finally achieved theological peace in the Formula of Concord. The king of Denmark, advised by theologians loyal to Philip Melanchthon, kept Denmark and Norway, which he also ruled, out of the agreement. The Calvinists were also troubled by internal dissent. In 1618, the Synod of Dort officially condemned a Dutch theologian named Jacobus Arminius. Though there was some dissent, for the time being anyway Calvinism spoke with one voice, echoing John Calvin.

For all three churches, it was the age of orthodoxy. Using the tools of Aristotelian philosophy, theologians of each tradition attempted to define their heritages as closely as possible, readily attacking the other traditions and one another in the process. They were intent on enforcing consensus among themselves.

The scandal of warfare, in the field and in classroom polemics, effectively undermined the standing of the church in public life. Those representing the Prince of Peace were directly implicated in the constant conflict. In this context, another movement arose which could also trace its roots to the Reformation and particularly to Luther and his nominalism. This came to be called the Enlightenment. Though it lasted from the later sixteenth into the seventeenth and eighteenth centuries, its legacy is still very much a part of European life, and even North American life through immigration. It can be said that in the twentieth century, the Enlightenment came to be the officially established way of thinking.

Peter Gay, one of the historians of the Enlightenment, describes a "sacred circle" which effectively controlled public discourse in the early modern period.[14] It united the hereditary nobility, the leaders of the church, and the text of the Bible and was exercised through the divine right of kings, to place its rule beyond challenge.

---

14 Peter Gay, *The Enlightenment: An Interpretation: The Rise of Modern Paganism* (New York: Norton and Co., 1995).

A disparate group of philosophers—among them David Hume in England, Voltaire in France, and Immanuel Kant in Germany, with many others scattered elsewhere—attempted to break the grip of the sacred circle to, in Kant's terms, free human thought. As Leo Strauss of the University of Chicago pointed out in a classical study, *Natural Right and History*, virtually all of them were sons of the rising classes of the new European economy, with roots in the old upper classes. They were thus wealthy and privileged, eager to break free from the restraints of a tradition they viewed as confining. Significantly, they were virtually all single.[15]

The Enlightenment used a set of three tools to break through the restraints. The first was empiricism. They demanded that all thought had to be publicly, outwardly demonstrable. With this, second, they sought to be rigidly scientific, disciplining thought according to methods taken over from the emerging sciences that had claimed new authority following the Reformation. Third, with the sciences, they applied the canons of historical study to what had previously been authoritative tradition. This was the beginning, for example, of biblical criticism. The Bible was not the book to be accepted on the basis of claims to biblical authority, but a book which collected the attempts of various times and sources to come to terms with the problems of their day.

The Enlightenment targeted the doctrine of revelation and natural law, which were seen as authoritarian vehicles for the entrenchment of the sacred circle. That which the church had claimed as revealed by God had to stand the empirical tests of the sciences. Historical methods, applied to Scripture, demonstrated that doctrines such as the Trinity or Christology, which had been supported by appeals to revelation, had developed over time, reflecting the interests of theologians in cities like Alexandria, Antioch, and Constantinople. Detached from God, revelation lost its authority and became a collection of historical opinions.

Natural law received the same treatment. The Greco-Roman tradition, taken over by the Early Church, had spoken of the law as inherent in the creation, holding all things in their proper place in the hierarchy

15 Leo Strauss, *Natural Right and History* (Chicago: University of Chicago, 1953).

of being. Using the tools of nominalism, Luther had found the Law summarized in the Ten Commandments, approached in the demands and conditions of creaturely life. The Enlightenment argued that it is logically impossible to deduct an *ought* from an *is*, that the structures of life do not necessarily indicate what should be. So they treated the Law as a set of concepts or ideas, without any basis in the structures or being or the workings of things, and so sought to reduce the Law to human terms, making it one idea among many.

This was not, as it might appear, the end of the Law anticipated. Tearing down the divine superstructure that had traditionally held the Law in place, Immanuel Kant attempted to rebuild it on the basis of human consciousness, appealing to what he termed the categorical imperative. Other Enlightenment figures, such as John Locke in England, appealed to what they termed the "social contract." Lacking divine endorsement or a necessary place in the workings of public life, the Law arises out of human agreement about what should be required or prohibited. In fact, the Enlightenment has generated a legal tradition that can trace itself back to these origins and has shaped Western political life.

Significantly, in the place of natural law the Enlightenment appealed to natural rights. Though there are no universal obligations built into the nature of things, each person as person had a set of entitlements, which can be invoked from nature. So Thomas Jefferson, one of the founders of the American republic, said in its founding document, "We hold these truths to be self-evident, that all men are created equal, that they are endowed by their Creator with certain unalienable Rights, that among these are Life, Liberty and the pursuit of Happiness." As evident as they were to Jefferson, they were not equally so to his 160 slaves, who had to be sold at his death to pay off his debts. Neither were they evident to Sally Hemmings, a slave whose services he required in his bed.

That is the fundamental flaw in the Enlightenment. Eagerly asserting human prerogative, making humanity the measure of all things, regarding the self as its own creator, it did not recognize the *incurvatus in se*, the power of the root or person sin—as Luther called it—that turns humanity in on itself. While looking past the sacred circle to denounce the church and its theological heritage as the source of the warfare and contention in the sixteenth and seventeenth centuries, seeking to liberate itself by reason alone, the Enlightenment did not develop an adequate understanding of the perversity at the center of the human heart. Carl Lotus Becker, a historian from the University of Wisconsin early in the twentieth century, wrote a book entitled *The Heavenly City of the Eighteenth-Century Philosophers*. They displaced the creation and the Creator in favor of their own creativity. So doing, they laid the foundations for the centuries of warfare that followed.

Early in World War I, Austrian medics and chaplains charged with ministering to wounded soldiers began reporting back the horrific quality of the wounds they encountered. New artillery, designed empirically according to the scientific methods of the Enlightenment, had been created to leave their victims wounded beyond measure. If anything, these early incidents were relatively tame when compared to what followed. The V-rockets in England, the firebombing of civilians in Hamburg and Dresden, had their logical conclusion in Hiroshima and Nagasaki. More recently, as archives in what was the Soviet Union have been opened to historical research, the true scope of World War II in the region between Poland's original German border and the Ural Mountains has become evident. Six million Jews went into the ovens on the basis of race alone. With them, Stalin and associates systematically eliminated equal numbers of Eastern Europeans.

It might be argued, as it certainly should, that the warfare that has followed in the wake of the Enlightenment could be considered sufficient grounds to reexamine theologically some of its illusions about human enterprise. But instead, Western culture has pushed Enlightenment assumptions further in an attempt to eliminate the Law from personal standing. This, though disputable, is the purported second end of the Law.

This alleged end is not, like the Enlightenment, the product of a group of philosophers. It cannot be traced to an individual either. Rather, it is the product of a community of inquiry, sharing assumptions and end endeavoring, without clearly defined intentions, to free the individual from external restraints.

Similar to the Enlightenment, this way of thinking begins with a hard view of what can be known for certain. Only scientifically established facts that can be tested, measured, and independently repeated can be regarded as true beyond doubt. Thus "the truth," which outside of the Church sounds like an old-fashioned concept, is strictly limited to the sciences themselves.

This makes it impossible to use the term *truth* for anything that concerns human relationship. Such knowledge is participatory; it requires the involvement of the people concerned. It is therefore subjective, a matter of personal observation. As such, it reflects the historical experience of the individual as this person has attempted to deal with the circumstances and demands of life. In American parlance, it shows "where you're coming from" and therefore cannot claim any particular value for others.

This is the "fact/value distinction." The sciences have an exclusive claim on the truth. Everything else is a value—subjective, arbitrary, personal, shaped by one's own history. Simplistic, vague, and questionable as it is, this is the claimed end of the Law. Armed with this distinction, even a confirmand—caught in the throes of adolescence, just getting a hint of adult realities—upon hearing one of the commandments can quip, "That's just where you are coming from" and dismiss Moses altogether.

The combination of this simple but effective distinction with the language of rights makes it especially troublesome. In popular culture, desire creates an identity and this identify in turn can claim a right, an entitlement. Where Descartes said, "I think, therefore I am," the self-seeking self now says, "I desire, therefore I am." The old Adam becomes the only definitive ethical standard. Like Agricola's end of the Law, there is no real termination—denied entry through the ear, the Law is driven underground where it works out its consequences.

The impact registers most compelling in matters of marriage and the family. Marketers have detached sexual relations from their original context in marital relationships and made them an end in themselves, to be pursued by the individual through various products and personal relationships. Since this detachment took place, in the 1950s and 60s with the emergence of the mass media, the institution of marriage has been transformed. It is no longer a vocation or calling God has established to serve the neighbor and the earth. It is now a means to self-gratification and fulfillment in which couples that are so inclined contract with each other, as they desire, for an indefinite period. According to the Centers for Disease Control and Prevention, 40 percent of the children conceived in the United States are born out of wedlock.[16]

Once again, as in the Enlightenment, the Law has been reduced to a set of ideas or concepts created and emplaced by the community for its own purposes. The Law, by definition, can have no basis in nature. Neither can the requirements of Law be more provisionally arrived at, as Luther did, using the Decalogue to spell out what is essential to the workings of life itself. This is free-will theology run to its logical conclusion: there can be no givens; everything is an alternative or choice that the sovereign self selects, as though shopping.

To take just one example, surely it is possible without using philosophical arguments to arrive at the conclusion that human children, by the very demands of life itself, must necessarily be cared for and that the consequences of neglect will show themselves evidently in personal and public life. A child's cry leaves no alternatives—neither hunger nor dirty pants negotiate.

Gustaf Wingren used to tell a story about divorce law in the early history of the USSR. Marxism is also part of the legacy of the Enlightenment. So Lenin and the early leaders of the USSR made the standard, Enlightenment critique of marriage and put in place a law that made divorce available on demand. Within ten years, Wingren said, the Marxist-Leninists reconsidered and passed a much more conservative restriction of divorce. A decade was long enough for the leadership to recognize the disastrous impact unrestrained divorce laws were having on the children. The same impact can be discerned in contemporary

16 See www.cdc.gov for more facts on unmarried childbearing. This data was provided for 2015.

societies.[17] But where the Law has allegedly ended, where desire creates an entitlement, a similar correction is not available.

SEEKING ALTERNATIVES

Classical, confessional Lutheranism insists on the proper distinction of Law and Gospel. Christ is the end of the Law. He takes on the accusations of the Law as they sound in the conscience and silences them in the forgiveness of sins. With this, He sends His Spirit to work in the heart, creating a new, freedom-borne obedience that turns to the neighbor in joy and service. In the grip of the Gospel, believers do joyfully without the Law what the Law requires.

While Christ puts the Law to its terminus in the conscience, He at the same time establishes the significance of the Law. The Law can no longer make ultimate claims for itself—salvation belongs to Christ and to Him alone. But reduced to terms, kept in check, there are some things the Law can do very well. It can provide for a rudimentary form of order, restraining hearts bent on themselves. More than this, it has a genius for accusations. In fact, once it gets loose it keeps ascending into the conscience until it becomes a terror.

The Gospel is the proper calling of the Church. It is an alien word that comes from outside of human calculations and stands contrary to all expectation. Christ Jesus justifies sinners, raises the dead, and binds the strong man, chaining the devil. The Church exists to say this, over and over again, declaring it in Word and Sacrament.

Because the Church knows and proclaims the ultimate word, God has called it also to the declaration of the penultimate. So, Luther begins both the Small and Large Catechism with a down-to-earth and careful exposition of the Ten Commandments. He is not making philosophical, conceptual arguments about theory. Informed by the Gospel, informed also by what he has heard in the confessional and seen in the home and the street, he is spelling out the elemental requirements of creaturely life

17 Wingren told this story in one of his classes at the University of Toronto, Canada, in the winter of 1980.

in relation to the Creator—the first three commandments—and other creatures, the remaining seven. The wording of the Ten Commandments may be dated, reflecting other times and historical situations. (It is currently difficult for most people to locate a neighbor's ox or his ass.) But that said, there is compelling public evidence available to reason which demonstrates that we are not our own creators shopping amongst alternatives but live out our lives within the limits and conditions imposed by the fact that life is not our possession but arises out of a complex web of interdependence overseen by God, who shapes it through the neighbors, near and far.

The alternative to the decimation of public life is not far away. The Law/Gospel distinction is totally misunderstood when pastors claim that the Gospel takes them beyond the Law. Instead, God calls preachers—whom according to Ezekiel 34, He holds accountable for those entrusted to them—to the faithful proclamation of both Law and Gospel. This involves joining parents in the teaching of the Commandments around the family table or instructing adolescents, just beginning to learn all that God has given them, in the disciplines of public life. It further calls pastors to join parishioners in a continual clarification of what God both demands and gives.

THE PROBLEM OF FREEDOM TODAY AND THE THIRD USE OF THE LAW

Biblical and Theological Considerations

Stephen Hultgren

Recent years have seen considerable interest in the topic of the third use of the Law. While I do not pretend to have surveyed every recent publication on the topic, one can quickly see that the interest spans biblical,[1] church-historical,[2] historical-theological,[3] as well as doctrinal and pastoral dimensions.[4] While multiple reasons may account for this interest, one factor is the sense among some Lutheran theologians that construals of Law and Gospel inherited from the middle and latter half of the twentieth century have left the Lutheran churches of the West vulnerable to assaults on doctrinal authority and Christian ethical teaching.[5] I write this contribution out of the same concern. The specific context in which

---

1 See, e.g., the essays in Charles A. Gieschen, ed., *The Law in Holy Scripture: Essays from the Concordia Theological Seminary Symposium on Exegetical Theology* (St. Louis: Concordia Publishing House, 2004).

2 See Scott R. Murray, *Law, Life, and the Living God: The Third Use of the Law in Modern American Lutheranism* (St. Louis: Concordia Publishing House, 2002).

3 See the study of the Second Antinomian Controversy leading up to the Formula of Concord: Matthias Richter, *Gesetz und Heil: Eine Untersuchung zur Vorgeschichte und zum Verlauf des sogenannten Zweiten Antinomistischen Streits* (Göttingen: Vandenhoeck & Ruprecht, 1996).

4 The July/October 2005 issue of the *Concordia Theological Quarterly* (vol. 69:3–4) is dedicated to the topic of the third use of the Law.

5 Gieschen, *Law*, 13–14; Murray, *Law*, passim. For a succinct diagnosis of the problem, see David S. Yeago, "Gnosticism, Antinomianism, and Reformation Theology: Reflections on the Costs of a Construal," *Pro Ecclesia* 2 (1993): 37–49.

I wish to address the question of the third use of the Law is the *crisis of freedom* in the West, which I will take up at the end of the essay.

It will be my contention that when we reflect on Law, freedom, and sin from a biblical-theological perspective, a third use of the Law is, among the options available to Lutherans, the most adequate biblical teaching on the nature of Christian freedom and obedience. Moreover, when understood properly, this teaching can be a great gift to men and women today. After bringing to the surface some problems that Article VI of the Formula of Concord presents, we shall review the major issues of debate in the Reformation period that led up to the article, as well as issues arising from the discussion of the third use of the Law in the modern period. We shall then turn to biblical-theological reflections on Law, freedom, and sin. From there we turn to the question of evangelical freedom, the third use of the Law, and New Testament *parenesis*. We conclude with thoughts on the Lutheran witness in the midst of the crisis of freedom today.

PROBLEMS PRESENTED BY ARTICLE VI OF THE FORMULA OF CONCORD

Article VI of the Formula of Concord affirms a third use of the Law distinguishable from the first and second uses. That affirmation, however, does not come without certain ambiguities. Others have noted them,[6] and the ambiguities have led some scholars to conclude that the Formula does not in fact teach a third use of the Law distinguishable from the first and second uses.[7] The ambiguities become evident when

---

6 E.g., Werner Elert, *Law and Gospel*, trans. E. H. Schroeder, (Philadelphia: Fortress Press, 1967), 41–42; Hans Philipp Meyer, "Normen christlichen Handelns? Zum Problem des tertius usus legis," in *Widerspruch, Dialog und Einigung: Studien zur Konkordienformel der Lutherischen Reformation*, ed. W. Lohff and L. W. Spitz (Stuttgart: Calwer, 1977), 223–47, here 230–31; Richter, *Gesetz und Heil*, 345–51; cf. also Ragnar Bring, "Gesetz und Evangelium und der dritte Gebrauch des Gesetzes in der lutherischen Theologie," *Zur Theologie Luthers: Aus der Arbeit der Luther-Agricola Gesellschaft in Finnland* (Helsinki: Akateeminen kirjakauppa, 1943), 43–97, here 83–87.

7 That is, Article VI does not know of a third use of the Law for the *reborn* that differs from the first or second uses. Already some sixteenth-century Lutherans argued this. See Lauri Haikola, *Usus Legis*, 2nd edition (Helsinki: Luther-Agricola-Gesellschaft, 1981), 32, 76. With respect to the Formula, see Bring, "Gesetz und Evangelium," esp. 54, 88–89, 90 n. 7, 91; Werner Elert, "The Third Use of the Law," *The Lutheran World Review* 1:3 (1949): 38–48,

one asks *why* the Law needs to be preached to the justified. On the one hand, the preaching of the Law is necessary because the old Adam still clings to the justified.[8] The justified are not totally reborn, and so the old Adam must still (like a stubborn donkey) be taught, admonished, warned, threatened, coerced, and even punished by the Law.[9] The Law also continues to function as a mirror for Christians, reminding them that they remain imperfect and impure in this life.[10] Here we recognize the first and second uses of the Law. On the other hand, the Law is necessary for the justified when they have been reborn through the Spirit because it depicts for them the will of God; it is the rule by which they are to order their lives. Moreover, the justified need the Law so that they do not invent their own form of obedience apart from God's Word or commandments.[11] In these latter functions, it seems, we have a genuinely third use of the Law, giving guidance to the reborn specifically. The different reasons for preaching the Law to the justified given here do not have to be mutually exclusive. They make good sense together. So far, so good.

The ambiguities become evident when one looks more deeply into the question of how the justified, insofar as they are reborn (*quatenus renati*), relate to the Law. We should be clear, first of all, that the dispute was not over whether the Law should be preached to the justified—even opponents of the third use of the Law agreed that the Law must be preached to the justified insofar as they remain sinners.[12] The point in

---

here 38–39: Article VI "knows nothing of a purely informative function of the Law"; cf. Elert, *Law and Gospel*, 42–43; William H. Lazareth, in his introduction to Paul Althaus, *The Divine Command*, trans. F. Sherman (Philadelphia: Fortress Press, 1966), vii; Lazareth, *Christians in Society: Luther, the Bible, and Social Ethics* (Minneapolis: Fortress Press, 2001), 243; Meyer, "Normen christlichen Handelns?" 227–31; Oswald Bayer, "Gesetz und Evangelium," *Leibliches Wort: Reformation und Neuzeit im Konflikt* (Tübingen: J. C. B. Mohr [Paul Siebeck], 1992), 54–55.

8 FC SD VI 7–8, 18–19, 23–24; cf. FC Ep VI 4. Book of Concord quotations in this chapter are from Kolb-Wengert.

9 FC SD VI 9, 12, 19, 24; cf. FC Ep VI 4, 7.

10 FC SD VI 21.

11 FC SD VI 1, 3, 4, 20.

12 Meyer, "Normen christlichen Handelns?" 227, 228. After the resolution of the first antinomian controversy, it was not in dispute that the Law should be preached in the Church (FC

dispute was whether the Law should be preached to the justified insofar as they are reborn ("new persons" in Christ). The Formula states that the justified, insofar as they are reborn, actually do not need the Law, or to be more exact, *should* not need the *coercion* of the Law. They perform works (better: bring forth fruit) of the Spirit freely and spontaneously, with a merry spirit and a willing heart. They do so "according to the unchanging will of God, as comprehended in the Law," but without the coercion of the Law,[13] for, being reborn in the inner person, they delight in the Law, rather than being coerced by it.[14] They act according to what Paul calls the "Law of my mind" (Romans 7:23)[15] and the "Law of Christ" (Galatians 6:2).[16] As such, they are not actually under the Law but under grace.[17]

But the Formula is not able to maintain this view consistently. The Formula distinguishes between the justified as old Adam, who needs to be compelled by the Law, and the justified as reborn (*quatenus renatus*), who does not need to be compelled. The Formula appeals to the Pauline anthropological distinction between the old person and the renewed person, which also becomes a distinction between the "flesh" (*caro=sarx*) and the "inner person" (*homo interior=ho esō anthrōpos*). But the distinction is not completely clean. The Formula holds that renewal in this life involves only what Paul calls the "inner person." And yet even the renewal of the inner person is incomplete, because it continues to be opposed by the flesh.[18] And just here is the problem: what the article in one place seems to presuppose in theory—that the justified inhabit a

V 24). The only question was for which purpose(s) it should be preached.

13 FC SD VI 17, 18, 23; FC Ep VI 7.

14 FC SD VI 5, 18, 23.

15 Unless otherwise noted, Scripture translation is the author's.

16 FC SD VI 17; cf. FC Ep VI 6.

17 FC SD VI 17, 23; cf. FC Ep VI 6.

18 FC SD VI 5–8, 18, 23–24. The point is especially clear in FC Ep VI 4: Even if the justified are reborn and "renewed in the spirit of their minds" in this world, that renewal is not perfect. The old Adam still resides in *all* the powers of the reborn. Note that in SD VI 5 the inner person (*interior homo*) of the reborn does not need to be coerced by the Law, for he delights in it; yet according to VI 7 the old Adam continues to hang on to the inner powers (*interioribus viribus*) of the reborn.

realm of freedom in which they have no need for the Law and yet live according to the Law—in another place it denies in reality: the justified, even *quatenus renati*, ultimately still need the *prodding* of the Law, because even the "inner person" is corrupted by the old Adam. The article, in effect, wants to have it both ways: the justified, insofar as they are reborn, do nothing from the coercion of the Law; they act freely according to the Law, but without the Law's coercion. At the same time, because the old Adam continues to "hang" on to the justified until the end, even the inner person continues to struggle against the flesh, and so the justified as a whole, concrete person still needs the coercion of the Law.[19] A further tension appears when in one place the Formula confidently declares that the justified as reborn do the will of God freely, in the power of the Spirit, without the coercion of the Law, while in another place it declares that believers require the Law so that they do not "establish their own service to God on the basis of their own choice, without God's Word or command," under the "appearance of God's Spirit."[20] The latter statement appears to be a clear affirmation of a third use of the Law, but it stands in tension with the earlier declared confidence in the power of the Spirit alone, without the coercion of the Law, to lead the Christian in doing the will of God.

The root of the problem lies in how the article views the state of the justified (reborn), as is illustrated by comparing the following two citations. From the perspective that the justified, insofar as they are reborn, act freely and spontaneously by the power of the Holy Spirit, the article holds that,

> if the faithful and elect children of God were perfectly renewed through the indwelling Spirit in this life, so that

19 FC SD VI 18–19. The problem can already be seen when one compares the opening of Article VI in the Epitome (VI 1) with the opening in the Solid Declaration (VI 1–3). The Epitome states that the third use of the Law is necessary to give the reborn a rule (third use), for the reason that "the flesh still clings to them," while the Solid Declaration makes no mention of the flesh in this connection, but presupposes the freedom of the reborn. Meyer, "Normen," 227 n. 32, regards the language in the Epitome to be a secondary amendment, removing an originally more Melanchthonian formulation (cf. also 228).

20 Cf. FC SD VI 17, 23 with VI 20.

> in their nature and all their powers they were completely free from sin, they would need no law and therefore no prodding.[21]

But the faithful have *not* been so (perfectly) renewed. Only in the resurrection will the justified reach such perfection; then they

> will need neither the proclamation of the law nor its threats and punishment, just as they will no longer need the gospel, for both belong to this imperfect life. Instead, just as they will see God face-to-face, so they will perform the will of God by the power of the indwelling Spirit of God spontaneously, without coercion, unhindered, perfectly and completely, with sheer joy, and they will delight in his will eternally.[22]

At heart, clearly, is an anthropological problem. The article speaks of the "reborn" in two different ways: abstractly (or theoretically), as inhabiting a realm of freedom in which the justified can and do live according to the Law, but without the coercion of the Law; and concretely (or practically), as not fully reborn, not even in the inner person, still under the power of the flesh, and therefore needing the coercion of the Law until the Last Day.[23] Since the article, following Luther, reads Romans 7 as depicting the situation of the Christian, the article must apply to the Christian the paradoxical situation in which the "I" is able, on the one hand, to identify an inner "I" that delights in the Law (Romans 7:22), and yet, on the other hand, must acknowledge that it (the "I") in its totality is fleshly, "sold under sin" (7:14).[24] From here it is easy to see why many scholars have denied that the Formula actually teaches a truly *third* use of the Law for the reborn. A fundamental question for us, then, is this: Do the justified inhabit a realm of freedom in which they can obey the

---

21 FC SD VI 6.

22 FC SD VI 24–25.

23 Cf. Richter, *Gesetz und Heil*, 345–46.

24 On this aspect of Romans 7, see Paul Althaus, *Paulus und Luther über den Menschen: Ein Vergleich* (Gütersloh: Gerd Mohn, 1963), 63–64.

Law freely, without coercion, or not? Can there be a truly third use of the Law different from the first and second uses? The anthropological presuppositions of the article will need to be examined.[25]

The Formula's discussion of Law and freedom raises another question. The Formula acknowledges that at times Scripture (even Paul) speaks in terms of "Law" (*nomos*) for the justified. At the same time, the Formula wishes to avoid the idea that the justified, insofar as they are reborn, are *compelled* by the Law; for, as Paul says, to be under grace is to be no longer under the Law (Romans 6:14), and to live by the Spirit is to be free from the Law.[26] Thus to live by the "Law of Christ" is actually *not* to live by (under) Law.[27] At the same time, the article affirms that the Holy Spirit uses the Law to teach the justified what is pleasing to God![28] The Law for the justified is the "unchanging will of God, according to which human beings are to conduct themselves in this life"; such works that are done in accordance with this Law are works of the Holy Spirit, not (properly speaking) coerced works of the Law.[29] All of this raises the question: How does (or can) one reconcile the freedom and spontaneity of life in the Spirit with the concept of a Law for the justified, which ought to be noncoercive? This, indeed, is how the Formula itself frames the debate.[30]

---

25 In particular, is the article correct to adduce Romans 7 as evidence that the justified are opposed by the flesh in such a way as to preclude a free obedience to the Law? It is obvious that underlying the article's ambiguities regarding the relationship between the justified and the Law lies Luther's view of the Christian as *simul iustus et peccator* (supported by his reading of Romans 7–8). Wilfried Joest, *Gesetz und Freiheit: Das Problem des tertius usus legis bei Luther und die neutestamentliche Parainese* (Göttingen: Vandenhoeck & Ruprecht, 1968), demonstrates the complexity of the matter already in Luther. For Luther, the justified lives with both an inner freedom in the Gospel and a need for the Law to conform the flesh to the inner man. See especially pp. 57, 76–77, 99–109. Luther's *simul* was at the center of the debates on freedom and Law in the period between Luther and the Formula. More on this below.

26 FC SD VI 17. Although the Formula does not cite it, one thinks of Galatians 5:18 here.

27 FC SD VI 17, 23.

28 FC SD VI 12.

29 FC SD VI 15–17; cf. FC Ep VI 5–7.

30 SD VI 2–3. See Charles P. Arand, Robert Kolb, and James A. Nestingen, *The Lutheran Confessions: History and Theology of the Book of Concord* (Minneapolis: Fortress Press, 2012), 198–99, on Article VI as a compromise position between the views of Melanchthon and Musculus (Law vs. spontaneity in the Spirit).

Finally, a last question is worth raising. According to the Formula, perfect renewal (which remains an exclusively eschatological reality) obviates the need for a (prodding) Law. Yet, as the Formula recognizes, the first human being was not without Law before the fall.[31] If, before the fall, the first humans lived in a state of (perfect) righteousness, why did they need a Law?[32]

Our review of Article VI has raised a number of questions that need to be discussed in any fresh, biblical examination of the third use of the Law. Below we will make our questions more precise. For the moment, however, we note that if our ultimate aim is to ask whether a third use of the Law is faithful to *Scripture*,[33] then that means asking whether the anthropological presuppositions for a truly third use of the Law are scriptural and whether the concept of a Law that freely (not coercively) guides the justified is scripturally justifiable.

ISSUES ARISING IN THE REFORMATION ERA

Article VI is a compromise statement, reflecting the intense debates of the so-called second antinomian controversy leading up to the Formula of Concord, which in large part explains its ambiguities. As already indicated, the Formula itself, in the introduction to Article VI, summarizes the main point of debate as being over the question whether the reborn do good works spontaneously and solely by the prompting of the Holy Spirit, free from the coercion of the Law, or whether the reborn, although being motivated by the Holy Spirit and acting freely, nonetheless serve God according to His written Law and Word, which the Holy Spirit Himself uses and which is a rule and guide for living a godly life according to God's eternal and unchanging will. At this point, it will be helpful

31 FC SD VI 5; cf. FC Ep VI 2 (the first parents).

32 The Formula makes an interesting exegetical move here. First Timothy 1:9 states that the Law is not laid down for the righteous, but for the unrighteous. The Formula rejects an interpretation of this verse that would draw from it the conclusion that the righteous have no need of a Law; the fact that the first human being had a Law immediately after his creation shows that Law is given for the righteous in some sense (FC SD VI 5).

33 To my mind, this question is more important than whether a third use of the Law is faithful to *Luther*. The debate has largely centered on the latter question.

to review some of the issues in the debates leading up to the Formula. When one reviews those debates, three areas in particular can be seen to have called forth sharp division—namely, in the understanding of the nature of Law, in the meaning of "necessity," and in anthropology.[34]

The issues that Article VI discusses can be traced back in large measure to the debates that erupted over Georg Major's proposal that good works are necessary for salvation (or "blessedness"; *Seligkeit*).[35] In response to this proposal, one view was that, while within the doctrine of justification good works cannot be said to be necessary for salvation (contra Major), it was acceptable nonetheless to hold that theoretically, within the framework of the doctrine of the Law, good works are necessary for salvation.[36] In other words, one can speak of the righteousness of the Law *abstractly*: if there were no sin, as in the antelapsarian state, humans could fulfill the Law, and such fulfillment of the Law would lead to righteousness and eternal life.[37] Sin, of course, prevents anyone from obeying the Law perfectly so as to obtain such life. That is why such talk about the necessity of the Law for salvation must always remain abstract.

An opposing view rejected speculation about the Law in the abstract and argued that we can only know about the Law in the concrete, postlapsarian situation.[38] The view that good works are necessary for salvation within the doctrine of the Law is not scriptural.[39] We know only of a Law that reveals sin, makes demands, terrifies, accuses sinners, and

---

34 I rely here on the extensive and impressive study of the historical documents in Richter, *Gesetz und Heil*.

35 Ibid., 94–169; Haikola, *Usus Legis*, 13–18. The definition of *Seligkeit* in these debates was imprecise. See Kolb-Wengert, *The Book of Concord*, 578 n. 145.

36 The Eisenach Synod (1556) affirmed such a view, although it warned about using such language, since it is open to confusion. See Richter, ibid., 145–51. Some wanted to distinguish between speaking of the necessity of good works for salvation in the doctrine of the Law (permitted) from speaking about the necessity of good works in the preaching of the Law (to be avoided). Ibid., 164–65.

37 Ibid. See esp. on M. Chemnitz (p. 105), M. Flacius (pp. 102, 156, 162–69, 323), and J. Wigand (pp. 162–69, 338). See also pp. 110, 126, 135, 144, 148, 151.

38 See esp. ibid., 134–35, 151–57 (on N. von Amsdorf). See further pp. 127, 193.

39 Ibid., 149, 154, 182 n. 65 (the notion of salvation "before the fall" is not scriptural), 184–85, 193.

condemns them to death;[40] we do not know of a Law that could be fulfilled by sinners, even theoretically. Any talk of a necessary fulfillment of the Law for salvation, even in the abstract, can lead only to a false doctrine of merit or works-righteousness and/or put the doctrine of justification into doubt.[41] It cannot be said that the Law "promises" life if the Law makes the promise of life dependent on obedience.[42] Moreover, the Law is fulfilled by Christ and through our faith in Him, not by our works.[43] God owes us no reward for our works, for they are our duty (Luke 17:7–10).[44]

It is apparent that the different sides in the debate worked from very different conceptions of Law. For those who upheld the necessity of the Law for salvation within the doctrine of the Law, the Law represented God's eternal order, His unchanging will for humans, which humans are obligated to obey at all times. The Law is first written in the hearts of humans and then also revealed in biblical Law.[45] Justification in Christ brings freedom from the condemnation of the Law, but it does not remove from the justified the obligation to obey God's unchanging will as contained in the Law.[46] Those who opposed this view saw the Law as God's instrument to coerce and to accuse.[47] The Law always accuses us, even the justified, as sinners. The Law applies only to the old Adam.[48] A so-called third use of the Law would only really be coercion and would delude the justified into trying to obtain through the Law the righteousness that is theirs already and only through faith in Christ.[49]

In addition to different conceptions of Law, there were different conceptions of "necessity." The Augsburg Confession (VI 1) had, of course,

---

40 Ibid., 155–57. See further pp. 173, 176–83.

41 Ibid., 154, 157, 158. See further pp. 181, 183, 228–29, 287–88.

42 Ibid., 156, 194.

43 Ibid., 139, 155–56, 159–60, 179–80.

44 Ibid., 188.

45 Ibid., 166, 168. See also pp. 200, 241–42, 248–49, 341.

46 Ibid., 241, 245.

47 Ibid., 225, 309.

48 E.g., ibid., 309.

49 Ibid., 284.

already declared that faith ought (is obligated to: *soll*; *debeat*) or even must (*musse*) bring forth good works (cf. XII 6: *debent*; XX 27: *sollen und mussen*; *necesse sit*).[50] In the Majoristic dispute, it was recognized that one can and must distinguish between saying that works are necessary in the sense that they are the cause of justification and saying that they are necessary in the sense that they are the effect of justification,[51] a distinction that the Formula of Concord also makes.[52] There were, however, further disagreements. As we saw, those who opposed a third use of the Law for the justified tended to view the Law as coercive. Thus they tended to equate the concept of the necessity of the Law with coercion. Justification was understood to be liberation from the coercion, and hence the necessity, of the Law. On this view of things, the justified act spontaneously and freely. Good works flow forth from the justified spontaneously in the power of the Holy Spirit. Necessity and freedom are mutually exclusive. Just as a tree does not need a law to bring forth good fruit, so the justified do not need the Law to bring forth good works.[53]

Those who argued in favor of a third use of the Law denied that a doctrine of the necessity of the Law implied coercion or a denial of freedom. For them, necessity referred to the divine order and the obligation (*debitum*) to obey it to which humans are bound.[54] Necessity in the sense of obligation to obey had been important in the debate from the very beginning.[55] (And it should be noted that Article IV of the Formula recognizes divine order and the human obligation to obey it, rather than coercion, as the proper sense of necessity.)[56] Obedience to the divine Law does not by any means cancel freedom. For example, in

---

50 Leif Grane, *The Augsburg Confession: A Commentary*, trans. J. H. Rasmussen (Minneapolis: Augsburg, 1987), 83, sees here the clear influence of Melanchthon over against Luther, who resisted such language. See also Wilhelm Maurer, *Historical Commentary on the Augsburg Confession*, trans. H. G. Anderson (Philadelphia: Fortress Press, 1986), 291, 370–71.

51 Richter, *Gesetz und Heil*, 99–117. See also p. 134.

52 FC SD IV 14–29; cf. FC Ep IV 7–9.

53 Richter, *Gesetz und Heil*, 227–32 (on A. Musculus).

54 Ibid., 126 (on Melanchthon), 235–50, esp. 241–42, 244–46 (on A. Praetorius), 337.

55 According to Richter (ibid., 96 and n. 14), Major himself had argued that good works are necessary, not in the sense of gaining merit, but in the sense of obligation to obey.

56 FC SD IV 16.

an important insight, Flacius argued that the first humans (before the fall) had God's Law and were obligated to obey it and yet were free, in a threefold freedom: free from committing sin, free from the punishment of sin, free from the necessity (compulsion) of acting (i.e., with a sound, free will, they acted in conformity to God's Law).[57] The Holy Spirit and the Law are not opposed to each other in the sense of freedom opposed to coercion. Rather, the Holy Spirit Himself uses the Law to teach and to guide the justified.[58] Indeed, it may be a case of sheer enthusiasm to argue that Christ or the Holy Spirit would work apart from the Word of God (the Law).[59]

Finally, and closely connected to the debates over necessity and freedom, different anthropologies were at work. The anthropological ambiguities in Article VI noted at the outset now become readily comprehensible. All sides recognized the importance of the Pauline distinction between the old person (Adam) and the new person in Christ. However, very different consequences were drawn from the distinction. Those who opposed a third use of the Law tended to argue either that the justified, living in the freedom of the Holy Spirit, had no need of the Law[60] or that, at most, the justified needed the Law only to the extent that the old Adam still remained.[61] The justified *quatenus renati* had no need of the Law. They had come into a new relationship to the Law, without the compulsion and necessity of the Law.[62] Faith, not the Law, is the font of good works.[63] Some argued that the justified lived by a new law—namely, the law of Christ or the law of the Holy Spirit.[64] That view could take the form that it was Christ or the Spirit Himself who performed the good

---

57 Richter, *Gesetz und Heil*, 166 n. 266; cf. Lauri Haikola, *Gesetz und Evangelium bei Matthias Flacius Illyricus* (Lund: Gleerup, 1952), 62, 80, 330.

58 Richter, *Gesetz und Heil*, 340, 342 (J. Wigand).

59 Ibid., 329 (J. Mörlin).

60 E.g., ibid., 226, 314.

61 Ibid., 270, 271, 313–14. Others argued that remnants of sin in the old Adam were not to be resisted with the Law (of Moses) but with the Law of the indwelling Christ or the Holy Spirit (ibid., 226, 284).

62 Ibid., 231, 283.

63 Ibid., 314.

64 Ibid., 233–34, 262, 289, 314, 316.

works in the justified, leaving no place for the Law[65] or even for action or cooperation on the part of the justified.[66] Some (citing Luther) argued that the justified were so intimately united with Christ, even becoming one person with Him, that the justified person, in and with Christ, became "Lord of the Law" and as such was above Law.[67]

Those who favored a third use of the Law viewed the relationship between the old Adam and the new person in Christ differently. The justified, though united with Christ, remains a subject of action.[68] To argue that the justified become united with Christ, even one person with Him, in such a way as to rise above the Law, is to approach blasphemy.[69] Since the Law is God's unchanging and eternal will, a person will always have a relationship to the Law, regardless of the state in which he or she is found. As we shall see, these disagreements over anthropology had deep roots in Luther's theology and in the reception of it.

ISSUES ARISING IN THE MODERN LAW-GOSPEL DEBATE

As an entrée to issues in the modern period, we begin with Gerhard Forde's helpful historical study of the development of the modern Law-Gospel debate.[70] Forde finds the genesis of the modern debate in disputes between (the heritage of) Lutheran Orthodoxy and the theology of *Heilsgeschichte*, the latter particularly as represented in the theology of J. C. K. von Hofmann (1810–77), over the doctrine of atonement and the place of the Law in it. Forde shows that the modern Law-Gospel debate must be understood as resulting from Hofmann's attack on the Orthodox doctrine of vicarious satisfaction. Orthodoxy worked with a formal and abstract understanding of God's righteousness, the Law, and Christ's

65 Ibid., 182, 232, 264, 266, 267 (Christ and the Law cannot exist together in the conscience).

66 Ibid., 229, 232–33. Cf. p. 329.

67 Ibid., 231, 233, 270, 280–81. Cf. 298, 304, 309–15 (M. Neander). See 267 n. 92 for appeal to Luther's statement about the Christian (with Christ) being lord of the Law.

68 E.g., ibid., 243 (*cooperatio*), 340 (A. Praetorius, J. Wigand).

69 Ibid., 324; and in reference to M. Neander's claim that, because the justified are united with Christ, they have no need even for prayer! (Ibid., 315.)

70 Gerhard O. Forde, *The Law-Gospel Debate: An Interpretation of Its Historical Development* (Minneapolis: Augsburg, 1969).

atonement. To be righteous before God (justified) requires perfect conformity to the will of God. The Law is (theoretically) the way to salvation and (eternal) life, but sin blocks the way to life through the Law; that way is no longer open to humans. Instead they stand guilty before God, under God's wrath, and are subject to His just punishment. Yet the demands of the Law must still be satisfied. Christ's atoning death takes care of this situation in that He both bears the punishment of sin and satisfies God's requirement of perfect obedience. This whole complex of ideas functions as a timeless order of things, within which Law, atonement, justification, and so on, each has its fixed position.[71]

Hofmann found the Orthodox doctrine to be an abstract, conceptual scheme that was too dependent on human ideas about justice. He thought that a less juridical and more historical approach was needed to grasp what Christ had done, one that took account of the historical forces that led to Christ's death.[72] His understanding of atonement was accordingly established on the basis of an elaborate history of salvation (*Heilsgeschichte*). Hofmann rejected an interpretation of Christ's death as a vicarious punishment or satisfaction.[73] Instead of that, Christ's death was part of the realization of God's will to love humanity in Christ and to reestablish His relationship with humanity.[74] Humanity fell into sin when it was deceived by Satan to turn away from God.[75] As a result of this fall away from God, humanity came under God's wrath.[76] But God's will to love mankind, to be in communion with humans, persisted. God's love came to full realization in Christ. In His life and death, Christ took upon Himself all the forces of evil in the world, evil that resulted from God's wrath.[77] In His resurrection, Jesus won the victory over Satan, and humanity was freed from its entrapment by Satan. In Christ, God regains

---

71 Ibid., 3–11.

72 Ibid., 36–39, 44, 46, 65.

73 Ibid., 38, 55–56. Cf. pp. 40–44.

74 For the following, see especially the helpful summary in ibid., 44–45 (cf. p. 109).

75 Ibid., 25–26.

76 Ibid., 44, 47.

77 Ibid., 65–66.

humanity as the object of His love. Thus, Christ's death and resurrection marks the beginning of a new stage of humanity, determined no longer by sin but by the righteousness of the Son of God.[78]

What is most important for our purposes is the consequences of Hofmann's approach for the place of the Law. In Hofmann's scheme, the Law is not the eternal order that forms the framework for atonement along juridical lines.[79] Rather, the Law is an interim measure. It is only a part—and a temporary one at that—of God's overall plan to realize His love for humanity. In a certain sense, the Law is only a consequence of humanity's fall into sin and of God's wrath.[80] God's wrath is not directed at human failure objectively to live up to God's standard as revealed in the Law. Rather, His wrath was due to the fact that humanity has turned away from Him.[81] God gave the Law as part of His larger plan of reunion. The Law served to single out Israel as God's people and to prefigure the end. But the Law itself could not accomplish the reunion of God and humanity. Therefore the Law needed to be superseded in history, through Christ. Christ brings a new stage in human history, characterized essentially by freedom from the Law in the Spirit.[82]

Forde goes on to show that debates over Law and Gospel in the later nineteenth and twentieth centuries were definitively shaped by the fundamental alternatives established by Orthodoxy and *Heilsgeschichte*:[83] Is the basis of atonement God's love or wrath? Is Law to be understood as an eternal order essential to God's righteousness and demanding human obedience or as a temporary dispensation? Does Law remain essential for a proper understanding of Gospel, or does the Gospel represent a new "stage" that leaves Law behind for good?

---

78 Ibid., 29, 39, 44, 47.

79 Ibid., 30–32.

80 Ibid., 32: Forde quotes Hofmann thus: "God's wrath against sin placed Israel under the Law of commandments and prohibitions." Cf. p. 65.

81 Ibid., 26.

82 Ibid., 29, 31–32.

83 Ibid., 69, 78, 81–134.

We must now consider a few other dominant voices in the twentieth-century debate in order to gather from them the issues that must be considered in any fresh look at our question. We take as our starting point Karl Barth's essay on "Gospel and Law."[84]

Barth argued that the Lutheran order Law-Gospel was wrong as an overall conception. The primary reason is that, by placing Law before Gospel, the Lutheran order allows one to define Law without respect to the Gospel, with the danger that it is no longer God's Law that is in view.[85] Since the Gospel is the fulfillment of the Law, one must understand the Gospel before one can understand or define the Law. Gospel and Law are united as the one Word of God, and the content of both is grace. The fact that God addresses us at all, even in the Law (indeed, even in judging us through the Law, which leads to salvation), is grace.[86]

For Barth, we must speak of the Gospel first because God's grace *is* Christ, the incarnate Word of God. Christ saves us by becoming our representative in obeying God. He lives out for us the life of faith and obedience that is the path to salvation and so accepts on our behalf God's offer of grace in the Law, which humanity refused. In defining Law, we must begin with the Gospel; for it is Christ and the apostolic Gospel that define for us what the Law is, in the Ten Commandments, in the Sermon on the Mount, and in the apostolic parenesis. The message of grace in the Law, as understood through the Gospel, is "you *shall* be perfect" (not "you must be perfect") (Matthew 5:48); that is, it is a promise

---

84 Karl Barth, "Gospel and Law," in *Community, State, and Church: Three Essays*, ed. W. Herberg (Garden City, NY: Doubleday & Co., 1960), 71–100. German original: *Evangelium und Gesetz* (Munich: Chr. Kaiser, 1935). Citations follow the English translation.

85 In historical context, Barth was concerned that Lutheran theology allowed "Law" to be defined nonscripturally; that is, other than by divine revelation, the consequence of which is that Law could be defined by history, reason, or the laws of a people (ibid., 91). Law is to be defined only by Christ and the apostolic witness (pp. 76–84). Against the threat of National Socialism and "German Christianity," the Barmen Declaration, under the strong influence of Barth, declared that "Jesus Christ, as he is testified to us in the Holy Scripture, is the one Word of God, whom we are to hear, whom we are to trust and obey in life and in death." In a 1939 letter, Barth states that Lutheran Law-Gospel theology served to confirm German paganism ideologically, allowing for the rise of Hitler. Karl Barth, *Eine Schweizer Stimme (1938–1945)* (Zurich: Evangelischer Verlag, 1945), 113.

86 Ibid., 71–73.

that through Christ we will become who we are meant to be in faith and action.[87] By faith, we participate in Jesus' humanity—that is, in His life of obedience leading to salvation. Our justification lies in such participation, the goal of which is our sanctification. Thus, as Barth famously put it, "Law is nothing else than the necessary *form of the Gospel*, whose content is grace."[88] God's grace makes at one and the same time both a claim and a demand on us.[89]

Barth's essay provoked strong responses from Lutheran theologians, including Werner Elert.[90] Elert vigorously rejected Barth's attempt to unite Gospel and Law. For Elert, Law and Gospel stand in "substantive opposition" to each other and can never speak together. When one speaks, the other must be silent.[91] To counter Barth's emphasis on the unity of Gospel and Law in the one Word of God Christ, Elert argued that Law and Gospel are two different words of God; the Law must be given its due as a Word of God apart from Christ.[92] Against Barth, it cannot be said that God's Word is always grace; the scriptural witness is that the Law condemns and punishes, so that Barth's schema unjustifiably renders the Law impotent.[93] In the post-fall situation, the Law always and only accuses.[94]

The Gospel does not reestablish the Law. Christ in His Gospel ministry did not seek to make sinners righteous through the Law. Rather He forgave sinners in a way that opposed the Law's principle of retribution. To be sure, in Christ Law and Gospel converge in a certain sense. Jesus' encounter with people condemned them, for those who accepted Him saw the distance that separated them from Him and that showed them

---

87 Ibid., 73–78, 81, 98.

88 Ibid., 80.

89 Ibid., 79, 81–84.

90 Werner Elert, *Law and Gospel* (see n. 6). German original in Elert, *Zwischen Gnade und Ungnade: Abwandlungen des Themas Gesetz und Evangelium* (Munich: Evangelischer Presseverband für Bayern, 1948), 132–69. Citations follow the English translation.

91 Ibid., 1, 5, 48.

92 Ibid., 4.

93 Ibid., 5–6.

94 Ibid., 7–13.

to be sinners. But the outcome of this "condemnation," at least for those who (unlike the self-righteous) accept the truth that they are sinners, was not punishment but forgiveness. Christ acts against the Law of retribution. Something similar happens in Christ's innocent death under the Law and His resurrection. Jesus' death fulfills the Law of retribution, but at the same time He forgives those who kill Him. Christ fulfills the Law but also acts against it. Law and Gospel do, in a sense, converge in the cross, but they are not finally united. If that were so, then the death of Christ would have to be God's last word. But the resurrection is God's last word. Only the resurrection shows that God has substituted a new order of forgiveness (Gospel) for the old order of a Law of retribution.[95] At this point, only the Gospel sounds. The Law is silenced.[96]

Law and Gospel, then, cannot be united, nor can one say that "judgment is grace." The old Adam is judged, but a new person is created by grace. The new person lives under grace, not under Law. And the new person has no need of the Law to guide his or her life. Christ becomes the new standard of life, and the Christian does not need to be told not to sin. Law is always coercive, and it works by way of threat and reward. But the Christian lives in the freedom of the Spirit. Law and Spirit are opposed just as Law and Gospel are opposed. The Law has no third use in constructing the life of the new person. Even for the Christian, the Law always accuses and can do no other. Only in that accusing sense could one speak of a third use of the Law after the Gospel. There can be no purely *informative* use of the Law.[97]

Despite Elert's vigorous rejection of a third use of the Law and of Barth's attempt to unite Law and Gospel, Paul Althaus took up the question "whether the traditional doctrine of the *tertius usus* may not contain an element of truth" and the question whether Barth might not have seen something true in the point that the Gospel entails certain

95 Ibid., 17

96 Ibid., 16–30. Cf. p. 48.

97 Ibid., 31–43.

imperatives.[98] Althaus agreed with Elert's view that Law and Gospel are opposed to each other, and that one cannot speak of a third use of the Law. But Althaus wanted to make room for a "Gospel imperative" in Christian ethics. Noting that much of the New Testament seems to prefer the term "commandments" or "the will of God" to "Law," Althaus proposed that the New Testament writings make a conscious distinction between "God's eternal will" and "Law" and that such a distinction should also shape our terminology. "Law" is only "one limited and temporary form of this eternal will" of God. We should speak of the Gospel imperative as "divine command" or as "God's will" for humans rather than as "Law." The influence of Luther is clear.[99]

The divine command comes originally (Genesis 1–3) in a situation characterized by divine love and by God's seeking fellowship with humans. The original command to humanity is a summons to surrender to the divine love and to fellowship with God and so to appropriate the life that God offers.[100] Through humanity's fall, however, a fundamental change occurs. Because of sin, God's will takes the form of Law. If the original summons to humans is to live in the freedom of love, now a Law with specific prohibitions must be given, in order to protect creation from humanity, indeed, to protect humanity from itself (first use). But this Law also, of course, exposes sins and condemns humans as sinners to the core of their being (second use).[101]

Christ is the end of the Law, but He is not the end of the command. In the Gospel, God acts against the Law, acquitting those who under the Law are guilty. The Law that condemns comes to an end. But the validity of the command continues. Humans are led back into a relationship of trust that was lost through the fall, even if not perfectly. The Christian

98 Paul Althaus, *The Divine Command: A New Perspective on Law and Gospel,* trans. F. Sherman (Philadelphia: Fortress Press, 1966), 1–2. German original: *Gebot und Gesetz: Zum Thema "Gesetz und Evangelium"* (Gütersloh: C. Bertelsmann, 1952). Citations follow the English translation.

99 Ibid., 3–7. Cf. pp. 29, 45. On the distinction between Law and commandment in Luther, see Lazareth, *Christians in Society*, 71–84; Joest, *Gesetz und Freiheit*, 72–78.

100 Althaus, *The Divine Command*, 8–11.

101 Ibid., 12–21.

is to fulfill the command of love, which is the original commandment. Since the justified remain sinners, however, this command to love takes shape not only in positive commandments but also in prohibitions, as in the New Testament *parenesis*. This command should not be called Law. One cannot speak of Law following the Gospel. One can only speak of command following the Gospel. Law and Gospel are opposed to each other; Gospel and command are not.[102]

For the Christian, then, the essence of God's enduring will is that he or she trust in God's love and live in this love. Love is expressed in doing the commandments, although love goes far beyond the commandments to do more than is necessary. What that means in any given situation, however, may not be known beforehand. God's will confronts the Christian ever and again as something new. The Christian knows God's will in the Holy Spirit. The "mature" Christian seeks God's will but is aware of the limits to knowing that will. Good works flow forth from faith both by an inner necessity of faith and as personal response to the divine command. This is a life of "free obedience." Although Christians are led by the Spirit and learn God's will from Him, the inconstancy of the flesh means that the Christian will still need to heed the apostolic imperatives of the New Testament and the Ten Commandments, so as not to confuse the directives of his or her own will and spirit with God's will and Spirit. This life of obedience to the New Testament moral teaching must not, however, be called a third use of the Law, because Law and Gospel are in opposition to each other, because the word "Law" implies legalism, and because use of the term "Law" can imply that only the imperatives in the Scriptures are of moral significance, whereas other genres in Scripture (examples, narrative, etc.) also provide guidance.[103]

About the time that Elert's and Althaus's essays on Law and Gospel appeared, Wilfried Joest's study on Law and freedom, more specifically, on the third use of the Law in Luther and New Testament *parene-*

102 Ibid., 22–32.

103 Ibid., 33–47.

sis,[104] presented a view that differed from the aforementioned authors in important ways. Not unlike Barth, Joest raised the question whether (German) Lutheranism had erred in opposing Law and Gospel in such a way that, with Law treated as God's penultimate word, the Church no longer had any binding Word of God to speak to the state on matters of Law, effectively sanctifying the state's laws developed on the basis of its own ideologies. Does Lutheranism need a stronger sense of the unity of Law and Gospel, or does such a unity endanger both Law and Gospel? Should we speak of a third use of the Law, and if so, is that to be identified with the New Testament *parenesis*?[105] We cannot undertake a full summary of Joest's book here, but we must note three important insights that required (and still require) a revision of many of the positions taken by Elert and Althaus.

First, whereas Elert and Althaus argued that for Luther (and against Barth) Law and Gospel are in fundamental opposition to each other, Joest showed that this was not an in-principle opposition. Gospel is opposed to Law in the sense that the latter demands righteousness and accuses the conscience, whereas Gospel grants righteousness and consoles. But it is the Law as external demand, not Law as an expression of God's will, that is opposed to the Gospel. The Law, although silenced with respect to the guilty conscience when it is consoled by Christ, remains God's Law.[106] Indeed, Luther can speak of the justified's love for and delight in God's commandments, because in Christ God comes onto the side of the justified, and now the justified, knowing that God is on their side, approve God's Law, revere it, and freely will its fulfillment. The Law no longer confronts the justified as a demanding and merely external Law.[107] Certainly the natural law as the expression of God's enduring will is not opposed to the Gospel.[108]

Second, Joest's nuanced treatment shows how complex the evidence

---

104 Wilfried Joest, *Gesetz und Freiheit* (see n. 25). Citations follow the 1968 printing.

105 Ibid., 9–13.

106 Ibid., 18–21. Cf. pp. 35, 195.

107 Ibid., 22–23, 110.

108 Ibid., 28–29.

is on the question whether a third use of the Law is derivable from Luther.[109] Against those who would deny a basis for a third use in Luther,[110] Joest finds in certain texts of Luther a potential opening to the idea. A third use is not to be found explicitly in Luther, but it is implicitly there. For Luther, New Testament imperatives help preserve and nourish faith and begin to heal the sickness of sin. They help the Christian to know what works to do rather than choosing his or her own works. The Law helps the Christian to mortify the flesh. The Law is an additional testimony, along with the example of Christ, of the good works that we are to emulate. However, the New Testament imperatives do not make the justified into persons that they are not already; the imperatives do not shape the justified as moral beings. Rather, they aim at actualizing the righteousness that is already possessed. Joest mitigates these findings to some extent by arguing that Luther still works within a basically twofold use of the Law, and that indeed Luther in these contexts tends to avoid use of the word Law (*lex*) in favor of other terms.[111]

One of Joest's most important points is that Luther's views with respect to a possible third use must be understood from his perspective on the Christian as *simul iustus et peccator*. In one sense the Christian is *totus iustus* and *totus peccator*. In another sense, however, the Christian is *partim iustus* and *partim peccator*. The life of the Christian as *partim iustus* and *partim peccator* is a struggle for the realization of the total righteousness already given in justification over the human's total fallenness. But this is not to be understood in the sense of the progress of an ethical subject, the Christian's moving forward from an incomplete reality toward a complete ideal. It is rather two complete wholes (complete righteousness and complete fallenness) battling each other. Here the Law has an important role. The Law disciplines the "flesh." Christians obey

109 See ibid., especially pp. 55–82. Joest attributes the complexity to the fact that Luther's *simul iustus et peccator* has both *totus-totus* and *partim-partim* dimensions. As we shall see below, the reception of the *simul* by Luther's heirs was a major factor in the disputes over the third use of the Law.

110 Ibid., 80.

111 Ibid., 73, 74, 78. See, however, the citations on p. 75, where *lex* does occur! Cf. also p. 132.

the Law for the sake of the kingdom of this world, for their own good and for the good of others, and they do this out of Christian freedom. Moreover, the Law has a role in conforming the Christian's own "flesh" to the "inner person." The Law actualizes the inner person's will against the flesh. In this sense, the Law does not so much limit the Christian's freedom as it realizes it. Thus, while for the flesh the Law remains a foreign will, in faith one's own will comes to consent to the Law. The Christian lives from faith and in the righteousness of Christ, and in that faith and righteousness the command no longer takes the form "you must, in order to" but rather "you may, because."[112] At this point, Joest makes the striking claim that for faith, Law and Gospel even become one.[113]

That said, Joest finally rejects the derivation of a third use as such from Luther, on the grounds that it places Law where only Christ should stand salvation-historically, and because use of the specific term "Law" would imply that the Christian remains in the position, as prior to justification, in which he or she must fulfill the Law over against God. Joest prefers to speak of a "practical use of the Gospel" and of *parenesis* and *paraclesis* in terms of "Gospel encouragement" ("*evangelischer Zuspruch*"): in faith, the Christian may or even will (not must) do what God wills, because Christ has already done everything.[114]

Finally, Joest shows that Law and spontaneity of life in the Spirit are not in contradiction to each other in Luther. Faith acts spontaneously, to be sure, from an inner necessity, as it were, rather than by compulsion from an external norm. But faith also leads to a new situation vis-à-vis the Law. The Law is an external, coercing power only so long as the "I" is understood as an ethical subject that seeks to establish itself over against God. This establishment of the self (*Selbstbehauptung*) happens not only in rebellion against God, but it can even happen in obedience to the Law, when one (sinfully) obeys only to establish the self over against God. In such a case, the "I" is not totally obedient to the Law. Indeed, the

112 Ibid., 99–108, 124–25, 131.

113 Ibid., 125. See also p. 131.

114 Ibid., 131–33.

"I" is not even the subject; the Law is the real subject. The "I must do" includes a hidden "I do not want to do." But faith frees one from this relationship to the Law. Precisely because the justified is freed from the condemnation of the Law and from the demand of the Law, the justified can love the Law and delight in the Law in the combat against the flesh. The crown of Christian freedom is to say yes to God's Word, including His command.[115] For the justified, the Law is no longer a Law that *must* be fulfilled, but a Law already fulfilled (by Christ); hence the Law *may* be fulfilled with and in Christ.[116] In the justified, it is Christ or the Spirit who acts, not the "I" as a being over against God.[117] Hence the "I" does not need to "achieve" over against God, but can will the works of God and work with God.[118]

As already indicated, Joest himself did not argue that a third use of the Law should be derived from Luther, nor did Joest himself advocate a third use. His work is important, however, for it offered grounds for challenging Elert's view that Law and Gospel are for Luther in *substantive* opposition to each other and Elert's tendency to define Law in purely negative terms (accusation, retribution, coercion). Joest's work is also helpful in excavating from Luther's works the roots of the debates of the sixteenth century leading up to Article VI of the Formula, particularly questions about anthropology, whether the freedom of the justified is such as can be shaped by Law, and whether one should speak of the justified as an ethical subject. At the same time, Joest opened up possible bridges between Luther and the Formula of Concord, which Elert and others have tried to close down.

Much more could be said about the twentieth- and early twenty-first-century debate. For example, one notes in the last decades a willingness to see in Luther's catechisms and sermons a third use of the Law.[119] In any case, the main points that require discussion have been

---

115 Ibid., 21–24, 109–13.

116 Ibid., 116. Cf. pp. 126, 132, 195–96.

117 Ibid., 110, 114.

118 Ibid., 113–16.

119 Cf. Murray, *Law*, 176–77, 199. See also Paul Althaus, *The Theology of Martin Luther*, trans.

laid out. It is now time to turn to biblical-theological reflections. Our historical review shows that any fresh, biblical-theological approach to the question of a third use of the Law must confront three major questions in particular: (1) Can freedom in the Spirit and life shaped by Law be reconciled with each other or not? (2) Do the justified inhabit a realm of freedom that can be *positively* shaped by Law (and not just coerced by it)? (3) Is it proper for Lutherans to speak of the justified as an ethical subject whose freedom is to be shaped by Law?[120] The claim to be defended here is that there are biblical grounds for giving an affirmative answer to all these questions. Moreover, it will be argued on biblical-theological grounds that we should regard Law (*nomos*) primarily as a (normative) structure for the proper exercise of authentic freedom, rather than as a coercive entity. All of this, I shall argue, will provide a possible way through some of the problems that Article VI of the Formula of Concord raises and open a way to affirming the article's basic intentions.

LAW, FREEDOM, AND SIN IN BIBLICAL-THEOLOGICAL PERSPECTIVE

Before we come to the biblical texts, a note on method is in order. Any confessional and biblical-theological approach to the question of the third use of the Law must take its bearings from the biblical canon in its totality. The Formula of Concord speaks of the third use of the Law

---

R. C. Schulz (Philadelphia: Fortress, 1966), 272–73; further Holsten Fagerberg, *A New Look at the Lutheran Confessions* (1529–1537), trans. G. J. Lund (St. Louis: Concordia Publishing House, 1972), 82–87; Bernhard Lohse, *Luthers Theologie in ihrer historischen Entwicklung und in ihrem systematischen Zusammenhang* (Göttingen: Vandenhoeck & Ruprecht, 1995), 202–3, 293. On Luther even more broadly than the catechisms, see recently Edward A. Engelbrecht, *Friends of the Law: Luther's Use of the Law for the Christian Life* (St. Louis: Concordia Publishing House, 2011). I am not actually convinced that Engelbrecht's book proves that Luther taught a third use of the Law as this has usually been understood. But it is not my area of expertise. In any case, the catechisms remain important evidence.

120 Lutherans need to acknowledge that the fact that the last question even has to be asked would strike many non-Lutheran Christians as odd. It is indicative of the difficulty that Lutherans have had historically in speaking about normative Christian ethics and of a (in my view) troubling aspect of the Lutheran heritage. Yet the question must be asked. As we have seen, there is a history in Lutheranism, beginning with Luther himself and continuing in the debates of the sixteenth century, of speaking of union with Christ and of Christ or the Spirit as the actual subject of the good works of the justified in such a way as to call into question whether the justified should be regarded as an ethical subject at all.

in terms of the "unchanging will of God." If there is such a thing as a third use of the Law, and if Scripture has something to teach about God's unchanging will, then our investigation will require that we look at the whole canon to discern what in fact is *unchanging* across the Testaments. What that means is that we must read the Old and New Testaments together in the conviction that the Old Testament provides the foundations of the New Testament and that the New Testament opens up the meaning of the Old Testament in a decisive way. We will initially follow the biblical narrative and by means of it reflect on the relationship between Law, freedom, and sin.

Our starting point must be Genesis 2:16–17.[121] God gives Adam a commandment. This commandment actually consists of two elements, a positive "commandment" (permission) and a negative commandment (prohibition).[122] The positive reads: "You may certainly eat of every tree in the garden." Included in this commandment, of course, is permission to eat of the tree of life (2:9). The fact that the commandment relates to eating indicates that it has fundamentally to do with the *source* of life. Adam is to know that to have *lasting* life, a life that transcends the possibilities of natural life, entails being in relationship with God, who is the source of life (cf. 3:22). Thus, the positive commandment contains within itself a promise of life. Promise and Law cannot yet be distinguished.[123] The promise is *not* yet conditional upon obedience, but is simply an offer to accept the life that God has to give. Nor is this commandment coercive.

Besides offering life, God's first, positive commandment opens up for Adam a realm of freedom ("you may eat"). Adam was created, of

121 The first commandment given to humanity by God in Scripture appears in Genesis 1:28. I focus here on Genesis 2:16–17 because that is the commandment most relevant to the discussion of Law, freedom, and sin.

122 Strictly speaking, the positive "commandment" is not a commandment at all (Hebrew imperative); it is an emphatic verbal form (infinitive absolute plus imperfect), connoting permission. However, this permission is included in God's "command." Elsewhere the infinitive absolute plus imperfect can virtually function as an imperative (e.g., Deuteronomy 6:17). For simplicity, we shall refer to this positive permission as a commandment.

123 Cf. Luther's comment on Genesis 3:1: God's commandment to Adam in Genesis 2:17 was both "Gospel and Law" (AE 1:146; cf. 1:105–6).

course, with a kind of natural freedom—that is, freedom over his worldly affairs ("to till and to keep" the garden; 2:15). But the freedom opened up by the first, permissive commandment, which includes the offer of unending life with God, is an offer of *authentic* freedom: living in unbroken relationship with God, open to eternal life with Him. Adam differs from the animals around him in that he is capable of self-transcendence. God speaks to Adam, which means that Adam is able to know the ground of his being (God). Adam has a conscience (3:7). He is able to rise above and rule his world (1:28). Such self-transcendent freedom is a gift. The danger of such freedom, however, is that Adam can believe that his self-transcendence reaches to the heights of heaven. He can attempt to make himself God. Hence the negative commandment.

The negative commandment reads: "But of the tree of the knowledge of good and evil you shall not eat, for in the day that you eat of it you shall die" (2:17).[124] The fact that this commandment relates to eating from a tree of knowledge of good and evil, which is God's province (3:5, 22), indicates that death, the end of a life-sustaining relationship with God, comes through seeking to replace God with oneself as the ultimate arbiter of good and evil, the ultimate judge of right and wrong.[125] This prohibition is to protect Adam's authentic freedom. Once again, this commandment is not coercive. Rather, it puts proper limits on Adam's freedom, shaping his freedom in a way that is suitable for his existence as a creature, rather than creator. These are limits to which Adam, still in communion with God, can willingly submit. Adam is not to abuse his freedom. The possibility of being like God comes to humanity as a divine gift (1:27); it is not something to be grasped (cf. Philippians 2:6). If Adam seeks to go beyond the proper limits of his freedom, he will die. Communion with God will be broken; freedom will be lost. Thus, obedience to God's commandment, both in its positive and negative aspects, becomes

---

124 Scripture: NRSV.

125 On the tree of knowledge as a symbol for human, moral autonomy without reference to divine wisdom and the divine, revealed will, see Gordon J. Wenham, *Genesis 1–15* (Waco: Word Books, 1987), 63–64. By contrast, the tree of life alludes, among other things, to divine wisdom (cf. Proverbs 3:18). Wisdom, and hence life, is to be found with God.

both the source and the proper form of Adam's authentic freedom, the structure of a freedom that is open to eternal life with God. We must disagree with Althaus, then, when he states that negative commandments (prohibitions) are only a feature of infralapsarian (post-fall) Law.[126] A negative commandment is issued already before the fall, and its purpose is to help shape authentic freedom. It belongs to the original divine command and is essential to authentic freedom.

In sum, God's giving of the commandment(s) to Adam is *at the same time* His gift of authentic freedom. By giving Adam the positive commandment, God makes known to Adam that authentic freedom is not autonomy, but a freedom that is grounded in his relationship with God and open to eternal life with Him. By giving the negative commandment, God makes known to Adam that his freedom has a limit. The limit is for Adam's own good, because it is appropriate to Adam's status as creature. It sets the appropriate bounds for a life lived in authentic freedom before God. From these reflections, we gain an insight of the highest importance: Law is first and foremost *a structure for the exercise of authentic freedom open to life with God.* The highest form of freedom is not the freedom *to* choose between good and evil, but precisely the freedom *from* the compulsion to choose between good and evil. Such authentic freedom entails directing one's will fully and completely to God's will.

Adam's fall is the tragedy of human freedom. Precisely because it was the *commandment* that opened up authentic freedom and life, it was also the commandment that, if transgressed, could close down authentic freedom and life. An abused freedom could turn on itself and become unfreedom. And that is what happens. Adam, or rather Eve and then Adam, exercise their freedom, but they exercise it wrongly.[127] They are misled. Sadly, and ironically, in the very exercise of a presumed "freedom

---

126 Althaus, *The Divine Command*, 12–16. See esp. p. 13: "The command is wholly positive. . . . To be sure, there is always a negative element corresponding to this positive one; there is always a prohibition corresponding to the command. . . . But in the original relationship, there is no expression of this negative element." See further pp. 26–27.

127 Genesis 3:22 suggests that Adam and Eve chose to eat of the tree of knowledge *rather* than the tree of life! They chose autonomy rather than communion with God.

to choose" whether to accept the God-given limit to their freedom or to transcend it by seeking to become the arbiters of good and evil, they are overcome by evil. And they are trapped.

The author of this tragedy is a talking serpent (Genesis 3:1–6). That the serpent does this signifies that the origin of this evil is neither God nor human, but some third entity. No serpent can really talk. But just as God opened the mouth of a donkey to speak in the language of humans (Numbers 22:28–30), so the serpent becomes the mouthpiece for a lying voice that says "you will not die." Adam and Eve believe the lie and suffer the consequences. Adam and Eve's sin (their violation of God's commandment) and the consequences that follow from it are, mysteriously and paradoxically, at once both self-chosen destiny and the work of an entity beyond them that tempts them to transcend the limits of their freedom. They are put out of the garden and must die, possibly forever (3:23–24). That is the condemnation of God's Law. But this condemnation is not in the first instance an act of *retribution* on the part of God. No, the death is due to the fact that Adam and Eve abuse their freedom. They destroy *themselves* by reaching beyond the limits that were set for their own good, and they also break communion with God. In fact, in their abuse of freedom Adam and Eve become anti-gods,[128] no longer fit for life with God.[129] That is, because they chose to exercise a false freedom, they forfeited the only authentic freedom that they ever had: a life in trusting and obedient relationship to God, open to eternal life with Him.

The expulsion from the garden and the separation from the tree of life indicate that, after Adam and Eve's fall, humans no longer live in

---

128 Note the intimate connection between Genesis 3:5 and 3:22–23: God does not deny that Adam and Eve, by eating of the tree of knowledge, have, in a sense, become "like God." That the serpent said truly. The serpent's lie was that eating from the tree would not lead to death. Adam takes it into his own hands to become "like God," an ultimate arbiter of good and evil. But his being "like God" is actually being an anti-god. The result is that he chooses no longer to live with and for God. Cf. Ezekiel 28:1–19: The prince (king) of Tyre presumed to become his own god, with a corrupted wisdom, with the result that he was no longer fit to live in the presence of God.

129 The Eden story contains temple imagery, which indicates that expulsion from the garden is expulsion from the life-giving presence of God. See Wenham, *Genesis 1–15*, 62, 65, 86.

eternal life–sustaining communion with God. Adam does not die a physical death immediately, which indicates that the death that he must die "on the day" of his disobedience (2:17) is a spiritual death, a death that consists in spiritual self-dissolution and separation from God, potentially forever. Adam's offspring will be born outside of the garden (4:1), which means that humanity inherits a situation in which, because of Adam's fall, they are destined to die in the absence of eternal life–sustaining communion with God. Henceforth only God can restore such communion and life (cf. Revelation 22:2).

Sin corrupts human freedom (Genesis 6:5). Nonetheless, when we follow the biblical narrative we can see that the relationship between Law and freedom that characterized life in the garden is reestablished for Israel, although in a diminished way. After God frees Israel from slavery in Egypt, He gives them a Law. This Law opens up a realm of freedom and life for Israel, at least in temporal terms (Leviticus 18:5; 25:35–46; 26:1–46; Deuteronomy 28),[130] just as God's commandment opened up a realm of life and freedom for Adam. From the perspective of Christian faith, of course, it will ultimately be seen that this Law has the effect of trapping people under sin, just as the commandment given to Adam had the effect of trapping him in sin (although that was not its original purpose). One can also see that God placed a promise of life in the Law to point forward to Christ (Romans 10:4–13; cf. Galatians 3:21–22). Nonetheless, the fact remains that the Law of Moses contains a promise of life and a vision of freedom shaped by the commandments.

It is Paul, in fact, who most profoundly opens up for our reflection the relationship between Law, freedom, and sin. In Romans 7–8, Paul gives for Christian faith a definitive treatment of the topics first raised in Genesis 2–3, to which he almost certainly alludes. Paul makes clear that the enemy of freedom and life is *not* Law as such, which in itself is holy, just, and good (Romans 7:12), but Sin,[131] understood as a transpersonal,

---

130 See especially the warning in Deuteronomy 28:47–48: When Israel, because of its disobedience, goes into exile, the judgment will be: "Because you did not serve the LORD your God . . . you shall serve your enemies." Scripture: NRSV.

131 I capitalize Sin to indicate that we are dealing not with individual transgressions but with a

even cosmic power. God's commandment is meant for life (7:10), but Sin is such a pernicious power that it uses even something as inherently good as the Law to trap people in Sin and thus to condemn them to death (7:11, 13).

Romans answers at least two questions left open in Genesis. First, we learn that the "third entity" that is the author of the tragedy of human freedom is Sin. Paul does not reflect on the origin of moral evil, as one finds in some strands of Jewish apocalypticism. Why there is Sin or moral evil in a world created by a good God remains something of a mystery; however, we learn that Sin is a spiritual malady. As freedom is a spiritual phenomenon, so also the corruption of freedom is a spiritual phenomenon. Sin is of neither divine nor human origin. It originates in the spiritual realm,[132] but it is able to corrupt human freedom in both spiritual and material dimensions. It sets the human against God and thus out of communion with God. It causes the human to transcend the proper limits of freedom that God established for humanity's own good. The healing of Sin must also come from the spiritual realm.

Second, we learn from Romans that Sin is a power stronger than Law. As we have seen, divine Law opens up authentic freedom for Adam. But Sin is able to use human freedom to close down *authentic* freedom. And here even Law is of no help. Sin overcame God's commandment in the garden; it even overcomes the Law of Sinai. So strong was the power of Sin that it took the death and resurrection of the Son of God to overcome it (Romans 8:3). Now it becomes clear, as it could not have been clear to Israel before the coming of Christ, that the Law exposes and condemns human sinfulness, but it cannot overcome it. An overwhelming spiritual malady required an even greater spiritual healing.

Sin's power over the human has been broken in the death and resurrection of the Son of God, who died to Sin and rose beyond it once and

---

spiritual power.

132 Presumably Paul holds a view along the lines found in some strands of Judaism (e.g., 1 Enoch 10:8), according to which moral evil is introduced into humanity from out of the (fallen) angelic realm. Sin comes from spiritual forces, distinct from God, which can determine the human.

for all (Romans 6:10). Henceforth Christ restores authentic freedom and lasting life—that is, a life in which Sin is broken as a determining power, and which is open again to eternal life with God—to those who share in His death and life through the Holy Spirit (Romans 8:1–11). Authentic freedom and lasting life are thus *not* characterized primarily by deliverance from Law as such (although they do involve freedom from the *condemnation* of the Law and from the Mosaic Law), but deliverance from the overwhelming power of Sin that corrupts human freedom and that closes down eternal-life-sustaining communion with God. Christ reopens for the human eternal life (by restoring communion with God; Romans 5:2, 11) and a realm of authentic freedom open to such life, life and freedom that God first opened up when He gave the commandment(s) to Adam, but which were lost in the fall.

As Paul sees it, this restored freedom must be shaped. Although Paul speaks of freedom from the Law (Romans 6:14; 7:1–6; 1 Corinthians 9:20; Galatians 2:19; cf. 5:18), he is not afraid to use the words Law (*nomos*) or commandments (*entolai*) in various contexts to speak of a principle or rule (or rules) that should shape Christian freedom (Romans 8:2; 13:9; 1 Corinthians 7:19; 9:21; Galatians 6:2). That suggests that with Paul, as with the commandment to Adam, Law (*nomos*) for the justified is best understood in terms of a *normative structure for the exercise of authentic freedom open to life with God.* We need to give Law (*nomos*) in Paul a much more positive sense than is often done. We shall consider Paul's attitude toward the Law later. For the moment, we note that for Paul the Spirit both opens up and shapes authentic freedom, freedom open to eternal life with God (Romans 8:1–13), just as the commandment(s) to Adam did. Law and Spirit therefore have a formal likeness to each other, and we should not be too quick to place them in opposition.[133]

Our biblical-theological reflections thus far must cause us to challenge some of the ways that opponents of a third use of the Law have

---

133 Galatians 5:18 contrasts the Spirit with the *Jewish* Law specifically and cannot be used to oppose Spirit and *nomos* in an absolute way.

spoken about Law. To begin, Althaus's treatment of Law must be corrected in at least two ways. In his thoughtful presentation, Althaus correctly observes that what God offered to Adam in the divine command, what was lost in his fall, and what is restored in Christ is a fellowship of love and trust between God and humans and an offer of life from God to humans. For Althaus, the original divine command is to love, more specifically, to live in the "freedom of love," and Christ's restoration of life also includes the command to love. What Althaus did not observe, however, is that the commandment(s) given to Adam opened up a particular kind of freedom before God, with a specific shape and with specific limits. That is why the commandment to Adam included a prohibition, which Althaus ignores, assigning prohibitions exclusively to the post-fall situation and New Testament *parenesis*.[134] Moreover, when we define Law (*nomos*) essentially as a structure for the exercise of authentic freedom, and see the continuity and formal similarity between the commandment given to Adam, the Law of Moses, and Paul's use of *nomos* and *entolai*, there are no grounds for adopting Althaus's distinction between Law and commandment.[135]

Furthermore, the story of Adam and Eve teaches us that Law is neither essentially coercive nor retributive (contra some opponents of the third use in the sixteenth century and contra Elert). Nor is Law in the first instance (i.e., antelapsarian Law) *essentially* opposed to promise in the sense that Law makes eternal life dependent on obedience (as some opponents of the third use in the sixteenth century argued). In the first instance, Law is a divine *offer* of authentic freedom and eternal life through unbroken communion with God. The commandment given to Adam is a reminder that his capacity for self-transcendence may be

134 Althaus, *The Divine Command*, 13, 26–27. For Althaus, the original command can be summarized as love, more specifically, "love, and do what you wish!" (p. 14).

135 Although it is true that New Testament authors at times seem to prefer to speak of the "will of God" rather than Law, the New Testament does not seem to draw any fundamental distinction between *nomos* and *entolē*, as Althaus himself acknowledges (p. 3). Althaus's proposal also misses the *continuity* between the Law from Sinai and the New Testament *parenesis*, on which see below. Lazareth, *Christians in Society*, 71–74, writes of the difficulty Luther has in distinguishing between Law and commandment.

directed properly or improperly, and he is to direct it properly. Perhaps this insight answers one of our questions raised above in connection with Article VI. Why was a commandment given to the first human before the fall, if he already lived in a state of perfect righteousness? Answer: the Law was given to open up and shape authentic freedom and life before God.[136]

Our biblical-theological reflections further suggest that what is really at issue in the doctrine of the Law is not the abstract question whether humans might "merit" salvation in a speculative, prefall world, or the question whether they might justify themselves through perfect fulfillment of the Law, and so the question whether a third use of the Law also implies that Christians merit salvation or justify themselves, questions that occupied the sixteenth-century debate.[137] All of that seems to be beside the point. The point rather is that divine Law established for Adam an authentic freedom in communion with God that was open to eternal life. Such communion with God was (and still is) broken by Sin, but it is restored by Christ, who frees from the power of Sin and reconciles us to the Father (Romans 5:10). The Spirit reopens authentic freedom, which is to be shaped by normative structures for the exercise of authentic freedom (*nomos*). On the basis of Genesis 2–3 as well as Paul, one can say that it is unbroken communion with God, not meriting salvation, that is essential for eternal life, even within a doctrine of the Law.[138] That applies not only to Adam (contra opponents of the third use in the sixteenth century), but also to the life of the Christian (contra Joest).[139] The formal

136 We recall Flacius's point that the freedom of the first human couple was not only a freedom from committing sin and from the punishment of sin, but it was also the freedom of a truly free will, a will in free conformity to God's will (Law) and so *free from compulsion*.

137 Richter, *Gesetz und Heil*, 134, 154, 157, 158–60, 284, 288; Haikola, *Usus Legis*, 14–16, 65–69.

138 Formally one may speak of obedience to the Law as preserving innocence before God and life with Him rather than of meriting salvation. This, however, would apply only to prefall humanity. For the justified sinner, salvation is preserved only by faith (FC IV 34). Cf. Haikola, *Gesetz und Evangelium*, 81, 85; Haikola, *Usus Legis*, 15, 67. Nonetheless it remains acceptable to think of good works performed according to the Law as preserving the justified in their calling and preventing them from falling into sin (FC IV 33). Thus there remains a formal analogy between the commandment given to Adam and Law for the justified in preserving authentic freedom. More on this below.

139 Joest, *Gesetz und Freiheit*, 132–33.

likeness between Genesis 2–3 and Paul means that we cannot dismiss consideration of Genesis 2–3 in these matters as involving useless "speculation" about Law and salvation in the antelapsarian situation. Paul opens up the meaning of Genesis 2–3 in light of Christ in the deepest way, and that is not mere speculation.

LUTHERAN OBJECTIONS TO VIEWING THE JUSTIFIED AS A FREE, ETHICAL SUBJECT POSITIVELY SHAPED BY LAW, AND A RESPONSE

Our biblical-theological reflections on Law, freedom, and sin have led us to answer our first question affirmatively: Law and freedom in the Spirit can be reconciled with each other and should not be opposed to each other. We must now take up our other two questions: Do the justified inhabit a realm of freedom that can be *positively* shaped by Law (and not just coerced by it)? And is it proper for Lutherans to speak of the justified as an ethical subject whose freedom is to be shaped by Law? To answer these questions, we will continue to look to Scripture. We take up these questions under a new section, however, because we must also confront certain weighty construals of Pauline theology in the Lutheran theological heritage that would lead many to answer these questions negatively. I shall discuss three of those construals and give a response to each: (1) reading Romans 7 as a description of the situation of the Christian; (2) existentialist reception of Law-Gospel theology; and (3) an overwhelmingly negative view of Law.[140]

(1) The first construal is a reading of Romans 7:14–25 as primarily a depiction of the life of the Christian. The identity of the "I" of this passage has long been a point of debate in interpretation. The fundamental question is whether it depicts the life of the Christian or the non-Christian. Luther read this passage along the same lines as Galatians 5:17 (which is clearly directed toward Christians): the Christian exists as a battleground

140 Another important factor that has led to the rejection of the Law as shaping Christian life and doctrine in recent decades is "Law-Gospel reductionism," or simply "Gospel reductionism." I do not take that topic up here, since I wish to focus on biblical texts, but see Murray, *Law*, 103–7.

in the conflict between the (human) spirit and the flesh.[141] The Christian is *simul iustus et peccator*, at the same time justified and sinner.[142] Luther comments on Romans 7:18: "the spirit accomplishes the good it wants to do when it acts without protest according to the Law of God. But this cannot be done in this life" (because of the resistance of the flesh).[143]

For Luther, when the "carnal man" (unconverted person) does the Law, the person actually does it unwillingly, under coercion; for within the person that does the Law is an "I," standing against God in *Selbstbehauptung* (self-assertion), who does not want to do the Law. The Law is the actual subject of action.[144] When one believes in Christ, Christ enters the "inner person" and becomes one with it. Luther associates the "inner person" closely with the conscience. The Law ceases to burden the conscience with demands of works necessary for salvation. The inner person is "spiritual," totally freed from the Law. But the "outer person" remains "fleshly" and requires the Law. The situation, then, is that the Christian, insofar as he or she is led by the Spirit, can be viewed (abstractly) as totally free from Law, but insofar as the Christian is still fleshly, he or she can be viewed (also abstractly) as totally enslaved to sin and so must be coerced by the Law. The Law can, indeed, become an "ally" of the free, "inner person" in loving service to others and in the battle against the flesh.[145] But the justified cannot really be viewed as an ethical subject for whom Law can become the form of his or her freedom.[146] The Christian's freedom is constituted by the person of Christ (or the Spirit) who is the actual "ethical subject" of action and is above the Law. Here the Law has a role to play, but it is to combat the flesh, not to shape freedom.[147]

141 Wilhelm Pauck, ed., *Luther: Lectures on Romans* (Philadelphia: Fortress Press, 1961), 199–209 (see AE 25:327–36). It is with the gift of the Spirit that the battle first begins. Cf. Althaus, *Paulus und Luther*, 51, 75.

142 Pauck, *Luther: Lectures on Romans*, 204, 208 (see AE 25:332, 336).

143 Pauck, ibid., 204 (see AE 25:331).

144 Joest, *Gesetz und Freiheit*, 22–23; cf. Bring, "Gesetz und Evangelium," 67.

145 Joest, ibid., 35, 76–77, 101–9; Bring, ibid., 51–54, 56–61, 66, 69; Althaus, *Theology*, 269–71.

146 Haikola, *Usus Legis*, 105, 142–52.

147 Joest, *Gesetz und Freiheit*, 101–10 (esp. 110: "Christus ist das 'ethische Subjekt' des Gehorsams geworden, mit dem der Christ dem Gesetze gehorcht"); cf. pp. 94, 115–16. Joest (p. 125) does speak, to be sure, of the Law that confronts the Christian (*qua* "new person")

If one follows this view of things, it is easy to conclude that the Law can have no role in shaping Christian freedom. Abstractly conceived, insofar as the inner person is free in the Spirit, united with Christ, there is no place for the Law. Insofar as the Christian remains flesh, the Law continues to apply.[148] For the sake of the unity of the *concrete* person one must say that the Law applies to the whole person; this is not, however, for the sake of shaping freedom, but for combating the flesh.[149] It was just here, however, that Luther's heirs diverged.[150] Opponents of the third use of the Law adopted Luther's conception of the Christian as *simul iustus et peccator* in a *totus-totus* sense (the Christian is totally justified, and so totally free from Law with respect to the spirit; and totally sinner, therefore needing the compulsion of the Law for the flesh).[151] The early orthodox proponents of the third use found this conception to be unreal and to endanger ethical responsibility.[152] They preferred to think of the Christian as *simul iustus et peccator* in a *partim-partim* sense and to speak of the inner freedom of the Christian being normed externally by Law.[153] We can see here the roots of the anthropological ambiguity in Article VI.[154] The article, of course, follows Luther's reading of Romans 7 as depicting the

---

as bringing full freedom, but this is still not the shaping of an ethical subject. See further Haikola, *Usus Legis*, 146–47. Luther could speak of the justified externally following (more than just internally delighting in) the Law (or commandments) in a noncoercive way, but this does not seem to be the norm. Cf. Engelbrecht, *Friends of the Law*, 273, citing AE 24:102 (where, however, in context Law is still thought of as basically coercive). Note also that in the catechisms (Prefaces; LC II 69) Luther speaks positively of doing the Ten Commandments, as shaping Gospel freedom and following from delight in God's commandments.

148 Joest, ibid., 57, succinctly summarizes the paradox in Luther: If there are to be true Christians in the world, faith must act in freedom from the Law and without internal struggle; but there can be no such Christians, because Christians remain part of a fallen world.

149 Haikola, *Usus Legis*, 75; Bring, "Gesetz und Evangelium," 56–57, 60.

150 Haikola, *Usus Legis*, 73–83; Bring, ibid., 60, 65.

151 Haikola, ibid., 74–81.

152 See also Fr. H. R. Frank, *Die Theologie der Concordienformel*, 4 vols. (Erlangen: Theodor Blaesing, 1858–63), 2.352–54, who judges that viewing the justified as two "men" in one person, the Law applied to the person only as "old man," while the reborn man is merely "passive material" in which Christ works, leads finally to the corruption of evangelical ethics.

153 Haikola, *Usus Legis*, 53, 75, 77, 81.

154 James A. Nestingen, "Changing Definitions: The Law in Formula VI," *Concordia Theological Quarterly* 69 (2005): 259–70, here 268–69, remarks on the Formula's dissolution of the *totus-totus* into the *partim-partim*.

life of the Christian. But it tries to reconcile the very different views given: the justified need the Law to combat the flesh; the justified live with a spiritual freedom that needs no Law; *and yet* the justified live with an inner freedom that is to be normed by an external Law. The result of the compromise is that the Law can hardly be anything but coercive in the end, no matter how much the Formula insists on the Christian doing the will of God as comprehended in the Law from a "free and merry spirit."

Scholars have long recognized that Luther's reading of Romans 7, though following a time-honored tradition,[155] is *exegetically* problematic.[156] With many recent commentators, I take it that Romans 7:14–25 depicts the situation of a person under the Law before (or without) faith in Christ, but from the perspective of one who through faith in Christ has been delivered from that situation and is now able to see life under Law in its true colors.[157] That does not mean that the Christian cannot identify with the depth of the problem of sin of which the passage speaks.[158] After all, even on the reading favored here, it is only from the perspective of faith in Christ that one can see the *full* depth of the problem of sin: that is the "moment of truth" in Luther's exposition.[159] Nonetheless, it

155 Luther followed the later Augustine in reading Romans 7 in reference to the Christian. See the brief historical overviews in Althaus, *Paulus und Luther*, 31–32; and Werner Georg Kümmel, *Römer 7 und die Bekehrung des Paulus* (Leipzig: J. C. Hinrichs, 1929), 90–95. Augustine's views had changed. Augustine's later reading served him in the struggle against Pelagianism, although the reasons for the change were apparently exegetical. See Kümmel, ibid., 93–94; Althaus, ibid. Luther's reading of Romans 7 as speaking of the Christian rather than the non-Christian was influenced by Luther's interest in avoiding synergism (Althaus, ibid., 59–60).

156 Althaus, *Paulus und Luther*, 36–41; Kümmel, *Römer 7*, 90–104. See further Wilfried Joest, "Paulus und das Luthersche Simul Iustus et Peccator," *Kerygma und Dogma* 1 (1955): 269–320.

157 See, e.g., Arland Hultgren, *Paul's Letter to the Romans: A Commentary* (Grand Rapids: Eerdmans, 2011), 685; Peter Stuhlmacher, *Paul's Letter to the Romans: A Commentary*, trans. S. J. Hafemann (Louisville: Westminster/John Knox Press, 1994), 114–15.

158 There are Christians today who report that Romans 7 describes the division of the self that first begins when the Spirit comes upon them. While preparing this essay, I came across the following letter to the editor of an Australian Christian newspaper: "Romans 7 is all about our battle. When I was a heathen, I had peace. But when the Holy Spirit of God came into me, the war began" (Rolf Vaessen, "Grace Plus," *Eternity*, May 2014:15). Luther himself said that the "carnal man does not fight with the flesh," only the spiritual man does (Pauck, Lectures, 201; cf. p. 207. See AE 25:328, 335).

159 Althaus, *Paulus und Luther*, 40.

makes better sense *exegetically* to understand the "I" of Romans 7:14–25 as depicting the situation of the person under the Law and *before* faith in Christ, divided under the power of Sin between the "inner person" who delights in the Law and the "members" that do not do the Law—the paradoxical situation (visible only from the perspective of faith in Christ) that one can delight in the Law and seek to do it and yet remain a sinner before God and not please Him (8:7–8).

In that case, we must take Romans 8:1–17 as referring to the life of the justified who has been delivered from the situation depicted in chapter 7, when the Spirit begins to free one from the power of Sin and opens up a realm of genuine freedom in which the justified willingly submits to God's will. According to Paul the Christian does *not* live fundamentally in a struggle between spirit and flesh. Nor does Galatians 5:17 speak of such a struggle in the Christian. Rather Paul *presupposes* that the Christian is set free from the power of the flesh through the (Holy) Spirit and will *not* be determined by the flesh.[160] Of course, to live according to the flesh (Sin) always remains a real temptation for the Christian. The "works of the flesh" (Galatians 5:19–21; cf. Romans 1:29–31) run deep, to the inner workings of the heart. I do not want to deny that there is a certain theological legitimacy to Luther's deepening of Paul's sense for the problem of Sin, even in the Christian, for example, in the violation of the First Commandment.[161] Still, for Paul Sin is no longer the determining

---

160 On this, see the excellent essay of Otfried Hofius, "Widerstreit zwischen Fleisch und Geist? Erwägungen zu Gal 5,17," in his *Exegetische Studien* (Tübingen: Mohr Siebeck, 2008), 161–72. Hofius makes a convincing case that according to Paul flesh and (Holy) Spirit are not in a struggle with each other, but are simply (and absolutely) opposed to each other. The justified have been freed from the flesh and exercise their will under the guidance of the Spirit. Paul assures the Galatian Christians that if they walk according to the Spirit, they most certainly will not gratify the desires of the flesh. "[E]in Nebeneinander beider Größen [ist] schlechterdings nicht denkbar" (p. 170) ("a simultaneity of both entities [Spirit and flesh] is simply unthinkable").

161 As Althaus points out (*Paulus and Luther*, 91–95), Luther's sense, on the basis of Romans 7, for the problem of the "flesh" even in the Christian (as manifest in unbelief, mistrust, ingratitude, and other sins before God, in other words, in violations of the First Commandment) is, though not really exegetically defensible, theologically not unjustified as an extension of Paul's insights into the problem of the "desires of the flesh." When Paul speaks of such sins of the flesh or of unbelief, he has crass, Gentile sins in view, or the unbelief of Israel—but in any case, a kind of sin that the Christian has left behind—whereas Luther interprets them in

reality in the believer. Therefore, even if one would not want to say that the Christian is ever without Sin—for who of us can know the full truth about ourselves this side of heaven?—the question remains whether one can really appeal to Paul to speak of the Christian as *simul iustus et peccator* in the *totus-totus* sense, and then draw from it the implications about anthropology, Law, and freedom that Luther draws from it.

It will not do, then, to say that only Christ or the Spirit is the "ethical subject" of the Christian. The Christian is a free and responsible subject. Under Sin and the Law, I find within myself an "inner person" who delights in the Law (Romans 7:22), the person who I am meant (by God) to be but am not (and cannot be) under the power of Sin.[162] I can distinguish this person from the Sin that dwells within me and that determines me (7:20), as I can distinguish this "inner person" from my "members" that are enslaved to Sin (7:23). But such distinctions do not exonerate the total "me" from responsibility for my sin (7:14). When I am in Christ I find that my "inner person" is being renewed (2 Corinthians 4:16).[163] The power that determines me now is *not* Sin (as one might think if one read Romans 7 as a depiction of the Christian) but (the Spirit of) Christ, who lives in me (Galatians 2:20; cf. Romans 8:10) and who frees me to

---

a deeper sense, present even in the Christian (pp. 85–86).

162 The "inner person" (*ho esō anthrōpos*) in Romans 7:22 is best understood in the sense of the human as he or she is meant to be (by God), in distinction from the human as he or she really is. So Nikolaus Walter, "esō, etc." *Exegetical Dictionary of the New Testament*, ed. H. Balz and G. Schneider (Grand Rapids: Eerdmans, 1990–93), 2.64–65, here 65; Christoph Markschies, "Innerer Mensch," *Reallexikon für Antike und Christentum*, 18:266–312, here 281. It is more an aspect of the person than a part of the person. It is related to, but probably not identical with, the mind (*nous*) (Romans 7:23). The *nous* is the seat of discernment of God's will and is capable of renewal (Romans 12:2), which governs (but is not identical with) the renewal of the total, "inner person" (2 Corinthians 4:16). See the next note.

163 The "inner person" (*ho esō anthrōpos*) of 2 Corinthians 4:16 is best understood in the sense of the (Christian) person in the aspect of his or her transformation through the Spirit. Markschies, ibid., 280, with further references. By being conformed to the death of Christ in His apostolic ministry and so to all appearances being destroyed (4:10, 16), Paul at the very same time and paradoxically is manifesting the life of Jesus (4:10; cf. 12:9; 13:4) and is being transformed into the glory of Christ through the Spirit (3:18). Indeed, one may say that the inner person here is the "Christ coming into being in the Christian" (Galatians 2:20) (Hans Lietzmann/Werner Kümmel, *An die Korinther I-II* [Tübingen: J. C. B. Mohr, 1949], 117). It is the beginnings of the eschatological redemption of the total person (*sōma*) and adoption as son of God, which will entail conformity to Christ (Romans 8:18–30).

start to become the person that I am meant (by God) to be.[164] But the Christ who lives in me does not *replace* "me" as a responsible subject (Galatians 2:20)—I who "live to God" (Galatians 2:19) in freedom from Sin (Romans 6:11) and who am called to remain in freedom from Sin (6:12–23)[165]—any more than Sin previously replaced "me" as the responsible subject of my sin.[166] My "inner person" is not my conscience (so Luther) that knows itself to be totally freed from the coercion and accusations of the Law; rather, it is that aspect of my existence in which I have been freed from the power of Sin, whose freedom must now be shaped.

Although scholars have long recognized the difference between Paul's view of the Christian and Luther's interpretation of Paul, it does not seem that Lutheran theology has grappled seriously enough with the implications of this difference for a doctrine of a third use of the Law. The anthropology of Article VI—that even the Christian's "inner person" remains inescapably corrupted by the old Adam, so that even the justified must be coerced by the Law, which led Elert, for example, to reject a truly third use of the Law[167]—seems unduly pessimistic. For Paul, it is rather the case that the power of Sin has begun to be broken in the Christian and, although the Christian still remains an "old" person, on the way to death,[168] he or she inhabits a realm of freedom that can and

---

164 While Paul's use of *ho esō anthrōpos* does not have exactly the same sense in Romans 7:22 and 2 Corinthians 4:16, the common denominator is that the "inner person" is the person as he or she should be and, through transformation, can be and will be. It is the person as he or she is capable of being when not determined by the power of Sin, but by Christ. Cf. Johannes Behm, "esō," *Theological Dictionary of the New Testament*, 2.698–99, here 699. The Spirit frees one from slavery to sin to be the creature that God intended (Althaus, *Paulus und Luther*, 117).

165 Cf. Hofius, "Widerstreit," 170 n. 44: The Spirit's leading does not exclude but includes human activity. Cf. FC SD II 88, 90: the reborn cooperates in the works of the Holy Spirit.

166 Note the parallelism: "Now if I do (*poiō*) what I do not want, it is no longer I (*ouketi egō*) who do (*katergazomai*) it, but sin that dwells within me (*en emoi*) (Romans 7:20). "It is no longer I (*ouketi egō*) who live (*zō*), but Christ who lives (*zē*) in me (*en emoi*). And the life I now live (*zō*) in the flesh . . ." (Galatians 2:20). The force of the Greek word order in Galatians 2:20a (*zō de ouketi egō*) is difficult to capture in English: "I live, though it is no longer I who live, but Christ who lives in me." Scripture: NRSV.

167 Elert, *Law and Gospel*, 41–42.

168 It has been observed that the Pauline dialectic is more *simul novus et vetus* (both new and old) than *simul iustus et peccator* (Hultgren, *Romans*, 261), or that the Christian lives between life and death. Cf. Althaus, *Paulus and Luther*, 79–80. See also (though more cautious-

should be shaped in a positive way by normative structures of existence (*nomos* in the broad sense) and not only coercively. It seems, then, that Melanchthon and other early, orthodox Lutherans, such as Flacius, who argued that the Law no longer confronts the justified fundamentally as a divided self, but rather as one whose will has been freed, who can avoid intentional sins, whose conscience is not attacked by the Law, and whose freedom can be positively (not coercively) normed by Law,[169] may be closer to Paul than Luther was.

In Romans 8, Paul does not describe the situation of the Christian as entailing obedience to Law as such. Yet he is not afraid to use the words "Law" (*nomos*) and "Spirit" together (8:2). It is evident that Paul plays on the word *nomos* with a double meaning. On the one hand, the Spirit is an "ordering rule (or principle)," in the sense that, as life-giving power (cf. 8:10–11), it overcomes and so frees us from the "law of sin and death"—that is, from Sin's power likewise to order our lives (7:23) on the way to death (7:24). On the other hand, the Spirit inaugurates a new "order" or "rule" in the Christian's life in the sense of a structure of existence. From a number of places in Paul's letters, we can see what this new "rule" of the Spirit looks like: putting to death the deeds of the flesh and producing the fruit of the Spirit (Galatians 5:16–24; cf. Romans 8:13); honoring God with the body, particularly in abstaining from sexual immorality (1 Corinthians 6:19–20; 1 Thessalonians 4:3–8); general moral purity (1 Corinthians 6:9–11); and living in the gentleness, humility, and unselfishness of Christ (1 Corinthians 4:21; Galatians 5:25–6:2; Philippians 2:1–11). This new order or rule takes the place of the Law (of Moses) (Romans 7:6; 2 Corinthians 3:7–11). We cannot fail to note, however, that since this Spirit is precisely the Spirit of the new covenant

ly) Joest, "Paulus," 271–72, 280.

169 See Haikola, *Usus Legis*, 21–23, 49–52, 140–41; Haikola, *Gesetz und Evangelium*, 330, 331, 333. On Melanchthon, see Meyer, "Normen," 224–25, 228, 234: The new person in Christ should not simply be collapsed into the old, fleshly person. He or she can, then, in freedom be positively shaped by Law as guide, and does not simply have to be coerced. Similarly see Richter, *Gesetz und Heil*, 340–42, on Wigand. Article II of the Formula of Concord teaches that the reborn are freed in their will (FC SD II 67), although even this free will is said to be weak, since Romans 7 is taken to speak of the state of the Christian (II 17–18, 64–65, 68, 84–85). On the Christian's avoidance of intentional sins, see FC SD IV 15.

(2 Corinthians 3:6), although the Law of the Spirit is not identical with the Law of the old covenant, yet it stands in continuity with it and is the fulfillment of it: for it is precisely obedience to God's *Law* (in the Spirit) that is promised in the new covenant (Jeremiah 31:33; cf. Ezekiel 36:27).[170]

From Romans 6, we see that the rule of new life in the Spirit has a specific *shape*. Those who have been set free from the power of Sin, so as no longer to obey their fleshly desires (6:12, 14; cf. 8:2, 13), have a new life (6:4) that entails obedience to a particular pattern of teaching (*typos didachēs*), which has been given to them as a matter of apostolic tradition (*paradosis*) (6:17). The Roman Christians, Paul says, are to turn away from impurity and Lawlessness (*anomia*) and toward righteousness leading to sanctification. As the similar language in 1 Thessalonians 4:1–8 shows, Paul probably has sexual purity especially in mind.[171] The more important point here, however, is that the Thessalonian passage confirms what we find in Romans 6, that the rule of the Spirit in the life of the Christian (1 Thessalonians 4:8) goes hand-in-hand with specific apostolic instruction (4:2). That means that, on the basis of Paul, we cannot set Christian freedom in the Spirit and a normative structure for the exercise of that freedom in opposition. The purpose of such a structure of freedom is to prevent the justified from misusing their freedom and so falling back into the realm of the flesh and into enslavement to sin (Romans 6:12–23).[172] When we consider that for Paul the rule of the Spirit is the fulfillment of God's promise of a new covenant in which God's people will obey His Law from the heart, we understand Paul's positive use of the word *nomos* and should be open to the fact that even

---

170 Stuhlmacher, *Romans*, 117–21.

171 Note the parallels: the Thessalonians received (binding) divine instruction from Paul (4:1–2) (cf. Romans 6:17); this instruction in the "the will of God" is to lead them away from impurity (*akatharsia*) to sanctification (*hagiasmos*; 4:3, 4, 7) (cf. Romans 6:19, 22); such a life is in contrast to the Thessalonians' (Gentile) past (1 Thessalonians 4:5) (cf. Romans 6:17, 19); this has happened in connection with the giving of the Spirit (1 Thessalonians 4:8), presumably through Baptism (cf. Romans 6:1–4).

172 This is one important way that Article IV of the Formula speaks of good works: they keep one from falling back into concrete sins (FC SD IV 32–33; cf. Ap XX 13).

for Paul Christian freedom can be positively shaped by *nomos* (in the broad sense).

(2) Closely related to the foregoing is another legacy of the Lutheran theological heritage that has caused Lutherans to deny that the justified inhabit a realm of freedom that can be positively shaped by Law—namely, existentialist theology.[173] Drawing on Luther's conception of the Christian as *totus iustus* and *totus peccator*, the emphasis here falls on the Christian's encounter with the Word of God at a radical level: the Word, functioning as Law and Gospel, absolutely kills my old Adam and raises up a completely new person. Thereafter the Law must remain silent—for the old has passed away and the new has come—until the Law accuses me again.[174] The Christian life is a continuous dialectic, a constant *transitus*, to use Joest's term (drawing on Luther), between being *totus peccator* and *totus iustus*.[175] Such a scheme leaves little room for the Christian as an ethical subject, as we saw above.

It must be said that such a view of Christian life is not congruent with Scripture. Paul, after all, speaks of increase in love and growth toward the goal of blamelessness at the day of Jesus Christ (Philippians 1:9–11; 1 Thessalonians 3:12–13). He speaks not only of old and new persons but also of *transformation*, which presupposes a subject capable of change (2 Corinthians 3:18). It is difficult on biblical grounds to see why one cannot speak of progress, even visible progress in the Christian life.[176] Does not the existentialist view encourage a kind of overly realized eschatology, in which my existence is reduced to a totally

173 For the profound influence of existentialist theology on the denial of the third use of the Law, see Murray, *Law*, esp. 41–74, and 100, 112, 128, 129, 131, 140, 144. Closely related to existentialist theology is situation ethics (ibid., 59, 82 n. 94, 84 n. 132, 129, 160 n. 244).

174 See on Elert above.

175 Joest, *Gesetz und Freiheit*, 60–62, 92.

176 Cf. Althaus, *Paulus und Luther*, 73–74. Second Corinthians 4:16, 18 should not be taken in the sense that renewal in the Spirit is essentially invisible. In context, the point is that what looks like the apostle's participation in death is actually a participation in Christ's life (4:10–11). It would be illusory, of course, ever to assume that one has reached perfection. Any progress only reveals how much further one has to go! On the problem of "progress" in Luther, see Joest, *Gesetz und Freiheit*, 82–99, and Althaus, ibid., 74–80. See also the critique of Joest in Theodor Dieter, *Der junge Luther und Aristoteles: Eine historisch-systematische Untersuchung zum Verhältnis von Theologie und Philosophie* (Berlin: Walter de Gruyter, 2001), 306–8, 317–35, 343, 346. Dieter shows, on the basis of Luther's understanding of

actualized status *coram Deo* (I am totally condemned and totally freed from condemnation by God)? As a Christian, my *eschatological* status before God can never be *totally* actualized in this life.[177] I must still make choices of right and wrong, choices that have a real bearing, if not on my justification before God by faith, yet on how I exercise my freedom, which God will judge and which can lead me away from faith.[178]

This, in my view, is one major area where Forde's and Elert's proposals go astray. Forde was critical of both the Lutheran Orthodox and the *Heilsgeschichte* approaches to Law, because, in his view, neither approach took the Law seriously enough. The Orthodox attempt to make the Law, understood as an eternal order, as the foundation for atonement is too abstract and conceptual. The Law merely becomes part of a "system" that has no actual or existential relevance. On the other hand, the *Heilsgeschichte* approach is also too conceptual. It consistently seeks to remove the threat of the Law. The Law is a temporary dispensation, and God's wrath is not taken seriously. In Forde's view, the historical approach also obscures the newness of the Gospel, since the Gospel is only seen as the inevitable unfolding of a historical process, a foregone conclusion, as it were.[179] Forde argued that these earlier approaches to the Law and atonement needed to be corrected by an "actualizing" approach, where atonement is not primarily thought about in abstract terms of a system, but as an actual, eschatological event.

motion, that Luther's *simul* does not exclude, but includes (even requires) progress in righteousness, which happens through continual repentance.

177 Cf. Murray, *Law*, 195.

178 Joest, *Gesetz und Freiheit*, 65, 124–29 (cf. p. 80), raises the question about Luther: Does Luther's radical vision of the Christian as, in effect, inhabiting two realities at once, split between total slavery to sin and total freedom in Christ, correspond to reality? Is the Christian not one "I," one person, capable of progress? Luther's answer, according to Joest, is that the Christian is indeed one person, spirit and flesh, but that his or her total, concrete person, even the will, is wholly "flesh." As we have seen, it is precisely this view of things, and disagreement over it, that led to the anthropological ambiguities in Article VI. To explain how the Christian, who remains wholly flesh, can nonetheless agree with and do God's will, Luther must appeal to a nonbiblical, human "super-will" ("einen Überwillen haben"), which struggles even against the will of the redeemed. The Christian can never know that he or she can follow the Law other than by external compulsion; the Christian can only believe that he or she can do so.

179 Forde, *The Law-Gospel Debate*, 69–74. See further pp. 78, 120, 131, 134.

Forde was undoubtedly right that any adequate account of Law and Gospel must include an actualizing moment in the life of the believer. But by so emphasizing the eschatological newness of Gospel as an event discontinuous with Law (by which Forde hopes to overcome the problem that Orthodoxy, *Heilsgeschichte*, and liberal theology all emphasized too much the continuity of Law and Gospel[180]), Forde, it seems to me, risks losing sight of the continuity of the old Adam and the new person in Christ as *personal ethical subject*.[181] While Forde would (rightly) insist that the Law never ceases to carry out its condemning function on the justified, since they remain liable to sin, it seems that in his proposal the new person in Christ is deprived of any normative structure for the right exercise of freedom. A sharp discontinuity between the old Adam and the new person in Christ may be effective homiletically;[182] whether it is capable of rendering a coherent biblical anthropology or ethics is another question.[183] A similar critique can be made of Elert.[184]

(3) A third construal of Pauline theology that can lead Lutherans to object to the notion that Law can positively shape Christian freedom is an overwhelmingly negative, even crass, characterization of Law. There has been a tendency to ally Law uncritically with sin and with God's wrath. Luther himself was aware that for Adam before the fall, the Law was not a burden, but a joy, and it could be fulfilled. Luther was also aware that the

---

180 Ibid., 72, 74–76, 78, 121, 134–35, 191–92, 200, 213–14, 218–19.

181 Cf. Murray, *Law*, 129–30. On the continuity of old and new man in Paul, see Althaus, *Paulus und Luther*, 65–66 (though later on p. 66 Althaus moves dangerously close to synergism! Cf. pp. 6–7).

182 Note Forde's emphasis on proclamation rather than theology as such (*The Law-Gospel Debate*, 190, 213).

183 Cf. the remarks on the distinction between Law and Gospel in Robert W. Jenson, *Lutheran Slogans: Use and Abuse* (Delhi: ALPB Books, 2011), 31–36. Forde's radical separation of the old and new ages and his confining even the new life in "this age" prevent him from giving any clear, positive, biblical content to the new life (pp. 221–33). Forde recognizes the dangers of his approach (p. 215).

184 Elert (see above) distributes Law and Gospel thus: the preaching of the cross functions as Law to crucify the old man. The resurrection, however, has the last word. As Gospel, it raises up a completely new man, ruled only by grace. Here the Law can no longer speak. The result of Elert's distribution of Law and Gospel is that, not only is there no substantial unity between Law and Gospel, but there is no real continuity between the old man and the new.

Law was not originally an instrument of God's wrath.[185] When it came to speaking about life after the fall, however, and even about the life of the Christian, Luther could ally Law, sin, death, and the wrath of God in a way that makes it almost impossible to distinguish between them. "These three—Law, sin, and death—are inseparable," he could say.[186] For Luther, God Himself uses the Law to drive humans deeper into sin. In that sense, Law itself can even be a manifestation of God's wrath against sin.[187]

Following Luther, some opponents of a third use of the Law in the sixteenth century argued that the only Law about which we know is one that coerces, demands, accuses, and terrifies. The *Heilsgeschichte* approach makes Luther's view of Law normative for a history of salvation in which the Law plays only a temporary and negative role. In Forde's presentation of Hofmann, Law is regarded as a manifestation of God's wrath, and God's wrath occupies a stage of history beyond which we move in Christ. In Forde's own existentialist approach, Law is regarded as a "power" of "this [old] age," which, because it always accuses us, we seek to "get rid of."[188] Forde opposes Karl Barth's formula, "Law is the necessary form of the Gospel, whose content is grace," the formula that the Law is the "form of this age."[189] As such, the Law has almost exclusively a negative valence.[190] Elert treats "Law" as essentially retributive. The principle is *lex semper accusat*: the Law always accuses, from which Elert draws the conclusion—not very clear in its logic—that the Law can never do anything other than that.[191]

---

185 Althaus, *Theology*, 174; Joest, *Gesetz und Freiheit*, 112.

186 WA 39/I,354.24

187 Althaus, *Theology*, 175–76.

188 Forde, *The Law-Gospel Debate*, 211, 213. By this, of course, Forde does not mean to take an antinomian position in terms of *theology*. The sense, however, is that we seek to become free from Law existentially.

189 Ibid., 207, 211, 214–15.

190 Forde, ibid., 215, recognizes the danger that "speaking of Christ as the 'end' of the law (and thus of this age) will become almost exclusively a kind of *negative* theology . . . in which it is difficult to give positive content to the new life in this age."

191 Elert, "The Third Use of the Law," 42: "Law is *unable* to perform any other function because it is always retributive. This is not only the teaching of St. Paul. It is already contained in the Decalogue." Similarly, Elert, *Law and Gospel*, 36 (and cf. pp. 7–13, 42). Elert's logic seems to be that since the pedagogical function of the Law is either the first (Melanchthon) or

In response, it must be said that one cannot be too careful in making right distinctions when Paul speaks of Law, sin, and God's wrath. It is true, of course, that Paul says that the Law effects wrath (Romans 4:15), that the Law came "in order that trespass might increase" (5:20), and that the Law was given "for the sake of transgressions" (Galatians 3:19). It would be easy to draw from these verses an exclusively negative view of the Law, in which God gives the Law primarily or even exclusively as an instrument of accusation or retribution. But that would be a gross misreading of Paul.

What does Paul actually say about the purposes of the (Mosaic) Law? In the first instance, the Law instructs about God's will (Romans 2:18–20). In addition, in the time before Christ the Law functioned as "disciplinarian" (Galatians 3:24); that is, it chastised, disciplined, constrained, and guarded Israel.[192] From the perspective of faith, one can see that it had an additional function. It imprisoned all who came under it under the condemnation of sin until Christ should come, so that we might be justified by faith (3:23–25; cf. Romans 3:9, 19–20, 21–26). The Law condemns the sinner to death (2 Corinthians 3:6–11; cf. 1 Corinthians 15:56). But God's wrath works already apart from the Law of Moses (Romans 1:18–32); already the conscience accuses the human of sin, the Law being written on human hearts (2:15). The Law of Moses brings God's wrath to bear in a more intense way, because the Law reveals in a clearer way that sin (committed with or without a Law; cf. Romans 2:12) is in fact trespass (4:15), transgression of God's holy will (5:20; Galatians 3:19), thus "magnifying" sin (Romans 5:16, 20) by revealing the "sinfulness" of sin (Romans 7:13), and leaving humanity without defense before God (Romans 3:19).

---

second (Luther) use, the Law can have no purely instructional use. Elert defines the third use narrowly as pedagogical ("instructional") and then dismisses it on the grounds that the pedagogical use refers to something else. That is an inadequate treatment of Law in biblical-theological perspective. Against Elert, one can say that in all three uses the Law has both positive and negative functions, always laying down a norm, and always exposing sin. See Haikola, *Usus Legis*, 30–31 (cf. p. 128).

192 The term *paidagōgos* in Galatians 3:25 probably encompasses a number of dimensions. See Richard N. Longenecker, *Galatians* (Dallas: Word, 1990), 146–48.

Luther's reading of Paul in the sense that God gave the Law to incite sin or to manifest His wrath does not seem warranted.[193] Paul is careful to make clear that the Law is not a cause of sin. We must distinguish between Law as such, which is good (Romans 7:12), and Law that is misused by Sin to corrupt and to condemn.[194] Thus people rightly wish to be freed from the *condemnation* of the Law in Christ; but that is different from wanting to escape God's Law as such (e.g., Forde), on the (false) grounds that Law as such is *essentially* retributive or indissolubly mixed with sin.[195]

Another long line of interpretation, stretching from Luther to Bultmann to Althaus to Forde, and even including Barth, holds that a (even the) chief mark of sin is the human's misuse of the Law for his or her own purposes. The effort or even the desire to be righteous before God on the basis of the Law is itself sinful;[196] for that is *Selbstbehauptung* (self-assertion) before God: with the Law I sinfully try to establish my own righteousness before God. Underlying my "obedience" to the Law is actually a will set against God. Thus the Law places the human in opposition to

---

193 Althaus, *Theology*, 176 n. 41.

194 In Romans 7:7, 9 Paul clearly does not mean to say that the Law is the cause of sin. Rather, Paul is expressing the paradox that even when a good Law is given, the power of Sin finds a way to misuse it for its own purposes (7:8, 10, 11, 13). At the same time, once Sin has gained power over a person, the Law brings that Sin to deeper consciousness. The Law does not "increase" Sin in the sense of *causing* it, but in the sense of becoming an opportunity for Sin, exposing it, and making humans liable for it. Romans 7:6–13 is, among other things, a defense of the Law, showing that Law and Sin must be distinguished.

195 Paul's harshest words about the Law come in Galatians 4:3, 8–10, where he puts Torah on the side of paganism and its superstitious belief in the "elements of the universe." It is possible that the Jewish Christianity that was infiltrating Galatia included syncretistic elements not unlike the Colossian heresy (cf. Colossians 2:8, 20). Cf. Eduard Schweizer, *Der Brief an die Kolosser* (Zurich: Benziger/Neukirchen-Vluyn: Neukirchener, 1976), 101. Paul may be concerned that the Galatian adoption of certain parts of the Jewish Law made them particularly susceptible to pagan beliefs. But Paul's rebuke in Galatians 4:10 should not be read apart from Romans 7:12; 14:5 in grasping his overall view of the Law.

196 This view appears in Luther's 1535 *Lectures on Galatians* (AE 26:253–54: the "very keeping of the Law" for the purpose of being righteous before God is sinful). Rudolf Bultmann takes up this notion in his *Theology of the New Testament* trans. K. Grobel, 2 vols. (New York: Scribner's, 1951), 1.247–48, 263–67: the "desire" of which Paul speaks in Romans 7 includes the zeal to be righteous in the Law; Althaus, *The Divine Command*, 16–17; Forde, *The Law-Gospel Debate*, 206, who further states, "there should be no quarrel on this point"; also, though from a different overall perspective, Barth, "Gospel and Law," 84–89.

God, not only when the human rebels against the Law, but even when the human obeys. Althaus even considers the effort to be righteous before God on the basis of the Law to be a repetition of the primal sin of Adam: "the effort to live before God by something other than God's own love."[197]

It is difficult to find such a view in Paul. It is true that for Paul unbelief, which accompanies Israel's rejection of God's righteousness in Christ in favor of its own righteousness (Romans 10:3), is sin (transgression) (11:11); and Luther (not without good reason) considers unbelief the chief sin against God.[198] When Paul actually comes to discuss the relationship between Sin and the Law (Romans 7), however, *Selbstbehauptung* does not appear to be essential to the problem of Sin and Law.[199] Moreover, Paul does not teach that the *Christian* who has been freed from the power of Sin and who, in faith and freedom, wishes to have his or her freedom shaped in accordance with God's will is sinning. To seek to be *justified* before God on the basis of the Law after coming to faith is wrong (and causes one to fall away from grace; Galatians 5:2–5). If one seeks to follow the Law without justifying faith, one is still trapped in Sin (Romans 14:23). It is surely sinful when the Law—paradoxically—becomes an occasion for behavior contrary to God's will (cf. Romans 7). And it would be sinful if the Law were to cause one to become conceited toward God or others (Galatians 5:26; Philippians 2:3; cf. Luke 18:9–14). But the desire itself to live in conformity to God's Law (or will) is not sinful, nor is that desire contradictory to being in a right relationship to God through faith.[200] Here again one must say that some of the early orthodox Lutherans seem to stand closer to the biblical witness than Luther does.[201]

---

197 Althaus, ibid., 16–17.

198 Althaus, *Theology*, 144–50.

199 As the linguistic similarities between Romans 7 and Galatians 5:16–18 show, the "desire" of which Paul speaks in Romans 7 is almost certainly desire eventuating in concrete works of the flesh that are against God's will (Galatians 5:19–21). It is not the desire to establish one's own righteousness before God by one's own efforts.

200 Was the son who stayed home and never broke one of his father's commandments (Luke 15:29, 31) a sinner simply because he wanted to remain in a right relationship with his father through obedience to the commandments? At most, we may say that he sinned in being self-righteous or resentful toward the grace shown to his repentant brother (15:28).

201 Haikola, *Gesetz und Evangelium*, 85–88, points out that for Flacius righteousness by faith

EVANGELICAL FREEDOM, THE THIRD USE OF THE LAW, AND NEW TESTAMENT *PARENESIS*

Our reflections thus far lead us to the view that we must not oppose freedom and Law in the Christian life, and that we should think of *nomos* in terms of a structure for the exercise of authentic freedom. Furthermore, Lutheran objections to speaking of the justified as inhabiting a realm of freedom that can be *positively* shaped by Law and as an ethical subject whose freedom is to be shaped by Law seem unwarranted. But is it biblically legitimate to speak of *nomos* as a structure for the exercise of Christian freedom (rather than as a coercive Law)? Have we not overlooked some crucial texts? Does not Paul teach that the Law and the Spirit (or Christian freedom) are mutually exclusive and that Christians are not under the Law (Romans 6:14, 15; Galatians 5:18; cf. 5:1, 13)? A response is necessary.

First, the Galatian struggle was over the question whether the Gentile Galatian Christians must adopt the specifically *Jewish/Mosaic Law* in order for their *justification* before God to be complete (Galatians 5:2–4; cf. Acts 15:1–5). The answer was clear: no. But that does not mean that Paul thought that Law (better: *nomos*) in the sense of a normative structure for the exercise of freedom was of no relevance to Christians.[202]

Second, it is true that Paul states that those who are led by the Spirit are not "under Law" (*hypo nomon*), by which he means the *Mosaic* Law. But as we have already seen in Romans 6–8, Paul teaches that precisely those who are free, who are no longer under Law (6:14–15), have their lives shaped by a normative pattern of ethical teaching based on apostolic tradition. Paul uses the word *nomos* in a variety of ways, and we cannot

and righteousness through the Law were congruent in Adam's original state, whereas only after the fall are the two kinds of righteousness opposed to each other. For Luther, this opposition is an in-principle one: to be righteous by faith is precisely not to be righteous through the Law, ever. See further Haikola, *Usus Legis*, 135–36.

202 After all, Paul acknowledges that the Jewish Christian may continue to follow the Law (Romans 14:14; 1 Corinthians 9:20) without injury, as long as he or she does not see in it the cause of justification (Romans 4:12) or make it a requirement for Christian unity (Galatians 2:11–14; Romans 14). Paul's acknowledgment, it seems to me, strikes a blow against any claim that *nomos* is in principle antithetical to evangelical freedom.

reduce it down to any one of them (e.g., Law in its condemning function) without doing damage to Paul's overall view of Law. We concluded that *nomos* for the justified is best understood in the sense of a *normative structure for the exercise of authentic freedom open to life with God*. But that raises the question: Which *nomos*? This question requires a consideration of the foundations of Paul's ethical teaching.

The foundations of Paul's ethical teaching are multiple and complex, but they are neither indiscernible nor incoherent nor illogical. It is helpful to begin by recalling that Paul can speak of a *nomos* of the Spirit (Romans 8:2) and of a *nomos* of Christ (Galatians 6:2; cf. 1 Corinthians 9:21). He can also speak of *not* being *anomos* with respect to God (that is, of not being free with respect to God's Law; 1 Corinthians 9:21), which appears to be largely synonymous with being in the Law of Christ.[203] Finally, he can speak positively of Christians fulfilling the (Old Testament) *nomos*, including the second table of the Decalogue and the commandment to love the neighbor as oneself (Leviticus 19:18; Romans 13:8–10; Galatians 5:14).[204] As we shall see, he can even uphold commandments of the Mosaic Law where they are presented as universally binding. We have already considered the topic of the Law of the Spirit in Paul. Let us look at the other instances of Paul's use of *nomos*.

In two places, Paul speaks of the "Law (*nomos*) of Christ" (Galatians 6:2; cf. 1 Corinthians 9:21), while in a number of other places he holds up Christ as a model for imitation (Romans 15:3, 5; 1 Corinthians 11:1; Philippians 2:5). In the latter texts, the contexts make clear that Paul is thinking in terms of the "Law of Christ," for what it means to imitate Christ is basically synonymous with what it means to fulfill the Law of

203 1 Corinthians 9:21 contains a play on words. To those without the Law (*anomois*), Paul became as one without Law (*anomos*), although he is not Lawless with regard to God (*anomos theou*), but is in the Law of Christ (*ennomos Christou*). "Not being *anomos theou*" is used primarily to limit the meaning of the preceding *anomos*.

204 Paul's commendation to "observe the commandments" in 1 Corinthians 7:19—markedly *excluding* the commandment to circumcise!—most likely intends the Decalogue, or any commandment that belongs to loving the neighbor as oneself (cf. Romans 13:9). Cf. 1 Corinthians 7:19 with Galatians 5:6: circumcision and noncircumcision are contrasted respectively with keeping the commandments and with love, suggesting an equivalence.

Christ. The basic outlines of this *nomos* are easily and concisely summarized. The Law of Christ is essentially to seek the good of others, rather than one's own good (1 Corinthians 10:24, 33; Philippians 2:4). That happens by bearing patiently with the weaknesses, failings, and burdens of others (Galatians 6:2; cf. Romans 15:1), gently correcting them where necessary (Galatians 6:1) (not "tolerating" them!). All of this has the aim of edifying others and strengthening their faith (Romans 15:2; 1 Corinthians 10:23) on the way to eternal salvation (1 Corinthians 9:19–23; 10:33). When one compares such behavior with the Jesus of the Gospels, it is no wonder that Paul calls it the "Law of Christ."

With respect to the Old Testament Law, Paul urges Christians to fulfill it by loving the neighbor as oneself and (more specifically) by obeying the commandments of the second table of the Decalogue (Romans 13:8–10; Galatians 5:14). Thus while keeping the Law of Moses as such is no longer a requirement for justification, the commandment to love (as manifested in keeping the commandments of the second table of the Decalogue) remains binding on the Christian. From that fact, one could easily conclude that Paul has a minimalistic ethics, largely reducible to love of the neighbor, and a minimalistic view of the role of the Law of Moses in the Christian life. That, however, would be a mistake.

In the first instance, one must note that love (*agapē*), even before it is a matter of how one treats the neighbor, is a matter of how one's own life is shaped. From 1 Corinthians 13:4–7, one can see that love includes even such apparently "presocial" characteristics as humility, nonirritability, joy in the truth, faithfulness, endurance, and hope. Indeed, love really embodies all the fruit of the Spirit (compare the list in Galatians 5:22–23).[205] It is noteworthy that Paul often discusses love in connection with putting to death the works of the flesh (Romans 13:8–14; Galatians 5:13–14, 22–24; 1 Thessalonians 5:7–8).[206] In other words, for Paul love

205 In other words, love is the chief fruit of the Spirit (cf. Romans 5:5), which then manifests itself in the other fruit. See further Philippians 2:1–11.

206 If disordered desire (*epithymia*) is the chief manifestation of sinful life in the flesh (Romans 7:7–12), and if love is the chief fruit of the Spirit, then, when the Spirit frees us from living toward the flesh, it is no surprise that love is accompanied by putting to death the deeds of

entails a certain way of being in the world, a structure of existence, as it were, that precedes how I treat other people. The love of Christ totally constrains me, so that I do not live for myself but for Christ (2 Corinthians 5:14–15). Love by its very nature puts limits on its own freedom (1 Corinthians 8–10).

Second, one must observe that the Old Testament (Mosaic) Law provided the underlying framework for ethics in the apostolic Church, and that Paul accepted the ethical consensus of the apostolic Church on that basis. For example, on the basis of Leviticus 17–18, the apostolic Church regarded commandments against idolatry and sexual immorality as *universally binding* on Christians, Jew and Gentile alike (Acts 15:19–21).[207] Such commandments were therefore in something of a different class from commandments that applied only to the Jewish people (e.g., regarding food and days). Paul apparently agreed with the apostolic consensus (1 Corinthians 5–10; 1 Thessalonians 1:9; 4:3).[208] Nor does Paul question the Torah's teaching that God created man and woman for each other in marriage (which of course applies to Jew and Gentile alike). While the Gospel frees a person from the Torah's command to marry (1 Corinthians 7), it does not free the Christian from respecting God's created order for sexuality.

Scholars in recent years have become increasingly aware of just how deeply Paul's ethical and disciplinary instruction is rooted in the Old Testament and even in Jewish Torah exposition (*halakha*).[209] This may

---

the flesh.

207 The reason is that the Torah makes such commandments binding on both the Israelite and the foreigner who lives among Israelites. Leviticus is the most likely origin for the apostolic decree, as the reference to Moses (Acts 15:21) indicates. One may compare how rabbinic Judaism regarded the so-called Noachide laws as universally binding, in contrast to laws specific to Israel.

208 Paul does not explicitly prohibit consumption of blood. It is possible that consumption of blood was not a significant enough issue among his Gentile Christians for Paul to address. Although consumption of blood was not unknown in ancient paganism—there being no universal taboo against it—sacrificial blood tended to be reserved for the souls of the dead (poured out to them at the grave) or for the gods, and consumption of blood was regarded by many as barbaric. See Walter Burkert, *Greek Religion* (Cambridge: Harvard University Press, 1985), 59–60; Burkert, *Homo necans* (Berlin: Walter de Gruyter, 1972), 64, 68–69, 272.

209 See, e.g., Brian S. Rosner, *Paul, Scripture, and Ethics: A Study of 1 Corinthians 5–7* (Grand

seem odd to those who are accustomed to viewing Paul as an opponent of Law. It makes sense, however, when one rightly distinguishes between justification by faith *coram Deo* without works of the Mosaic Law and the project of shaping Christian freedom, for which Paul gladly appealed to the Law, which he honored and in which he delighted (Romans 3:31; 7:12, 16, 22). Moreover, one can see that Paul's concept of participation in Christ and life in the Spirit was easily congruent with the apostolic Church's teaching, based on Mosaic Law, on matters relating to idolatry and sexual immorality (1 Corinthians 6:12–20; 10:14–22). In other words, despite his frequent distinction between Law and Spirit, for Paul, when it comes to shaping the ethical life, Spirit stands in considerable continuity with Old Testament Law. After all, the Law itself is spiritual (Romans 7:14)!

Indeed, although the foundations of Paul's ethical teaching are multiple and complex, it is crucial to see their basic coherence. Life in the Spirit, conformity to Christ, love, the continuing validity of those elements of the Mosaic Law that are universally binding and that cohere with the Gospel—all of these hang together as a piece. For the Christian, all of these together become *nomos*, a normative structure for the exercise of Christian freedom. It is in their interconnectedness that they become a coherent structure. For example, *love*, in the sense of an unselfish seeking of the good of the neighbor (1 Corinthians 13:5; Philippians 2:2–4), of building up the neighbor (1 Corinthians 8:1), and of bearing with the neighbor (Romans 15:1–6) *is* the *Law of Christ* (Galatians 6:2). In faith, I follow this Law. I imitate Christ (1 Corinthians 11:1). But not only do I imitate Christ, I also become conformed to Him (2 Corinthians 3:18). Precisely because it is the Spirit of *Christ* that inhabits me as a believer (Romans 8:9–10; cf. Galatians 2:20), and because I am spiritually united to Him (1 Corinthians 6:15, 17), it is Christ's own person that shapes my Christian existence and structures (puts limits on) my freedom in the *Spirit* (1 Corinthians 6:15; 10:21). Also, because I am joined to the

Rapids: Baker, 1999); Rosner, *Paul and the Law: Keeping the Commandments of God* (Downers Grove: InterVarsity Press, 2013); Peter J. Tomson, *Paul and the Jewish Law: Halakha in the Letters of the Apostle to the Gentiles* (Assen: Van Gorcum, 1990).

cross of Christ in Baptism, I put to death the deeds of the flesh (Galatians 5:19–21), including those that are prohibited by the *Law of Moses* for all people, Jew and Gentile alike.

For Paul, then, while the Christian is free from the Law of Moses with respect to justification, it is too simple to say that the Christian is free from *nomos* as such. Freedom and *nomos* are not opposed to each other in the Christian life. On the basis of Paul, we should understand *nomos* for the Christian not in the sense of the Mosaic Law, nor as an accusing or coercive Law, but in the sense of a (normative) ordering of exercise of freedom in the Spirit. This *nomos* is fundamentally the rule of the Spirit, but it stands in considerable continuity with the Mosaic Law, while it is also shaped by life in and according to Christ. It seems to me quite right and proper, then, to speak with the Formula of Concord of a third use of the Law for Christians in terms of God's "unchanging will." This is Law (*nomos*) in the sense of a normative structure for the exercise of Christian freedom. That is, Law is not "the form of the Gospel, whose content is grace" (Barth), nor is it merely the "form of this age" (which ends with the Gospel) (Forde). Law is the proper form of *authentic Gospel freedom*, the content of which is obedience to the will of God as revealed through the prophets and apostles, in openness to eternal life with God.

We need to resist construals of the third use of the Law that dismiss it on the grounds that it reintroduces merit or works-righteousness after justification (as in the sixteenth-century debates; also Joest; Bring);[210] or that the attempt to perform the Law always constitutes sinful self-assertion before God; or that there can be no third, pedagogical use of the Law because the Law always accuses (Elert). All of this is beside the point. Biblically considered, a true third use of the Law has the primary purpose of preserving and properly shaping authentic freedom open to eternal life with God and of preventing the Christian from submitting to the realm of the flesh, just as God intended His first commandment(s) to preserve for Adam an authentic freedom open to eternal life with God.[211]

---

210 For the sixteenth century, see earlier in this essay; Joest, *Gesetz und Freiheit*, 132–33, 134, 193, 195, 198; Bring, "Gesetz und Evangelium," 62, 63.

211 By this, I do not mean to deny that the third use of the Law can have other purposes such as

This structure of freedom is not, of course, simply equivalent to the Mosaic Law or even a part thereof. As we see from Paul, the structure for the exercise of Christian freedom has multiple roots, including the Law of Christ and the Law of the Spirit. Moreover, Jesus and the apostles alternatively abolish, affirm, clarify, and deepen or intensify different aspects of Old Testament Law. We cannot make blanket statements about the Law in the New Testament. But any church that calls itself apostolic will need to examine carefully the basic patterns laid down by Jesus and the apostles for relating Old Testament Law to life in the Gospel and respect those patterns.[212]

The last point, it seems to me, is extremely important. One argument against regarding Law as an eternal order (and hence against a third use of the Law) has been that God has apparently given different laws in different situations:[213] Adam and Eve were not given the whole Law, but only one commandment. Israel had its Law, but it no longer applies to Christians (as national law). Luther and the Confessions, when they speak of an unchanging or universal will of God, tend to identify it with the Decalogue, understood as a restatement of natural law, which is further summarized in the law of love (the application of which for Luther, however, becomes highly dependent on situation and vocation: one can even say a kind of situation-love ethic).[214] So what is God's unchanging will? Is there one?

In response, I would say that a biblical view of reality, and a sense for God's will and ways, must be based on the whole of Scripture, in its

are outlined in Article VI of the Formula.

212 We have focused on Paul, because he is thought to be the primary witness against a third use of the Law. A full biblical account would, of course, have to include other New Testament voices, especially James and Matthew. One would also have to think through how one arbitrates between the various voices in the New Testament and their relative authority. Finally, one needs to acknowledge that the apostles themselves attribute varying levels of authority to their *parenesis* (e.g., 1 Corinthians 7). All of this, however, would go well beyond the scope of this essay.

213 Cf. Forde, *The Law-Gospel Debate*, 176–78.

214 On unchanging Law in Luther, see Lazareth, *Christians in Society*, 148–49, 228–30; Forde, *The Law-Gospel Debate*, 176–77; Haikola, *Usus Legis*, 99–101, 111, 148–49; Haikola, *Gesetz und Evangelium*, 94–95; Bring, "Gesetz und Evangelium," 64. On situation-love ethics in Luther, see further n. 232 below. For the Confessions, see LC II 67; Ap IV 6–8; FC SD VI 12.

overall canonical shape. We have already seen that Genesis 2–3 and Romans 7 open each other up for understanding the relationship between Law, freedom, and sin. It is not as though Genesis 2–3 reveals one reality and Romans 7 another. For the Christian, Genesis and Romans read *together* reveal the reality of the human situation.

In the same way, I would argue, for Christians the New Testament opens up God's will as it always existed but either remained unrevealed or lay latent in the Old Testament. A fine example is Jesus' teaching on marriage. What Jesus teaches was *always* God's will for marriage (from the garden onward; cf. Mark 10:6–8), and will always be God's will for marriage, even though God, in His patience with human sin, allowed for divorce and remarriage in the Law of Moses (Mark 10:2–9). In other words, the Law of Moses intervenes with certain purposes (cf. Galatians 3:19–22), but it does not change God's enduring will for His created people. We must read Genesis and the Gospels together to understand what is unchanging in God's will. In general, the New Testament gives the decisive interpretation and application of Old Testament Law, helping us to distinguish between what in Old Testament Law is of enduring validity and what was of only passing significance for the nation of Israel. Moreover, Paul has a strong doctrine of natural law (Romans 1:18–32; 2:12–16, 25–29). It seems doubtful, therefore, that one can say that because Adam and Eve had only one (or two) commandment(s), they did not know God's will (before their fall into sin).

Thus God's unchanging will does, indeed, consist above all in the commandment of love and the Decalogue (as these are interpreted in the New Testament and not merely as the national law of Israel),[215] but from a canonical perspective one must say that it includes more than that (e.g., what Scripture has to teach about marriage). Moreover, it is clear that one needs the whole canon to discern God's unchanging will. One can argue at point after point that the New Testament opens up God's Law in

215 For Luther on the Decalogue as universal, natural law (as distinct from Mosaic Law), see Lazareth, *Christians in Society*, 227–29.

its depth and enduring validity.[216] In other words, we ought not to think of God's will for humanity as changing. God's will for humans has always been the same; it is only that we have received a fuller revelation of it (indeed, the fullest revelation of it this side of heaven) through Jesus and the apostles. Accordingly, as Christians we are that much more accountable to it.[217] That means that the third use of the Law is not simply the first or second use of the Law applied to the justified, as has sometimes been argued.[218] A third use of the Law calls the justified to something higher than the first use does; the latter applies to all people, justified or not. Nor does this "higher" Law imply a theologically poorly grounded pietism, a special ethic of the "reborn," as Bring claims.[219] It represents God's will for *all* Christians.[220]

That means that the Church should not be afraid to take New Testament *parenesis* seriously in terms of *Law*. As Luther already observed, one of the functions of New Testament *parenesis* is to make the condemnation of sin sharper than the Old Testament alone could do (in other

---

216 E.g., who is the neighbor whom I am to love as myself (Leviticus 19:18)? The neighbor includes my (supposed) enemy (Luke 10:30–37; cf. Matthew 5:44). What kinds of behavior does the commandment against adultery (Exodus 20:14; Deuteronomy 5:18) include? It includes a man taking a second wife, with or without divorce (Mark 10:2–9; previously allowed under Mosaic Law), with certain exceptions (Matthew 19:9; 1 Corinthians 7:15). And so forth.

217 That implies no injustice on God's part. God seeks from us what He has always sought from people. But through Christ and the apostles, we have been given a deeper knowledge of God's will than generations before Christ came. And to whom much is given, from that one much is required! One can ask why God chose to reveal His will in the fullest way only through Christ and the apostles rather than at the beginning of Israel's history. That is part of the mystery of God's providence. Undoubtedly it has to do with the fact that God's revealed Law first took form as a national law of Israel. The question is not really different from the question why salvation in Christ came so "late" in Israel's history. Why did God not send the Messiah at the beginning of Israel's history? Jesus came at the "right time" (*kairos*) in God's providential ordering.

218 E.g., Werner Elert, *The Christian Ethos*, trans. C. J. Schindler (Philadelphia: Fortress Press, 1957), 299. Better is Piotr J. Malysz, "The Third Use of the Law in Light of Creation and Fall," in Gieschen, ed., *The Law in Holy Scripture*, 211–37, here 234: The third use of the Law is the first use without its alien character. It is "a return to creation in its primeval beauty." (However, it should be noted that the first use of the Law basically applies to the post-fall situation. It restrains the sinful nature. Cf. AE 26.308–9; FC SD VI 1; SA III 2.)

219 Bring, "Gesetz und Evangelium," 48–55, 89.

220 Why else does Paul call his Gentile Christians to a new way of life, and to a way of life that entails more than an abstract concept of love or spontaneity in the Spirit?

words, the second use of the Law).[221] That makes good sense. If the Holy Spirit, through the teaching of Jesus and the *parenesis* of the apostles, does not convict us, then it is impossible for Christians to recognize "how deeply [the Law] has cursed and condemned" them, as the Formula puts it in Article V.[222] In other words, the Gospel itself exposes and condemns sin to a depth that even the Law of Moses does not attain.[223] But if the teaching of Jesus and the apostles is to function in principle as *Law*—in the second use—even for the justified (and New Testament *parenesis* is addressed to the justified), then it is difficult to see why it should not also function as Law in the third use—for the justified.[224]

Thus in my view, to speak of a third use of the Law is to be preferred to speaking of a "practical" use of the Gospel (Joest),[225] or of a "second" or "parenetic" use of the Gospel (Lazareth),[226] or of the "[Gospel] command" (Althaus).[227] The latter terms have been thought necessary to safeguard the Gospel, so that Law will not stand where only Gospel can stand. The effect, however, is to undermine the Gospel; for if one tries to shape Christian freedom on the basis of the Gospel alone, without biblical Law, the Gospel will always be transformed into a new law,[228]

---

221 Joest, *Gesetz und Freiheit*, 72–73.

222 FC SD V 10.

223 E.g., if Matthew 5:28 is not in some sense "Law," can the Christian be condemned for using pornography?

224 It is worth noting that even Luther, for all of his emphasis on the Christian's freedom in the Spirit, not needing the Law, and on love overruling the Law, finally acknowledges that the Christian needs to abide by the apostolic imperatives of the New Testament. His famous statement that Christians can establish new Decalogues as Jesus and the apostles did is immediately qualified by the statement that, since we are inconstant in the spirit and since the flesh fights against the spirit, we need to adhere to apostolic mandates, lest the Church be torn to pieces (WA 39/1.47,51–58. See AE 34:112–13). These apostolic imperatives can be called Law in a sense. Note again, however, that for Luther they are needed primarily to combat the flesh and not to shape freedom.

225 Joest, *Gesetz und Freiheit*, 132, 134. Joest's claim (e.g., pp. 184–85) that New Testament parenesis has the main function of driving the Christian back to justifying faith rather than shaping Christian life in a normative way is untenable. It does not take seriously enough the specific shape of life that Paul sought to inculcate in his churches.

226 Lazareth, *Christians in Society*, 198–99, 244.

227 Althaus, *The Divine Command*, 28–29.

228 It has often and correctly been said that when one dispenses with the Law in the name of the Gospel, Law always comes back in, often under the guise of the Gospel, thereby corrupting

whether that is a "law" of absolute freedom (anarchy, leading to the triumph of the will to power),[229] the law of love (Ritschl),[230] or laws of human invention.[231] The law of love, left to itself, becomes no less demanding, coercive, or convicting than Law otherwise conceived: "You need to be more loving!" And since the New Testament *parenesis* has been made optional, "love" can become whatever I want it to be.[232] A third use of the Law, when understood as a normative structure for proper exercise of evangelical freedom, does not undermine the Gospel

---

the Gospel. This is as true of the second use of the Law as it is of the third. See, e.g., Rudolf Mau, "Gesetz V," *Theologische Realenzyklopädie* 13.82–90, here 86 (Agricola); Forde, *The Law-Gospel Debate*, 119, 134; Murray, *Law*, 107, 123, 145. Articles V and VI of the Formula of Concord are important precisely for guarding against this corruption of the Gospel. In particular, Article V helps to set clear limits to the way in which the Gospel can be understood to function as "Law."

229 E.g., Robert J. Hoyer, "On Law and Gospel," *The Cresset* 29:2 (February, 1966): 8–9, here 9: Since the Law only condemns, it "forbids our setting up categories of good and bad either of person or act" and actually functions "to deny validity to any ethical pattern in relationship to God." Hoyer, "On Second Thought," *The Cresset* 32:1 (November, 1968): 17, goes so far as to propose "anarchy" (absence of Law), which "is one of the things we hope for in paradise," for the Church. Hoyer dreams of a Gospel utopia in which the Spirit "check[s]" every "believer's desire to impose his will on others." We "deny . . . grace if within the fellowship of the Spirit we promote control by law because we fear anarchy." How can this not lead to the triumph of the will to power?

230 See Forde, *The Law-Gospel Debate*, 96–119, esp. 111. Albrecht Ritschl rejects the orthodox understanding of Law and atonement. The love of Christ (Gospel) is realized in the Law of love within the Christian community, a Law which is immanent rather than transcendent. Now the Gospel-Law of love becomes the mandate for the Church's legalistic efforts to construct the kingdom of God on earth, as we see in liberal Protestantism today.

231 Once God's Law is thrown out, a new Law must take its place. One may take as an example the 2009 social statement "Human Sexuality: Gift and Trust," of the Evangelical Lutheran Church in America. While highlighting the commandment of love, the statement ignores most biblical laws relating to sexual behavior, substituting for them all manner of new imperatives regarding what the Church "must," "should," and "will" do in this realm, whether guided by Scripture or not. See www.elca.org/Faith/Faith-and-Society/Social-Statements/Human-Sexuality (accessed November 20, 2014).

232 Love can become mere tolerance of the neighbor's lifestyle, or it can be defined as seeking the "good" of the neighbor, but where the "good" is defined exactly as I or the neighbor wants it, rather than biblically. It is rather dubious that "love" can become the grounds for overruling God's Law, as one can find in Luther and some of his heirs (Haikola, *Usus Legis*, 80–81, 145–46). God's love frees us from the condemnation of the Law, but it does not overturn God's Law in the sense of His enduring will for humanity. When Jesus in the Gospels challenges the validity of certain laws of the Torah, He challenges them on the basis of other competing or, more often, more important *imperatives*, based on God's creative will, the imperative to preserve life, other commandments (the Decalogue), or discipleship to Him, not on the basis of an abstract principle of love.

of justification, but rather serves it, by preserving the Gospel as Gospel and by helping to keep the justified from falling back into the power of the flesh.[233]

CONCLUSION: THE CRISIS OF FREEDOM TODAY AND THE LUTHERAN WITNESS ON LAW AND GOSPEL

Our study leads to the conclusion that, when we reconsider in light of Scripture the problems that have attended the doctrine of a third use of the Law, from Luther and the Confessions up to the present, a number of major problems disappear. Much of the opposition to the third use of the Law has been based on views of Law or of the human person that are not biblically defensible. A major reason for the rejection of the third use of the Law has been that it was difficult to define the relationship between the Law and the justified insofar as they are reborn (*quatenus renati*): *either* the Law must coerce the old Adam in the justified; *or* the justified are reborn and led by the Spirit in such a way that they do not need the Law. Either way, there seems to be no place for a truly *third* use of the Law. But when one considers Law in a total biblical-theological perspective, it makes better sense to speak of Law (*nomos*) for the justified in terms of a *structure for the exercise of authentic freedom in the Spirit*. The third use of the Law is not coercive, nor does it reestablish the Law as a means for self-justification, nor does it entail sinful self-assertion before God, nor does it deny the guiding power of the Spirit.

Important steps in reaching this conclusion have come through rethinking the concept of Law in biblical-theological perspective and through distinguishing Paul's anthropology from Luther's reception of it. Reconsideration of Genesis 2–3 and Romans 7–8 has enabled us to see that Law is *essentially* neither coercive, nor retributive, nor a means to merit, self-justification, or self-assertion. Rather, divine Law originally constitutes and shapes authentic human freedom. Such freedom finds its

233 Cf. here the Formula's warning against the "false Epicurean delusion . . . that faith and the righteousness and salvation we have received cannot be lost through any arrogant and intentional sin or evil work" (FC SD IV 31).

origins and self-transcendent goal in a relationship to God, characterized by willing obedience to God as His creature, open to eternal life with Him. Reconsideration of Paul's anthropology has enabled us to see the shortcomings in the anthropological presuppositions of Article VI of the Formula. It has enabled us to see that Christ reopens for the justified a realm of authentic freedom, open to eternal life with God, which can and should be positively shaped by *nomos* of a kind. Just as the commandment(s) given to Adam constituted and shaped his authentic freedom in openness to eternal life, so the Spirit constitutes and shapes the authentic freedom of the justified, open to eternal life with God, not in opposition to *nomos* but in congruence with it. This certainly does not mean that the Christian, as reborn, does not also remain old Adam, does not continue to sin, or does not still need the accusation or coercion of the Law. It simply means that the Christian should not be viewed as fundamentally determined by Sin.[234] In a blessed irony, biblical study allows us to exercise a critique of the Formula's interpretation of Scripture, which enables us in turn to affirm the Formula's basic intention in teaching a third use of the Law specifically for the justified.

As we noted earlier, theologians in the period of the Second World War and immediately afterward, from both the Reformed tradition (Barth) and the Lutheran tradition (e.g., Joest), raised the troubling question whether the Lutheran distinction of Law and Gospel had not contributed to the political crisis that engulfed Germany in the years of the Third Reich. Had Lutheranism made the distinction so sharp that it actually separated Law and Gospel, in such a way that the Church no longer had any word of binding Law to speak? In that context, Lutheran theologians were forced to reconsider the relationship between Law and Gospel.

The circumstances today are different, but we, too, live at a critical point in the history of the West. Freedom is in crisis—questions about the origins, the meaning, and the ends of freedom stand before us as

234 Why can the Law not accuse me of sin, coerce my "flesh," and shape my freedom from Sin all at the same time?

perhaps never before. The triumph of free-market economies and of democracy after the end of the Cold War has brought material blessings and personal freedoms to people who formerly did not enjoy them. But at what cost and to what ultimate ends do such blessings and freedoms come? The amassing of personal wealth leads to new oppressions, with the creation of a permanent underclass. The middle class in America, it seems, is being squeezed to the ends of the economic spectrum. The lust for wealth and the ideological commitment to freedom from taxation lead to a selfish hoarding of resources and to a situation where future generations are increasingly burdened by the debts of their parents and grandparents. What will the effects be on the long-term stability of developed nations? As the global economy develops, as consumption grows, and as environmental degradation worsens, humanity faces the possibility that it will destroy its own planetary home.

Meanwhile we witness the move toward ever-expanding personal autonomy, in the form of the right to destroy human life in the womb, expansive sexual expression, the redefinition of marriage, and even the right to change one's "gender identity" on the basis of subjective feeling.[235] At the same time as these personal freedoms expand, we witness the curtailment of free speech and freedom of religion. There is a hollowing out of civil society: the lack of confidence in the ability to define and to pursue a common good and shared truths, through which a free people can be sustained, leaves us increasingly in a situation where individuals feel compelled to define and zealously protect their own private goods and freedoms, at no matter the cost to society. A hardened

235 In an interview, Dr. Grégor Puppinck, Director General of the European Centre for Law and Justice, speaks of a new era of "post-human" and even "trans-human" rights in Europe. Whereas human rights have been based on notions of human nature and dignity, a new anthropology is leading to post-human rights (rights based on the individual will, e.g., abortion and euthanasia prevailing over rights based on human nature and dignity, e.g., the right to life) and even to trans-human rights (rights based on the creation of an "increased human nature" through technology, e.g., eugenics prevailing over the right to life). The new anthropology and understanding of rights are based on a concept of personal freedom as the "undefined will of the individual," www.zenit.org/en/articles/how-human-rights-are-becoming-post-and-trans-human-rights (accessed November 27, 2014); see also the interview published in French by Flora Thomasset, *La Croix* (October 31, 2014): 11.

individualism, focused on the satisfaction of personal desires and freedoms, comes to underlie both public and private life.[236]

The crisis of freedom in the public realm increasingly permeates churches. The "freedom of the Gospel" becomes an abstract principle that can be used to deconstruct God's commandments in a way never intended by Jesus, Paul, or the other apostles. "Love," defined not biblically but as mere sentiment, becomes the primary (and perhaps the only) law in the church, which overrides biblical structures of human existence (such as marriage) and biblical structures for the exercise of freedom (such as chastity). Love becomes the law that condemns as "loveless" anyone who rejects the agenda. The same churches that celebrate this radical freedom pass resolutions condemning corporate greed, not seeing that it may be the very ideology of personal freedom underlying their sexual ethics that promotes the greed of those whom they condemn and the economic structures that oppress those for whom they claim to advocate. A coherent, biblical vision of authentic human freedom is profoundly lacking.

In a day when the question of freedom looms as perhaps never before, the Lutheran confessional witness on Law and Gospel can be a great gift to men and women, directing them toward true freedom through an encounter with the one Word of God speaking in two voices.[237] The Law, culminating in the Word of the cross (FC SD V 12), tells me that Christ died for *all* my sins as exposed by both Old and New Testaments and continually confronts me with the truth about my life. As Gospel, the same Word of the cross (and resurrection) truly frees me. It frees me from my past and from the guilt of my sins. It opens up for me eternal

236 For a brilliant, concise diagnosis of the problem in the American public realm, see Yuval Levin, "Taking the Long Way," *First Things* 246 (October, 2014): 25–31. The impoverishment of American political culture lies in the fact that the "idea of liberty that both progressives and conservatives generally articulate takes the person capable of freedom for granted without pausing to wonder where he might come from" (p. 27). True liberty "requires not only that people be free to choose but also that they be able to choose well." "To be capable of freedom . . . we need more than the liberation of the individual from coercion. We need a certain sort of moral formation" (p. 28).

237 While Barth's formulation regarding Gospel and Law was wrong, he was surely right to question whether the Lutheran schema of Law and Gospel has left the Church vulnerable to

life with God. It frees me from the fear of death, from my obsession with the things of this world, and from my sinful and selfish lusts. The Spirit, having opened up authentic freedom before God, shapes my freedom in accordance with God's enduring will as revealed in the Old and New Testaments (Law).[238] A third use of the Law protects me from an illusionary "freedom of choice," where I get to choose my own works apart from God's Word or command;[239] such illusionary "freedom of choice" is actually the chief occasion for sin, whereby I, under the power of Sin, continually choose falsely against God's will and fall back into Sin's captivity.[240]

It is my hope that confessionally minded Lutherans (or at least Book of Concord Lutherans) will be able to come to some consensus on this matter. Such a consensus could not only aid Lutheran unity, but it could also bring Lutherans closer to other orthodox Christians, who live in the midst of the same crisis of freedom as we do, but who do not carry all the unhelpful "baggage" that Lutheran Law-Gospel theology carries. Law-Gospel theology, when it is not integrated into the full witness of the biblical canon, is sometimes met by our ecumenical partners with suspicion and even bafflement, not always unwarranted. Our ecumenical dialogue partners who are committed to orthodoxy need Lutheran

---

ideological distortions of Law and to insist that we learn to hear Law and Gospel speak together as Word of God. Elert's view that Law and Gospel cannot speak together because they are in substantive opposition to each other is, in my view, profoundly unbiblical. Article V of the Formula should warn us against subscribing to such a view.

238 For a proposal for Lutheran ethics along lines similar to those developed here, including divine Law and communion with God as the form of authentic human freedom, see Reinhard Hütter, "The Twofold Center of Lutheran Ethics: Christian Freedom and God's Commandments," Karen L. Bloomquist and John R. Stumme, ed., *The Promise of Lutheran Ethics* (Minneapolis: Fortress Press, 1998), 31–54. See further Hütter, *Bound to Be Free: Evangelical Catholic Engagements in Ecclesiology, Ethics, and Ecumenism* (Grand Rapids: Eerdmans, 2004), 111–67. Hütter deconstructs the modernist, post-Kantian dichotomization of Law and freedom in favor of Luther. One can argue, however, that the dichotomy is already found to some degree in Luther and some of his followers.

239 FC SD IV 20; VI 20.

240 Proponents of unlimited access to abortion are fond of speaking of women's "freedom to choose." But how often do women who procure abortions actually act freely? How many are coerced by men? How many are pressured by their economic situation to choose abortion? How many are pressured by the inconvenience that pregnancy and child-raising cause to the pursuit of education and career? Where is the freedom? Is not this supposed "freedom" actually very often unfreedom?

counterparts who take their confessions seriously. That does not mean that our confessions stand above criticism, even from ourselves. But neither can the Lutheran theological heritage as a whole—or, for that matter, Luther himself—be immune from criticism. In every case, we must submit what we have received to careful study and critical engagement with Scripture. I offer this essay in that spirit of critical engagement.

PREACHING LAW AND GOSPEL

Repentance and Faith from the Penitential Psalms in Lent

John T. Pless

The penitential psalms (6, 32, 38, 51, 102, 130, 143) have long been associated with Lent. Pope Innocent III (r. 1198–1216) ordered that all seven psalms were to be prayed each day, while kneeling, during the Lenten season or if this proved unfeasible, at least on Fridays. In the Middle Ages, these psalms were associated with the seven deadly sins: Psalm 6 was said to address anger. Psalm 32 was associated with pride. Psalm 38 with gluttony. Psalm 51 with luxury. Psalm 130 was directed against envy and Psalm 143 against sloth.[1] Luther would value the penitential psalms, especially Psalm 51, but instead of linking them to deadly vices, the reformer would read these psalms as expositions of God's work of bringing sinners to repentance and faith through the preaching of His Law and Gospel.

Luther lectured on the penitential psalms in 1517, and he revised these lectures and republished them in 1525. Luther would provide a

1 See Mark A. Throntveit, "The Penitential Psalms and Lenten Discipline," *Lutheran Quarterly* (Winter 1987): 495–512. Throntveit writes: "The connection between the psalms and these applications are tenuous, usually linked to a single word, and probably have more to do with the similarity in number between the psalms and the sins than with exegetical precision. More damaging in my opinion, is that such an application misses one of the crucial points these psalms strive to make, namely the distinction between a cataloguing of specific sins, as in the individual laments and the recognition of sin as part of our human condition: 'Behold, I was brought forth in iniquity, and in sin did my mother conceive me.' (51:5), 'If thou, O Lord, shouldst mark iniquities, Lord, who could stand?' (130:3), 'for no man living is righteous before thee' (143:2b)" (500).

fuller exposition of Psalm 51 in 1532.[2] Luther would see sinfulness not merely as individual deeds but as a state of being that embraces all of man's existence which he has inherited from Adam; this is the root sin from which man cannot deliver himself.[3] In this commentary, Luther observes that David confesses not simply his adultery and murderous plot against Uriah but the corruption of all his powers both inwardly and outwardly.[4] Luther writes:

> He [David] is not saying, "My mother sinned when she conceived me"; nor is he saying, "I sinned when I was conceived." He is talking about the unformed seed itself and declaring that it is full of sin and a mass of perdition. Thus, the true and proper meaning is this: "I am a sinner, not because I have committed adultery, nor because I have had Uriah murdered. But I have committed adultery and murder because I was born, indeed conceived and formed in the womb, as a sinner." So we are not sinners because we commit this or that sin, but we commit them because we are sinners first. That is, a bad tree and bad seed also bring forth bad fruit, and from a bad root only a bad tree can grow. (AE 12:348)

Five years later in the Smalcald Articles, Luther is insistent: "The foremost office or power of the law is that it reveals inherited sin and its

2 For background on Luther's 1532 exposition of Psalm 51, see Martin Brecht, *Martin Luther: Shaping and Defining the Reformation 1521–1532*, trans. James L. Schaaf (Minneapolis: Fortress Press, 1990), 456–58. Brecht says "When confronted with the great Psalm 51 and its main thrust of repentance and justification, Luther felt that he was truly a student who needed the Holy Spirit as his schoolmaster. Nevertheless, his commentary may be called a masterpiece" (456).

3 Here see Robert Kolb, "The Lutheran Doctrine of Original Sin" in *Adam, the Fall, and Original Sin*, ed. Hans Madueme and Michael Reeves (Grand Rapids: Baker Academic Press, 2014), 109–27. For an explicit treatment of "root sin" in Luther's interpretation of Psalm 51, see Robert Kolb, *Luther and the Stories of God: Biblical Narratives as a Foundation for Christian Living* (Grand Rapids: Baker Academic, 2012), 104–6.

4 See Kolb, *Luther and the Stories of God*, 104. "In breaking the fifth and sixth commandments, David has defied and despised the Lord and thus has become guilty of blasphemy against the first commandment. David thus served as an excellent example of the interconnectedness of individual sinful acts and their root in the rejection of God and doubt of his Word."

fruits" (SA III 2, 4).[5] This statement is foundational for Luther's discussion of repentance. The Law is retained, Luther says, in the New Testament in order to work repentance: "Now this is the thunderbolt of God, by means of which he destroys both the open sinner and the false saint and allows no one to be right but drives the whole lot of them into terror and despair" (SA III 3, 2). Luther equates the Law with the hammer of which Jeremiah speaks (Jeremiah 23:29). In opposition to papal theology, Luther asserts that the Law does not work an "active contrition" or a "contrived remorse" but a "passive contrition; true affliction of the heart, suffering, and pain of death" (SA III 3, 2). Contrary to the antinomians, Luther argues that repentance is produced by the Law not the Gospel. But to the office of the Law, "the New Testament immediately adds the consoling promise of grace through the gospel" (SA III 3, 4). Where the Law is preached without the Gospel, there is only death and hell. The Law never provides consolation. Instead, as Mark A. Seifrid, in commenting on Romans 7:24–25, points out,

> The Law tells us a story about ourselves that we are unable to tell and unwilling to hear. It carries us on the "journey to [the] hell of self-knowledge"—and in the knowledge of Christ back from there to heaven itself. Only those with ears to hear, who know the apostle's shout of thanksgiving, can listen to the story and see the image of our person reflected in the Law.[6]

The papists do not preach genuine repentance for they fail to see both the Law and sin for what they are. They continue to hold out hope for some uncorrupted part of man retaining the capacity to will the good.[7] This leads to what Luther condemns as an "active contrition" where penance is parsed into three parts: contrition, confession, and satisfaction. "In this way, they directed the people who come to penance to place

5 Book of Concord quotations in this chapter are from Kolb-Wengert.

6 Mark A. Seifrid, "Romans 7: The Voice of the Law, the Cry of Lament, and the Shout of Thanksgiving" in *Perspectives on Our Struggle with Sin: 3 Views of Romans 7*, ed. Terry L. Wilder (Nashville: B & H Academic, 2011), 114.

7 Here also see Article II in the Augsburg Confession and the Apology.

confidence in their own works" (SA III III 13). This, Luther concludes, is a Christless procedure: "Here we see how blind reason gropes around in the things of God and seeks comfort in its own works, according to its own darkened opinions" (SA III III 18).

Luther holds up John the Baptist as the model preacher of repentance, for his preaching of the Law condemns the totality of sin whether it is inward or outward (see SA III III 30–32). The repentance which John preaches is not uncertain or fragmentary (SA III III 36). Likewise, the forgiveness which John proclaims is inclusive for he preaches Christ, the Lamb of God who takes away the sin of the world (SA III III 38). This repentance is not confined to a single episode in the life of the Christian; it is ongoing: "This repentance endures among Christians until death because it struggles with the sin that remains in the flesh throughout life" (SA III III 40).

The understanding of repentance laid out by Luther in the Smalcald Articles is evident in his exposition of the Psalter.[8] Luther says that the Psalms might be called a "little Bible" for they show us Christ and His kingdom: "The Psalter ought to be a precious and beloved book, if for no other reason than this: it promises Christ's death and resurrection so clearly—and pictures his kingdom and the condition and nature of all Christendom—that it might be called a little Bible. In it is comprehended most beautifully and briefly everything that is in the entire Bible. It is really a fine enchiridion or handbook" (AE 35:254). Luther sees the Psalms as God's words to us; words which we in turn are authorized to speak to Him in lament and praise, confession and thanksgiving. Because the Psalms are God's Word, they give us certainty in our speaking.

Luther sees the Psalms as universal. They apply to all the saints: "Hence it is that the Psalter is the book of all saints; and everyone, in whatever situation he may be, finds in that situation psalms and words that fit his ease, that suit him as if they were put there just for his sake,

8 For an introduction to Luther on the Psalms, see Carl Axel Aurelius, "Luther on the Psalter" in *Harvesting Martin Luther's Reflections on Theology, Ethics, and the Church*, ed. Timothy J. Wengert (Grand Rapids: Eerdmans, 2004), 226–39.

so that he could not put it better himself, or find or wish for anything better" (AE 35:256). When it comes to the preaching of repentance and faith, the Psalms are indispensable, for in them, Luther says, "There you have a fine, bright, pure mirror that will show you what Christendom is. Indeed, you will find in it also yourself and the true *gnothi seauton,* as well as God himself and all creatures" (AE 35:257).

Luther came to understand that the knowledge of self without the knowledge of God leads to despair and that knowledge of God without the knowledge of sin leads to presumption.[9] Psalm 51 gives us both. The preacher may wish to set the psalm in the context of 2 Samuel 11:1–12:15, unfolding the dynamic of Nathan's proclamation of God's Law to David, which brings about the knowledge of self. See Psalm 51:3, "For I know my transgressions, and my sin is ever before me."[10] Here the preacher could explore the connection that is entailed in this self-knowledge. Ash Wednesday is a day for self-examination. Recall the words of the Exhortation in Corporate Confession and Absolution (*LSB,* p. 290): "It is proper that we diligently examine ourselves, as St. Paul urges us to do, for this holy Sacrament has been instituted for the special comfort of those who are troubled because of their sin and who humbly confess their sins, fear God's wrath, and hunger and thirst for righteousness. But when we examine our hearts and consciences, we find nothing in us but sin and death, from which we are incapable of delivering ourselves."[11]

The somber words of the Ash Wednesday liturgy announce to us what deep down we already know, that we are dust and to dust we must return. But the problem is not merely mortality. It is not just that we die but that we die as sinners under God's judgment. It is a judgment that is

---

9 On this point, see Dennis Ngien, *Fruit for the Soul: Luther on the Lament Psalms* (Minneapolis: Fortress Press, 2015), 29.

10 Scripture quotations in this chapter are from the ESV.

11 Note Hans Joachim Iwand: "Our knowledge of God will only be true insofar as the essence of sin is taken into account and is understood. Likewise, our knowledge of sin will only be genuine if it is at the same time understood and recognized in connection with God's Being, for the one includes the other." *The Righteousness of Faith according to Luther*, trans. Randi H. Lundell (Eugene, Oregon: Wipf and Stock Publishers, 2008), 26–27. Used by permission of Wipf and Stock Publishers. www. wipfandstock.com.

not misplaced; it is justified (Psalm 51:4). It is a verdict of condemnation that falls not simply on miscalculated choices and perverse deeds; it falls on me, my person. It falls on the one who was a sinner before he first cursed, lusted, lied, hated, or killed. It falls on the one who was brought forth in iniquity and conceived in sin (Psalm 51:5).[12]

To confess your sin is to agree with God's evaluation of your life. To confess your sin is to cease the futile attempt to self-justify. Rather it is to join with David in saying to God: "Against You, You only, have I sinned and done what is evil in Your sight, so that You might be justified in Your words and blameless in Your judgment" (Psalm 51:4). In confession, the sinner acknowledges that God is right. It is to agree with God's verdict: Guilty.[13]

But to speak of guilt requires some clarification today, for another word has come to attach itself to guilt. So we speak of guilt feelings. Guilt is seen as the subjective reaction of the doer to the deed, i.e., how I feel about what I have done.[14] But this is not the case with the Scriptures' use of the word *guilt*. In the Bible, guilt has not so much to do with emotions as it does with what happens in a courtroom when a judge declares the defendant guilty. The criminal may or may not have reactions of remorse, regret, or shame. It doesn't matter. The verdict of the judge establishes the reality. God's Word of Law unerringly establishes His judgment. There is no appeal.

To deny the verdict means that the truth is not in us, says the apostle John. But denial can never bring release. Only God's absolution can release from the accusation of the Law and unlock the sinner from his sins.

---

12 Hans-Joachim Kraus *Psalms 1–59*, trans. Hilton C. Oswald (Minneapolis: Fortress Press, 1993), 503. "Misleading are the statements of H. Gunkel that the OT does not recognize the total depravity of human nature but only affirms weakness vis-á-vis what is good, and that thus the OT statements are 'a preparation for the church's doctrine of original sin.' On the contrary, the OT emphasizes the total depravity, the degeneracy of guilt of human existence with an altogether different force than the church's doctrine of original sin."

13 Kraus, *Psalms 1–59*, 503. "In a confession of guilt over against God himself, the petitioner submits to the righteous judgment of Yahweh."

14 On this point, see the discussion of Werner Elert, *The Christian Ethos*, trans. Carl Schindler (Philadelphia: Fortress Press, 1957), 163–73. Elert traces the subjective understanding of guilt to F. Schleiermacher.

Lutheran theology is nothing if it is not realistic![15] Like the Scriptures, Lutheran theology does not start with notions about human freedom and the potential (great or small) that human beings have. Theologies that start with assumptions about human freedom end up in bondage.[16] Lutheran theology begins with man's bondage in sin and ends up with the glorious liberty of the Gospel. The bondage to sin is not a slight defect that can be corrected by appropriate self-discipline. Neither is it a sickness that can be cured by the appropriation of the medication of regular doses of God's grace. Sin is enmity with the Creator that carries with it God's verdict of guilt and a divinely imposed death sentence. To be a sinner is to be held captive in death and condemnation. The distance between God and humanity is not the gap between infinity and the finite but between a Holy God who is judge and man who is the guilty defendant.

Confession is the acknowledgment of this reality. The sin is named not in an effort to "get it off my chest" but to acknowledge it before the Lord, to whom no secrets are hidden. Where sin is not confessed, it remains festering and corrosive, addicting the sinner to yet another attempt at self-justification. Confession admits defeat and so leaves the penitent open for a word that declares righteousness, a verdict that justifies. That word is called absolution. It is absolution alone, says Gerhard Forde, that is the answer: the absolute claim of God, who is inescapably present to the sinner.[17]

It is with the absolution, the word by which God declares sinners righteous for Christ's sake, that the bones God has broken with the hammer of His Law are brought to rejoice. The Gospel alone puts joy and gladness into the ears of sinners (Psalm 51:8). For in this verdict, the

---

15 Here note the German New Testament exegete Udo Schnelle's comment on Pauline anthropology: "his view of human beings is not merely pessimistic, but realistic" in *Theology of the New Testament*, trans. M. Eugene Boring (Grand Rapids: Baker Academic Press, 2009), 319.

16 On this point, see Gerhard Forde, *The Captivation of the Will* (Grand Rapids: Eerdmans, 2005), 21.

17 Gerhard Forde, "Absolution: Systematic Considerations" in *The Preached God: Proclamation in Word and Sacrament*, ed. Mark C. Mattes and Steven Paulson (Grand Rapids: Eerdmans, 2007), 153.

judge of heaven and earth is hiding His face from our sins and scrubbing us clean from all iniquity (Psalm 51:9). The flip side of God's hiding His face from our sins is His causing His face to shine on us (Numbers 6:24–26).[18]

This salvation is completely the work of the triune God. In forgiving sins, the God who created the heavens and the earth is bringing forth a new creation. Just as by His Word God called all things into existence at the beginning, so now by His Word He is creating a clean heart and renewing a right spirit (Psalm 51:10; also see 2 Corinthians 4:6).[19] Hans-Joachim Kraus observes about Psalm 51:

> The petitioner knows that he is entirely dependent on the merciful activity of God. From God's mercy alone he expects the blotting out of the guilt which is looked on as corruption (v. 5) that totally permeates the human being. Only God can eliminate the threatening, dark wall of separation, sin, that separates God and human beings, and blot out what is intolerable. Only by God's creative, renewing power can the heart be cleansed and led to a new obedience. Also the future is in the hands of God alone. If God sends the Spirit of willingness and constancy, then the psalmist is saved from fickleness and unfaithfulness. Even the witness of thanksgiving (v. 15) is exclusively left in the hands of powers furnished by Yahweh. Everything is God's act. The *sola gratia* shines forth from every verse. No gift, no condition comes between God and man. No sacrifice has an effect on Yahweh. Only the pleading and trusting human

18 For more on this point, see Claus Westermann, *The Living Psalms*, trans. J. R. Porter (Grand Rapids: Eerdmans, 1989), 98.

19 Here see Mark Seifrid on 2 Corinthians 4:16, "Paul simultaneously defines salvation as an act of creation and presents creation as an act of salvation. They are bound together not only in their like action but also in their form: just as the creation of light is the work of the word of God, so the Gospel is God's effective word that creates light in the darkness of the human heart. In this effective word, that performs what it says, God's person and work are revealed. Salvation is coming to know and confess God as the Creator of our life." *The Second Letter to the Corinthians* (Grand Rapids: Eerdmans, 2014), 200.

> being is the sacrifice, he who with body and life surrenders himself to God, who has nothing to offer but a heart that is bruised and broken (v. 17). The human being presents himself to God for what he is. For him nothing remains except to plead for forgiveness and confess his guilt. In its extreme of knowledge and wisdom (v. 6) which has been won from the prophetic word of the OT, Psalm 51 stands out in the Psalter. Its peak statements are unique. And its fullness of insights is incomprehensible.[20]

Only where there is the forgiveness of sins can God be rightly honored and praised. Apart from God's forgiveness, we open our own mouths and we know what spews forth. It is not the confession of Christ's righteousness, but blasphemous assertions of our own righteousness. The sin of the heart defiles the lips. Here the preacher may wish to draw out connections with the Second Commandment and its explanation in the Small Catechism.[21] Christ's absolution is the key which unlocks lips to praise His name by confession of His righteous deeds.

In Psalm 51, David links this praise of God with sacrifice (also see Hebrews 13:15–16). Sacrifice is not a means that we use to placate a wrathful God. On account of Christ's once and for all sacrifice for sin on the cross, the category of sacrifice gets relocated as we see in Romans 12:1–2. Now by the mercies of God, the redeemed offer their bodies as living sacrifices not to achieve God's favor or to merit reconciliation with Him but for the sake of the neighbor. This is nicely put by Steven Paulson: "God is keeping his Christians and their churches in this old world as a sacrifice of the body for the neighbor. He does this along with the appeal that they endure suffering, not for their salvation, but for the sake of the old world, that it might be sustained for now, and that the

---

20 Hans-Joachim Kraus, *Psalms 1–59*, 507.

21 For more on this, see John T. Pless, *Praying Luther's Small Catechism* (St. Louis: Concordia Publishing House, 2016), 19–21. Also see Albrecht Peters, *Commentary on Luther's Catechisms: Ten Commandments*, trans. Holger Sonntag (St. Louis: Concordia Publishing House, 2009), 149–65.

preacher arrives in time to those who have not heard."[22] Here the preacher could draw out the implications of the Christian life as one of sacrifice as the answer or response of the one who is justified by faith. Good works are completely withdrawn from the equation of justification before God. They are relocated in the world for the well-being of the neighbor. God does not need or want your sacrifice (Psalm 51:16), but the neighbor needs it and so freed from the burden of self-justification we are liberated to live for the sake of the world.

Luther sees both Law and Gospel at work in Psalm 51.[23] Through the Law comes the knowledge of self—that is, a knowledge of sin which is always directed against God. Repentance is to be crushed with this knowledge imparted by the Law. The Law allows no space for self-justification. It is the Gospel, however, that gives broken sinners the knowledge of God's mercy in Christ Jesus. Preaching the Psalms gives us a true knowledge of self (repentance) and a true knowledge of God (faith).[24] Luther recognized that in the penitential psalms, God gives us the words to cry out to Him in our distress, lament our sins, and confess trust in the promise of His righteousness in which alone is our sure and certain hope.[25] To preach the penitential psalms is to proclaim both the Law

---

22 Steven Paulson, "The *Simul* and the Two Kingdoms: The End of Time Twice," *Logia* (Reformation 2016), 20. The whole of chapter 11, "The Fruit of Faith" based on Romans 12:1–2 in Paulson's book, *Lutheran Theology* (New York: T & T Clark, 2011), 228–43 is especially helpful in preaching the "new obedience" of which David speaks in Psalm 51:16–19. © Steven Paulson, 2011, *Lutheran Theology*, Bloomsbury T & T Clark, an imprint of Bloomsbury Publishing Plc.

23 Here see James A. Nestingen, "Luther on Psalm 51," *Lutheran Theological Journal* (December 2016): 201–12. Particularly: "Luther argues throughout the Commentary on Psalm 51, both Law and Gospel are required for the preaching of genuine repentance. The Law must be preached to faithfully expose the bondage of original sin, to confront the pious and dislodge the smug. But the best it can produce, by itself, is cynicism, despair, and finally death. The Gospel brings the Law to its proper goal in Christ, who is 'the end of the Law that all who believe may be justified' (Rom. 10:4). It enables the good resolve, or better yet it creates the faith that makes it possible for the sinner to tell the truth about the self in faith and hope" (208).

24 A comprehensive guide to the preaching of the Psalms is to be found in Sidney Greidanus, *Preaching Christ from Psalms* (Grand Rapids: Eerdmans, 2016). Greidanus includes extensive treatments of three of the penitential psalms: Psalm 51 (pp. 240–71), Psalm 32 (pp. 272–95), and Psalm 130 (pp. 364–79). Sample expository sermons are also included.

25 On Luther's understanding of the lament psalms, see Ngien, *Fruit for the Soul*. For exegetical

and the promise. Luther's commentary on Psalm 51 provides preachers with an example of how this is done so that the finality of God's promise in Christ Jesus remains the only security for those broken by sin and crushed by the Law.

---

and historical treatments of these psalms see Philip Johnston, "The Psalms and Distress" in *Interpreting the Psalms: Issues and Approaches*, ed. David Firth and Philip Johnston (Downers Grove: InterVarsity Press, 2005), 63–84; Bruce Waltke, James Houston, and Erika Moore, *The Psalms as Christian Lament: A Historical Commentary* (Grand Rapids: Eerdmans, 2014); Claus Westermann, *Praise and Lament in the Psalms*, trans. Keith Crim and Richard Soulen (Atlanta: John Knox Press, 1981).

A ROYAL ASS

Steven D. Paulson

Evangelical theology must take up as its first question: What shall I preach? Answer: The Law, without diminishment; then the Gospel, without limit. But this central question is followed immediately with our second theological question: To whom shall I preach? The answer is surprising: Not to free, but bound wills.

Now, preaching to bound wills is either a curiosity to the world, or more often an affront. For what possible reason does a person speak to a bound will, since by definition it is a will that cannot be persuaded or moved? Yet this was exactly the task given to Isaiah, "Listen, you that are deaf" (Isaiah 42:18).[1] Only a preacher could ever say something so nonsensical, so against the grain, so impossible, or as Paul says, so foolish as to preach to deaf people. So here we have our basic Lutheran anthropology, which begins, in opposition to all others, not with the *essence* of the person (the quiddities or the realities that exist right now), but rather with the *hope* of the person. So, we start not with what "is" the case—the reality of the blood and bones—as a doctor would, nor do we start with the basic powers or circumstance of the person, such as "you are a 'political animal'" (as Aristotle assumed). Instead of all that, we begin with what the person is *not*, but *will be*—the hope. A true human being is a forgiven being, who does not look at his present circumstance, but lives in hope provided in the promise of forgiveness. But to be forgiven, there must first be the sin. And so we start our answer to the question "To whom do we preach" with what is surely outside the person in the form

1 All Scripture quotations in this chapter are the author's translation.

of a promise from Christ: "I forgive you." Only then do we figure backward as to what the reality, the condition, the nature of sin is, and what it means for the present circumstance. We work from the absolution backward to figure out to whom it belongs.

In turn, this means that we have to make a major distinction when we explore what is human. God Himself is not an essence or unity that we can grasp in Himself, since He purposefully hides Himself from us. This is not, as many have thought, to attract us more thoroughly to His sublime beauty, awe and, *mysterium tremendum*. God hides from us because He refuses to be found on our side, with favor toward us—*unless He is preached*. Therefore, God must be distinguished right from the start in our theology as either preached or not preached. Failing to make this distinction means all sorts of things will be imagined about God that are simply not true. Such as, that God is the highest good to which our desires must rise. Or that human nature is made to seek the higher, supernatural in order to become truly human. Or that the possibility of participation in the divine unity or Godhead is the motivation and goal of human life. Instead our baseline theology says this: God hides from you when you have no preacher; God seeks you when you do.

When we next turn to the matter of "to whom do I preach?" (so anthropology), we must make the same kind of distinction as with our doctrine of God. So just as God is either (1) not preached and hiding so as not to be found by you, or (2) preached and hiding a new way as to be found by you—in the Word, not outside it—just so the human person is either going to be considered with a preacher or without. Before a preacher or after. There is no such thing as considering the human *per se*, in himself, outside the presence of the preaching office.

When we ask to whom we preach, the answer is this: to those who have no preacher. And they are simply deaf. We preach to deaf people. How deaf? Well, when you get really good at preaching, like Christ is, you can take your time getting to your congregation and preach to people who have laid in the tomb long enough to stink, just as He did with Lazarus, saying to the corpse, "Rise!" Lazarus was very deaf when this sermon was given to him by Christ. Lazarus, we could say, didn't have much potential or possibility of changing; he had no quality or quiddity that we could call "free will." He was stone deaf, equally dead. Still, Jesus preached.

Indeed, we have a name for this human nature or person that exists before the preacher arrives, and that is simply *bondage*. Humans have bound wills. Or to put it in the terms of Luther's great sermon on this matter to Desiderius Erasmus, humans suffer from "the bondage of the will." This does not mean there is no will, or that the will cannot choose. Quite the opposite, it means the will is choosing too much, serially and obsessively. Admittedly, bondage is not quite a biblical word. I had a young Lutheran boy attending a Roman private school ask me where he could find the Scripture proof for the bondage of the will, since the nun teaching him could not believe he was saying anything like that in class—that a person's will is bound, not free. So the nun told him to put up or shut up, and prove it in Scripture. But she was never persuaded. It is hard to find one verse to seal the deal if you reject Paul's withering summation of Scripture with "O man, who art thou that contendest with God?" (Romans 9:20). Besides, the bondage of the will is a term in response to a dream, a fantasy, a fraud which is so common that the word becomes almost necessary: the dream of the free will.

Have you ever tried to prove to someone their will is not free, but bound? Apologetics doesn't work. But thankfully the preacher is not required to convince anyone of a bound will. Jesus did not reason with Lazarus about coming out of the tomb. It is not belief in bondage of will that is required for faith; indeed, faith understands that belief in bondage of the will is precisely what the will cannot produce or abide. Bondage of the will is sometimes suspected, as with Sophocles's *Oedipus*, but in reality it is always in need of revelation. There is a covering over your hearers' faces that is removed when you preach—as the Spirit wills. Bondage is revealed when you preach. So when you finally get a preacher, you come to see what you had not before: you are an ass. This is not in debate when it comes to Christ. Imagining you are something else, something greater, has caused great damage in the world, and is actually the death of faith. In fact, we could make up an imaginary proposition that you are something other than or higher than the creatures, especially the donkey—stubborn and willful—because of a quiddity or quality, *essentia* or accident in you as a human that makes you different from the animals. But that imaginary proposition is a true danger and exercise of the fall of Adam who especially misconstrues what dominion is.

But the real question is not whether you are in fact an ass or not but precisely what kind of ass, since there is not one species, but two. Which kind of ass you are makes all the difference in the world (or shall we say, in the next, in eternity?). To be very precise, we learn that we are two asses at once, which is called the *simul*. But before anyone attempts to investigate himself to find evidence of the kind of ass he is, he must learn to look away from himself to the external matter of lordship. The kind of ass you are depends not upon any choice you ever have made or ever will make, and requires no "consent" of a "free" will, but depends entirely on who is your lord, who is precisely the one who rides you. You are an ass ridden by your Lord.

Luther learned how to speak this way, in part, from the great anthropological psalm, 73:22, "I have become an ass to you." What Luther taught Erasmus on this matter, and how Luther was correcting the long patristic tradition of misuse of this psalm, has always been frightening—especially to Lutherans. In brief, the long exegesis of this psalm says this: being an ass means you have a power, or freedom, to obey. Whichever lord you obey determines which kind of ass you are. Obedience then is imagined as the power of the human to make its own lord. This, in turn, inevitably became the key theological difference between those who obeyed the Law and those who disobeyed it—between the saint and the sinner. But this theological anthropology is far from true. In fact, Luther agreed there was a power of the will, the *creatrix divinitatis*, that unseated the true God and put another—any other—in His place. Thus, it is not the question of whether or not I am an ass or whether or not I have a rider, but whether one is ridden by Satan or Christ. There are only two kinds of asses, servile and royal, and two kinds of riders.

Thus, evangelicals teach differently about who humans are than the normal theology of the Law with its implication of a free, neutral will who sits in the saddle. The lord of this world is Satan, not by self-appointment or power, but by service to the one and only God, the Creator of the universe, the Father Almighty. Job learned this by terrible experience. So did Peter. So did Luther. Now what the one true God is doing with this servant Satan (who serves as the lord of sinners) I don't know, other than to say that without a preacher theology freezes at this point, while with a preacher I have learned to run from this speculation. Fortunately, faith has a place to run which the world does not have. More of that in a moment, but meanwhile Satan rides the servile ass and does not miss a single human being—all of whom are born under the Law. He rides them into sin, and so they bear the wrath of God. America and the modern world was built upon denying this fact, so it will spend any effort to reject it.

Naturally, the self-discovery of being a servile ass with Satan as rider frightens everyone: even one as significant for Lutherans as Walther von Loewenich, who in his *Luther and the New Protestantism* says of Luther's comments on Psalm 73: "It seems flatly to put an end to man as a personal being," adding, "This was certainly not Luther's intention."[2] Then he added this: "Even with an unfree will, man remains a person, not an instrument." True, the person is not by nature a PVC pipe, or a rake for the garden, but neither is the person other than a creature—and this is part of the lesson for today. Indeed, there are few better descriptions of what the Spirit makes of a person in the office of preaching than PVC pipe. But aside from that office, a person is not either a free will, thank God, which is an abstract, imaginary dream spun to oppose what we really are—creatures of the Creator who receive all things needed for life as ridden by a proper lord. But sinners assume that the best thing about them is their *possibility*, even if that potential has never been realized even once in human history. They say to themselves things like this: "After all the mistakes I have made in life, tomorrow is another day." "I just may make a better choice than I made so far, and I must learn to live with no regrets." People picture themselves this way as possibilities—

2 Walther von Loewenich, *Luther und Der Neuprotestantismus* (Wittenberg: Luther-Verlag), 418.

"maybes"—and the experience of having this pure potentiality taken away is worse than bodily death. Yet, that theft is precisely what Christ aims to accomplish by sending a preacher. Christ intends to make us perfectly passive creatures who trust their Creator—to make us human—to unseat Satan and ride us Himself.

But there is a wholly different ass yet to be born. This happens when a Stronger One than Satan comes to bind the strong man (Mark 3:23–27), divides Satan's kingdom (Luke 11:21), and sets the captives free: "we are again slaves and captives—though this is *royal* freedom."[3] That means that you suddenly and all at once become a *royal ass*. The royal ass is no less ass than a servile kind, but now is a beast who is "royally free." She has a true Lord in the saddle for whom "we readily will and do what he wills."[4] And what is it that Christ wills? This is odd indeed! Christ does not will the Law, but wills the beast's forgiveness—apart from the Law. He rides strangely, by justifying a sinner. Christ's will is not "obedience" to Law, as it was for both the scholastics who preceded Luther and the orthodox who came after him. That kind of obedience takes time and implies a free will progressing in its pilgrimage from moment to moment. Instead, Luther says when Christ rides, the obedience is "ready," meaning instant—without the moment of potential, choice, decision, or the separation of will and act. This makes you a royal ass in perfect harmony with the Royal Highness, a true likeness with Christ, who did not count equality with God a thing to be grasped but became a servile ass.

So Luther assured Erasmus: "Thus the human will is placed between the two like a beast of burden." "Between" means not *in order to choose* one or another but *to be chosen*: "If God rides it, it wills and goes where God wills" as Psalm 73:23 says: "Nevertheless, I am continually with You, and You hold me by my right hand." "If Satan rides it, it wills and goes where Satan wills; nor can it choose to run to either of the two riders or seek him out, but the riders themselves contend for the possession and control of it."[5]

3 AE 33:65.

4 Ibid.

5 Ibid., 65–66.

But everyone knows what happens with this psalm and Luther—the charge of Manichaeism immediately goes up. So it happened also in the first and second articles of the Formula of Concord. As usual, Luther was far ahead of us theologically since he heard and experienced the one vital distinction that no one else was willing to make: the difference between God preached and not preached. This distinction is not merely an epistemological exercise of the limit of our knowledge of God, but an insistence that God finally is opposed to God. God is not united in the sense we want Him to be as one essence or one true vital characteristic (say, love) that, if really known, would be highly desired. In fact, the world does not need any preachers to make the assumption that love eventually must conquer evil. People naturally assume Manichaeism. Christ is not given in order to assure us of that. Nor is God (as the great theologians following Karl Barth, including Eberhard Jüngel teach) a being who "corresponds to Himself" in the end—which is a version of making God into nothing but the eternal Law itself.[6] But God opposes God in what only Luther learned to characterize as "the remarkable duel" in his Galatians commentary—the curse of Christ by the Father, and the overcoming of that curse at the resurrection.[7]

Precisely in that cosmic duel is the binding of the strong man, the overcoming of Satan that divests him of possession and control of you, personally. That fight of Christ over Satan is not Manichaeism, and indeed is the furthest thing possible from the modern version of this that we call *Star Wars*. Luther's point is the only true monotheism, unity of God, and so the only fulfillment of the First Commandment tells us we must become a new ass ridden only by Christ. That royal rider does not say, "Have you done?" but says, "I have done, for you." That is, the *servile* ass hears the Law and its accusation; the *royal* ass hears the promise of Christ in the forgiveness of sins. The great fear to which sinners cling is not the threat of two Gods who are locked in mortal combat, or Manichaeism. It is the self-confession that I am an ass, and that asses,

6 See Steven D. Paulson, "Luther's Dangerous Account of Divine Hiddenness," in *Indicative of Grace—Imperative of Freedom*, ed. R. David Nelson (New York: Bloomsbury, 2014), 203–18.

7 AE 26:370.

even royal ones, are ridden by their masters. They are forced to go where the rider takes them—thus the fear is that we are to live an animal life that does not choose what it desires, is coerced in the meanest fashion, and so lives the dreaded life of a slave according to the desires of another. And when a person lives long enough, they begin to suspect that everyone's wills in the whole world are contrary to my own—they are masters seeking a slave. Who would not refuse to submit to that? One does not need Hegel to tell him that the world is made up of masters and slaves, and it is better to be the former than the latter. So the dream of free will masks the truth.

Free will is a disguise for what is more properly the subject of a sinner's concern: desire. *Shuq*, or *teshuqa*, הקּוּשׁתּ in the Hebrew, is rarely used in Scripture, but it appears in the crucial description of the original desire of Adam for Eve and vice versa, and in the desire gone awry in Cain that led to Abel's murder. Paul dealt extensively with this "power" of desire in the Letter to the Galatians when it came to the male member and circumcision, and rabbinic literature is full of the *Yetzer ha-Ra*, the impulsive desire of the flesh. Desire is supposed to be a kind of tool that one can move in one direction or another, and the secret of life is to move one's desire to the higher rather than the lower things. Desire is then a kind of North Star that guides one's life, but that is a fraud that is revealed once a preacher comes. We can jump right to the conclusion of this desire. What the imaginary free will fears more than anything else in the world is the forgiveness of sin—since that word immediately takes away the free will's great dream of the Law. As the rabbis said: "So God says to the Israelites, 'I created within you the evil *Yetzer*, but I created the Law as a drug." And so the rabbis conclude: "If the Evil Inclination says to you, 'Sin, and God will forgive you,' *believe it not.*"[8]

The rabbis are better than Erasmus on this matter, who feared that whoever removed the basic created desire would take away the motor of Christian righteousness. This fear of forgiveness runs deep, in the form

8 C. G. Montefiore and H. Loewe, ed., *A Rabbinic Anthology* (New York: Schocken Books, 1974), 296.

of the teaching of love found especially in Augustine in which the erotic love, *eros*, must not lose its drive, but rather reorient itself to the proper goal: if you loved animal things, do not stop desiring, but desire the higher things, which would be God and His eternal Law. What made Erasmus modern, and so a template for our current lives, is that he operated with what Luther called a "moderate Skeptical Theology."[9] That was Luther's moniker for what he prophetically saw as the black hole that future theologians and religions would fall into: a mild skepticism. Mild skepticism hides beneath its humility the *desire to hang on to desire* as the motor, the future, the hope, the possibility of the human to transcend being merely a creature of the Creator. The desire is not to be an ass. The worst thing that could happen to a person, in this mild skepticism, was to have desires denied altogether—to have them stifled and blocked. In that case, my desires would not cease burning, but they would never achieve the pleasure of release that would come when the true object of desire was finally found. Erasmus's skepticism was humbly willing to give up many things worth knowing, that is to say that they were above and beyond our human knowing. That is not easy for a humanist to admit, including giving up things like whether or not God is triune or Christ is really one person with two natures. Most surprisingly, Erasmus was even willing to give up knowing for sure whether or not he had free will before God! Even that Erasmus was willing to question since he could not be sure of it in Scripture or in experience. But he was sure he had to be allowed to "infer" free will, not prove it, else humans would be nothing but asses. His was a theology based on an inference only, but without that inference, Erasmus complained, three things would be lost that really make up the whole of religion for him, especially Christianity.

First, if you give up free will in relation to God, then you have no just way of distinguishing the wicked from the righteous—which is of course the Law. Then, second, God would be revealed as unjust in judging some as falling short of grace. That is, you would end up saying God is cruel and blameworthy of evil. Who would desire to pursue His divinity then?

9 AE 33:34.

And so finally, the human would fall into a psychology of despair, since the only thing keeping humans going in life is to have incitement to "endeavor" in life—to risk the journey upward, to climb the ladder, to try to turn one's desire from natural to supernatural—that is, to participate in the being of God by transcending. Life is shedding the ass and becoming all flame.

So in the end, Erasmus cried out to Luther for relief: Perhaps you are right! Perhaps there is no free will! But then of what worth is a man if God works on him like a potter does a pot? Luther heard this confession, and responded: Well done, poor Erasmus! Finally, you have bottomed out, and are saying something worthwhile! That is a good question, "what worth is it to be a man if God works on him like a potter does a pot?" The same was asked by the Prophets and Paul, and with that question we finally reached the nadir of modern, moderate skepticism—not too much doubt, and not too little doubt, lest we become proud. Staying in the game, lest we stop striving to control the desire and lose our one great power in life that makes us greater than the ass: the power to obey the Law or to disobey it as the means to determine our righteousness. Between me and the ass lies the precious Law. If that is removed, what good is life?

This is the dying confession of the old Adam: "Has the potter no power over the clay to make out of the same lump one vessel for honor and another for dishonor?" (Romans 9:21). And of the same, Isaiah who was told to preach to the deaf: "Woe to him who strives with his Maker, an earthen vessel with the potter! Does the clay say to him who fashions it, 'What are you making?' or 'Your work has no handles'?" (Isaiah 45:9).

The great fear of the Lutheran teaching on the bondage of the will comes at this point. What sinners want is one thing: possibility, delay of the judgment giving time to our potential to become actual. That potential depends upon getting rid of the promise of forgiveness in Christ and replacing it with the inner self in the form of "desire" or impulses. The modern, moderate skeptic knows there are problems with life, and much of it comes down to the addictive, impulsive desires of sex, wealth, fame, and the like. But the hope remains that somehow we can get a handle on that desire and direct it to its proper end of obedience rather than disobedience to the Law. We assume that if the Law rode us we would magically become unassed, and like Pinocchio become a real boy. This "endeavor" as Erasmus called it is the "journey" of becoming human—it is the meaning of life, the goal of humanity. Aristotle called this the "education of desire" that teaches itself to desire less the lower, animal things and become truly human, like God, by making our desires fit God's—which is to contemplate perfect order and reason in the form of the Law. What does God do all day? Consider Himself, in the form of the Law. What must we do? Love the higher, not the Law, and in so doing participate in God's obedience to the Law.

True, this love has gone bad, but if it were removed, then my life would have no purpose. And worse, it would be a terrific suffering—to be forced to subjugate desires by a violent, external power. I would be coerced into imprisoning desires, rather than setting them free so they can endeavor—try, move by a motion of the will to the better, the higher, rather than the worse. Denying my transcendence is violence! To be forced, brainwashed, proselytized, inculcated, trained, programmed to sublate one's desire is a fate worse than death. It is to live without endeavor—without a journey. In fact, simple forgiveness perpetrates a double violence: it imprisons my desire inside me where the desire then festers. But to be free, I must release my desire, express it to the outside, or like a raisin in the sun, it will be a dream deferred, and one day not only dry and die, but explode and destroy the self and others in the process. But worse yet, the second violence is then to allow someone else's desires to dominate mine—to be someone else's ass.

Instead, sinners think, just as Aristotle taught in the theory of tragedy, what we need is *catharsis*, a release from enclosing one's desire. We must play them out rather than nurse and succor them. A desire unexpressed to the outside is not only the definition of bondage but is also dangerous to self and world. It is the source of violence, not the end of it. Another common way of expressing this Erasmian principle is to say that the human being, in order to be truly human, must not only be natural, but *supernatural*. The goal is set, and the human can reach the goal if the endeavor is there; the endeavor is there only so long as one believes in free will—literally puts one's trust there. So in a reply often attributed to Isaac Bashevis Singer, when asked if he believed in free will, he said, "Of course I believe in free will, I have no choice!"

When Lutherans intrude upon this moderate skepticism, they are going for the jugular, the root, inherited, original sin, and in doing so have to teach not merely the redirection of desire but its demise. They are destroying love in the form imagined to be original or essential to humans. So, if we must do this—and what else is a Lutheran to do?—then we should at least make it a clean cut. But the first thing we have to say is that bondage of the will is not referring to what sinners fear the most: bondage as restriction from my desires.

The bondage of the will is not a discussion of human essence as will in that sense. You have a will and it does desire, and indeed it cannot do anything other. The bondage of the will, however, is a quick reference to what it means to come under the divine work of preaching. If you do not learn what God is doing here in dethroning your old rider and giving you a new one, then of course it does not mean God is not doing it, but that you truly do become a pawn in God's game of chess. God is then doing something that you refuse to recognize. But putting your head in the ground like an ostrich does not make it go away. In fact, there are two activities of God regarding bondage of the will, at least when God brings redemption to you. The first is truly universal: it is not that God restricts you or denies you your desires, but rather "hands you over to them," as Paul clearly says (Romans 1:24). Bondage begins with this matter: you are left "freely," if you must, to nothing but your desires. This is why Luther preceded his comments on Psalm 73 and the royal ass by saying, "Now, by 'necessarily' I do not mean 'compulsorily' [*coacte*], but by the necessity of immutability (as they say) and not of compulsion [*non coactionis*]." A sinner "does not do evil against his will, as if he were taken by the scruff of the neck and forced to it, like a thief or robber carried off against his will to punishment, but he does it of his own accord and with a ready will [*libenti voluntate*]."[10] He does evil—freely, necessarily. That is, evil is the work of your freely operating desires that have you in a terrible bondage.

Here anyone who has been addicted to the bottle can understand what the bondage that hands you over to your desires feels like. Bondage is not tying you down so you cannot do what you desire—it is precisely doing the opposite, letting you bind yourself to exactly what you want. To be able to do what you want and have no one deny you. And what do people want? Well, Paul says, a man lays with a man—homosex. And why does a man desire this? First, because it is homo—self. Second, because it is sex, which is the power of procreation—but this time used not for God's purpose, but to transcend animal life as if that were for the lower class. It is sex for self, which is not production of life, but death. Freud fought for years against the truth that what humans want is death. He mused about this phenomenon appearing again and again on his couch *ad nauseum*, but I suppose this is what people figure they can in fact produce—all by themselves and without their Creator. Just so, the serpent lied by telling us that this was what it was like not only to *have* a God, but *be* one. I can put my seed in the anus of a man and have it die there—*ecce homo*, behold the man! Thus we have Nietzsche glorying in what Luther called "the will to act." And those who do not do this particular exercise, but stand by applauding and celebrating are no more righteous, and so fall also under God's cosmic wrath at human class transcendence. What is born of this is not life, but *resentment*.

As Luther and all the philosophers and psychologists worth their salt have noticed, "the will cannot change itself and turn in a different direction [than what it wants], but is rather more provoked into willing by being resisted, as its resentment shows."[11] My friend Jim Nestingen likes to say that your will is like a Lincoln Continental with no neutral—it is always in forward or reverse. Resentment is the hallmark of this "free will" that is bound to its desire. It resents everything. If it is denied, it

10 AE 33:64.

11 AE 33:64.

resents whoever said no. If it achieves its desire, it resents the fact that it has no happiness, and people have stopped applauding for my achievement. Even achievement doesn't remove the desire at all; it only makes it bigger and the ass smaller for having it and still failing to feel fulfilled.

This is the psychological side of things, the being handed over to your own desires that is the terrible withdrawal of the Holy Spirit, or having no preacher. There is also a theological side to this, which is to discover one day that these desires did not arise *ex nihilo* from you, nor were they the product of being "created good" by a loving God. Rather, one has had them whispered in the ear by the lord who is actually riding you—which marks the discovery of Satan as your lord. The preoccupation with Satan, like the endless desire of young people for vampire movies, or the desire to contact or manipulate what is recognized as some kind of power in the world, is one result. But as Scripture says, Satan is always a liar (John 8:44). What he lies about is the specific Word of God, and therefore the natural contact with God between Creator and creature is destroyed, or at least impossibly garbled. In place of the daily reception of God's Word and your trust, we have Satan riding the servile ass, which means God is not preached. He is utterly silent.

In this way, bondage is not only in reference to the psychological aspects of desire, but also this theological truth. "God withdrew His Spirit" means not that He is absent or gone, but that He isn't saying anything to me. This forces a person into the false theology that we call "theodicy," which defends God against accusation of allowing evil, and then makes a dramatic announcement of the human attempt to sever all ties with his Creator. We call this atheism, but it is really antitheism. Luther likens it to a play put on in an empty theater. It is the ass saying that there is *no one* in the saddle, and that we finally have to get used to being alone in the universe. But in point of fact, as we also know, the devil does not mind when people do not notice him. He is not a stickler for public recognition.

It is a terrible bondage of will that is forced to spend its time not in proclamation of the promises of Christ, but rather defending God to the society that cannot hear Him. This trades theological speculation, or apologetics, for proclamation. As Hegel observed, history then becomes nothing more than an explanation to the intellect about why God is not to blame for evil in the world. Luther could see that the final position of the modern world, in the person of Erasmus, would conclude that free will is a necessary, abstract hypothesis in order for humans to hold on to their dignity and escape despair (i.e., to keep "endeavoring"). The Pelagians at least honestly thought one had the tools in their created goodness to become righteous or to fail; it was now your fault. God was not at fault for your sin. But the new mild skepticism of Erasmus that has spread everywhere "stubbornly holds onto an empty term,"[12] Luther said, in order to keep this little light of "possibility." Maybe one day someone will use his will to choose the good and not the evil, proving that it was really there all the time—even though no one in all history has yet seen it done. So we say, "even though the whole world has failed, I just might be the exception to the rule. I may be that special one who breaks out!"

One would think that holding to an empty concept that has no reality would be neutral in the world—it may not be quite right, but at least it can do no harm. So what if I believe in free will; it isn't causing any trouble to anyone else! But Luther knew that the opposite is the case. Tolerating this is not like tolerating the king with no clothes, who insists on saying he is finely dressed. Who cares if the king is a fool? Instead, this lie puts salvation in direct danger. This is caused by the normal religious reasons offered. Perhaps I cannot quite say yes to God, but surely I have the power to say no, don't I?

Well, no! What we are revealing here is a fake theology that infers from the Law that there must be a means of doing what the Law says. If God gave the Law, I must be able to accomplish it. *Ought* implies *can*. This sinner's inference actually steps in to speak where God is silent. It tries to fill in for what God is not saying. But what this says is not the Gospel—it is not preaching. It is speculation, and it directly substitutes one's own words, or those of theology and religion, for God's own words.

---

12 AE 33:69.

This substitute theology stuffs the ear with lies. It occupies the deaf ear with a false hope: "you could hear if you tried." "Hear, o deaf," is then transposed into a self-reference to *endeavor*! Instead, the only answer to a bound will with an unpreached God is to get a preached God.

This change from an unpreached to a preached God is most decidedly not according to your will. It is not an obedience or choice of your own: "The riders themselves contend for the possession and control of" you, said Luther.[13] This is a cosmic battle that rages as we speak. It is not conducted transcendentally over your head; it is actually a battle over you, in particular. That the God of wrath (who has set His servant, Satan, in your saddle) would bother contending for you is amazing itself. That He actually wins you is more amazing yet. And then, whom He sets in the seat of you is the most amazing of all—His only begotten Son, crucified with your sins, and raised for your justification. All of a sudden, you are not a servile ass, but a royal ass.

What bothers the bound will most about this battle is that it is not waged under the good and gracious Law, but finally steps outside of it. The answer to a bound will is not the will unbinding itself or being unbound into the Law. That is what God did when He gave you up to your desires, not when He justified you. He made you an enjoyer of the very Law that is killing you. So the answer to a bound will is to get a new rider in your saddle, and this comes first by Christ crucified, who takes your sins upon Himself. But it is that sort of thing that the bound will literally believes is impossible.

Then even more strangeness follows. The way this change of riders happens is not by an inner movement or transcendence, but comes through the external preaching office. Freedom comes by getting a preacher, who is not you, sent by the Holy Spirit from outside. Freedom does not emerge from within. It comes externally through the preacher, who unseats Satan from your saddle and puts Christ there instead. You could not be more passive. But passivity does not hinder freedom in the slightest. The free will, imaginary as it is, thinks preaching uses words as

13 AE 33:66.

signs that trigger something in my mind so that if I apply myself I can decipher and use the words as a guide to make better decisions regarding my desires. It thinks of preaching as motivation of the will to endeavor. But the words of the preacher are not signs, and they are not waiting for the mind to absorb, decipher, recognize, accept, respond, decide, or in any way to "think" these words into action. Instead, the words are not aimed at the *thought*, but the *heart* of the person, that is faith, and they have power to accomplish what the free will could never do and what Satan could never do. Of course, a person is thinking while the preacher preaches, but that is the remains of the old ass.

Truly Satan can lie, which is a power of sorts, but he can't create with a word. The strangest thing that a preacher does, and this is done daily, is preach not to potential free wills but to bound wills. No rhetoric known to man could do this because such preaching is literally Paul's foolishness. This is precisely how you are a fool as a preacher: you speak not to persuade, but to do the two things God alone does—destroy the old and create the new. As Jesus said, if you had faith you would say to this mulberry tree, "Be uprooted, and planted in the sea," and it would be uprooted and planted in the sea (Luke 17:6). If you preach to the deaf, the word gives them the ears as the Spirit wants.

So we come again to the strangest sentence ever written: "Hear, o deaf" (Isaiah 42:18). This is what you do when you preach. The sentence contains the two necessary words. You are speaking to the deaf, and you command them to *hear*. This is a sermon to bound wills. We could go further, as Paul does: "you have died." This is how deeply bound the will is. It means not being able to do anything more before the face of God. Will reaches its end as an "endeavorer," a supernaturalist, a free-willer who is attempting to desire the proper object, the higher good, but has instead managed only to curve in upon itself, as Augustine liked to say. But Luther is correct, the will is not just curved inward—selfish—but bound. Humanity is not just crooked timber, as Kant liked to say, distorted, but is being ridden as a servile ass by a congenital liar. The only way to change this is to bind the strong man, pillage his house of you, and set you in a wholly new kingdom. That is, to bring the mesmerizing Law to an end, which is no less than a new creation.

This new creation is a creature. It is a servant; it is an ass. It has a saddle and is ridden, but all the difference between *imprisonment* and *freedom* is found in who is riding that saddle. When Satan rides, the Law accuses eternally. When Christ rides, the forgiveness of sins makes a sinner righteous by imputation. This is not a mere thought or perspective—even if divine—but is the reality of the new creation, with the actual Christ in your seat and you doing exactly what He wills, without so much as a moment's hesitation that would lead you to think you had a free will that was cooperating with Him: "Look at what royal ass I am, agreeing with my master's every command." Not at all. The royal ass has no introspection, no neutral time or reflection, because the one riding him is not the Law—for the first time in his life!

This does not denigrate humanity, except from the perspective of the bound will and Satan, but rather exalts it. It does not redirect desire; it destroys it. It does not leave you to fulfill the Law; that is fulfilled by Christ alone. What is the human then, if not a chooser, decider, endeavorer, and expresser to the outside world of the inner desire? The human is now the created creature of the Creator, who is created by God saying He forgives. That is, God's Holy Word is not the Law, but His only-begotten Son, Jesus Christ, incarnate deep in the flesh, born under the Law—who does not leave His creation to the creatures' own desires.

The human is the perfectively passive receiver of the promise of forgiveness, which is the freedom that comes from having no more to do, no more accusation, no more endeavor. Free. That means free to listen to what Christ is saying without interruption: "You are Mine, and I am pleased with you." Free choice is a divine term—alone, as Luther knew, without any cooperation of your own (as if you could add anything to freedom). And what God chooses when He sends you a preacher is you who has his sins removed and no Law added. This makes you a royal ass.

Now there is one final slip of the knot that Erasmus tried with Luther. He said of Luther, and the Lutherans, that they ought to stop talking and preaching about the bound will, which he called a "fable" and "useless." Ah, "*useless*!" The most American of words, the most pragmatic, the most like Emerson and Dewey. Instead (and here is the sly devil trying to take the seat back), Erasmus suggested that speaking of the bondage of the will should be replaced by preaching *only Christ crucified*, speaking wisdom among the perfect (1 Corinthians 1:23; 2:2ff). That is crafty indeed. What self-respecting Lutheran could resist it? Preach Christ alone, no bondage of the will! "Scripture," Erasmus argued, "has a language of its own, variously adapted to the state of the hearers."[14] We call this "contextuality," the snake of rational criticism! Erasmus was quite well aware that Luther demanded the context for every text. But now comes the form of modernity—you must adapt the Word to the context. The preacher's job is to alter the Word to become "hearable" in ever-new contexts. And of course, the primary "context" of our modern times says that in the sixteenth century people felt guilty so that Luther preached forgiveness of sins. But now my congregation does not feel guilty; they are concerned more with "meaning" or "recognition," and so, how they fit into the church and feel welcome.

Watch out! Erasmus suggested the same thing to Luther—and they were both from the sixteenth century. The context of our time, Erasmus argued, requires teaching charity—*caritas*—that says God's kind of love reorders desire to its godly goal by means of a preacher using the Law in its most Christian sense. That is, preachers must teach what is expedient or useful to the neighbor. Luther responded, "we too teach nothing but Jesus crucified. But Christ brings all these things with him"[15]—that is, He is sitting in the saddle; you are not. The useful and practical is not turned back to you, but stays with Him. Your will is no longer bound, but is in service to Him alone. So Luther concluded his overall review of Erasmus's preface to the *Diatribe* by saying this kind of evangelical preaching to the deaf is wisdom hidden in a mystery, and "pertains to the perfect, not to mere children of a Jewish and legal people that glories in works without faith . . . unless you want the preaching of Christ crucified to mean nothing other than the making of the bare statement, "Christ has

14 AE 33:71.

15 Ibid.

been crucified."[16] So the final lie by Satan is just to say: "Christ has been crucified!" There you have what all theology wants—a crucified God who stoops down to suffer what we suffer and know what we feel like, and so we imitate Him by loving the lowly. Instead, the evangelical preacher applies the pronoun: Christ's crucifixion is a promise "for you"—not a new Law. And that "you" is free from bondage, free from *caritas* in particular, which has nagged at Christian teaching's penchant for humility for so long. It really is the Gospel alone—the absolving "I forgive you on account of Christ's cross"—that works the seating of Christ in your ass's saddle. Then and only then He makes you royal. Nothing else ever did or will make you royal, including your usefulness to your neighbor in charity.

Divine necessity, what God insists on doing, is Christ, not the Law. This is a great shock to a servile ass. But it is the glorious freedom of the royal ass, who is a creature made so new by God that he cannot sin, just as the servile ass was a creature who could not but sin. The servile ass has the Law ever before him; the royal ass has the Law behind him—eternally.

---

16 AE 33:71.

LAW AND GOSPEL IN MISSION THEOLOGY

Albert B. Collver III

Thesis 1: The doctrinal contents of the entire Holy Scriptures, both of the Old and the New Testament, are made up of two doctrines differing fundamentally from each other, viz., the Law and the Gospel.

Thesis 3: Rightly distinguishing the Law and the Gospel is the most difficult and the highest art of Christians in general and of theologians in particular. It is taught only by the Holy Spirit in the school of experience.[1]

INTRODUCTION

The statement that Law and Gospel applies to mission theology for a Lutheran is or should be obvious. How this is carried out in practice has demonstrated that the obviousness of the statement is much harder to execute. In one sense, the application of Law and Gospel to a particular people group is contextualization. The noun "contextualization" is one that has had a relatively short usage in the English language, being used for approximately one hundred years. Its usage in the field of missiology is even more recent, appearing in the early 1970s but gaining popularity in the 1980s. By the early twenty-first century, "contextualization" has become an undisputed dogma in the field of missiology and

1 Carl Ferdinand Wilhelm Walther, William Herman Theodore Dau, and Ernest Eckhardt, *The Proper Distinction between Law and Gospel: 39 Evening Lectures*, electronic ed. (St. Louis: Concordia Publishing House, 2000), 1.

missionary practice. The idea of contextualization has so penetrated the life of the Church that it is discussed not only with application to "overseas" mission but also to domestic mission. One cannot have a thought of planting a new congregation, or discussing the revitalization of an existing congregation, without addressing the thought of contextualization and its application to ministry, outreach, and worship. In some ways, "contextualization" is the perfect postmodern word and discipline.

Emerging from linguistic interpretation, to the field of hermeneutics, to the practice of mission within the Church, the etymological roots of the Middle English word from the Latin *con-* (together) and *texere* (weave) cannot really describe the full force of the abstract noun "contextualization" which has grown beyond these humble etymological roots. Contextualization no longer merely involves how to best understand a literary text or how to best translate an idea from one language to another, but has emerged as one of the key hermeneutical concepts needed to communicate the Gospel of Jesus Christ in the culture. In fact, some might well say there can be no mission without contextualization. A failure to contextualize, or undercontextualization, can result in the hearers not receiving the message of the Gospel as for them but rather viewing it as an alien or foreign message.

The practice of contextualization in the field of missiology has varied greatly. At times, contextualization results in a better communication of the Gospel within a particular culture. At other times, contextualization seems to result in the alteration of the historic Christian message. For instance, a group of Bible translators made the choice in the name of contextualization to translate John 1:29 as "Behold the pig of God that takes away the sins of the world."[2] For the people of Papua New Guinea, an animal despised by the Judeo tradition (and Islamic tradition) has

---

2 Charles E. Farhadian, ed., *Christian Worship Worldwide: Expanding Horizons, Deepening Practices* (Grand Rapids: Eerdmans, 2007), 14. "For instance, the social and religious life of the indigenous inhabitants of the island of New Guinea is centered on the pig. They use pigs for every important transaction between themselves and beings of the spirit world, and domesticated pigs hold the highest prestige and exchange value. . . . Highland Papuans keep ordinary pigs and sacrificial pigs, the latter whose blood has to be spilt during critical rituals to appease angry spirits. Moreover, the distribution of the meat of the sacrificial pig is highly

become the chief or best animal to represent God. Does such a contextualized message go beyond what is permissible, particularly when such a contextualized application would require recontextualization to the Church catholic? No doubt contextualization plays an important role in the communication of the Gospel, but what are its limits and bounds to remain within historical Christianity?

Klaus Detlev Schulz notes that some terms are essential to the communication of the Gospel, whether or not they can be easily contextualized. In these cases, teaching and catechesis need to take place to convey the proper conceptualization. He writes,

> In this case, the missionary would be required to use the indispensable meaning, even if that concept is foreign. The idea of indispensable meaning explains why missionaries in areas such as Papua New Guinea or among the Inuit in Alaska have continued to teach the biblical theme of shepherding sheep, even though that concept is foreign to the natives. The same can be said of the Kalanga people in northern Botswana and southern Zimbabwe who, though not familiar with the biblical concept of wine, vineyard, and fruits of the vine, were nonetheless familiarized with them. Thus, if the missionary considers the literal meaning of the biblical message indispensable, he may have to import its meaning and complement that with proper catechetical instruction.[3]

formalized, similar to the way in which the bread is distributed during the celebration of the Lord's Supper and thus have [sic] missiological significance. Papuans assume that the pig's blood guarantees reconciliation and peace among the environment, human beings, and the spirit world. For Euro-North Americans, it may be meaningful to learn that the Christ is the incarnate Logos or the Lamb of God—these biblical notions hold much weight, especially for those socialized into the worldviews of Lambs and Logos. However, New Guineans have never seen a lamb, and the concept of Logos is so abstract that it is nearly impossible to make sense of it to a common villager. To many New Guineans, Christ is like a pig. . . . He is the pig of God who takes away the sin of the world."

3 Klaus Detlev Schulz, *Mission from the Cross: The Lutheran Theology of Mission* (St. Louis: Concordia Publishing House, 2009), 177–78.

At times, to communicate the Gospel, no "contextualization" is possible and an idea that is foreign to the culture needs to be introduced and taught.

Although Eugene Nida does not use the term "contextualization" in his 1960 book *Message and Mission: The Communication of the Christian Faith*, his ideas about communication were developing around the same time and can be applied to the concept of "contextualization." Nida describes two communication techniques: the "common ground" approach and the "point of contact" approach.[4] The common-ground approach seeks to demonstrate how certain practices of pagan religion are similar to practices of the Christian faith. It sought to subsume or transform pagan practices into Christian ones. For instance, pagan temples would not be destroyed but consecrated for Christian use. Pagan festivals would be transformed into Christian saint days or other holy days. Nida cites this approach as that of the Roman Catholic Church from the fifth until the sixteenth century. He cites a letter of Pope Gregory regarding the conversion of the English. He writes, "What Pope Gregory undoubtedly wanted was a different basic set of beliefs with essentially the same cultural forms. What he got was a continuation of the same cultural forms and beliefs, with only a different nomenclature, for there was no significant change in the religious concepts of the English people until several centuries later."[5] Nida notes that Roman Catholic missionaries tended to focus on similarities in ritual and worship, whereas Protestant missionaries instead focused on conceptual similarities. "While some Roman Catholics would take over pagan symbols, many Protestants would almost as eagerly adopt pagan beliefs, at least in a provisional form and on an elementary level. For example, some missionaries have regarded pagan sets of beliefs and practices as constituting the 'Old Testament' of the indigenous society."[6] Both the Roman Catholic tendency of finding

4 Eugene Albert Nida, *Message and Mission: The Communication of the Christian Faith* (Pasadena: William Carey Library, 1960), 15.

5 Ibid., 16–17.

6 Ibid., 17.

common ground with pagan ritual and the Protestant tendency of finding common ground with belief can lead toward syncretism.

Nida contrasts the "point of contact" approach to the "common ground" approach with the following example. "The parallelisms are emphasized in order to provide one with an intelligible basis for communication, without involving any initial field of agreement. Thus in certain aspects of Buddhism we recognize a number of similarities to Christianity not as common bases of belief, but as elements that make communication possible."[7] Nida prefers the "point of contact" approach to the "common ground" approach because "it is impossible to take any element of belief out of its context and still have the same belief."[8] Nida notes although Islam and Christianity both have concepts of revelation, each religion has such different beliefs about revelation that they cannot serve as a common ground of belief but only as a point of contact. Nida sees finding a "point of contact" not as the basis for a common belief but as the starting point for having an intelligent conversation. Nida's insights into communication theory help us see that "contextualization" can be used both as a "common ground" methodology or as a "point of contact" methodology. Nida's "point of contact" approach is fraught with fewer theological problems than the "common ground" approach. A difficulty with the term "contextualization" is that when a person says the Gospel must be "contextualized," it is not immediately apparent if a "common ground" approach, a "point of contact" approach, or some other approach is intended. Oftentimes, the term "contextualize" means little more than communicate the Gospel effectively (whatever that might mean). Contextualization often becomes the catchall phrase for communicating the Gospel across linguistic, cultural, philosophical, and theological lines.

In this postmodern era, where expediency is often sought on the basis of what seems best to an individual or to a particular culture, this paper would like to propose a theological standard rather than an

7 Ibid., 18.

8 Ibid.

anthropological, cultural, or linguistic standard to guide the extent of contextualization so that the contextualized message indeed remains within the historic Christian faith. To that end, contextualization is the application of Law and Gospel to a particular people group. The application of Law and Gospel to a particular people does not occur in a mechanistic manner but in a way that takes seriously language, culture, and philosophy (a people group's outlook on life). In the end, it must apply the Scripture to a people in a way that convicts them of their sin and provides them with the saving comfort of the Gospel of Jesus Christ.

BACKGROUND

The terms "contextualize" and "contextualization" first appeared connected to a discussion on the renewal of theological education.[9] David Bosch notes that the term "contextualization" first appeared in connection with the Theological Education Fund but soon became a blanket term for a variety of theological models.[10] In 1956, the General Secretary of the International Mission Council approached John D. Rockefeller to assist with theological education in the developing world.[11] Rockefeller agreed to contribute $2 million (approximately $16.6 million adjusted for inflation in 2016) to the International Mission Council, provided that a number of mission boards and societies would contribute an additional $2 million over a period of five years.[12] These donations formed the corpus of the Theological Education Fund (TEF). "In January 1958, the

---

9 Paul Duane Matheny, *Contextual Theology: The Drama of Our Times* (Eugene, Oregon: Pickwick Publications, 2011), 62. "Most scholars pinpoint the original impulse to 'contextualize' theological and ecclesial work as a response to the expectation of the Theological Education Fund."

10 David J. Bosch, "Mission as Contextualization" in *Transforming Mission: Paradigm Shifts in Theology of Mission* (Maryknoll, NY: Orbis Books, 1996), 420–21. "The word 'contextualization' was first coined in the early 1970s, in the circles of the Theological Education Fund, with a view particularly to the task of the education and formation of people for the church's ministry. It soon caught on and became a blanket term for a variety of theological models. . . . In my view, only the inculturation model in the first type and only the revolutionary model in the second qualify as contextual theologies proper."

11 Charles W. Ranson, "The Theological Education Fund," *International Review of Mission* 47, no. 188 (October 1958): 432.

12 Ibid. The eight mission boards that agreed to contribute to the Theological Education

Theological Education Fund was launched by the International Missionary Council at its Assembly in Ghana."[13] The intention of the TEF was to foster ecumenical cooperation in the area of theological education.[14] Eventually, the administration of the TEF shifted from the International Mission Council to the Division of World Mission and Evangelism of the World Council of Churches (WCC).[15]

The TEF can be divided into three mandates.[16] The first mandate spanned 1958–65 and consisted of grants to institutions in Africa, Asia, Latin and Central America, and the Middle East. It also provided textbooks and began library development. The TEF's Textbooks Program had the following goal: "In each major language area, to help provide, where they do not exist, or to supplement where they exist in part, the books needed for a full course of theological education, to the number of about fifty. They will consist of Basic Texts and Essential Texts."[17] The

---

Fund were the Board of Missions of the Methodist Church ($750,000), the Board of Foreign Missions of the Presbyterian Church USA ($500,000), the American Baptist Foreign Mission Societies ($175,000), The American Board of Commissioners for Foreign Missions ($150,000), The United Christian Missionary Society ($150,000), the National Council of the Protestant Episcopal Church ($100,000), the Board of Foreign Missions of the United Lutheran Church ($100,000), and the Board of Foreign Missions of the Evangelical and Reformed Church ($75,000).

13 Charles W. Ranson, "How the Theological Education Fund Began," in *A Vision for Man: Essays on Faith, Theology, and Society in Honor of Joshua Russell Chandran*, ed. Samuel Amirtham (Madras: The Christian Literature Society, 1978), 130.

14 Ibid., 134. "The missionary movement, despite its many shortcomings, had in fact been a pioneer of united Christian action, and displayed a wider range of interdenominational co-operation than any other activity of the Church. The purpose of the proposed fund was to strengthen training. But the *primary* goal of the Fund would not be Christian unity but better seminaries, though in most cases the goal could best be achieved by united action."

15 Leonard Kaufmann, "Theological Education in the 1970s: A Working Policy of the Theological Education Fund," *AFER* 15, no. 3 (1973): 250. "In the last 15 years the TEF has played an important role in promoting theological education in the Third World. As sponsored agency first of the International Missionary Council and then of the Division of World Mission and Evangelism of the World Council of Churches it has been a centre of reflection and an instrument of action with vital influence on the whole field of theological studies."

16 Dietrich Werner, David Esterline, Namsoon Kang, and Joshva Raja, ed., *Handbook of Theological Education in World Christianity: Theological Perspectives, Ecumenical Trends, Regional Surveys* (Eugene, Oregon: Wipf & Stock Publishers, 2010), 17. "The work of the TEF is best understood in terms of its three mandate periods and their respective commitments." Used by permission of Wipf and Stock Publishers. www.wipfandstock.com.

17 Ranson, "How the Theological Education Fund Began," 139.

Textbook Program may have been the most useful aspect of the TEF, and it shows how the production of books in indigenous languages is among the most important activities for ongoing theological education and mission work in a given place.[18] The first mandate primarily approached the quality of theological education from a Western perspective.

The second mandate spanned 1965–70. It continued to support theological education through grants, provided for faculty development, supported curriculum development, and promoted the development of theological associations. "The primary questions in this period had to do with the relevance of theological education and formation for ministry in the face of poverty and the political powerlessness of many people."[19] If the first mandate focused on bringing Western standards of theological education to the non-Western world, then the second mandate focused on indigenization. The first two mandates of the TEF primarily were under Western leadership. The third mandate shifted leadership to the "Third World."[20] The third mandate spanned 1970–77.[21] The third

---

18 Ibid., 140. "In the early stages of the programme [sic], production plans were in motion under local committees in twenty-three different language areas. By 1965, there were one hundred and thirty-nine new books in print in sixteen different languages. By 1969, the total number of titles issued had risen to four hundred and fifteen and the number of language areas receiving assistance to twenty-seven. On any reckoning, this was a remarkable achievement. The Textbooks Programme [sic] has received far less public notice than some other activates of the TEF. But it may prove to be the most useful and durable of the results of the whole enterprise."

19 Werner et al., *Handbook of Theological Education in World Christianity*, 17.

20 Shoki Coe. "In Search of Renewal in Theological Education," *Theological Education* 9, no. 4 (1973): 233. "During the first two Mandates the TEF was under mainly Western leadership, its first and second directors being Dr. Charles W. Ranson and Dr. James F. Hopewell; and its first and second chairmen Dr. John Coventry Smith and Dr. Charles W. Forman. Now, in the Third Mandate period, the leadership is marked by its emphatic shift to the Third World, with Bishop Sarkissian as chairman, and four of the five directors coming from Asia, Africa, and Latin America."

21 Ranson, "How the Theological Education Fund Began," 141. "There were a number of new and distinctive features in the operation of the TEF which distinguished it from most other missionary and ecumenical organizations. . . . Ecumenical (and other) organizations have the tendency to perpetuate themselves. It is often harder to stop one than to start it. The TEF was conceived, from the outset, as an interim operation. It sought and received a mandate with a time limit of five years. As the work proceeded and the end of the five year plan would be substantially completed . . . and that the TEF has done little more than scratch the surface of the task assigned to it." Because of this, the TEF continued in total for twenty years for phases 2 and 3 to be completed.

mandate began with two years of study followed by the publication of *Ministry in Context*.[22] The terms "contextualize" and "contextualization" emerged and became popularized from this third mandate. The TEF approached theological education like a Hegelian dialectic with the first mandate the bringing of Western standards as the thesis, the second mandate of indigenization as the antithesis, and the third mandate of contextualization as the synthesis.

Shoki Coe, the developer of the term "contextualization," explains why it as a term is preferred over the older term "indigenization." He writes, "Indigenous, indigeneity, and indigenization all derive from a nature metaphor, that is, of the soil, or taking root in the soil. It is only right that the younger churches, in search of their own identity, should take seriously their own cultural milieu. However, because of the static nature of the metaphor, indigenization tends to be used in the sense of responding to the Gospel in terms of traditional culture. Therefore, it is in danger of being past-oriented."[23] Coe notes that a given location might have multiple overlapping contexts, but that the missiologist does not necessarily consider every context seriously "because they are not equally strategic for the *Missio Dei* in working out His purpose through history."[24] Coe also notes how other disciplines such as sociology and anthropology are helpful in determining the context. He next identifies two dangers of contextualization. He writes, "Dr. Jürgen Moltmann warns of the danger that academic theology may become so contextualized that it becomes fossilized theology, and all the more dangerous because we are not aware of it. But equally there is a danger of contextual theology becoming chameleon theology, changing color according to the contexts."[25] Coe does not offer any solution on how to avoid these two dangers other than "missiological discernment."

---

22 Kaufmann, "Theological Education in the 1970s," 251.

23 Shoki Coe. "Contextualizing Theology" in *Mission Trends No. 3: Third World Theologies*, ed. Gerald H. Anderson and Thomas F. Stransky (New York and Grand Rapids: Paulist Press and Eerdmans, 1976), 20.

24 Ibid., 21.

25 Ibid.

DEVELOPMENT OF CONTEXTUALIZATION

Even in the early 1970s, some had voiced concern that "contextualization" might cause a loss of the catholicity of the Gospel. Coe, while stating that "contextualization" is a missiological necessity, asks if it is a "theological" necessity.[26] David Bosch regards "contextualization" as the incarnation of the message of the Christian Church in those who embrace it.[27] If missiology is praxis and theology is theory, Bosch would see contextualization as the dialectic between the two. Bosch would argue that contextualization is necessary to theology. Bosch sees the development of contextualization (or the recognition of its importance) as a question of epistemology. Bosch writes, "The traditional way of knowing considers the truth as the conformity of the mind to a given object, a part of Greek influence in the western philosophical tradition. Such a concept of truth only conforms to and legitimizes the world as it now exists. But there is another way of knowing the truth—a dialectical one."[28] In other words, experience provides the framework to understand or to know truth. The recognition that theology was conditioned by its environment led to the developments of form criticism and higher criticism. Bosch goes further: he states the people who recognized that theology was conditioned by the situation it developed in failed to realize their own theology was equally conditioned.[29] Bosch sees literary criticism as moving beyond higher criticism. However, he argues that the new hermeneutic approach where the reader "creates" the text when he reads it does not go far enough.[30] Bosch states, "Interpreting a text is not only a literary

---

26 Ibid., 22.

27 Bosch, "Mission as Contextualization," 421. "A basic argument of this book has been that, from the very beginning, the missionary message of the Christian church incarnated itself in the life and world of those who embraced it. It is, however, only fairly recently that this essentially contextual nature of the faith has been recognized."

28 Ibid., 424.

29 Ibid., 423. "They did not realize that their own interpretations were as parochial and as conditioned by their context as those they were criticizing."

30 Ibid. "Where this state of affairs is recognized, scholars may succeed in moving beyond the important accomplishments of the historical-critical method and of the form and redaction critics of the middle twentieth century. Paul Ricoeur and other recent literary critics have, in a great variety of ways, advanced the view that every text is an interpreted text and that, in a sense, the reader 'creates' the text when she or he reads it . . . is not going far enough."

exercise; it is also a social, economic, and political exercise. Our entire context comes into play when we interpret a biblical text. One therefore has to concede that *all* theology (or sociology, political theory, etc.) is, by its very nature, contextual."[31] So to answer Coe's question whether contextualization is theologically necessary, Bosch would answer in the affirmative.

Bosch recognizes that contextualization can lead to the danger of relativism. In fact, Bosch would caution against an overcontextualization that creates an "isolated theological world in itself."[32] At the same time, Bosch is no fan of the Reformation confessions, either Lutheran or Reformed, or of systematic theology. According to Bosch, the Lutheran Confessions, Augustana VII, defines the Church passively as a place where something is done but not as an organism that is doing something.[33] Bosch argues that such a confessional view hindered missions for centuries. Bosch sees confessions of the Church as stating truth without engaging in the context.

Bosch writes,

> The Christian faith was based on eternal, unalterable truth, which had already been stated in its final form, for instance in ecclesiastical confessions and policies. Ostensibly, of course, Protestants did not ascribe the same status to their traditions and creeds as they did to Scripture. Even so, the sixteenth-century Protestant confessions were soon treated as universals, valid in all times and settings and, through the missionary enterprise, exported in their unaltered—and unalterable—forms to the younger churches in the Third World.[34]

---

31 Ibid.

32 Ibid., 427.

33 Ibid., 238. "In all these instances the church was defined in terms of what happens inside its four walls, not in terms of its calling in the world. The verbs used in the Augustana are all in the passive voice: the church is a place where the Gospel is taught purely and the sacraments are administered rightly. It is a place where something is done, not a living organism doing something."

34 Ibid., 427.

Bosch holds contextualization above the Reformation confessions. Bosch calls the Gospel the *norma normans* (the norming norm) and context the *norma normata* (the normed norm).[35] Confessional Lutherans typically describe the Holy Scriptures as the *norma normans* (the norming norm) and the Book of Concord (the Lutheran Confessions) as the *norma normata* (the normed norm). For traditional Lutherans, the Holy Scriptures and the Book of Concord form a hermeneutical circle. For Bosch, the hermeneutical circle is between the Gospel and contextualization. Bosch states that contextual theologians do not write systematic theologies; rather, he says, "we need an experimental theology in which an ongoing dialogue is taking place between text and context."[36]

CONTEXTUALIZATION AS LAW AND GOSPEL

As noted above, the term "contextualization" appeared in connection to the Theological Education Fund (TEF) in the early 1970s and has had various usages and meanings since it was coined. In the present day, it is difficult to imagine a person talking about missions without also talking about contextualization. This was not always the case. Dr. Udo Etuk of Nigeria says that the mission effort in Africa passed through three periods: (1) the period of iconoclasm; (2) the period of adaption; and (3) the period of contextualization.[37] The period of iconoclasm was when the West sought to Christianize the "Dark Continent," and copy cultural patterns from the West. The period of adaption occurred when the West recognized that African culture had aspects worth preserving and that made contributions to the Church. The final period is contextualization, called by some Roman Catholics "incarnational theology."[38] He writes,

35 Ibid., 430. "This means that it is the *Gospel* which is the *norma normans*, the 'norming norm.' Our reading of the context is also a norm, but in a derived sense; it is the *norma normata*, the 'normed norm.' Of course, the Gospel can only be read from and make sense in our present context."

36 Ibid., 427.

37 Udo Etuk, "The Theology of Contextualization in Africa: A Cover for Traditional Cultural Revival," *Concordia Journal* 11, no. 6 (November 1985): 214–22.

38 Ibid. "Now we are in the third period, the period of contextualization or, in contemporary Catholic thinking, 'incarnational theology.'"

"The reasoning behind the theology of contextualization or incarnation is this: God became man in order to save man. Christ literally took on Himself the form of a servant in order to redeem all men. Now by virtue of that fact, the Christian Gospel must assume the forms and expressions of the different cultures of the world if it is to redeem these cultures."[39] In the context of Nigeria, "contextualization" would "Africanize Christianity."[40]

What precisely it means to "Africanize Christianity" would depend upon the person defining it. Etuk offers caution in contextualizing to the point of creating an "Africanized Christianity." He writes, "The difficulty with the theology of contextualization and the call for an African Christian theology is that what emerges is neither Christian nor theological, but a capitulation to traditional cultural practices."[41] Etuk argues that those who seek an "African Christianity" are primarily those who were educated in the West or to Western standards. They are those who make a decision to reject aspects of their Western education and to return to the culture of their homeland.[42] He writes, "Black theology, or liberation theology, comes when people are better educated and better informed, and are in a position to ask questions about their origins, their identity, their values, about equality, liberty, and justice, and can oppose or throw off what they do not want."[43] Etuk says that Christians should be concerned by this form of contextualization "because the trend to Africanize Christianity is a neo-heathen trend. It adds Jesus Christ to the African pantheon merely as one more mediator, and not the Mediator,

---

39 Ibid.

40 Ibid., 215. "What does it mean to 'Africanize Christianity'? To give a clear meaning to these concepts would force a long digression. In my mind, however, these developments pose grave and subtle challenges to Christian witness in Africa today."

41 Ibid., 217.

42 Ibid., 218. "Those Africans who advocate a return to traditional ways of doing things—including our traditional worship of ancestral gods, traditional cures and healing methods, marital patterns, and so on—or, in words popularized by the philosophy of Négritude, a 'return to our sources,'—are not the uneducated, unenlightened African peasants. Rather, they are those who have in all likelihood lived and studied in the Western world, highly qualified in some modern discipline, and have then rejected certain Western values in preference for their own."

43 Ibid.

between God and men. Further, the Supreme God whom all traditionalists acknowledge is seldom mentioned as causing misfortunes or even as directly involved in the affairs of men."[44] Examples of this can be seen in syncretistic forms of Christianity in Africa, or among members who attend church on Sunday but make sacrifices to the ancestors during the week. It also manifests itself in some forms of Pentecostal worship that seeks to reach the "mediator Jesus" through the Spirit. Etuk concludes that "The Christian's loyalty in Africa and elsewhere must be first and foremost to his Lord and Master, before the claims of tribe, culture, traditions, political parties, and schools of thought."[45] Etuk's rejection of the "Africanizing of Christianity" is not a rejection of cross-cultural communication, or the acceptance of ignorant or paternalistic missionaries. Westerners must learn from and work with Africans. A better understanding of the culture allows for a better application of the Law and the Gospel.

In some ways, because of the vast changes to Western society caused by industrialization and urbanization, Africans have a readier understanding of the plain text of the Scriptures. For instance, when Isaiah 53:7 says Jesus was led like a lamb to the slaughter, few people in the West have experienced a lamb being led to the slaughter. Yet in Africa, even in urban areas, it is common to see sheep and goats on a vacant property marked with paint (often bright orange or pink) for the slaughter. It is common to see a lamb with bound feet carried away for the slaughter. It is not unusual in some places to see a lamb or goat slaughtered in the common area of an apartment complex in an African city. In this case, the African Christian does not need to "contextualize" the Scriptures because he sees it every day and it relates to his experience. Instead, the Westerner has a more difficult time understanding what the text says. The Westerner is more likely to need this text explained and "contextualized" to fully understand it than a person living in Africa.

44 Ibid., 220.

45 Ibid.

The image from Africa, in this case Ethiopia, of the lamb or goat with the bright pink paint can serve as an illustration for Christian doctrine. It can be used to explain original sin. The lamb in the pen with the pink mark does not recognize or know that it is marked for death. In a similar way, every person has the mark of original sin and is condemned to death just as surely as the lamb with the pink mark. Apart from the revelation of the Scriptures, a person is much like the lamb marked for death; he is unaware that he is under the condemnation and judgment of God. In this way, an item common to the culture—a lamb marked for slaughter—can help teach the Law, in this case original sin.

While Africa for a variety of reasons has one of the fastest-growing Christian populations, the same growth has not been seen in other parts of the world. Dr. Makito Masaki[46] notes "Christianity never became a part of Japan."[47] Yet the reason for this is not due to a lack of contextualization or for a lack of enculturation. Western materialism and consumerism very much are a part of Japanese culture. Makito Masaki points out that nearly every "methodology" employed by Western churches has been tried with limited to no success in Japan. His brother, Dr. Naomichi Masaki,[48] notes that the Japanese are masters at marketing and contextualization. He notes how Japanese corporations design their products for each country. "In Japan, the Honda Accord is a completely different model in size and design than in North America or, for that matter, in Europe. While the Accord in Japan is narrower and more 'high-tech oriented,' the American Accord is longer, wider, and smoother."[49] Dr. Makito Masaki points out that Christians have tried two approaches to evangelize Japan. One approach attempted to Westernize Japanese

46 Dr. Makito Masaki serves as the President of Kobe Lutheran Theological Seminary in Kobe, Japan.

47 Makito Masaki, "The Use of Luther's Theological Anthropology in Addressing Current Japanese Thought" (STM thesis, Fort Wayne: Concordia Theological Seminary, 1992), 3.

48 Dr. Naomichi Masaki is associate professor of systematic theology and director of the Master of Sacred Theology program at Concordia Theological Seminary in Fort Wayne, Indiana.

49 Naomichi Masaki. "Liturgy and Culture: Can the Liturgy Be Made to Reflect a Particular Culture?" in *Through the Church the Song Goes On: Preparing a Lutheran Hymnal for the 21st Century*, ed. Paul J. Grime, D. Richard Stuckwisch, and Jon D. Vieker (St. Louis: Commission on Worship, The Lutheran Church—Missouri Synod, 1999), 130.

people so that they would become Christian. The other approach was to create a Japanized Christianity. Neither approach has proven very effective. Both approaches involved some form of "contextualization."

Dr. Makito Masaki provides an analysis of Japan based on Luther's writings on the Turks. Masaki notes that the Japanese are like the Turks in the sixteenth century, whose identity as a nation was connected to its religious heritage.[50] Masaki notes that Japan is deliberately anti-Christian to protect itself from Western colonization.[51] "Japan is, therefore, a country of deliberate contamination of the Two Kingdoms, the Kingdom of the Left and the Right, so that the religious system may serve the government by providing for the unity of the people in the national interest."[52] Masaki notes that Japan is similar to Turkey in the sixteenth century, where the government represented both civic and religious life.[53] Masaki then provides a brief history of Christianity in Japan, which tried to deal with both Japanese and Christian identity. He identifies three periods in Japanese Christianity where the theological message said Japan must Westernize and Christianity can help it do so.[54] This theological approach in Japan created a Japanese version of "Social Gospel." It was believed to make Japan more "Western," Japanese people would need to become more individualistic. Masaki noted that some Christian leaders developed Christian counseling methods to enhance the Japanese sense of individualism and self.[55] Masaki contrasts this period of openness

---

50 Makito Masaki. "The Use of Luther's Theological Anthropology," 67. "Japanese mentality is similar to the Turks whose religion was a part of their national identity. Although Japan issued its new Constitution after World War II with a clear statement on the freedom of religion, the government has tried to unite the Japanese people by mingling Japanese identity with the philosophy of the National Shintoism."

51 Ibid., 97.

52 Ibid., 98.

53 Ibid. "Today Japanese Christians are living in a country somewhat similar to Turkey in Luther's day, the country ruled by the government under which Luther would have rather be [sic] dead than alive."

54 Ibid., 94. "The first, third and fifth 20-year periods after the Meiji Restoration, Christian leaders developed the theology which presupposed the need for Westernization. They presented Christianity as the appropriate helper for the nation to be westernized at both the social and individual levels."

55 Ibid., 99. "At the individual level, Christian leaders referred to psychologists and philoso-

to the West with three periods of Christianity under Japanese nationalism. During periods of Japanese nationalism, the Church's theological message was "the church should give its loyalty to the nation."[56] He noted others tried to develop Christian theology according to the Japanese sense of beauty and to Japanese philosophy. Meanwhile, recognizing the civic and religious role of the government in Japan, some Reformed and Roman Catholic theologians tried to place a church leader in both the spiritual and secular realms.[57] Dr. Masaki maintains that a contextual approach that properly distinguishes the Law from the Gospel is the key to helping Japanese churches out of their theological confusion.[58]

Dr. Masaki provides a few examples where Law and Gospel were confused in contextualizing the Christian message in Japan. One of the primary examples of the confusion of Law and Gospel identified by Masaki was the mixing of civil and religious realms. Masaki states that national pride and patriotism exist in the realm of the Law and not in the realm of the Gospel. A contextual theology will take into account patriotism as a First Article gift and not confuse it by connecting it to the Gospel of Jesus Christ. Masaki writes that Japanese Christians need "to learn that patriotism should stay in the realm of the Law. In the past, they promoted social movements in the name of the Gospel. They have attempted to develop Japanese theology in the realm of the Law and call it Gospel.

phers in Japan who pointed out that Japanese people needed to gain a more individualistic personality. In the modern secular society, with its decreasing communal and interdependent characteristics, the traditional pattern of relationship was no longer seen as appropriate. They said that human Japanese people needed to have a more independent and autonomous personality, like the people of the West had developed over the years. At present, some Christian leaders, especially those who are engaged in Christian counseling, are trying to develop a Christian interpretation of individual self along this line."

56 Ibid. "In the periods of nationalism, the second, fourth, and sixth 20-year periods, the opposite opinion was developed. They often admitted that Japan was the Kingdom of Kami, and the Christian church should give the nation its loyalty."

57 Ibid., 100. "The churches with Reformed try to make their church a leader in both the spiritual and secular Roman Catholic background try realm [sic]. How Lutherans in Japan deal with this situation is a very important matter for further discussion. Luther believed that the relationship to the temporal authority has to be Biblical so that the message of the church may be purely Gospel oriented."

58 Ibid., 101–2. "This section has shown how the proper distinction between Law and Gospel can serve Japanese churches and help them come out of their theological confusion."

They need to know the importance of the distinction between Law and Gospel in the social setting."[59] Masaki notes that before and after World War II, Japanese Christians took on a Barthian theology that rejected natural law. This allowed Japanese Christians to attend church on Sunday but then serve Shintoistic Nationalism and the emperor during the week.[60] A substantial portion of Masaki's analysis deals with properly teaching the Law. This is in part because without the proclamation of the Law, the Gospel and what Christ has done for me cannot really be heard. Another recognition from Masaki is that Japanese philosophy is not "merely philosophy but a religion which denies the Creator God and makes universal life their god."[61] This can make it more difficult to have natural law points of contact in the contextualization process.

A significant argument in Masaki's thesis is that Westerners and even Christians in Japan have tried to present Christianity to the Japanese beginning with the doctrine of God.[62] For example, there is a Creator God who made you. This approach has typically not worked well and led to the use of contextualization to make a "Japanized Christianity." Masaki argues that a better contextualization of Christianity in Japan is to begin with the doctrine of man. This is accomplished by preaching the Law to weaken a Japanese person's confidence in his oriental morality. The preaching of the Law demonstrates that there is no intrinsic goodness in the Japanese person (or any person) and prepares him to hear the saving message of the Gospel. Because the "context" in Japan swings back

---

59 Ibid., 100.

60 Ibid., 101. "Thirdly, they need to learn not to throw the Law away. Christian leaders, before and during World War II, took on Barthian theology as their excuse to serve the Shintoistic Nationalism. Their interpretation of Christianity as a nonreligion was that they should be faithful to God in the church, but they should give their loyalty to the emperor as citizens. They needed to learn the basic principle that the Law is of God (Acts 4:19; 5:29). Under persecution, Christians do not fight back against the government as people of the church, but live as justice-loving citizens."

61 Ibid., 106.

62 Ibid., 124. "The presenter's premise is that one needs to start his theology from the doctrine of man as opposed to the doctrine of God in order to properly present the theology of the cross. If one starts by discussing the creation, God, and nature, he tends to look at man positively with some strength left in him by which he can please God. Luther's view of man carefully and powerfully denies this kind of theology."

and forth between internationalism and a desire to embrace Westernism (perhaps including Christianity) and nationalism coupled with Japan's philosophical system that is intermixed with religious thought, Masaki's "contextual" solution to approaching evangelism is to distinguish between Law and Gospel, while teaching the Law.[63] What Masaki shows with his insight into Japanese culture is that knowing the culture and people (or contextualization) allows one to apply the Law of God with precision in a way that prepares hearers for the Gospel. Masaki's study also helps demonstrate, to use Nida's language, the "point of contact" between the Scriptures and a culture or between two cultures is in the area of the Law. This is not surprising when one considers it is natural law and the things people around the world share because of life under creation. Finding these natural law or First Article points of context are key to contextualization.

CONCLUSION

"Contextualization" as a term did not appear in theological usage until the early 1970s. When it appeared in the early 1970s, "contextualization" appeared in the "context" of theological education as dialectic between Western theological standards and the indigenization of theological education. Prior to this time, "contextualization" was not discussed in theology, let alone missions. Continuing with a dialectical explanation, missions prior to the mid-twentieth century was colonialist or paternalistic (or as Bosch described it, "the era of non-contextualization"),[64] where the indigenous people were expected to conform or adapt to Western ideals. This colonialist or paternalistic period of missions was followed by an indigenization of the mission. The dialectic of these two is contextualization. Some would say "contextualization"

63 Ibid., 126–27. "The way to cope with the repetitious shifts between nationalism and internationalism is to keep the relationship with the temporal authority in the realm of the Law. If philosophical discussion is kept in the realm of the Law, then Christians can dialogue with Japanese philosophers without fear. Japanese people have not been confronted by the Law so they are sleeping in false security."

64 Bosch, 427.

occurred prior to the use of the term. People who argue this usually intend to say that good or effective mission work always has taken into account the culture and indigenous habits of people even if such activity was not described as "contextualization." Contextualization as a dialectic has not existed nor could have existed prior to Hegel in the nineteenth century and Barth in the twentieth century. Some Japanese philosophers (Nishida) saw Hegel as the West's solution to the dualistic nature of Western philosophy[65] first found between Plato and Aristotle and later in Kant's *phenomena-noumena* dualism.[66] Instead of a dualistic philosophy, the Japanese favored a monistic worldview. These thoughts, while not having a widespread influence on contextualization around the world, did influence how the Christian message was contextualized in Japan. Nishida's insight into Western dualistic tendencies and the West's struggle to overcome this is helpful in seeing how the discussion about contextualization has been influenced by philosophy, which influenced the linguistics and anthropology upon which it is based.

The fact that the term "contextualization" developed in connection to theological education helps to demonstrate the connection between theological education and missions. Around the same time the term "contextualization" emerged, The Lutheran Church—Missouri Synod (LCMS) experienced a "contextualization" trend before the term was in general use. Lawrence Rast notes, "Little by little this theological shift permeated areas of the synod, most notably the seminary at St. Louis (and the Mission Board). Though initially somewhat surreptitious in character, eventually this perspective dominated. The 'Mission Affirmations' of 1965 are a key link in the process of 'A Statement' and what became Seminex."[67] What Rast demonstrates is that "relativism" affected the realm of theological education, which in turn influenced the

65 Perhaps Nishida was not entirely familiar with the Western philosophical tradition. Western philosophy was represented in various modes of philosophy: monism (Spinoza), dualism (Descartes), pluralism (Leibniz). It is true that contextualization philosophically followed the pattern of synthesis from Hegel and Barth.

66 Makito Masaki, "The Use of Luther's Theological Anthropology," 104–5.

67 Larry R. Rast, "1938, 'A Statement,' and the LCMS Today" in *Lord Jesus Christ, Will You Not Stay*, ed. J. Bart Day, Jon D. Vieker, and Albert B. Collver (Houston: The Feuerhahn Festschrift Committee, 2002), 288.

mission field. Rast notes how John Tietjen, the now former president of Concordia Seminary, no longer considered it possible to transfer the Reformation theology of the sixteenth and seventeenth centuries without accommodating the twentieth century.[68] Rast quotes Tietjen:

> Certainly we cannot simply transfer Reformation theology from the sixteenth to the twentieth century without accommodating it or applying it to twentieth-century conditions. But must we begin with justification at all? In fact, do we begin the theological task with some basic thematic expression of the Gospel? No! Not if we want to assure a relevant proclamation of the Gospel! For theology to be relevant, the theological task has to begin not with the Gospel but with the situation to which it is to be addressed. The first step in theological formulation is to analyze the conditions of the world for whose sake the Gospel is to be proclaimed. "The world writes the agenda," we are being told these days. True as that may be in other areas, it is true also for theology. The situation in our world should help shape our theology. Why? Because there is no "Gospel in a vacuum." The Gospel cannot be dealt with by itself apart from the situation to which it is addressed. It is ever so much more than a set of religious propositions, spiritual truths, or divine principles. If it were only that, it could be passed on unchanged from generation to generation. The Gospel must always be addressed to particular conditions and circumstances. Therefore, it cannot be formulated in terms enduringly valid for every age and condition.[69]

The idea of changing the Gospel to fit particular conditions and circumstances is behind some forms of contextualization.

---

68 Rast, "Response to Walter Sundberg," *Journal of Lutheran Mission* 1, no. 1 (March 2014): 16–19, 18.

69 Ibid. Originally John H. Tietjen, "The Gospel and the Theological Task," *Concordia Theological Monthly* 40 (June–July–August 1969): 438–39.

In a sense, contextualization emerged from relativism. Or rather, contextualization assumes relativism. Philosophically, this is certainly the case. In the late twentieth and early twenty-first centuries, New Relativism emerged in analytical philosophy to address perceived limitations of contextualization.[70] "*Contextualists* about (for instance) moral, aesthetic and epistemic discourse will view moral, aesthetic and epistemic expressions likewise as indexical expressions but (as we'll see) with some difficulty explaining apparent genuine *disagreement* in these areas of discourse. On this point, New Relativists claim an important advantage over contextualists. *New relativism*, by contrast with contextualism, aims to achieve this advantage *via* a much less familiar form of context dependence."[71] Contextualists claim to evaluate positions based on the "context of use" while the new relativist claims to evaluate positions independent of the context of use by means of the context of evaluation. Rather than a synthesis of positions, the new relativist considers both positions true depending upon which person is making the judgment. The end result is that propositional truth is no longer tenable. Contextualization runs into difficulty with examples as was cited above in Papua New Guinea, "the pig of God." New Relativism would allow the lamb to remain for cultures that have lambs and pigs for cultures that do not have lambs. No need to reconcile since both are true depending on the perspective. Both end up losing propositional truth. Schulz's solution to this problem was to teach the culture without lambs what a lamb is. In a sense, contextualization attempted to hold back the flood gates of relativism. As will be noted below, contextualization preserved some in the Global South from the relativism that inundated the West.

As the people charged with spending the large grant for theological education around the world, they struggled to define its shape around the world. Not surprisingly, theological education was first established in patterns that mirrored the West. Lacking the support institutions for university-style education such as prep schools and so

---

70 Maria Baghramian and J. Adam Carter, "Relativism," *The Stanford Encyclopedia of Philosophy*. Metaphysics Research Lab, Stanford University, 2016. https://plato.stanford.edu/archives/win2016/entries/relativism/.

71 Ibid.

forth, it is not surprising that attempts were made at making education more indigenous. The "contextualization" of theological education did not change the institutions or the preparatory systems as much as it changed the philosophy behind education. Education after all is primarily a school of thought influenced by philosophy and the zeitgeist. Contextualization emerged during a period when the West in general developed a mistrust of institutions and tradition, seeking to leave the past behind. Since contextualization emerged from an education setting, it did not take long for it to be spoken upon the lips of theologians, missiologists, and missionaries. In less than a decade from the adoption of the term "contextualization" among theological educators, the field of missiology could not avoid speaking about contextualization.

By the 1980s and 1990s, the concept of contextualization gave legitimatization to nearly every type of theology, from black theology to liberation theology, from African theology to Asian theology, from feminist theology to identity theology of the early twenty-first century. For example, the book *Queering the Ethiopian Eunuch* argues that the Ethiopian eunuch in Acts 8 was a man who was not a man, a homosexual, but was accepted by St. Luke as a man, providing a way for the church today to accept homosexuals.[72] The voices from the emerging two-thirds world often provided insights not readily identified by Western theologians with the risk of departing at times from the historical, biblical witness. At the same time, contextualization and the development of African and Asian theologies in some ways protected the two-thirds world (for a time) from the West's total departure from the historic, biblical teaching on marriage and sexuality because feminism and the acceptance of homosexuality were not part of these cultures.

---

72 Sean D. Burke, *Queering the Ethiopian Eunuch: Strategies of Ambiguity in Acts* (Minneapolis: Fortress Press, 2013), 15, 17. "In order to make this argument, I will employ queer theory, which I here define in a preliminary way as a constellation of approaches to issues of identity, deference, and ambiguity that have emerged in the cultural and intellectual context of postmodernism. . . . I will follow the example of queer theorists and focus first on gender and sexuality. . . . I will begin by addressing the question of whether it is legitimate to read the Ethiopian eunuch as a castrated male. . . . I will introduce queer theory and will examine several strategies that queer theorists have developed for engaging issues of identity, difference, and ambiguity."

David Bosch demonstrated in his brief overview of contextualization that the term in and of itself can take on virtually any usage and meaning. He acknowledges the dangers of both over- and under-contextualization. For Bosch, contextualization replaces historic confessions (i.e., Reformed and Lutheran Confessions) as the *norma normata* (normed norm) and is in a dialectic with the Holy Scriptures to produce mission. Such a view cannot be accepted by a Lutheran who pledges himself to the Holy Scriptures and the Book of Concord. Ultimately then, to speak about a naked contextualization is not helpful. To speak helpfully about contextualization requires a definition of it as a prolegomena for its use in mission.

Contextualization most helpfully or at its best is the proper distinction between Law and Gospel to a particular people group. The proper distinction between the Law and Gospel for a particular people or culture requires the practitioner to know the people and the culture and how to establish "points of contact" with the Law. The establishment of these points of contact certainly can make use of linguistic, anthropological, and philosophical insights to find where the Law can cut to the heart as Masaki demonstrated in his thesis. Placing "contextualization" within the framework of the proper distinction of Law and Gospel provides a theological guide that allows for the evaluation of various "contextual theologies," while keeping contextualization within the historic biblical confession. The use of the proper distinction between Law and Gospel breaks the dialectical paradigm for contextualization. Applying the Law and Gospel to a particular people and culture is no easy task; in fact, it is much more difficult than "contextualization" as it has generally been practiced for the past several decades. Yet this is the task given to the biblical, confessional, and Lutheran Christian.

WHAT HAPPENS WHEN THE THIRD USE OF THE LAW IS REJECTED?

Roland Ziegler

1. INTRODUCTION

What happens when the third use of the Law is rejected? Maybe you think the answer is simply this: one goes down the road of antinomianism, the road of moral decay. In this paper, I want to show that this thesis is false. It *can* be the case, but it does not *have to be* the case.

Before we go into the topic proper, though, it is appropriate to define some terms. When Lutherans talk about the third use of the Law, they mostly talk about Law as informative for the Christian (*usus didactictus*), as distinguished from the political use of the Law (*usus politicus*), the Law functioning to uphold external order by threats and rewards, which not only exists in the positive laws of the state and natural law but also in the orders of creation, suprapersonal structures in which human beings find themselves. The theological use of the Law is the Law convicting man of his sin, also known as *usus elenchticus* or *paedagogicus*. Lutheran orthodoxy distinguished four uses of the Law, distinguishing in the second use of the Law the *usus elenchticus*, which shows sin and the *usus paedagogicus* which indirectly leads to Christ.[1] The third use of the Law,

1 Heinrich Schmid, *Die Dogmatik der evangelisch-lutherischen Kirche*, 7th ed. (Gütersloh: C. Bertelsmann, 1893), 378f.

the didactic use of the Law, is taught in the Formula of Concord, Article VI, even though rather in passing. Mostly, FC VI talks about the Law as convicting the Christian.

In the title of the conference, antinomianism and legalism are mentioned as the two dangers of a false understanding of Law and Gospel. The term "antinomianism" is not a very old term. Theodor Mahlmann has found the oldest reference in the second edition of Johann Hoornbeeck's *Summa controversiarum* in 1658.[2] Luther seems to be the first to coin the term "antinomer" (antinomians) in the controversy with Johann Agricola. In this context, antinomianism has nothing to do with libertinism. Agricola's contention was rather that repentance is only caused by the Gospel, not by the Law. The Law has only a function in the civil realm, hence his famous statement that the Law belongs to the city hall, not the church. The antinomian controversy was thus about the *usus elenchticus*. Agricola did not discuss the question how the Christian knows what good works are. This became an issue only in the so-called second antinomian controversy after Luther's death. When people use the term *antinomianism* today, it does not refer to the antinomian controversy between Luther and Agricola, but the second one, where it pertains to the question of the *usus didacticus*. Antinomianism as a term has its use also in the history of the Reformed churches. Especially pertinent in this country is the controversy connected with Anne Hutchinson who was condemned as an antinomian and exiled from Massachusetts.

Antinomianism is also used as a general term describing attitudes in the history of Christianity where the proclamation of freedom from the Law is understood in the terms of libertinism, (i.e., that the Christian can do whatever he or she wants and that sinful behaviour is no longer sinful). In this sense, the term has also been used to describe certain tendencies in radical Jewish mysticism that is associated with *Sabbatai Zevi*.[3]

---

2 Theodor Mahlmann, "Antinomismus," in *Die Religion in Geschichte und Gegenwart*, 4th ed., (Tübingen: Mohr Siebeck), vol. 1, col. 549.

3 Gershom Scholem, *Major Trends in Jewish Mysticism* (New York: Schocken Books, 1995), 310–15.

Theodor Mahlmann makes the distinction of a denied antinomianism (antinomianism 1): Here it is affirmed that the Law precedes the Gospel. Therefore, the sequence "Gospel and Law" (Barth) is rejected.[4] Affirmed antinomianism denies that the Gospel itself is Law or needs the Law as a necessary affirmation. The Gospel gives; the Law demands. Both positions are complementary and exclude that the antionomianism develops into libertinism, since the Law is imprinted in the conscience (BSLK 961, 17–19).

Maybe you think that the notorious study of the ELCA on human sexuality is an example for a denial of the third use of the Law. But it is indeed not. Yes, it states that Luther taught only two uses of the Law, not surprising, since this is the common opinion in Luther scholarship. But it describes the functions of the Law also thus: "As Lutherans, we believe that God has given the Law not only to reveal sin and order society (1 Timothy 1:9), but also to point us to God's intentions and promises for our lives."[5] Here, clearly besides the *usus politicus* and *elenchticus* also a *usus diadacticus* is taught. Therefore, the discussion on human sexuality is not framed in pro-third use and anti-third use; the divisions are somewhere else. That the third use is not the decisive issue is also shown in that opponents of the third use in the ELCA (or formerly in the ELCA), like the school of Gerhard Forde, are against the statement on human sexuality.

2. WERNER ELERT

Werner Elert is certainly the most famous—or infamous—Lutheran theologian denying the third use of the Law, not the least because of his polemical streak. Who else would speak of "a theological forgery" when a student uses the scheme of the three uses of the Law he knows in his

---

4 Mahlmann, "Antinomismus." Cf. also *Die Bekenntnisschriften der evangelisch-lutherischen Kirche,* 5., durchgesehene Auflage. (Göttingen: Vandenhoeck & Ruprecht, 1963), 956, 42–957, 3. This edition will be abbreviated as "BSLK."

5 "A Social Statement on Human Sexuality: Gift and Trust." Page 6 of the PDF file available at http://download.elca.org/ELCA%20Resource%20Repository/SexualitySS.pdf. Accessed June 21, 2017.

notes of Luther's disputation, but which is not by Luther?[6] It seems to be quite certain that Luther did not use the terminology of the third use, that this is rather a Melanchthonian scheme. This does not answer, of course, the question if Luther teaches what is meant by the third use of the Law. This is, though, not our topic.[7]

2.1 Werner Elert's Understanding of the Relation of Law and Gospel[8]

What does Elert mean by Law? Law is not limited to statutory law for Elert. Law denotes our entire reality as the realm ordered by God, but therefore also as a realm of coercion (CE, 81). The Law encounters us as aspect of God's governance, legislation, and judicature.

God's governance as Law manifests itself in Him giving a person a certain place that comes with certain obligations. Thus, there is a certain ontological structure of the world that has moral implications. For Elert, these are the orders of creation. On the lowest level, these are the physical and biological laws, over it the institutions of marriage, family, tribe,

6 Werner Elert, "Eine theologische Fälschung zur Lehre vom tertius usus legis," *Zeitschrift für Religions- und Geistesgeschichte* 1 (1948), 168–70.

7 Most of modern Luther research rejects the presence of a third use in Luther. Fairly typical is Hans-Martin Barth, *The Theology of Martin Luther. A Critical Assessment* (Minneapolis: Fortress Press, 2012), 147f: "Certainly it is a disputed question whether according to Luther the Law can really have a positive significance for the orientation of the justified. In that case, there would be a third function (*tertius* usus) for the Law as applied to believers. The Law should then 'be kept so that the saints may know what works God demands, in which they can practice obedience to God.' This passage, as Werner Elert has demonstrated, was interpolated into Luther's text. At the same time, of course, there are many statements by Luther in which the Old Testament commandments or the New Testament instructions are received positively. But for believers they no longer function as 'Law' that threatens them; their fulfilment is a matter of course for the serious Christian. The good tree bears good fruit without needing any instructions or aids to orientation!" For a more nuanced view, cf. Paul Althaus, *The Theology of Martin Luther* (Philadelphia: Fortress, 1966), 266–73.

8 The subsequent overview on Elert is based on Werner Elert, "Gesetz und Evangelium," *Zwischen Gnade und Ungnade* (München: Ev. Presseverband für Bayern, 1948), 132–69 (abbreviated as GE) and Elert, *Das Christliche Ethos* (Tübingen: Furche Verlag, 1949) (abbreviated as CE).

legal community, people, state. These are givens; we find ourselves in them. The Ten Commandments presuppose that there is family, body, property, law, and honour/reputation (Eighth Commandment). Our place is our s*tand* or "walk of life." Elert does not simply identify the existing ordered structures with the will of God. It is an act of faith to see them as orders of God, and they can devolve into something demonic.

God is also legislator. God gives commands and prohibitions. This is no longer in the simple realm of being, but it is an order of ought (*Soll-gefüge*). The Law of God protects the order of being (*Seinsgefüge*) against the powers of chaos. This is the equivalent of the *usus politicus.*

The centre of Elert's thinking of the Law is God as the one who judges. To be a human person means to be under the judgment of God, to be responsible and answerable to God. That God truly judges is most clearly seen in the death of Christ. Since man is a sinner, the Law is for the sinner a threat, with death as punishment for sin.

The death of Christ shows us also that there is no escape from the condemnation of the Law. We cannot claim to have the centre position (*Mittelpunkthaltung*), so that we ask objectively for God. We are not even the morally free persons. As Paul shows, the Law does not help us in this situation; it rather exacerbates it and drives us deeper into sin.

The Law is therefore not, as ethicists believe, marking the borders of the straight and narrow way over which man sometimes strays (trans-gression!). But that is not our situation. The doctrine of original sin means that man is outside of the road (GE, 138f), and that means always condemning.

The Gospel is not denying the validity of the Law. Rather, in the death of Christ, who suffers the Law, we see the right of the Law. In Christ and for Christ's sake, God gives Himself to man as Father; therefore, man can believe that he is not simply condemned by God's judgment. The Gospel can be understood as an expression of God's will, but this can be misleading. Since every expression of God's will is binding on us, a consequence presenting itself to us is to understand the Gospel in parallel to the Law as a demand, and then we are not far from understanding the

Gospel as a rule for good life.[9] Elert can take up positively the definition of the Gospel suggested by Friedrich Gogarten at the oecumenical conference in Lausanne, 1927: The Gospel is the message about Christ who was delivered for our sins and was raised for our justification— essentially Romans 4:25. Elert acknowledges that the Gospel is a word, just as the Law, but that the Law here is a person. Content is not only what Jesus said, but what happened to Him—the crucified and raised Christ. Third, it is *euangelium*, Good News, because it contains "for our sins" and "for our justification." This is not a specific Pauline position. The Gospels have the same Christ and the same events as content as the *kerygma* of Paul, only that Paul presupposes the Gospels and gives more of an interpretation of the significance of the events than the events themselves. Christ, even though He also preaches the Law, does not give the preaching of the Law as a sign for the fulfillment of the Old Testament promise, but the preaching of the Gospel to the poor (Matthew 11:5; GE, 146). He becomes the friend of sinners (Matthew 11:19). The Pharisees, on the other hand, want to understand the Law as rule of life, but not as God's judicature.

The sinner realizes in his encounter with Christ that Christ is not a sinner and he sees his distance from Christ, a distance that is not constituted by individual acts, but is a difference in person. Jesus is not only the truth in itself, but He is also the truth for them. The sinners see their truth in Him. But the moment He becomes the friend of the sinner, the moment there is Table fellowship, they are like Him; they are no longer sinners. The question is simply if they can believe it. What happens here does not happen according to the Law. The Law condemns sin; Christ forgives sin. "There is either recompense or forgiveness" (GE, 151).

The purpose of the condemning Law is therefore to drive man to the Gospel of Christ's alien righteousness. This is not a one-time act; rather, the preaching of the Law is ongoing in the Church. It serves the destruction of the old man, not the building up of the new man. With this, we are at the topic of the third use.

---

9 The following according to GE, 143–45.

Elert parallels the fear of those who think that without the Law the Christians would fall into libertinism with the fear of the Pharisees when they saw Christ associating with sinners without Jesus making preconditions. The answer is the same: Christ transforms people. Where He enters, the demons are silent (Mark 1:24). Christ is the *master*. He is the standard of all things, in doing, in omitting, in loving, in suffering (GE, 147). What the personal presence of Christ accomplished in His earthly life, He does now through His Spirit. The children of God are led by the Spirit (Romans 8:14). Since this is not the spirit of fear, they cannot live in fear of the threats of the Law, neither are they longing for the rewards of the Law. In them, the Spirit of love operates, "in which the entire Law is fulfilled, even more than the Law can demand, joy, peace, faith (Gal. 5:22). . . . No, they have not received the Spirit through the works of the Law (3:2), and *because* they are governed by the Spirit, therefore they *are* no longer under the Law (5:18)" (GE, 158).

In this discussion, there is a strong anti-Calvinist emphasis in Elert. For Calvin, the third use is the preeminent use of the Law (Inst. II 7, 12).[10] For Elert, there is no Law that neutrally informs. Also, Elert understands Calvin in such a way, since the Law is according to Calvin "reigle de bien vivre et justement" that this is the final arrangement between God and man (CE, 395). Not the Law would have entered, but rather the Gospel would have entered and be in the service of the Law.

The new man, according to Elert, is not only freed from the curse of the Law, but also from the coercion of the Law. He is at the centre of his person one with the will of the Lawgiver. Therefore, he needs no instruction. On the other hand, the old man needs not only the instruction of the Law, but also the sanction of the Law. The old man never encounters simply the Law as instructing, but rather also as accusing and convicting. Thus, the *usus didacticus legis*, purely informative, is a "pure abstraction, which can only seduce to the *pestilentissma securitas* of the Pharisees

10 John Calvin, *Institutio Christianae religionis* 1559 II 7, 12: Joannes Calvin, Opera selecta, vol. 3 (München: Chr. Kaiser Verlag, 1928), 337, 23–25: "Tertius uses, qui et praecipuus est, et in proprium Legis finem propius spectat, erga fideles locum habet, quorum in cordibus iam viget et regnat Dei Spiritus."

(CE, 393). "Either the Law or the Gospel is the end of God's ways with humanity, but not both. They are against each other as life and death. We believe the second."[11]

How does Elert understand Article VI of the Formula of Concord? The summary is this: "One can summarize its position in this way: it denies the necessity of the informing function in the (unattainable) ideal case, affirmed in view of the factual state of the regenerate, but denies the possibility of a purely informative validity completely."[12] The ideal case is given in SD VI 6: "Indeed, if the faithful and elect children of God were perfectly renewed through the indwelling Spirit in this life, so that in their nature and all their powers they were completely free from sin, they would need no Law and therefore no prodding."[13] But this case never happens, because the Christian remains a sinner. They need the Law. But not for the purpose that the Law gives them the power to do good words or as *mere* information. The Law shows the regenerate what good works are and reproves them, for "reproof is the proper function of the Law" (SD VI 14). For Elert, the term "the regenerate" is used in two different meanings: it can mean the new man, who is no longer under the Law (SD VI 17; Romans 7:23; 6:14). Or it means man as he exists, who is pardoned, but also remains a sinner. There is a "personal union" between old and new man. These are not two parts of man, but two "sides" of man, defined by the purview of God, one as seen by God condemned by the Law, the other pardoned in Christ (GE, 164). For Elert, the third use of the Law is not another function of the Law, but it describes the significance of the Law for the regenerate in his earthly factuality (GE, 165).

What we see here is that Elert does not deny that the Law can tell us something. But it never simply tells us something—it condemns us.

---

11 Werner Elert, "Gesetz und Evangelium," *Zwischen Gnade und Ungnade*. (München: Ev. Presseverband für Bayern, 1948), 169.

12 "Man kann ihre Stellung dahin zusammenfassen, daß sie die Frage nach der Notwendigkeit der informatorischen Funktion im (unerreichbaren) Idealfall verneint, im Hinblick auf den tatsächlichen Zustand der Wiedergeborenen bejaht, die Möglichkeit einer rein informatorischen Geltung aber überhaupt verneint" (GE, 162).

13 Book of Concord quotations in this chapter are from Kolb-Wengert.

What about the relevance of the Decalogue for the believer? For Elert, the Decalogue marks borders and shows where the orders are endangered. It has significance for the *usus politicus*. But one cannot derive from the Ten Commandments what one concretely has to do. Elert thus thinks that the Law cannot do what one expects it to do: regulate one's life.[14] If I understand him correctly, here are some examples of what he means: How much money should one donate to church? Is it ethically justified that you spend money on alcohol or other nonessential things, while (a) the Synod has no money to pay missionaries, and (b) there are millions of malnourished children in the world? The Law cannot guide you in deciding how much money you will give to finance the college education of your child or maybe you give none and your child should get federal loans and get in debt for the rest of his or her life. The Law also does not answer the question what percentage of sales tax is moral.

Elert refers to Emil Brunner's ethics and points out that Brunner refers back to natural law in political questions, not the Decalogue, because the Decalogue consists in prohibitions, not commandments in the area of social questions. Any conclusions drawn from the Decalogue are human conclusions; as such, they have the problems of all human decisions (GE, 167).

Think of your own thinking: in many of these, especially political questions, you do not argue from the Decalogue, you argue from what the state is (i.e., from state as an institution of the gubernatorial rule of God).

The Law has its place because the Christian is also a sinner:

> Here the Law has its place in the preaching of the church, as in the life of its members, its continuing necessary place. It does not serve the edification of the new man, but the tearing down of the old. It has to tell us incessantly that

14 "Weder die kleinen Fragen unseres irdischen Lebens, ob und wenn einer heiraten, welchen Beruf einer ergreifen soll, noch die praktisch-sozialen des Arbeits-, Steuer-, Erbrechts, noch die großen politischen, Kommunismus, Sozialismus oder liberale Demokratie, lassen sich aus dem Dekalog beantworten" (GE, 159).

> we are lying if we say we have no sin. It exercises continually the *usus proprius*, because it is *semper accusans*, and because it cannot be anything else. To be led by the Spirit does not only mean to be led by Christ, but also to him, because we are continually afflicted by the accusation of the Law. The *usus proprius* of the Law is, in the language of the old dogmaticians, the *usus elenchticus*, and therefore always the *usus paedagogicus*, which drives us to Christ.[15]

But what forms the life of the Christian, if not the Law? For Elert, the place in which God has put us and the command to love our neighbour. Now, there is a place for the Ten Commandments, because they show us when a "walk of life" becomes demonic.

Albrecht Peters asks here the question with Peter Brunner: does there not arise the danger that the believer is formed by the powers of the world or pseudo-religious powers?[16] In Elert's understanding, the only means to prevent this is to preach the second use of the Law openly and continually, including the perversion of life in the "walks of life" and the institutions founded by God.

Peters sees a change in Elert after World War II. Now, so Peters, Elert also talks about "imperatives of sanctification and renewal" opposite of "imperatives of repentance and conversion." "These imperatives are not prescripts, not a legal command, but an offer . . . to let God give to one the concrete content of the newly gifted life, 'good deeds, which God has prepared, so that we shall walk in them' (Eph 2:10)" (CE, 295).[17] The Danish theologian N. H. Soe asked in a review of Elert's *The Christian*

---

15 "*Hier* hat das Gesetz in der Predigt der Kirche wie im Leben ihrer Glieder seinen bleibend notwendigen Ort. Es dient nicht dem Aufbau des neuen Menschen, sondern dem Abbau des alten. Es muß uns unablässig sagen, daß wir lügen, wenn wir sagen, wir hätten keine Sünde. Es übt unablässig den usus proprius aus, weil es semper accusans ist und weil es niemals etwas anderes sein kann. Vom Geist getrieben werden, heißt nicht nur von Christo, sondern auch zu ihm getrieben werden, weil wir unablässig von der Anklage des Gesetzes angefochten sind. Der usus proprius des Gesetzes ist, in der Sprache der alten Dogmatiker, der usus elenchticus und deshalb immer der usus paegadogicus, der zu Christo treibt" (GE, 161).

16 Albrecht Peters, *Gesetz und Evangelium* (Gütersloh: Gütersloher Verlagshaus Gerd Mohn, 1981), 184.

17 CE, 294d, 321, 349–51.

Ethos: "One wonders what indeed is the difference between the 'imperatives of renewal' and the *tertius usus legis* of his opponents."[18]

2.2 *The Christian Ethos:* An Example of Material Ethics: Marriage

What, then, does Elert's ethical teaching look like? Since marriage is always, but especially now, an interesting topic, let's have a look at it. Elert's book is entitled *The Christian Ethos*, not *Christian Ethics*. His ethos is not discussing the norms for human action; rather, the ethos of a person is defined by how God is judging a person. The quality of a person is only defined by God's judgment and is therefore distinct from moral philosophy. His book is divided in three parts: ethos under the Law, ethos under grace, and objective ethos. Marriage is treated in the first section, after the section on family.[19] Whereas the relationship between parents and children is naturally enduring and cannot be voluntarily ended, marriage seems to have no such natural lifelong aspect. No wonder, therefore, that the Enlightenment defined marriage as a contract for the purpose of procreation which can be dissolved if there is no offspring. The Church enumerated purposes of marriage: procreation, mutual help, protection from immorality. Melanchthon talks about the physical urge that God has implanted in humanity to fulfill His purpose (Ap XXIII 7), so that there is no need to talk about a purpose.

The Sixth Commandment presupposes marriage; it does not define it nor does it discuss how somebody got married. It demands that the order of marriage is not broken. The spouses are not only bound to each other, but also to a third, an estate or an order. It is an order because husband and wife cannot exchange places; it is an estate because it shows a place where we stand.

The difference from the theory of contract is that there is no recognition of the motives and feelings of the spouses. Marriage is not an "ought," a *Sollgefüge* (order of ought) but a *Seinsgefüge* (order of being). The connection between the two is that they *are* no longer the same as

18 Quoted in Albrecht Peters, *Gesetz und Evangelium*, 184.

19 This is §14, pp. 123–33 in the German of *Das christliche Ethos*.

before, each one body, but that they are now one body. Adultery is therefore not only breaking a contract, not only hurting one's spouse, not even only breaking a law, but the breaking of the order of being (*Seinsgefüge*) put together by God Himself. This means that marriage out of its being must be lifelong.

What about monogamy? After all, there are examples of polygamy in the Old Testament. The only command concerning a person who ought to have only one wife is the bishop (1 Timothy 3:2). Polygamy cannot be shown to be against the law of nature, but the development in history cannot be reversed. A Christian marriage is not a different marriage from the one governed by the Law; rather, the difference lies in the Christian realizing that marriage is governed by God's Law.

In a Christian marriage, *eros* remains *eros*, but it is not the only thing that binds the spouses. Between the spouses, there is also *agape*, which is also the norm for the life of the spouses. First Corinthians 13 is applicable also to marriage. To love one's neighbour is not simply to love somebody, but the neighbour who is given to me in a concrete ordering. For Elert, the nature of *agape* demands for the Christian monogamy. In polygamy, some spouse is always preferred to others, and this is incompatible with *agape*.

The Law fulfills also concerning marriage its twofold office. It reveals unchastity and prohibits therefore fornication before marriage. From the Fourth Commandment is derived the consent of the parents for a marriage. Because marriage is a public estate, secret engagements are invalid. Its public character follows from its significance for the orders of people and government. Because of the dangerous consequences of the marriage of close relatives, the order forbids them. But only the government can enforce that. The government has other interests in the order of marriage because marriage determines the relationship between two people, so the question of property rights and inheritance between spouses must be regulated. There is a difference between marriage recognized by the government and marriage recognized before God. If a couple consents and consummates the marriage, they are bound to each other. The church is also interested in this order. It cannot be disinterested if its members live according to divine order or in contradiction to it. Conversely, bride and groom will want to hear God's judgment on their marriage. A church needs its own order for marriage. It will follow the laws of the state unless the state laws indubitably violate divine Law. The government can appropriate the churchly order; in any case, it has the duty to oversee the orders of family and marriage and has therefore also the right of legislation in this area.

What about divorce? If marriage is essentially a contract, then it can be dissolved, except there is a public interest against it. The church is not against this view arguing from the letter of canon law or because of a Bible passage, but because it contradicts the natural order of marriage. Since there is a binding of the two spouses not only to each other but also to the estate of marriage, marriage is for life. What God has put together, no man can put asunder without being guilty. Traditionally, Lutherans therefore had no decree of divorce; rather, there were motions to allow remarriage. The judge did not grant a divorce. He stated that the marriage had been divorced, by adultery of the guilty party for which Matthew 19:9 was quoted. Adultery destroys the structure of marriage. If the wronged party wants to continue the marriage, then this can be a manifestation of *agape*, but it cannot be required. Churchly and secular laws need to help the innocent party to his or her right. It is the civic duty of any Christian to do his or her part in this question. Marriage serves the orders of people and government, but it can serve them only if the institution is respected by people and government.

In this lengthy summary, you see how Elert argues from the existing structure of marriage and develops from marriage as structure of being the ethical implications, without deriving it from a divine law. You see also that the Christian is not free from this order and its laws, because the Christian is in this gubernatorial order. The difference is that he or she lives this order in love. There is nothing antinomian about it.

3. STEVEN PAULSON

A more modern opponent of the third use of the Law is Steven Paulson, professor of systematic theology at Luther Seminary in St. Paul,

Minnesota, who published *Lutheran Theology,* an introduction to Lutheran theology but also a concise summary of his thinking.[20] The entire book is structured and dominated by the distinction between Law and Gospel. In his introduction, he defines the purpose of theology first as "to witness to sin and make it great, so great that it kills" (Paulson, 1). "The second task of theology is to make way for the declaration of a completely foreign, new righteousness that comes completely from the outside and is foreign" (Paulson, 2). "Virtue is not the goal of life, virtue is our problem. Religion is not given for morality; it is there to end it" (Paulson, 2). Sentences like that may confirm your fears and seem to contradict my opening statement that the third use of the Law does not lead to libertinism. But what Paulson means here by virtue and morality is not the same as good works. Rather, he identifies both with what he calls "the legal scheme." "The legal scheme refers to that teleological picture of life as a ladder on which life is a type of motion from earth's lowest level to the highest heaven by means of the exercise of the free will that either refuses the Law and fails to reach its proper goal or accepts the Law and fulfills it in order to arrive at the life of glory" (Paulson, 2f.). Paulson rejects the view that life either moves toward virtue or toward vice. But the goal of the Christian life is not virtue—it is Christ. Christ is to be imitated, but after the self has been killed and is dead to the Law. This strong and exclusive distinction between Law and Gospel means also a certain understanding of the Scriptures. "It is not a Law book at its heart, but the book of divine promises" (Paulson, 120). The content of the promise is Christ, the for is the forgiveness of sins (Paulson, 121).

In Baptism, man dies to the ruler to sin, and that means also to the Law (Romans 7) (Paulson, 155). Of course, Paulson does not deny the *simul iustus et peccator*. Rather, following Romans 7, he teaches that there are two persons: one entirely sin and dead, the other a person who is entirely just and alive, in contrast to an Augustinian understanding of

20 Steven D. Paulson, *Lutheran Theology* (London, New York: T & T Clark, 2011), abbreviated as "Paulson" in the references in the text.

the Christian being partially sinful and partially just. That means also that the Law continues its accusation and condemnation. It continues to do that what God wants it to do—namely, reveal sin of the old Adam. As such, the Law is *good* (Paulson, 182). Paulson rejects therefore with Luther antinomianism: "Luther's teaching is clear at this point: Law does not aid in making anyone righteous, yet it is necessary for true repentance or conversion" (Paulson, 184). Paulson describes the debate between Luther and Agricola and accuses Agricola of changing Luther's teachings from a Gospel of faith back to a Gospel of love (Paulson, 185). "Antinomians think sinners require only a midcourse correction of their desires in order to be free of the Law, and for them a carrot works much better than a stick: preach love, not wrath! But freedom does not come by abolishing Law in preaching—it comes by *fulfilling* the Law" (Paulson, 186). For Paulson, Agricola's antinomianism is in the end nothing but a return to the legal scheme, since it puts love in the place of faith. No wonder, therefore, that Agricola chose the wrong side once the Augsburg Interim was implemented. Agricola's problem was that he did not grasp the *simul* (Paulson, 187).

Paulson understands Romans 10:4, "Christ is the end of the Law" in both senses of the word *end*: it has been fulfilled, and it is over. The Law has been fulfilled by Christ and now remains as that which has been fulfilled in Christ. For this, he quotes the second series of the Antinomian Theses:

> 45. For the Law, as it was before Christ, certainly accused us; but under Christ it is placated by the remission of sins; and then it is to be fulfilled in the Spirit.
>
> 46. Thus after Christ in the coming life, there it will remain as fulfilled, when what it demands in the meantime is brought about—the new creature.
>
> 47. For never will the Law be removed in eternity, but it will remain, either as to be fulfilled in those damned or as fulfilled in those blessed (quoted in Paulson, 223). Thus, the Law is indeed eternal, its demand has to be fulfilled, but it

has been fulfilled in Christ and this fulfillment given to the Christian.

But now comes what you were waiting for: Paulson's critique of the third use. He accuses Melanchthon of introducing the novelty of the third use of the Law, the "Law as a guide to Christians that utterly confuses Paul's use of the *Simul* and freedom from the Law" (Paulson, 187). But then what does the Christian life look like? "[F]reedom from the Law is frightening for people who live in the old, secular Aeon because the end of the Law is chaos and hell according to the legal scheme" (Paulson, 170). But the result is not chaos and hell. Rather, the freedom to which Christ has set us free is the freedom from the teleological life, the life that aims at some kind of ideal. "[I]nstead, once the Law ends, one can truly begin to live—freely—without any purpose in the sense of a path to perfection" (Paulson, 223). In the new man who clings to Christ, the Holy Spirit produces fruit, "love that pours out its life in the body for the neighbour" (Paulson, 228). Love and the Law exclude each other, since love is immediate and relational. It exists between persons, but it is not a quality in a person, whereas in a legal relationship the relation is first to the Law, then to the person (Paulson, 229). If I understand Paulson here correctly, his point is that an action of love is done for the beloved's sake, not out of a sense of duty, as we also distinguish between these two. A husband can be caring about his spouse's needs and considerate and a good provider for her without loving her, out of a sense of duty. Love manifests itself in certain actions, but it is not exhausted in these actions.

Paulson does not want to abolish good works. "Lutherans ruin the idea that good works have any standing before God, but does that mean that there is no such thing as a good work? God forbid!" But a real good work cannot be an object of a person's trust (Paulson, 231). What do these good works look like? Paulson refers to Romans 12:9f, to love. Good works are works of love (Paulson, 235). This love "is a freedom of the *Spirit* which refuses to be bogged down in the letter of any law—including hierarchical lists of moral casuistry to which one could refer when two loves collide" (Paulson, 236).

"What do you, a baptized person, say when the Law (correctly) accuses you of sin? You do not claim that the Law made a false accusation. Nor do you claim that there appears to be a sin beyond Christ's reach, and therefore you must seek another remedy or rhubarb—like penance" (Paulson, 175). Rather, the answer to the accusation of sin is the return to Baptism. Sin is not reckoned to the sinner because he has been united with Christ's death (Paulson, 175).

Paulson is therefore taking up the continued significance of the Law for the Christian in its convicting power. The Christian, confronted with sin, will not say that it is not sin, that in Christ this has become an acceptable behaviour. Rather, he will accept the condemnation of the Law of the deed, but affirm that he is nevertheless free of the condemnation in Christ; in other words, he believes the promise. Good works are produced by the Holy Spirit in the new man. They are works of love.

So far, so good. But what is then the problem? Maybe you still fear that here is an enthusiastic misunderstanding, that in the name of love sinful acts are justified. But I do not see anything like that in Paulson. The remedy for such a course of action is the continued preaching of the Law that identifies what sin is.

4. JOSEPH FLETCHER

Joseph Fletcher (1905–91), an Episcopal priest and professor, brought on the scene of the sixties the concept of "situation ethics." The uses of the Law are a terminology specific to Lutheranism, so we should not expect Fletcher to give a discussion on the third use of the Law. But he certainly has an opinion on the Law, understood as unchangeable rules prescribing and proscribing certain behaviours, and its significance for the Christian.[21]

---

21 For our discussion, these books are used: Joseph Fletcher, *Situation Ethics: The New Morality* (Philadelphia: The Westminster Press, 1966) (abbreviated as SE) and Fletcher, *Moral Responsibility: Situation Ethics at Work* (Philadelphia: The Westminster Press, 1967) (abbreviated as MR).

But why choose Fletcher? After all, his books are not brand new. True, but it seems to me that the question he raises is still a living one, and if there ever was an antinomian as it is understood nowadays, then it was he. Now, Fletcher was not an antinomian according to his own understanding. Rather, he distinguishes three different approaches to making moral decisions: the legalistic, the antinomian, and the situational. "Situational" means that there is a principled approach to moral decisions, which is defined by two components: the principles and the situation. Actually, there is one principle or law in Christian situation ethics: love (SE, 30). All other rules are contingent; they are valid only if they serve love. Besides that, Fletcher rejects as demonic any notion that there are, as Sophocles put it, "immutable laws of heaven" (SE, 31). Principles below love are "maxims, or general rules"; they are "illuminators" but not "*directors*" (SE, 31). Thus, situation ethics, in the relation between Law and situation, finally lets love and reason be the guide for a moral decision (SE, 31). As such, the moral decision process takes into account four basic questions: the end of an action, what is the result; second, what are the means by which they can be acquired; third, the motive of the person; fourth, the foreseeable consequence (SE, 127f.). Thus, Fletcher disagrees with Kant, who denies that it can ever be right to lie, even if one would lie to a would-be murderer seeking his victim. In the end, the outcome defines if an action is good or bad, and thus Fletcher's ethic is a form of utilitarianism.[22] What counts is the result. "Are we not entitled to say that, depending on the situation, those who break the Seventh Commandment of the old Law, even whores, *could* be doing a good thing—*if* it is for love's sake, for the neighbor's sake? In short, is there any real 'Law' of universal weight? The situationist thinks not" (SE, 146). The examples Fletcher brings are a mother prostituting herself to feed her children or to serve their countries in counterespionage.

So, what about the Law, then? Fletcher's program is a reduction of the Law to the canon of love, for which he claims Jesus—as shown in

22 Klaus Bockmühl, *Gott im Exil? Atheismus in der Christenheit—Anfechtung und Überwindung. Zur Kritik der neuen Moral*, (Wuppertal: Aussat Verlag, 1975).

His teaching on the Sabbath—and Paul's teaching on the Law (SE, 69). Both replace *Torah* with *agape*. Thus, today we "follow Law, *if at all*, for love's sake; we do not follow love for Law's sake" (SE, 70). Fletcher rejects the thesis that by obeying the Law man serves love, since there is no real conflict. But is this not what Jesus said in Mark 12:29–32? "And Jesus answered him, The first of all the commandments is, Hear, O Israel; the Lord our God is one Lord: And thou shalt love the Lord thy God with all thy heart, and with all thy soul, and with all thy mind, and with all thy strength: this is the first commandment. And the second is like, namely this, Thou shalt love thy neighbour as thyself. There is none other commandment greater than these."[23] For Fletcher, the question is if we take loving one's neighbour as a compendium, that is as a collection of many laws, or rather as a distillation, where the essence is taken out of the legal code, "with the legal husks, or rubbish, thrown away as dross" (SE, 71). Thus, there is an inherent conflict between love and Law: "The situationist replies to all claims that love commands us to follow the Law, 'Yes, all right. We are willing to follow principles and precepts *if* they serve love, *when* they do. But just the same, there can be and often is a conflict between love and Law.' They cannot be partners; at best, love only employs Law when it seems worthwhile" (SE, 71).

If one wants to base ethics on natural law, one builds, so Fletcher, on quicksand. "There are no 'universal laws' held by all men everywhere at all times, no consensus of all men. Any precepts all men can agree to are platitudes such as 'do the good and avoid the evil' or 'to each according to his due.' What *is* good, when, and how, and what *is* due, is always widely debated in theory and hotly debated in concrete cases" (SE, 76).

Law as prescriptive, in the sense of what Lutherans would call the *political use of the Law*, does have a place in Fletcher's thinking. Even though morality cannot be legislated as the experiment with prohibition shows, laws can encourage certain behaviours: "But sometimes law can encourage and inculcate higher standards of behaviour, not reflecting present mores but nurturing and pioneering better ones. Situationists

23 Scripture quotations in this chapter are from the KJV.

acknowledge that law and order are not only necessary but actually good, wherever and whenever they promote the best interest of love" (SE, 100). Anarchism is therefore wrong, because justice needs both, love and order.

So, what does it look like concretely? For Fletcher, even adultery can be justified in a certain situation. He tells the story of a Mrs. Bergemeier, a woman who at the end of WWII was taken to a prison camp in Ukraine. Her husband came back from a POW camp, found their three children, and tried to get into contact with his wife. Somehow she learned about him. The only reason for early release were either illness, which would result in her being sent to a Soviet facility, or pregnancy. So to be with her family who needed her, she decided to get impregnated by a sympathetic Volga German prison guard. She went home, and husband and children were happy for her return and cherished the child born out this "sacrificial adultery" (SE, 164f).

How does Fletcher deal with the ethical evaluation of premarital sex? In a presentation of 1966, "Ethics and Premarital Sex," he first lays out the fact that premarital sex is widespread.[24] There are two camps in America: those who follow a divine sanction, broadly speaking the Judaeo-Christian ethics, then the secular one whose value commitment are to "human welfare and happiness" (MR, 132). Now, it is only an inference that the Bible allows sex only in marriage. What is forbidden is adultery. "Those Christians who are situational, refusing to absolutize any moral principle except 'love thy neighbor,' cannot absolutize Paul's one flesh (*henōsis*) theory of marriage in I Cor., ch. 6" (MR, 134). The question, if premarital sex is allowed, must therefore be answered by using the principle of love. First, no sexual act is "ethical if it hurts or exploits others. This is the difference between lust and love: lust treats a sexual partner as an object, love as a subject" (MR, 138). Second, "how can I act with the most certain concern for the happiness and welfare of those involved—myself and others?" We see here again the fundamental utilitarian character of Fletcher's ethic. The conclusion is therefore: "Sex

24 The following according to Fletcher, MR, 125–40.

is not always wrong outside of marriage, even for Christians; as Paul said, 'I know . . . that nothing is unclean in itself' (Rom 14:14)" (MR, 138).

5. CONCLUSION

What I wanted to show with this paper is that a denial of the third use of the Law as it is commonly understood among Lutherans does not lead in itself to libertinism. Neither Elert nor Paulson is a libertine. They both believe that the Law continues to convict the Christian of his or her sin. The message of the Gospel is not that sin is no more sin, that sin is suddenly something good, but that sin is forgiven.

For Elert, there is in this world no law that is not in the service of God's judicature. It can therefore never be simply informative; it is always also condemnatory. Elert also wants to avoid the thought that the Gospel is not the last word of God, that it is just the motivation for good works, and that therefore the determining relationship between God and the Christian is the Law. This is not rejected by the proponents of the third use of the Law. The difference, it seems to me, is in the question if the Law can have an informative use (not only, but also), and if the Holy Spirit uses the Law to identify what good works are. Against Elert, I think that the latter is true. Proponents of the third use of the Law nevertheless have to realize that the wording of the Ten Commandments by themselves is not sufficient to establish a moral philosophy. As Luther already did in his explanation of the commandments in the catechism, following the example of Christ in the Sermon on the Mount, the Law has to be interpreted and, so to speak, brought into the details of the common life, through the commandment to love one's neighbour. From Elert, one can also learn that the structures of being and of obligation, the orders of creation, and their inner logic have to be taken into consideration. What is lacking in Elert is the understanding of the Law as the immutable will of God. Also lacking is the conformity of the fruit of the Spirit with the demands of the Law, even though Elert does not deny it.

With our insistence on the third use of the Law, we should also remember that the Law does not give the power to do good works; rather the Spirit, who is not given through the Law, produces them in us.

In Fletcher, we see that libertinism is not simply tied up with the denial of the third use, but rather with a rejection of the Law and the replacement with a principle of love which is defined in a utilitarian way. But where in the Bible is the good defined in such a way? Here utilitarianism, always strong in Anglo-Saxon moral thinking, has overtaken the church. And what kind of God is it who is no longer the giver of Law and executor of Law? Not the God of the Bible. No wonder Fletcher became an atheist.[25]

And here seems to me to lie the challenge to the church today. First, not the denial of the third use of the Law, but rather that the content of the Law is defined differently. Proponents of same-sex marriage are not against the Law—after all, they want same-sex *marriage*, a legal institution. Our situation is not simply that of Greenwich Village in 1915 with Emma Goldman preaching free love—but now the proponents of same-sex marriage define the Law, the eternal will of God, differently.

Second, there is the challenge of a utilitarian or consequentialist ethics. What is right or wrong is defined by the outcome, the "greatest happiness for the greatest good." If this utilitarianism is combined with a wrong understand of what constitutes a human person, then one gets to statements like this by Fletcher:

> People in the Bards' situation have no reason to feel guilty about putting a Down's syndrome baby away, whether it's "put away" in the sense of hidden in a sanitarium or in a more responsible lethal sense. It is sad; yes. Dreadful. But it carries no guilt. True guilt arises only from an offense against a person, and a Down's is not a person. There is no cause for remorse, even though, certainly, there is for regret. Guilt over a decision to end an idiocy would be a false guilt, and probably unconsciously a form of psychic masochism.

---

25 "In the late 1960s, he renounced belief in God and publicly espoused humanism, although he maintained many of his ties to religious groups and members of the clergy." Peter Steinfels, "Dr. Joseph F. Fletcher, 86, Dies; Pioneer in Field of Medical Ethics," *The New York Times,* October 30, 1991, http://www.nytimes.com/1991/10/30/us/dr-joseph-f-fletcher-86-dies-pioneer-in-field-of-medical-ethics.html, accessed April 16, 2013.

> There is far more reason for real guilt in keeping alive a Down's or other kind of idiot, out of a false idea of obligation or duty, while at the same time feeling no obligation at all to save that money and emotion for a living, learning child. The learning child might be a retarded one with a viable potential, or just an orphan in need of adoption.[26]

And thus a good conscience in its murderous pursuits is given to a sinful world in the name of Christianity. Against such perversions of Christianity and against a false Law that is proclaimed in today's society, the Church is called to preach the Law without detraction, in its full force, concretely, and God will bless such preaching that will do its part to uphold public order, bring knowledge of sin, and guide Christians in their life.

---

26 Bernard Bard and Joseph Fletcher, "The Right to Die," *The Atlantic Monthly*, 221 (April 1968), 59–64, http://www.riverbendds.org/index.htm?page=fletcher.html, accessed April 16, 2013.

APPENDIX

LCMS, LCC and NALC Leaders Release Joint Statement on Scripture

As an important step forward in the ongoing consultation between representatives of the Lutheran Church—Canada (LCC), The Lutheran Church—Missouri Synod (LCMS) and the North American Lutheran Church (NALC), the participants who represented the three church bodies are releasing their joint statement on Holy Scripture, "God's Word Forever Shall Abide: A Guiding Statement on the Character and Proper Use of the Sacred Scriptures."

Representatives of the three Lutheran church bodies have been meeting twice a year since late 2011, with conversations focused on similarities and differences, as well as topics of common concern. Discussion regularly addresses the challenges to marriage, sexuality, the sanctity of all human life and religious liberty. From the beginning, however, the participants have been engaging in serious, in-depth conversation about the authority of Scripture, which is foundational to the church bodies' understandings of these other issues.

The two most recent consultations, Sept. 9-10, 2015, in St. Louis, and March 16-17, 2016, in Bradenton, Fla., resulted in the drafting of the common statement, understood as providing guidance to the participants in ongoing, future conversations. The introduction to the document states:

> *We confess that the Bible is God's written Word as part and parcel of our deepest confession — that Jesus Christ is the very Son of God, God incarnate, "very God of very God" and the Savior and Redeemer of all humankind. We confess that the Bible is God's Word because its entire message is focused on Jesus Christ and His saving work. He is the heart and center of Scripture and the key to its true meaning.*

Topical sections of the statement address: how did the Bible get here, what kind of book is the Bible, suitable methodology of interpretation and proper use of the Bible.

The statement is a reflection of the consensus of the participants and not an official document or doctrinal statement approved by any one of the three church bodies. It is intended to serve as a guideline for further joint study by the representatives and by other groups within the three denominations who are seeking to know more about each other. It also is hoped that it may help pastors and congregations who want to know more about the confessional Lutheran understanding of the truth and authority of Scripture on which the LCMS, the LCC and the NALC are founded.

The statement concludes:

> *We rejoice in our consensus in these truths. We pray that our shared understanding will be a sure and solid foundation for us to address future conversations and discussions, both in matters of agreement and areas where we do not share a common teaching or practice.*

Participants in the ongoing consultations between leaders of the LCMS, the LCC and the NALC have been the Rev. Dr. Albert Collver III (LCMS), the Rev. Dr. Joel Lehenbauer (LCMS), the Rev. Larry Vogel (LCMS), the Rev. John Pless (LCMS), the Rev. Robert Bugbee (LCC president), the Rev. John Bradosky (NALC bishop), the Rev. Mark Chavez (NALC), the Rev. Dr. Jim Nestingen (NALC), the Rev. Paull Spring (NALC) and the Rev. Dr. David Wendel (NALC).

"God's Word FOREVER *shall* ABIDE"

A GUIDING STATEMENT ON THE CHARACTER AND PROPER USE OF THE SACRED SCRIPTURES

NALC North American Lutheran Church
LUTHERAN CHURCH–CANADA ÉGLISE LUTHÉRIENNE du CANADA
The Lutheran Church Missouri Synod

God's Word FOREVER *shall* ABIDE"

A GUIDING STATEMENT ON THE CHARACTER AND PROPER USE OF THE SACRED SCRIPTURES[1]

God spoke, and it was so (Genesis 1). Together we acknowledge that God works by His Word. The Word of God brings creation into being in a way beyond human knowledge — a way that can only elicit doxology, not human understanding. Then, to a fallen world God spoke through prophets in great compassion with human speech for human comprehension (Gen. 15:1). And now "in these last days," with grace beyond comprehension, "he has spoken to us by his Son": the Word by whom He upholds His universe and, yet, the Word made flesh. The Son, who dwelt among us, reveals that God is love as He bears sin and death in a great exchange that grants us resurrection and eternal life (Heb. 1:2–3; John 1:1–4, 14, 18).

God's Word is not silenced. He speaks through human voices proclaiming His excellencies. He bespeaks us righteous in sermon and absolution. He declares His Word by human lips over baptismal water and eucharistic bread and cup. And He speaks with clarity and authority in the Holy Scriptures, which we recognize and confess to be "the only guiding principle and rule" for all Christian teaching, preaching, life and practice (FC SD Binding Summary 9).[2]

We confess together that the Bible is the written Word of God. We confess this even as we recognize that it is a collection of human writings spanning a time period of more than a thousand years in three different human languages. We confess this even as we recognize that the biblical texts address a variety of particular circumstances and exhibit the influence of cultural particularities, historical experiences, individual character traits and so forth.

We confess that the Bible **is** *God's written Word as part and parcel of our deepest confession — that Jesus Christ* **is** *the very Son of God, God incarnate, "very God of very God" and the Savior and Redeemer of all humankind. We confess that the Bible* **is** *God's Word because its entire message is focused on Jesus Christ and His saving work. He is the heart and center of Scripture and the key to its true meaning. We trust the Bible because it has led us to trust in Jesus as our Savior and Lord. As St. John reminds us: "But these are written so that you may believe that Jesus is the Christ, the Son of God, and that by believing you may have life in his name" (John 20:31; cp. John 5:39). We rejoice in the truth that comes in Christ*

[1] This statement, "God's Word forever shall abide" ("A Mighty Fortress Is Our God," verse 4; see *LBW* 228, 229; *LSB* 657), was conceived at the Sept. 9-10, 2015, meeting of representatives of the LCMS and NALC where we agreed to prepare a joint statement on the authority of Holy Scripture. The LCC representative for the ongoing discussions — although unable to be present for these discussions — affirmed both the goal and this document. The present document uses materials provided by both groups (see the attached bibliography for resources that informed our discussions) and is the result of further conversation and consideration at the March 16-17, 2016 meeting of the representatives. The statement's initial purpose was to serve as a foundation and guidelines for our deliberations, on the basis of God's Word, both in areas where we seek to express a common position and also regarding such topics and practices as may divide us. It is offered here as a report from the representatives involved in these discussions.

[2] Unless otherwise indicated, quotations from the Book of Concord are from *The Book of Concord: The Confessions of the Evangelical Lutheran Church*, ed. Robert Kolb and Timothy J. Wengert (Minneapolis: Fortress Press, 2000).

alone — the truth that is given by God's gracious act of sending His Son: "Long ago, at many times and in many ways, God spoke to our fathers by the prophets, but in these last days he has spoken to us by his Son, whom he appointed the heir of all things, through whom also he created the world" (Heb. 1:1–2).

With the Church of every era, we regard these texts as the authoritative Word of God, because the Gospel of Christ is known through them and they alone rightly guide the life of faith. Our Lord Jesus Himself declares the trustworthiness of the Hebrew Scriptures when He quotes their authority, saying time and again, "It is written" (e.g., Matt. 4:4, 7, 10; Luke 24:46). He also assures us that His apostles, whose testimony undergirds the entire New Testament, were inspired by the Holy Spirit and that their writings are trustworthy in every way: "But the Helper, the Holy Spirit, whom the Father will send in my name, he will teach you all things and bring to your remembrance all that I have said to you" (John 14:26).

Therefore, we joyfully confess that we are not strangers to God and His truth, for in justifying us sinners He has made us members of His household, "built on the foundation of the apostles and prophets, Christ Jesus himself being the cornerstone" (Eph. 2:19–20). The Scriptures' prophetic and apostolic testimony to God's work from creation until Christ's future return and renewal of creation is the only trustworthy basis for knowing God rightly. Its authority is complete. We receive it with joy and accept its truth without qualification.

Part 1: How Did the Bible Get Here?

1. Lutheran confessional theology teaches that God has given humankind a revelation of Himself in His works of creation. The self-disclosure of God in the realm of nature is called "general revelation." The revelation of God in nature, which does reveal God's wisdom and power (Rom. 1:20), nonetheless is finally a revelation of God's *law*.
    a. Ever since the entrance of sin into the world, the whole creation groans under the bondage of corruption (Rom. 8:19ff). Our whole physical environment witnesses to the judgment of God who visits *death* on the works of His own hands because of human rebellion against Him.
    b. Since general revelation does not witness to the grace that pardons but only to the wrath that punishes sin, the sinner responds to the revelation of God in nature by willfully suppressing the truth to which it witnesses (Rom. 1:18). The sinner either denies that there is a God (Ps. 14:1; 53:1) or invents an idol whose wrath can be appeased by human devices (LC I 18-23).
2. The revelation in which God makes Himself known as a *gracious* God is called "special revelation." While special revelation cannot simply be equated with the Holy Scriptures, since God spoke to His people in many ways before any Scriptures were written and has spoken to us in these last times especially in His Son (Heb. 1:1–2), it is nevertheless true that it is in the Scriptures that the knowledge of these special revelations of God's mercy has come to us.
3. The revelation given to us in the Scriptures about all that God has done in human history to effect our salvation *comes from God*. No prophetic teaching about what God was doing through His people to keep His promise of sending a Redeemer arose from any mere human reflection on an interpretation of Israel's history. But men spoke from God about these things as they were moved by the Holy Spirit (2 Peter 1:20–21).

    Apostolic proclamation concerning all that God did in Christ was "revealed … through the Spirit" and imparted "in words not taught by human wisdom but taught by the Spirit" (1 Cor. 2:10, 13; Gal. 1:11–12). The apostle Paul can declare of the Scriptures that nurtured Timothy (and us as well) that "all Scripture is breathed out by God" (2 Tim. 3:16). So also, he can claim the same Spirit as the One who inspired his own writings (Rom. 15:18–19; 1 Cor. 2:13; Eph. 3:4–5).
4. Scriptures inspired by God were written by *human beings*. God gave His Word to His Old and New Testament people through human beings whom He Himself chose and endowed to speak His Word to concrete situations and circumstances in the history of His people.

Part 2: What Kind of Book Is the Bible?

The Bible, inspired by God and written by men, is a divine-human book. However, this is not to say that these are two parts that can be separated. The divine and the human in the Bible are combined in an inseparable union analogous to the union of the two natures in the Person of Christ.

1. *A book written by human authors*

   Lutherans acknowledge and teach that the Bible, even though it is and transmits God's very own Word, is a thoroughly human book. They do not have a docetic view of the Bible.[3]

   a. One obviously human aspect of the sacred Scriptures is that the language of the Bible is *human language*, written to be read and understood by human beings. Accordingly, the Bible's language conforms to the usual principles of grammar and syntax. The biblical literature contains many of the literary forms and devices used by other literature for the purpose of effective communication.

   b. The Bible, considered as written communication, is human also in that it has a *history*.

      i. In a sense, the biblical literature represents a "development." The Bible did not fall full-blown from heaven, but grew upon earth. The biblical literature came into existence over a period of many centuries and was written *by* human beings *for* human beings who lived in varying cultures and conditions, but the message remains the same.

      ii. Inasmuch as the Bible was written in history by authors who were not insulated from the culture in which they lived and wrote, and inasmuch as its literature was not produced in a vacuum but was originally composed for and addressed to distinctively discreet situations and circumstances, this literature has a historical dimension that gives *it its own peculiar and concrete particularity*. In this sense, it bears the marks of a particular time and culture.[4]

2. A *book inspired by God*

   Lutherans, however, also teach that the Bible is a *divine* book.

   a. While Lutherans recognize that the Bible as an historical phenomenon is open to investigation by the historian, they believe and confess that there is a not-of-this-world dimension to the sacred Scriptures, not discernible by historical research. Lutherans, therefore, do not surrender the Bible to historians as though they could by their methods give a full account of the origin and nature of the biblical literature.

   b. Lutherans will not admit that the historian has the last word to say about the kind of a book the Bible is. They will not permit the historian to rule that the Bible is the product of precisely the same processes that produce other literature.

   c. Lutherans believe that in the history that occasioned the writing of the biblical literature God was active in a unique way, so that there is a qualitative difference between the inspired Scriptures and every other form of human expression.

3. *A perfect unity*

   Since *God* is their primary Author, the Scriptures differ qualitatively from other literature in that they possess such attributes as unity and complete truthfulness or reliability.

   a. Lutheran theology has always acknowledged that there is a certain progression discernible in the revelation that God gave of Himself and of His saving actions in history when earlier Scriptures are compared with later Scriptures (as when the Old Testament is compared with the New Testament.)

   b. Lutheran theology also acknowledges that there are in the Scriptures no conflicting or contradictory conceptions of God and His ways with humanity, but rather a perfect theological unity, despite different emphases in different biblical books and authors.

   c. For Lutheran theology, it is a self-evident truth that God's revelation of Himself in the sacred Scriptures is always perfectly consistent with itself.

   d. Lutherans have given deep consideration to the implications of our Lord's two distinct natures united in His person and the Bible's character as a book that is both human and divine.

      i. With the Church through the ages we confess that the divine and human natures and attributes of the incarnate Son of God relate to or "communicate" with one another. There is, no doubt, a mystery at work here not unlike that of the Father, Son and Holy Spirit in the undivided unity of the one God who made heaven and earth, redeemed all humanity and will renew the justified in the new creation. Nevertheless, even as we confess these great

[3] The docetists were a heretical group in the ancient church who denied the true humanity of Jesus. They held that He only appeared to be human.

[4] For example, the situation in Corinth which occasioned Paul's correspondence with that congregation had no precise parallel in any other congregation in apostolic times. If that particular situation had not occurred, Paul's letters to the Corinthians might not have been written at all or, at least, they would have had a different complexion.

mysteries, we also affirm these undeniable truths. As for the *communication of attributes (communicatio idiomatum),* we Lutherans have always confessed that which the Word of God makes clear:

1. What is true of each individual nature — the human and the divine — is true of the whole Christ, for He is one divine person (FC SD VIII 36). So it is that we confess the incomprehensible truth that in *the man* Christ Jesus, *God* died for us.
2. The one Christ, in His office, works "according to, with, and through both natures" (FC SD VIII 46-47).
3. In the personal union of the human and divine natures, the human nature of our Lord retains all its essential characteristics and traits, but alongside of them it has "special, high, great, supernatural, incomprehensible, indescribable heavenly prerogatives and privileges" both now and into eternity (FC SD VIII 51). And, with regard to this third point, we confess that we cannot limit or define the extent to which Christ's humanity shares in His divinity.

ii. With the Church through the ages we confess: The divine and human character of the Scriptures relate to one another in similar ways.

1. The Bible is fully human and fully divine — in its entirety. So we do read and study it, seeking to understand it as we would other historical documents. We also read it expectantly, for we believe its prophetic and apostolic character means that it is ever profitable to us in every way.
2. God is at work in Scripture — indeed, He is present and most profoundly present in the Person of the Son about whom all Scripture testifies (Luke 24). God is present wholly in His humanity and divinity wherever the Word is rightly preached and taught. This is of deep comfort, for Jesus has promised Christians "that not only His mere divinity would be with them (which to us poor sinners is like a consuming fire on dry stubble). But Christ promised that He — He, the man who has spoken with them, who has experienced all tribulations in His received human nature, and who can therefore have sympathy with us, as with men and His brethren — He will be with us in our troubles also according to the nature by which He is our brother and we are flesh of His flesh" (FC SD VIII 87).[5]
3. Our God's humble work in this divine-human book — a book as open to ridicule as was the Lord whose humility made Him the suffering servant of all — is nonetheless "special, high, great, supernatural, incomprehensible, indescribable." So much so, indeed, that we gladly confess that this book, like our Lord, is without fault, truthful in all things and given for our salvation (see John 20:31).

4. An *inerrant book* — a book that is completely reliable

Another qualitative difference between the Scriptures and other literature is that the Scriptures — like the God who gives them — are reliable and completely trustworthy, or as the Christian church has often asserted, they are inerrant.

a. We realize that the term "inerrant" (or terms like "infallible" or expressions like "completely reliable") is itself open to "errant" understandings and definitions. Not all Christians who confess the inerrancy of the Bible view this inerrancy in the same way or in a way that can be affirmed here. It should not be understood as implying that the Bible's complete reliability can be demonstrated on the basis of human reason, historical study, scientific evaluation and so forth, but as an article of faith that fully coheres with Scripture's character as the Word of God.[6]

b. Lutherans do hold that to declare the inerrancy or complete reliability of the Scriptures

[5] *The Book of Concord: The Confessions of the Evangelical Lutheran Church*, ed. Theodore G. Tappert (Philadelphia: Fortress Press, 1959).

[6] Lutherans are not "fundamentalists." We note that fundamentalism, historically, is a movement within Reformed theology holding to five fundamental doctrines and asserting that the inerrancy of Scripture is the only foundation for faith. Lutheran theology would hold that faith results from the Word as it is heard and received sacramentally. So faith in Christ, created by the Spirit through the Word, precedes and is the basis for confidence in Scripture's infallibility. Therefore, while denying that Lutherans are fundamentalists, we joyfully affirm that we confidently hold that the Bible speaks truthfully when it teaches such doctrines as the bodily resurrection of Christ or His virgin birth or God's miraculous interventions in history.

is to declare that what the Bible teaches to be true in any area of doctrine or life is so, but without any assumption that we can thereby resolve every difficulty of interpretation.

c. We may not simply reduce scriptural reliability to "spiritual" matters. To do so is to invite a Gnostic sort of faith that not only questions the Bible's truthfulness in such matters as creation, but in the whole of redemption as well, for the same Bible that tells us God is Spirit (John 4:24) also tells us that He creates the entire material world and has become man, embodied in flesh and blood (John 1:14; Heb. 2:14). So also, a limitation of biblical reliability to "spiritual matters" undermines biblical authority in matters of morality and ethics. Therefore, we affirm scriptural reliability in every matter of doctrine and life.

d. Lutherans believe that Scripture's reliability and trustworthiness does not suggest that it employs the technological precision of modern scientific study or contemporary historiographic methodologies. Only an anachronistic interpretive method would impose upon the Bible methodologies that have been developed centuries after its composition or would require the type of precision demanded by modern positivism or scientism.[7]

e. The Lutheran Confessions make a sharp distinction between the Scriptures and human literature: "no person's writing can be put on a par with it" (FC SD Summary 9), and clearly affirm that the imperfections that characterize human writings are not found in the Scriptures (Ap XXIV 94-95). Rather, the Word of God is "pure, infallible, and unchangeable" (Preface to the *Book of Concord* [BC Preface], 16; see also paragraph 20).

f. The Lutheran Confessions confess the truthfulness of the Scriptures with simple and forceful words: "They will not lie to you" (LC V 76; cf. also FC Ep VIII 13) and "God's Word cannot deceive" (LC IV 57). The Formula of Concord refers to Scripture's teaching on election as a "clear, certain, and unerring foundation" for faith (FC SD XI 12).

[7] Positivism and its synonym, scientism, assert that only the sciences can establish a valid truth claim.

g. Above all, Lutherans approach the Scriptures with humility, confessing with Luther: "The Pope, Luther, Augustine, Paul, an angel from heaven — these should not be masters, judges, arbiters but only witnesses, disciples and confessors of Scripture" (AE 26:58).

Part 3: Suitable Methodology of Interpretation

Lutheran theology has always recognized that because the Bible is written in human language, certain general principles of interpretation must be observed. Lutheran theology also recognizes that because the Bible is God's Word, certain other principles are basic to a correct understanding of its message.

A Human Book: General Principles

1. Because the Bible communicates God's eternal truth in literature, written by human authors employing human terminology and idioms, and comprises literary forms common to other human literature, it is self-evident that the best and most thorough biblical exegesis requires the following:
   a. A thorough knowledge of the languages in which the Bible was originally written;
   b. Acquaintance with and recognition of the literary forms employed by biblical authors for effective communication (address, oracle, prayer, creed, hymn, proverb, parable, historical narrative, edict, treaty, prose and poetry).
2. Because the biblical literature dates from various periods of human history and was addressed to concrete situations characterized by the particularity peculiar to everything that is historical, biblical interpretation needs to take this "historical dimension" of the Bible into account.
   a. The biblical literature cannot be treated as though every book and pericope was addressed to general situations, and as though everything that is said in every pericope is applicable immediately to every situation.[8]
   b. The interpreter will therefore want to understand:

[8] For example, concerning the Third Commandment, Luther said: "Therefore, according to its literal outward sense, this commandment does not concern us Christians" (LC I 82 [Tappert]). For a discussion of the specific application of specific texts to specific situations, see the Apology's treatment of Matt. 19:21 in Ap XXVII 45-50.

i. What the *original* situation was to which the words were first spoken;

ii. What the words meant in that *particular* historical context;

iii. What their *continuing* meaning is for subsequent times and circumstances.

c. Lutheran theology, therefore, gratefully uses all the information made available by historical and archaeological research relative to the history of Israel and of all the other nations whose history touches Israel's. Lutheran theology gratefully uses the gains of faithful New Testament scholarship, which broaden and deepen our understanding of the apostolic writings.

d. When Lutherans say that Scripture interprets itself, this is not to be understood as though historical research has no value for illumining the meaning of a biblical text.

Inspired by God: Other Principles

While Lutheran students of the Bible gladly avail themselves of any light that historical research can shed on the Bible as a historical phenomenon, they never forget that the Bible is at the same time God's eternal, immutable Word given to us by inspiration of God to make us wise unto salvation (2 Tim. 3:15).

1. Viewing the Bible in this way leads Lutherans to emphasize the following as they interpret the Scriptures:

a. The divine and saving wisdom that the Bible imparts can be understood and believed only as the Holy Spirit graciously empowers us to hear what God is speaking to us in His Word.

b. In His Word, God speaks to us His Law and Gospel, the Word that condemns and the Word that forgives. These must be carefully distinguished lest the Law be diluted and the Gospel perverted so that we receive from the Scriptures neither the knowledge of sin nor the assurance of grace. The central message of the Bible is the Gospel of God's free grace toward sinners in Christ Jesus — the Good News that through the cross of Christ, the condemning record of our sin has been erased.

c. God's Word is, therefore, always to be read and interpreted in light of the Gospel — its central message of Christ and His justifying work. Just as surely, only in the Bible's revelation of the Triune God and the Person and work of Christ can we know the Gospel authentically and truthfully. The Bible must be understood in this way, or it will not be understood at all.

2. With these indispensable emphases in mind, Lutherans employ principles for interpreting the Bible that flow from the fact that it is a divine book whose primary Author is the Holy Spirit.

a. Since it is the Holy Spirit who bears witness in all the Holy Scriptures to God's actions in human history for the salvation of the world, this witness is consistent with itself and true to the facts. Therefore, a basic principle for interpreting the Holy Spirit's writings is that they are characterized both by *unity* and *truthfulness.*

b. Because there is perfect unity in the scriptural witness to God and His mighty deeds for our redemption, Lutherans operate confidently with the principle that *Scripture interprets Scripture.*

i. It is the Spirit's authorship of the Scriptures that makes a meaningful application of this principle possible. If the Bible were merely a human book written from a variety of human perspectives and reflecting only human attempts to talk about God and history, then the unity necessary in order to use one part of Scripture to interpret another would be totally missing.

ii. Since the Spirit of truth is the Author of Scripture, the witness of Scripture to the history in which God acted savingly is true. This is not to say that the Scriptures are mere chronicles, or that they were written in the first instance to be a history of Israel and a biography of Jesus. The Bible reports history to show what God was doing through Israel and Jesus to accomplish His saving purposes. The history reported in the Bible is selective. In the Bible, God has given us a theology of history.

iii. While the history the Bible reports is selective, it is also wholly reliable. If the history is negated, then what God was doing in the history is negated too, and the Bible is turned into a book of mythology — humanly devised legends with no basis in fact — about the doings of the deity that have nothing to do with human affairs.

iv. It is a principle for Lutheran biblical interpretation that the Bible is not mythology, but a revelation from God Himself about what He actually did in the arena of human history in order to carry out His eternal counsels of salvation.

c. Lutherans hold that the Scriptures are clear in their saving truths (the perspicuity of Scripture). We must, with Luther, distinguish the inner clarity of faith and the external clarity of Scripture. No one — believer or unbeliever — can misunderstand the clear assertion that God created heaven and earth, for example. However, only faith believes this clear assertion. The Bible's essential message is unambiguous, but only faith appropriates its truth (Deut. 30:11–14; Rom. 10:5–13). This does not deny that there are passages we cannot understand either in part or fully. For this reason, we read what is unclear to us in light of the overwhelming clarity of the biblical message, confident that God has made clear everything we need for life and salvation in Christ Jesus.

d. In interpreting the Bible, Lutherans remember that the Spirit has spoken through *human beings* whose words must be understood in the light of their historical context. They remember, too, that the *Spirit* has spoken through human beings. This fact means that historical, human words are at the same time divine, eternal words that speak the truth about God's saving will and actions.

Part 4: Proper Use of the Bible

1. Because Lutherans believe, teach and confess that the words of the Holy Scriptures are from the Holy Spirit (Ap IV 107-108; AC XXVIII 49), they therefore hold that the Bible is qualitatively different from all other human literature (FC SD Summary 9; Ap XXIV 94-95). They do not hesitate to call the Bible the "pure, unadulterated Word of God" and "infallible" divine truth (BC Preface 5, 20).

2. Confessional Lutheran theology, accordingly, declares that "we base our teaching on God's Word as the eternal truth" (FC SD Summary, 13); "God's Word alone ought to be and remain the only guiding principle and rule of all teaching" (FC SD Summary 9); "Holy Scripture alone remains the only judge, rule, and guiding principle, according to which, as the only touchstone, all teachings should and must be recognized and judged as good or evil, correct or incorrect" (FC Ep Summary, 7); "the only rule and guiding principle according to which all teachings and teachers are to be evaluated and judged are the prophetic and apostolic writings of the Old and New Testaments alone" (FC Ep Summary, 1; cp. FC SD Summary, 3).

   a. These quotations from the Confessions leave little doubt about how they use the Bible, namely, as the *ultimate* and *absolute authority* for all that the church teaches in God's name.

   b. That is why the Symbols repeat over and over again such formulas as "Scripture teaches" (AC XXIV 28; Ap XXIII 11; FC SD I 46; FC SD III 30) and "it is written" (AC XXIV 26; XXVIII 51; Ap IV 263; SA III vii 1-2; III xiii 3; FC SD III 20, 57; VI 12; VIII 6; X 8 11; XI 7).

   c. That is why the Confessions, without concern that some might accuse them of making a legislative use of Scripture, firmly insist that where "we have the clear, certain testimonies in the Scripture … we should [*sollen wir*] simply believe" and "should not raise any objections" (FC SD VIII 53).

3. The sacred Scriptures are to the Lutheran confessors the source of doctrine.

   a. In contrast to the authority of the church fathers, the Smalcald Articles (II ii 15) set up the invariable rule: "This means that the Word of God — and no one else, not even an angel — should establish articles of faith." The Augsburg Confession (Preface 8; Epilog to XXI 2; XXI 4, German) and the Apology (I 2; II 32-43; IV 5, 166; XII 16; *et passim*) appeal to the sacred Scriptures as a whole as well as to individual passages as final authority.

   b. The "summary and generally accepted concept and form" that the Formula (SD Summary 1) regards as essential for basic and firm agreement in the Church is to be drawn from the Word of God. The prophetic and apostolic Scriptures of both testaments are "the pure, clear fountain of Israel" (FC SD Summary 3).

4. Lutherans think it is "rash" to teach something that passages of Scripture do not teach (Ap XII 138), and that it is "extreme impudence" to teach anything that is contrary to testimonies of Scripture (Ap XXIII 63).

   a. Lutherans, therefore, hold "that it is only from the Word of God that judgments on articles of faith are to be pronounced" (FC SD II 8). We accept without reservation that the only norm for the church's faith and practice must be the Scriptures of the Old and New Testaments, that is, the written Word of God.

   b. Lutherans appeal to and use the sacred Scriptures as a whole, as well as individual passages of Scripture, as the sole and final authority in the Church.

i. This means that biblical teaching about the foundational doctrines of Christianity such as the Trinity, the two natures of Christ and the justification of the ungodly by grace through faith in Christ Jesus — these great truths — is sure and certain.

ii. Just as certain is the biblical teaching on God's ordering of human life within His creation according to the commandments.

We rejoice in our consensus in these truths. We pray that our shared understanding will be a sure and solid foundation for us to address future conversations and discussions, both in matters of agreement and areas where we do not share a common teaching or practice.

Resources for Further Study

A Comparative Study of Varying Contemporary Approaches to Biblical Interpretation. St. Louis: LCMS Commission on Theology and Church Relations, 1973.

Bayer, Oswald. "Luther as an Interpreter of Holy Scripture." In *The Cambridge Companion to Martin Luther*, edited by Donald McKim, 73-85. Cambridge: Cambridge University Press, 2003.

Bayer, Oswald. *Theology the Lutheran Way*. Translated by Jeffrey G. Silcock and Mark C. Mattes. Grand Rapids: Eerdmans, 2007.

Braaten, Carl, and Robert Jenson (eds). *Reclaiming the Bible for the Church*. Grand Rapids: Eerdmans, 1995.

Franzmann, Martin. "Seven Theses on Reformation Hermeneutics." *Concordia Theological Monthly* 40:4 (1969): 235-246.

Gospel and Scripture. St. Louis: LCMS Commission on Theology and Church Relations, 1972.

Hultgren, Stephen J. "Canon, creeds, and confessions: an exercise in Lutheran hermeneutics." *Lutheran Theological Journal* 46:1 (May 2012): 26-50.

In Christ All Things Hold Together: Intersection of Science and Christian Theology. St. Louis: LCMS Commission on Theology and Church Relations, 2015.

Kolb, Robert. "The Bible in Reformation and Protestant Orthodoxy." In *The Enduring Authority of the Christian Scriptures*, edited by D.A. Carson, 89-114. Grand Rapids: Eerdmans, 2016.

Kolb, Robert. "Nowhere More Present and Active Than in the Holy Letters: Luther's Understanding of God's Presence in Scripture." *Lutheran Theological Journal* 49:1 (May 2015): 4-17.

Paulson, Steven D. "From Scripture to Dogmatics." *Lutheran Quarterly* 7:2 (Summer 1993): 159-169.

Paulson, Steven D. "Lutheran Assertions Regarding Scripture." *Lutheran Quarterly* 17:4 (Winter 2003): 373-385.

Pless, John T. *Word: God Speaks to Us*. St. Louis: Concordia, 2006.

Preus, Jacob A.O. *It is Written*. St. Louis: Concordia, 1971.

Preus, Robert. *Doctrine is Life: Essays on Scripture*. Edited by Klemet Preus. St. Louis: Concordia, 2006.

Preus, Robert. *The Inspiration of Scripture: A Study of the Theology of the 17th Century Lutheran Dogmaticians*. Edinburgh: Oliver & Boyd, 1957.

Reu, J. Michael. *Luther and the Scriptures*. Chicago: Wartburg Publishing House, 1944.

Reu, J. Michael. "What is Scripture and How Can We Become Certain of Its Divine Origin?" In *Two Treatises on the Means of Grace*, 1-38. Minneapolis: Augsburg Publishing House, 1952.

Sasse, Hermann. "Suggestions for Theses on Holy Scripture." In *Letters to Lutheran Pastors – Volume III*: 1957-1969, edited by Matthew C. Harrison, 537-543. St. Louis: Concordia, 2015.

Silcock, Jeffrey. "Luther on the Holy Spirit and His Use of God's Word." In *The Oxford Handbook of Martin Luther's Theology*, edited by Robert Kolb et al, 294-309. Oxford: Oxford University Press, 2014.

Stephenson, John. "Inerrancy" *Logia* 2:4 (October 1993): 4-8.

Yeago, David. "Authority in the Church," two unpublished papers presented at the NALC Pastors' Conference in Orlando, Florida, on 10 February 2015.